Proven Strategies *for* Building *an* Information Literacy Program

Edited by Susan Carol Curzon *and* Lynn D. Lampert

Neal-Schuman Publishers, Inc.

New York   London

Published by Neal-Schuman Publishers, Inc.
100 William St., Suite 2004
New York, NY 10038

Individual chapters © 2007 by the contributors

Printed and bound in the United States of America.

The paper used in this publication meets the minimum requirements of American National Standard for Information Sciences - Permanence of Paper for Printed Library Materials, ANSI Z39.48-1992.

Library of Congress Cataloging-in-Publication Data

Proven strategies for building an information literacy program / edited by Susan Carol Curzon and Lynn D. Lampert.
        p. cm.
    Includes bibliographical references and index.
    Includes index.
    ISBN 978-1-55570-608-1 (alk. paper)
1. Information literacy—Study and teaching. I. Curzon, Susan Carol. II. Lampert, Lynn D.
ZA3075.P76 2007
028.7071—dc22

                                                                    2007012844

In Memory of Ilene Rockman, 1950–2005,
because her passion for information literacy
inspired so many.

Contents

List of Figures

Foreword

by Hannelore B. Rader

In the twenty-first century, information is generated more quickly than ever before. The Internet and other new tools have changed the ways in which people seek information. Academic institutions in the electronic age have also undergone a variety of changes in order to prepare students for productive futures in this new environment. *Proven Strategies for Building an Information Literacy Program* will help readers teach students how to successfully negotiate the technological and digital information environment.

Proven Strategies for Building an Information Literacy Program includes advice from an impressive array of leading information literacy authorities. For example, Sarah McDaniel defines information literacy as compared to library instruction. Australian author Judith Peacock discusses sustainability. Gabriela Sonntag addresses librarians' significant and global role as full partners in student learning endeavors and Margit Misangyi Watts describes approaches that help librarians engage students in successful learning initiatives in higher education. Scott Walter writes on cultural impact, Eleanor Mitchell on timing, and Kendra Van Cleave on collaboration and partnerships. The work of these authors mentioned as well as the other excellent authors in this book combine to provide a broad yet practical view of information literacy.

This volume will be a significant addition to the continually expanding body of literature on teaching information skills to students. It provides readers with compelling analyses of the issues, with new thinking, and with clear directions to meet the challenges ahead. I know the wisdom in these pages will help readers develop an information literacy program that truly meets the needs of twenty-first century learners.

Preface

by Susan Carol Curzon
and Lynn D. Lampert

M any information literacy programs start with the best of intentions only to be defeated by politics, bad timing, lack of organizational readiness, or lack of administrative support. Librarians that fail to attend to such issues often are left frustrated, wondering why their program cannot get off the ground or, once launched, cannot really fly.

We believe that only a complete strategy will ensure the development, sustenance, and success of an information literacy program. While hundreds of articles and dozens of books have focused on one or several aspects of information literacy, we have designed *Proven Strategies for Building an Information Literacy Program* to address all aspects of this important topic. Our goal is to cover the full spectrum of information literacy issues, including the roles of school libraries and public libraries, which have not usually been discussed in other works to date. Twenty knowledgeable and experienced authors have contributed to this work, which we hope will be helpful both to librarians new to the field of information literacy and to librarians seeking to revive or improve existing programs.

In our introduction to each chapter, we share with the reader what makes each author uniquely qualified to comment on the particular topic. The contributors were chosen for their practical experience in information literacy and, as a group, reflect a wide range of backgrounds. Each contributor illustrates through research, experience, and examples the most important steps towards achieving information literacy success.

We include chapters focusing on school and public libraries in order to emphasize the importance of these institutions as partners for academic librarians. School libraries have an obviously critical role to play in teaching students foundational skills. University and college librarians look to school librarians to prepare students for the rigors of higher education.

Less recognized in the literature of information literacy is the role that public libraries can and should play. Clearly, public libraries serve many school-children and college students. When public librarians reinforce information literacy, students benefit from the additional exposure to these essential skills. Moreover, public libraries have a vast user base and frequently reach diverse audiences that may never have been exposed to information literacy instruction. There is little doubt that better information literacy skills could improve the lives of many members of the public, bringing them both concrete benefits and enjoyment.

HOW TO USE THIS BOOK

We developed the information literacy wheel, shown below and at the start of each chapter, to show that each element of an information literacy program is essential to the whole. Each of the 18 chapters in *Proven Strategies for Building an Information Literacy Program* focuses on a different segment of the wheel. As you read the book, the highlighted area of the wheel shown at the beginning of the chapter will remind you of that topic's place in the overall development of a successful program.

The wheel starts on the top right with Randall Burke Hensley's chapter on practical goals for information literacy programs in an academic environment. Sarah McDaniel then provides a comprehensive definition of information literacy.

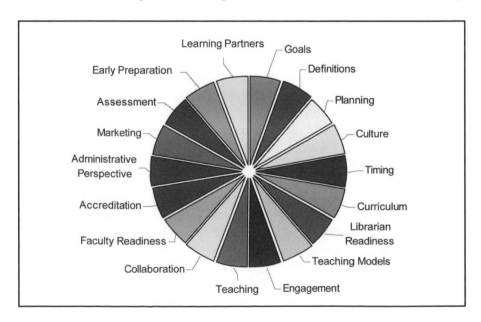

Judith Peacock writes on planning for a sustainable program, while Scott Walter discusses information literacy's cultural impact. Eleanor Mitchell advises readers on the importance of finding the best timing for an information literacy program. Lynn Lampert argues for the importance of academic librarians' involvement in curriculum development.

Jeff Liles introduces new ways to better prepare librarians for teaching information skills. Gabriela Sonntag's contribution shows a teaching model that includes librarians as significant partners, and Margit Misangyi Watts, on a related topic, demonstrates how librarians can truly engage students.

Michael Eisenberg's chapter outlines a conceptual and practical approach to teaching information literacy. Kendra Van Cleave addresses the importance of collaboration and partnerships in successful information literacy endeavors.

Rie Rogers Mitchell, Merril Simon, and Gregory Jackson, three professors from California State University, Northridge, describe the role of faculty readiness and how it contributed to their collaboration, which integrated information literacy throughout the graduate curriculum.

Stephanie Bangert encourages academic institutions to go beyond the requirements of accreditation to self-evaluation of what students are really learning in information literacy programs. James Mullins provides an administrative perspective, weighing in on issues related to resources, spaces, political support, and time. Marketing, discussed by Janeanne Rockwell-Kincanon, is another important aspect of effective information literacy programs. Bonnie Gratch-Lindauer investigates the role of assessment and the key features of a useful and accurate assessment.

Finally, Lesley Farmer and Virginia Walter take us into the worlds of school and public libraries. Lesley Farmer addresses information literacy skills in the K–12 curriculum and how instructors can grab students' interest. Virginia Walter discusses information literacy as a new initiative for public libraries.

We were delighted when Hannelore Rader accepted the invitation to write the foreword to our book. Hannelore's international contribution to the field of information literacy is well-known. Her work in the groundbreaking "Information Literacy Standards for Higher Education" issued by the Association of College and Research Libraries (ACRL) was pivotal. She is the author of over 100 papers relating to information literacy and library administration. Hannelore has received many honors throughout her distinguished career, including the ACRL's Miriam Dudley Award for Bibliographic Instruction and ACRL's prestigious Academic and Research Librarian of the Year award in 1999. Since 1997, Hannelore has been the Dean of University Libraries at the University of Louisville in Kentucky. Her M.L.S. is from the University of Michigan, where Hannelore also received an M.A. in German Literature, as well as a teaching certificate. We thank Hannelore very much for writing this foreword.

We have tried to ease the journey towards a successful information literacy program by providing information, examples, and advice in a logical and practical order. The wheel will help you keep your eye on the big picture even as you improve the individual aspects and details of your library's work. We hope that *Proven Strategies for Building an Information Literacy Program* will help you to effectively develop or sustain your own efforts.

Acknowledgments

We have dedicated this book as a special thanks and remembrance to Ilene Rockman, the manager of the Information Literacy Initiative at California State University (CSU). Her early passing saddened all who cared about the cause of information literacy and all who cared about a librarian who stood for excellence. Both of us were privileged and honored to work with Ilene.

We especially would like to recognize all our colleagues at the Oviatt Library at California State University, Northridge (CSUN) for their steadfast commitment to advancing student success.

We express our appreciation especially to two colleagues at the Oviatt Library: Joyclyn Dunham for her assistance with the photos in the book and Mickey Martinez for her assistance with the author contracts.

We also would like to express our thanks to each other. Editing a book is a unique experience! Sue would like to express her thanks to Lynn, and Lynn to Sue. We both appreciated the partnership and collegiality.

Both of us would like to express our thanks to our husbands. Lynn would like to thank her husband, Andrew Diekmann, who has always been there to support her during a weekend or weeknight of writing or editing on the laptop. Sue would like to express her thanks to her husband, Dr. Mohammad B. Ayati, for the enduring support that he has given for many years.

SPECIAL ACKNOWLEDGMENTS FROM LYNN

Many individuals, colleagues, and friends have encouraged and enriched both my understanding and advocacy of information literacy and the powerful role that it can play in both strengthening the educational mission of academic libraries and the educational experience of students. Special thanks go to several individuals who have been invaluable mentors and friends since my graduate school years at the University of California, Los Angeles (UCLA): Stephanie Brasley (CSU Information Competence Manager), Esther Grassian (UCLA College Library), and Joan Kaplowitz (UCLA Biomedical Library). I also want to thank my instructors at the 2002 ACRL Information Literacy Immersion Institute, Deborah Gilchrist, Randy Hensley, Sharon Mader, Karen Williams, and Beth Woodard, who collectively taught me so much about the information literacy.

Many thanks also deservedly go to my family for their encouragement of both my work and research as an academic librarian. In addition to my husband, Andy, I particularly want to thank my mother, Frances Lampert, for her love and support, and my late father, Howard Lampert, who I believe would have been really proud of my decision to become a librarian. My sister, Dr. Lisa Lampert-Weissig, also deserves recognition for her consistent support of her little sister. Lastly, I have to acknowledge my two favorite muses, my beloved beagles Daisy and Gatsby, whose unconditional love and support mean the world to me.

Proven Strategies for Building an Information Literacy Program

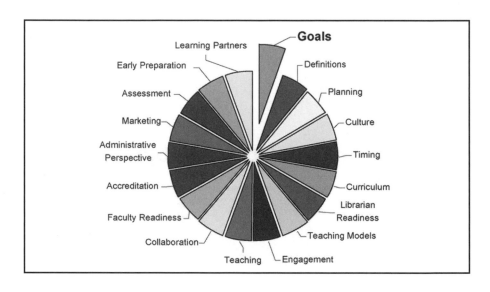

GOALS

A Word from the Editors

*W*e begin our book with a discussion on goals because knowing the direction of an information literacy program is vital for its success. Every program must begin with workable and sustainable goals that will carry the program through the years ahead. Without goals, we will not know where we are going with our programs, nor will we be able to measure our success as we would be able to with articulated goals. But how do we develop these goals? What should the goals say? What factors should we take into consideration as we develop our goals? Randall (Randy) Burke Hensley, the Student Learning Programs and Services Librarian at the University of Hawaii at Manoa, is our guide through the complexities of goal development. In this chapter, Randy helps us re-conceptualize the goal-making process by placing goals in the context of student learning, the curriculum, collaboration, motivation, and shared commitment with students. This innovative and sensitive approach to goals will help us secure and anchor our information literacy programs into the institution. As a member of the Immersion faculty of the Association of College and Research Libraries Institute for Information Literacy and as a recipient of the prestigious Miriam Dudley Instruction Librarian Award in 2002, Randy is very well-qualified to reflect upon information literacy. In his current position, Randy is responsible for developing programs and services that enhance the ability of undergraduate students to understand, appreciate, and perform original research. Randy's M.L.S. is from the University of California, Berkeley, and he also has an M.A. in Sociology from California State University, Chico, where he also held a position as a Social Sciences Librarian. Before that, he was the Assistant Head of the Odegaard Library at the University of Washington.*

Chapter 1

Getting to Goals:
New Influences on the Role of Goals in Active and Sustainable Information Literacy Programs

by Randall Burke Hensley

Goals provide a framework that guides subsequent action. Of all the elements of planning, they often reflect the perspective of the organization on the program. An alternative vision for goals is that they are indicators of what students need and good teaching should achieve. In this way, program goals become student-centered and effective devices for articulating how teachers will know they have accomplished objectives well. Furthermore, they can serve as motivation for executing an effective program.

There is now a greater understanding and appreciation for the ways that students learn effectively, just as there is a deeper appreciation for the involvement of the deliverers of any product or service in decision-making processes. These different perspectives are moving organizations away from hierarchical forms of order, just as higher education is departing from content-focused curricula to inquiry or process-centered teaching and learning. The setting and articulation of goals can align with these trends.

TRADITIONAL GOALS

James Rice, Jr. in his 1981 text, *Teaching Library Use: A Guide For Library Instruction*, gives insight to the historical context of goals for instruction programs. He writes about eight steps for instructional design: 1. Developing goals, 2.

Developing objectives, 3. Assessing entry skills, 4. Developing strategies and techniques, 5. Choosing resources, 6. Implementing (teaching), 7. Testing, and 8. Feedback (Rice: 34). He states, "the reader will note that goals and objectives are set before entry skills are assessed. We are concerned with what should be known by all students in a certain situation or context. It is the aim of our program to insure a certain mastery level of ability" (Rice, 1981: 34). This prevalent approach to goal development assumes that there is an established content all students need to know. This type of goal setting does not consider what is now known about the learning process, and it does not allow for individualization of learning that so much of the contemporary literature about learning has come to consider significant. This type of goal setting assumes the hierarchical positioning of the teacher as the most knowledgeable member of the teaching program.

Library Instruction for Librarians by Anne F. Roberts and Susan G. Blandy brings to bear the idea of needs assessment as a prelude to goal setting. In their 1989 book, they state that "librarians can develop a profile of users' needs to help them with their library instruction program objectives. Or, the profile of users' needs may show that a library instruction program is not what is needed at all" (Roberts and Blandy, 1989: 29). Furthermore, "a needs assessment gives both the librarian and the user a heightened awareness of the library. Working together to find out about users and their needs in the library can give the library staff a team feeling, which can be a significant morale booster" (Roberts and Blandy, 1989: 30). This work represents a shift in the perception of the primacy of the librarian as source of goals to one that involves the student perspective on what learning should be. Furthermore, it identifies a relationship between goals and motivation to teach.

Another facet of goals and goal settings worthy of consideration is the larger institutional environment of higher education. John M. Budd's *The Academic Library: Its Context, Its Purpose, and Its Operation* discusses the problematical nature of the university as an organization. He refers to the work of Michael D. Cohen and James G. March, *Leadership and Ambiguity: The American College President,* to offer the view of the institution of higher education as one of "organized anarchy" (Budd, 1998: 154). "Organized anarchy presents some particular challenges for governance, because it is a realization that there are aspects of the environment that are independently influential and not easily controllable" (Budd, 1998: 154). When it comes to goals, setting them is often problematical.

> Problematic goals generally means that there is a fairly loose collection of changing ideas (that have a number of sources); the organization tends to operate according to a variety of inconsistent and ill-defined preferences (for instance, the decision to emphasize "teaching" as opposed to "research" without a clear definition of the two terms or a clear conception of the similarities in or differences between the two); the educational institution

discovers preferences through action more than it acts on the basis of preferences (that is, the pragmatics of everyday activity tend to suggest short-term direction or policy); and it is difficult for the institution to establish clear goals when what it wants to do is subject to change (although the overall direction or mission may be fairly stable, the means by which goals are achieved are at least somewhat malleable). (Budd, 1998: 154–155)

Once again, the tradition of attempting to articulate an information literacy program's goals from an institution's goals for the library or for teaching and learning is flawed. In fact, the many programs that over-emphasize program objectives over goals can be seen as a functional response to the state of institutional goal setting Budd describes.

PARADIGM SHIFTS

In their book, *Assessment in the Learning Organization: Shifting the Paradigm*, Arthur L. Costa and Bena Kallick build upon the literature of the learning organization to question the traditional perspective on organizations and activities planning as a linear enterprise. They articulate a non-linear approach to organizations where holistic and interdependent relationships are fostered within the goal-setting and assessment processes. They refer to this approach to organizational activity as systems thinking which "requires constant attention to the whole along with an analysis of whether its parts are, indeed, interdependent and interconnected" (Costa and Kallick, 1995: 4). The alternative to systems thinking is "combative relationships among various parts of a system that is permeated by top-down authoritarianism and fragmentation. The farther away you are from students, the greater the inconsistency in principles and practices" (Costa and Kallick, 1995: 3). Their touchstone is Peter Senge's *The Fifth Discipline: The Art and Practice of the Learning Organization* whose perspective they summarize as, "the learning organization is a place where people continually expand their capacity to create the results they truly desire, where new and expansive patterns of thinking are nurtured, where collective aspiration is set free, and where people are continually learning how to learn together" (Costa and Kallick, 1995: 3). Therefore, an information literacy program's goals need to be hallmarks for how the program is integrated in an interdependent manner with other aspects of the library organization and with its larger institutional setting, how the program will change and expand capacity, and how student needs are incorporated in a continually correcting pattern of measurable outcomes.

A critical ingredient for capacity expansion is the instructional librarian who becomes a part of the non-linear accomplishment of goals in a constantly changing and, hopefully, improving way. Crucial to the articulation of goals is the idea of vision. We can understand vision as a set of essential beliefs. "Visions die prematurely when they are merely hollow statements developed by leadership teams and when they attempt to impose false consensus that suppresses rather than enables personal visions to flourish" (Costa and Kallick, 1995: 100). A program's goals need to incorporate a vision for the student and how the institution relates to students in ways that allow for both individual instructional librarian and student to align their own versions of the vision with a broader agreed upon vision that has been incorporated into the goals. Another way to think of this articulation is that of flexible vision. Costa and Kallick quote from the work of Michael Fullan that, "the development of authentic shared vision builds on the skills of change agentry: personal vision building through moral purpose, inquiry, mastery, and collaboration. Collective vision building is a deepening, reinforcing process of increasing clarity, enthusiasm, communication, and commitment. As people talk, try things out, inquire, re-try—all of this jointly—people become more skilled, ideas become clearer, shared commitment gets stronger" (Costa and Kallick, 1995: 101). The vision which informs the goals comes from a continual process of examining the meaning of the information literacy program for all who are involved in it. As Jerry W. Gilley and Ann Maycunich point out in *Beyond the Learning Organization: Creating a Culture of Continuous Growth and Development Through State-of-the-Art Human Resources Practices*, "individual differences make us interesting, revealing areas of specialization, creativity, and unique success. When properly nourished, these differences lead to organizational initiatives that may bloom into new ideas, products, or efficiencies that capture the imagination (and potential customers)" (Gilley and Maycunich, 2000: 44). Furthermore, "unless organizations create conditions by which their employees can produce adequate products and services, organizational process goals will be jeopardized" (Gilley and Maycunich, 2000: 290).

For the information literacy program the starting place is student learning both from the perspective of the student and the instructional librarian. A process that involves goal-setting through a process of visioning that involves students might seem daunting. However, JoAnn Wong-Kam et al. in their book, *Elevating Expectations: A New Take on Accountability, Achievement, and Evaluation*, describe one simple tactic that is easily adaptable to multiple settings and grade levels. Their model involves students strongly: "I remember we would discuss what made excellent readers and writers. We would identify those characteristics and write them on charts. From there the children would pick what they thought would help them become better readers and writers. Sometimes they would choose very broad, perhaps unattainable goals. My dilemma was, should I guide them to something more appropriate, or do I let them go through their own discovery?" (Wong-Kam et al., 2001: 19).

This process was done with second grade students in an elementary school! If we accept the idea that information literacy program goals should incorporate a vision of student learning from the perspective of both the teacher and the student, and we accept that those goals and vision should be aligned with both library organizational and institutional ideas about effective teaching and learning, and, finally, we acknowledge the need for a program's goals and visions to be articulated in ways that facilitate alignment of individual visions with shared goals in a way that encourages a continually changing, dynamic, non-linear, and motivating set of principles to guide action, then there are some perspectives about teaching and learning that we can use to see our processes for establishing program vision and goals.

THINKING ABOUT THE TEACHER

Parker J. Palmer in *The Courage to Teach* provides some useful guideposts towards what our information literacy program goals might be. He describes the role of fear in our educational institutions, within our students, and as an aspect of our approach as teachers to teaching and learning. His antidote to fear is to embrace the need for connectedness in the educational enterprise. His paradigmatic change prescription involves our relationships to truth. For our purposes "truth" can be understood as instructional content. "If we regard truth as something handed down from authorities on high, the classroom will look like a dictatorship. If we regard truth as a fiction determined by personal whim, the classroom will look like anarchy. If we regard truth as emerging from a complex process of mutual inquiry, the classroom will look like a resourceful and interdependent community. Our assumptions about knowing can open up, or shut down, the capacity for connectedness on which good teaching depends" (Palmer, 1998: 51). Palmer also discusses the value of creative tension in the classroom that arises from an appreciation of paradox, the tension between opposing perspectives, and the suffering of relating individual student stories to the stories of the group or of others. He states, "the principle of paradox is not a guide only to the complexities and potentials of selfhood. It can also guide us in thinking about classroom dynamics and in designing the kind of teaching and learning space that can hold a classroom session" (Palmer, 1995: 73). Our program goals should articulate a desire to deliver instruction that is creative because it is not a dogmatic imparting of ways to do things. Furthermore, our goals should mandate an environment where individual perspective is examined in the context of the perspectives of others. In this way, we are less delivering content and more delivering process, a process that has the potential for the discovery of personal meaning. Finally, one of our goals must speak to the role of the teacher who, in order to engage multiple perspectives and foster creativity that arises from the tension of the "not right answer," acts as a participant in the learning environment.

In *What The Best College Teachers Do*, Ken Bain defines "best" as teachers who had a sustained influence on their students. "We were drawn to classes in which students talked not about how much they had to remember but about how much they came to understand (and as a result remembered)" (Bain, 2004: 10). Bain articulates a number of attributes of good teachers and by extension, good teaching. He summarizes,

> In general, the people we investigated tried to avoid extrinsic motivators and to foster intrinsic ones, moving students toward learning goals and a mastery orientation. They gave students as much control over their own education as possible and displayed both a strong interest in their learning and a faith in their abilities. They offered nonjudgmental feedback on students' work, stressed opportunities to improve, constantly looked for ways to stimulate advancement, and avoided dividing their students into the sheep and the goats. Rather than pitting people against each other, they encouraged cooperation and collaboration. (Bain, 2004: 35)

Bain's work concludes with a prescription for success: "Create a natural critical learning environment, get their [students'] attention and keep it, start with the students rather than the discipline, seek commitments, help students learn outside of class, engage students in disciplinary thinking, and create diverse learning experiences" (Bain, 2004: 99–117). Our instruction program goals will be better guides for articulating objectives, determining more meaningful assessment, and developing modalities for learning if they incorporate these ideas for how best to foster a learning environment that works for students.

In fact, work has been done to develop measurements that assess how well instruction is doing to engage students in learning processes that are effective. George D. Kuh and Paul D. Umbach discuss some ramifications of the attributes for learning embodied in the National Survey of Student Engagement in their article, "College and Character: Insights From the National Survey of Student Engagement" (Kuh and Umbach, 2004).

Their conclusion: "students must also be told early on, and then institutions must consistently reinforce the message, that opportunities will be presented for students to experience and integrate what they are learning from their courses with their social, political, and cultural lives. Then institutions must intentionally organize the students' in-class experiences so that they are exposed to the kind of activities and events that push them further along the character development path" (Kuh and Umbach, 2004: 50–51). They see character development as an intended outcome of the higher education experience.

Lastly, Maryellen Weimer offers an instructional scenario that is fertile for goal setting. Her book, *Learner-Centered Teaching: Five Key Changes to Practice* (Weimer, 2002), answers the question, "what should teachers do in order to maximize learning outcomes for their students?" She discusses the shift in the balance of power from teacher to student, the move in content from quantitative acquisition of knowledge to the qualitative appreciation of meaning, the role of the teacher moving towards a focus on actions that students take to learn so that the responsibility for learning more clearly lies with students in more self-directed ways, and that evaluation purpose and processes are designed so that the student more than the teacher understands what learning has occurred.

The information literacy program goals now begin to take shape. They form a scaffolding about the environment for learning, the expectations for the role of the student in the learning process, the approach to the role of teacher desired, the ways learning will be assessed, and the conduct of instructional situations.

TODAY'S STUDENTS

Much discussion has occurred about the nature of today's student. Certain attributes should be incorporated into the articulation of information literacy program goals. They serve to make relevant and student-centered the program scaffolding that goals represent and remind us that these goals will of necessity need to be habitually examined and re-articulated as the information literacy program develops and progresses. In a positive manner, Neil Howe and William Strauss develop a perspective about today's students that should encourage us to be better teachers. In their book, *Millennials Rising: The Next Great Generation* (Howe and Strauss, 2000), they argue that today's students are optimists, that they are cooperative team players, that they accept authority, and that they are rule followers and smarter than most people think. Especially important is the characteristic of belief in the future and that they see themselves as cutting edge. In a nutshell, they charge us as teachers to, "with Millennials rising, Americans need to start thinking bigger. Test them. Challenge them. Put difficult tasks before them, and have faith that they can do themselves, and their nation, proud. Lead them. Love them. And above all listen to 17-year-old Sarah Fulton when she says, 'celebrate the good! Celebrate the youth of America!'"(Howe and Strauss, 2000: 367).

Our information literacy program goals should take seriously the opportunity to make our learning environments student centered because those environments will incorporate a more effective role for teachers, be more the embodiment of accurate problem-solving and process oriented learning, be more life-long in their implications for our students' lives, and be more aligned with the perspectives and abilities our students are bringing to our institutions.

A MODEL

James Rice, Jr. provided a list of sample goals in his 1981 text, *Teaching Library Use: A Guide for Library Instruction* (Rice, 1981: 36). These goals are: 1) to motivate potential users to use a library, 2) to generate interest in research, 3) to promote reading as an activity, 4) to dispel anxiety about a library, 5) to justify the existence of the library, 6) to support an institution's curriculum, 7) to improve access to materials, 8) to upgrade the image of the library and librarians, 9) to enhance good citizenship and values, and 10) to improve the decision-making ability of any member of the public (by making him/her informed in library use and information access). By applying the considerations presented in this chapter, the following possibilities emerge:

The information literacy program will constantly gather information about changing student needs for effective use of information. This goal acknowledges the centrality of the student perspective on the information literacy program content (Roberts and Blandy, 1989).

The information literacy program will habitually monitor institutional modifications to curriculum and pedagogy. This goal acknowledges the influential yet sometimes anarchic nature of the higher education organizational context, especially at a time of educational reform, increased oversight by accrediting agencies, and generational change among faculty and higher education administrators (Budd, 1998).

The information literacy program will assess the impact of the program on the library and larger higher education institution so that synergistic benefit can be achieved. This goal acknowledges the interdependence of each part of an organization on the others so that capacity to achieve results can be increased (Costa and Kallick, 1995).

The information literacy program will regularly discuss the vision of the information literate student so that the goals and objectives of the program represent a shared commitment to students and the program it teaches. This goal acknowledges the importance of the collective vision as a motivating ingredient for goals (Fullan, 1993).

The information literacy program respects individual perspectives about how to translate the program's goals into measurable outcomes. This goal acknowledges how individual differences foster creativity, use of specialized knowledge, and unique experience (Gilley and Maycunich, 2000).

The information literacy program will emphasize approaches that promote connectedness between teacher and students. This goal acknowledges the critical nature of facilitating discovery among program participants for learning (Palmer, 1998).

The information literacy program will foster intrinsic motivators for learning through student-centered pedagogy. This goal acknowledges the advantages of students participating in the determination of the content of and approach to learning so that the student experience is habitually utilized in learning (Bain, 2004).

The information literacy program will incorporate national standards for character development and engagement so that holistic, lifelong learning is achieved for students. This goal acknowledges the integrated nature of students' lives among life, educational, and career experiences (Kuh and Umbach, 2004).

The information literacy program will use current student attributes in order to increase learning effectiveness. This goal acknowledges changing student values and characteristics for learning (Howe and Strauss, 2000).

THE FINAL WORD

Goals that address the nature of students, the challenging construct of higher education institutions, the manner in which teaching should occur, and the pedagogical approaches that are deemed effective for engaging students hold promise for increased effectiveness of information literacy programs. Goals that emphasize the importance of the student perspective on the program along with a constant examination of goals as part of an ever changing environment offer the best chance to articulate meaningful objectives that articulate content and specific action that can be assessed to promote an ever improving program.

REFERENCES

Bain, K. 2004. *What the best college teachers do*. Cambridge, MA: Harvard University Press.

Budd, J. M. 1998. *The academic library: Its context, its purpose, and its operation*. Engelwood, CO: Libraries Unlimited.

Costa, A. L., and B. Kallick, eds. 1995. *Assessment in the learning organization: Shifting the paradigm*. Alexandria, VA: Association for Supervision and Curriculum Development.

Fullan, M. 1993. *Change forces: Probing the depths of educational reform*. New York: Falmer Press.

Gilley, J. W., and A. Maycunich. 2000. *Beyond the learning organization: Creating a culture of continuous growth and developments through state-of-the-art human resources practices*. Cambridge, MA: Perseus Books.

Howe, N., and W. Strauss. 2000. *Millennials rising: The next great generation*. New York: Vintage Books.

Kuh, G. D., and P. D. Umbach. 2004. "College and character: Insights from the National Survey of Student Engagement." *New Directions for Institutional Research*, Vol. 122: 37–54.

Palmer, P. J. 1998. *The courage to teach*. San Francisco, CA: Jossey-Bass.

Rice, J. Jr. 1981. *Teaching library use: A guide for library instruction*. Westport, CT: Greenwood Press.

Roberts, A. F., and S. G. Blandy. 1989. *Library instruction for librarians*. 2nd rev. ed. Englewood, CO: Libraries Unlimited.

Senge, P. 1990. *The fifth discipline: The art and practice of the learning organization*. New York: Doubleday.

Senge, P. 2000. *Schools that learn*. New York: Doubleday.

Weimer, M. 2002. *Learner-centered teaching: Five key changes to practice*. San Francisco, CA: Jossey-Bass.

Wong-Kam, J., et al. 2001. *Elevating expectations: A new take on accountability, achievement, and evaluation*. Portsmouth, NH: Heinemann.

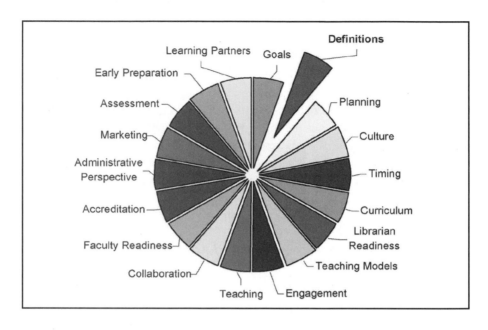

DEFINITIONS

A Word from the Editors

*W*e hear or read the phrase "information literacy" continually in our work-places, in the literature and at conferences. We all think we know what it means, but Sarah McDaniel, the Instructional Design and Assessment Librarian in the Doe/Moffitt Libraries at the University of California, Berkeley, challenges us to really understand the meaning of the term "information literacy." How, for example, do we differentiate it from bibliographic instruction? Taking us on a journey through the origin of the term, Sarah places it in historical context and also looks at its rela-tionship to technology literacy and library instruction. Sarah is also Assessment Con-sultant for Berkeley's Mellon Library/Faculty Fellowship for Undergraduate Research where she works closely with faculty fellows, librarians, and other academic support staff to embed the assessment of information literacy into undergraduate research as-signments. Sarah's M.L.I.S. is from the University of Wisconsin, Milwaukee, where she also took an M.A. in Foreign Languages and Literature. In addition to her pre-sentations and publications on instruction and information literacy, Sarah was the Instructional Services Coordinator at the University of Southern California. Writ-ing to the editors, Sarah has said that "information literacy has great potential as a framework for designing curriculum, assessing student learning, and strengthening the role of librarians in the broader educational enterprise. Until individual librar-ians gain a more complete understanding of information literacy in order to become more effective advocates and educators, the full potential of the information literacy movement will remain unrealized."

Chapter Two

Defining Information Literacy:
Conceptual Models and Practice

by Sarah McDaniel

Despite [the frequent use of the phrase information literacy], there are numerous definitions and there is resultant ambiguity. In order for information literacy to be embraced by non-librarians and academe at large, clarification of the definition is essential. In addition, librarians must identify the unique contributions that differentiate the phrase from bibliographic instruction (BI) and past phrases, not to mention differentiating it from education and learning in general. (Snavely and Cooper, 1997: 9)

Since the appearance of this challenge in "The Information Literacy Debate," a seminal article on information literacy terminology published nearly two decades ago, information literacy has gained wide acceptance as a key conceptual framework for discussing the knowledge, skills, and abilities individuals must develop to be successful in an information society. Yet many of the critical issues identified in "The Information Literacy Debate" remain unresolved.

In the library literature, numerous authors have addressed the definition and scope of the phrase information literacy and traced debates around its use; notable studies for those working in higher education are outlined in literature reviews by Grassian and Kaplowitz (2001), Rader (2002), and Eisenberg, Lowe, and Spitzer (2004). In her 2000 study, "Information Literacy Research: Dimensions of the Emerging Collective Consciousness," Christine Bruce traces the evolution of the information literacy research agenda over time and discusses the various disciplinary lenses, theoretical approaches, and research methodologies that have been used to define the problem. Bruce predicts that the field will continue to expand, with interdisciplinary collaborations resulting in a "firmer, more consolidated research agenda" with a continuing focus on "research in practice" conducted by librarians in the course of their work (Bruce, 2000: 95).

Professional organizations have made significant inroads in defining information literacy, promoting new scholarship and laying the groundwork for large-scale incorporation of information literacy into curricula. In a series of reports, standards, and other documents, the American Library Association (ALA) and the Association of College and Research Libraries expanded on emerging definitions of information literacy, set an agenda for research and action, and documented emerging good practices. This documentation has provided tools for librarians and libraries, academic institutions, consortia and university systems to promote information literacy in their own environments. Accrediting agencies have also become involved, influencing the systematic incorporation of information literacy into college curricula (Gratch-Lindauer, 2002).

Despite all of these developments, imprecision in the use of the phrase "information literacy" and a lack of consensus about the types of pedagogies and initiatives that promote it have persisted, both in the literature (Bruce, 1997) and among librarians in the field. For librarians, understanding information literacy is critical to effective participation in teaching and learning on college campuses, identification of new strategies to promote student learning, and development of information literacy programs and initiatives suited to particular campus environments. This chapter will provide some essential background on information literacy as a framework for the role of academic librarians in the educational process, tracing important developments in the emergence of the information literacy agenda, identifying some key elements of information literacy, and discussing relationships between information literacy and related concepts.

EMERGENCE OF AN INFORMATION LITERACY AGENDA

In 1987, then American Library Association President Margaret Chisolm charged a committee of librarians and educators to "define information literacy within the higher literacies and its importance to student performance, lifelong learning, and active citizenship" and to propose models for its development in various learning environments (ALA, 1989). Central to the committee's report was a discussion of forces that had created a need for a systematic program of education to create self-sufficient information users: an expansion in the amount of information and a profusion of technologies for organizing it, making access to information increasingly complex, economic factors intervening in individuals' access to information, and the need to promote an economically independent and informed citizenry. The report articulated a definition of information literacy that remains widely used:

> To be information literate, a person must be able to recognize when infor-
> mation is needed and have the ability to locate, evaluate, and use effec-
> tively the needed information. . . . Ultimately, information literate people
> are those who have learned how to learn. They know how to learn because
> they know how knowledge is organized, how to find information, and
> how to use information in such a way that others can learn from them.
> They are people prepared for lifelong learning, because they can always
> find the information needed for any task or decision at hand. (ALA, 1989)

This broad and ambitious definition places information literacy at the very
heart of the educational process and lifelong learning.

User education in libraries can be traced back to the nineteenth century
(Grassian and Kaplowitz, 2001), and a focus on librarians' role in developing
students' self-sufficiency as researchers emerged in the literature in the 1960s
(Bruce, 1997: 5). The phrase "information literacy" was first used to describe citizens' ability to use a range of information sources to solve real problems in a 1974
report to the National Commission on Libraries and Information Science. The
report's author, Paul Zurkowski, discussed the increasing importance of information in society, as well as the emergence of a multiplicity of information sources and
approaches to the information seeking process. He called on the federal government to develop and fund a universal program to promote information literacy.
While Zurkowski's concern with empowering citizens to use information to solve
authentic problems has continued to gain currency, his call for the development of
a universal program to promote information literacy never garnered wide interest.

The ALA Presidential Committee's "Final Report" (1989) took up many of
these same themes, but proposed a more distributed approach to the development of information literacy programs and initiatives. The report called for a
"re-conceptualization of the role of information in daily life" through scholarship and demonstration projects, advocacy by librarians, and the broader education community to align information literacy with related initiatives,
inclusion of information literacy in curriculum at all levels, and the establishment of a coalition to coordinate these efforts. The recommendations focused
on top-level initiatives to involve constituencies in libraries, education, government, and industry in promoting information literacy. A subsequent "Progress
Report" (ALA, 1998) documented the success of this distributed approach,
summarizing developments and proposing some new directions to pursue.

Drawing on previous scholarship, the committee framed information literacy
as a set of foundational skills and abilities that are central to the educational
process and learning itself. These skills and abilities were framed as characteristics of the information literate individual. This focus on characteristics of the
learner constituted a significant realignment of librarians' role with the larger
educational process; instead of focusing on a narrow set of information-seeking
skills, librarians would now be engaged in a broader effort to develop a student's

foundational knowledge, skills, and abilities. The project of developing an information literate citizenry became an important organizing theme for many sectors of librarianship and education internationally.

THE HIGHER EDUCATION CONTEXT

The ALA Presidential Committee's "Final Report" (1989) was widely discussed in the higher education community, and the Association of College and Research Libraries (2000) subsequently charged a committee to develop "The Information Literacy Competency Standards for Higher Education." "The Standards" situated information literacy within broader trends in higher education, presenting both an argument for developing students' information literacy as an integral part of the educational process and a set of standards to further define and assess information literacy. "The Standards" provided a new and powerful tool for the development and implementation of information literacy pedagogies, programs, and initiatives in educational institutions.

The first section of "The Standards" endorses the work of the earlier ALA Presidential Committee and situates information literacy in the context of broader discussions about pedagogy and accountability in higher education. "The Standards" cite the "Boyer Report" (Boyer Commission on Educating Undergraduates in the Research University, 1998), which recommends improving the quality of education at large research institutions by involving undergraduates in active research that connects them to library collections and requires them to engage with content through inquiry, problem-solving, and critical thinking. "The Boyer Report" cites the importance of involving the entire campus community in the effort to integrate research-based learning into the undergraduate experience and staging the required skills across the undergraduate curriculum. The authors of "The Standards" observe that "such learning environments require information competencies" (ACRL, 2000: 5) and make the case for working collaboratively on college campuses to weave information literacy competencies "into the curriculum's content, structure, and sequence" (ACRL, 2000: 5).

The familiar definition of information literacy is presented in the form of six standards. "An information literate individual is able to:

- Determine the extent of information needed.
- Access the needed information effectively and efficiently.
- Evaluate information and its sources critically.
- Incorporate selected information into one's knowledge base.
- Use information effectively to accomplish a specific purpose.
- Understand the economic, legal, and social issues surrounding the use of information, and access and use information ethically and legally." (ACRL, 2000: 2–3)

The standards are subdivided into 22 performance indicators, each with learning outcomes detailing observable behaviors that an information literate student should demonstrate.

In their language and structure, "The Standards" are designed to align with broader movements toward accountability and assessment in higher education. "The Standards" "outline the process by which faculty, librarians, and others pinpoint specific indicators that identify a student as information literate" (ACRL, 2000: 5), bringing focus to what a student knows or is able to do as a result of his or her educational experiences. "The Standards" provide a blueprint for assessment: learning outcomes detail specific behaviors that an information literate student should demonstrate. Some have criticized this behaviorist approach as resulting in a list of general skills that have little meaning when viewed individually (Webber and Johnston, 2000). A closer look at the language employed is helpful in understanding the tension between "The Standards" as a comprehensive description of information literacy and the specificity of the discrete performance indicators and learning outcomes provided for each standard.

A National Center for Educational Statistics (NCES) "Working Group Report" published a few years after "The Standards" provides a useful exploration of the language of competency-based education, observing that "many terms are used interchangeably to describe learners and the results of the learning process" (Jones, Voorhees, and Paulson, 2002: 7). The working group proposed the following hierarchical relationship between commonly used terms:

- A student begins with a foundation of traits and characteristics.
- A student develops skills, abilities, and knowledge through learning experiences.
- Competencies result from integrative learning experiences in which skills, abilities, and knowledge are brought to bear on a particular task, and are applied in demonstrations that may be assessed. (Jones, Voorhees, and Paulson, 2002: 7)

The specific skills, abilities, and knowledge to be developed and assessed may be articulated in the form of learning outcomes, "the essential and enduring knowledge, abilities (skills), and attitudes (values, dispositions) that constitute the integrated learning needed by a graduate of a course or program" (Battersby, 1999: 8). Learning outcomes emphasize what students need to know and be able to do, and make explicit the development and assessment of generic abilities (Battersby and LON, 1999: 9). In "The Standards," each performance indicator encompasses a range of potential learning outcomes at various levels of cognitive complexity, supporting curricular integration and assessment of information literacy at every level, from assignment and activity design to the development of courses and curricula.

In environments where the call for accountability and assessment has been particularly forceful, the alignment of "The Standards" with the language of competency-based education and learning outcomes has positioned information literacy to become central to curriculum planning and assessment efforts. While in some settings "The Standards" have been formally endorsed and adopted in their entirety, they are more frequently used as a basis for conversations about information literacy and its place in the curriculum.

A. Relationship of Information Literacy to the Broader Educational Enterprise

"The Standards" position information literacy as a conceptual framework for the educational process itself. Shifting the focus of education from content knowledge to learning skills and incorporating active engagement with content through resource-based learning are hallmarks of a wider movement toward constructivist and learner-centered approaches in higher education (Weimer, 2002). Providing students with "The Standards," or with learning outcomes for a specific course or assignment, can also facilitate a "metacognitive approach to learning, making them conscious of the explicit actions required for gathering, analyzing, and using information" (ACRL, 2000: 6).

Information literacy encompasses a set of interrelated learning outcomes that are attained throughout the educational process, concurrently with a student's intellectual development. Many of the skills and abilities articulated in "The Standards" may be attained to some degree by the novice learner, but will be performed at increased levels of sophistication throughout a student's education, often as students gain greater knowledge of disciplinary content and methodologies. Some professional organizations and other discipline-based groups have adapted "The Standards" to be subject-specific or integrated elements of information literacy into existing professional standards (ACRL Instruction Section, Teaching Methods Committee, 2006). Efforts to map "The Standards" to disciplinary curricula should take into account both local structures (e.g., requirements for the major) and the relationship of information literacy competencies to disciplinary knowledge and methodologies.

The authors of "The Standards" hoped that educators would use their document as framework for curriculum development. In *Integrating Information Literacy into the Higher Education Curriculum: Practical Models for Transformation*, Ilene Rockman (2004: 16) describes an information literacy curriculum as:

> campuswide, problem-based, inquiry-based and resource-based (that is, it uses a variety of information resources); makes effective use of instructional pedagogies and technologies; is learner-centered; and is integrated and articulated with a discipline's learning outcomes. It enhances and expands student learning through a coherent, systematic approach that facilitates the transfer of learning across the curriculum.

Information literacy is one among many competing frameworks that shape curricula, and effective models for curricular integration vary according to local structures and governance, campus culture, and factors such as accreditation cycles.

B. Relationship of Information Literacy to Library Instruction

Since librarians first involved themselves in user education, there have been transitions in both nomenclature and models for librarians' involvement in the educational process. Woodard and Janicke-Hinchliffe (2001) note of the transitions from library orientation to bibliographic instruction to library instruction, "as the terms came into use, the programs that were described by the newer term often included everything indicated by the previous term, in addition to newer developments and initiatives" (178). In the same way, the phrase information literacy instruction has become widely and somewhat inaccurately used to describe the instructional activities of librarians. Snavely and Cooper (1997) defined library instruction as a situation-specific response that is a component of and contributes to the broader educational outcome of information literacy. Information literacy provides a framework for a learner-centered and process-oriented re-conceptualization of librarians' instructional activities, but is not synonymous with library instruction.

Setting librarians' instructional activities in the context of a broader educational enterprise, that of producing information literate learners, presents new challenges. Library instruction is a contribution to the educational process that is relatively straightforward to measure and value: instruction sessions and students in attendance can be counted, a specific set of learning outcomes can be addressed, and librarians' expertise and contributions are clearly delineated. Information literacy brings new measures of success based on student learning outcomes. In 1990, Lori Arp wrote, "With information literacy we must recognize that we have an expected product—the information-literate individual—and that we will be expected to produce this product" (Arp, 1990: 47). While librarians increasingly measure success in student learning outcomes, their contributions to student learning occur in the broader context of active collaboration with faculty and other campus stakeholders. Student learning outcomes are attained not just in library sessions, but through assignments, courses, and curricula, and may be attributed to a variety of factors, not just the instructional intervention of the librarian.

Librarians' contributions to the learning process have also become much more diverse: "Librarians engaged in information literacy instruction become involved with a wide variety of educational activities both in the traditional library setting as well as in non-traditional settings" (Woodard and Janicke-Hinchliffe, 2001: 180). Characteristics of pedagogies and collaborations that support information literacy initiatives are addressed in the document "Characteristics of Programs of Information Literacy that Illustrate Best Practices: A Guideline" (ACRL Instruction Section, 2006).

C. Relationship of Information Literacy to Computer Literacy

The relationship between information literacy and computer literacy has continued to evolve with shifting relationships between information and technology, emerging conceptions of computer literacy, and changing attributes of successive generations of students. Early definitions of computer literacy focused on a set of lower order skills needed to operate hardware and software. "The Standards" further distinguished between the two, defining information literacy as a distinct and broader area of competence that information technology skills are interwoven into and support.

In 1999, a major report, "Being Fluent with Information Technology," proposed a new and broader conception of computer literacy. The report defined fluency with information technology (FITness) as a set of skills and abilities required for success in the information age: "People fluent with information technology (FIT persons) are able to express themselves creatively, to reformulate knowledge, and to synthesize new information. . . . FITness entails a process of lifelong learning in which individuals continually apply what they know to adapt to change and acquire more knowledge to be more effective at applying information technology to their work and personal lives" (CITL, 1999). The report takes a constructivist approach, incorporating higher-order skills, abilities and understandings in three areas: contemporary skills that enable an individual to use computer applications and information technology for current needs, understandings of the foundational concepts behind computers, networks and information, and the intellectual abilities that enable an individual to apply information technology to complex situations (e.g., applying problem-solving and critical thinking skills). FITness garnered a high degree of interest on many campuses and provided a basis for hybrid conceptions of information literacy such as information fluency (Arp and Woodard, 2002: 126) and Information and Communication Technology Literacy.

ALTERNATE CONSTRUCTS AND DEFINITIONS

Snavely and Cooper (1997: 10) observed that "disagreement about the term *information literacy* is fairly strong and seems to be widespread," but stemmed more from terminology than from philosophical disagreements. Concerns that the term literacy connoted a remedial skill set failed to take into account the existing uses of literacy to describe a continuum of knowledge (Arp, 1990), advanced knowledge of a particular subject or field, or being knowledgeable and well educated (Snavely and Cooper, 1997). Alternative formulations have stemmed in part from lingering negative connotations around the terms literacy and illiteracy. Most significant alternative or hybrid formulations of information literacy, however, were born not just out of debates around terminology, but also to capitalize on opportunities presented by emerging local and national trends in higher education.

A. Information Competence

The California State University system launched its Information Competence Initiative in 1995, when a working group of librarians, faculty, support staff, and administrators was charged to recommend "basic competence levels, and to recommend processes for assessment of student information competence" (Rockman, 2002: 190). The following definitions were developed at a system-wide workshop:

- "Information competence, at heart, is the ability to find, evaluate, use, and communicate information in all of its various formats. . . .
- Information competence is the fusing or the integration of library literacy, computer literacy, media literacy, technological literacy, ethics, critical thinking, and communication skills" (Work Group on Information Competence, 1995: 8).

The Work Group on Information Competence identified three additional emphases for the initiative: ethical and legal dimensions, media literacy, and the production and application of information in various media.

These definitions and concerns place information competence in nearly complete congruence with information literacy, and in fact "The Standards" are the primary document used to articulate the integration of information competence into the curriculum. The definitions and emphases developed at the workshop align information competence more explicitly with FITness, and in recent years, the CSU system has been highly involved in the development of Information and Communication Technology (ICT) Literacy.

The term "competence" evokes the framework for competency-based education proposed by the NCES (2002), with its focus on assessment and the integration of a range of competencies in solving real problems. By using terminology and selecting areas of focus that resonate with the goals, culture, and mission of a particular university system, CSU launched a highly successful initiative with programming across its more than 20 campuses (Rockman, 2002).

B. Information Fluency

In some liberal arts colleges and consortia, information literacy has been promoted as part of a larger concept of information fluency. The Associated Colleges of the South (ACS) used fluency with information technology as a point of departure to "further define and articulate a congruence of critical thinking, information literacy, and computer literacy" (Arp and Woodard, 2002: 126) and to foster collaborative information fluency initiatives among librarians, information technologists, and faculty. The ACS defined information fluency as "the optimal outcome when critical thinking skills are combined with information literacy and relevant computer skills" (Moore, 2002: 5). Curriculum and assessments are developed from both information literacy and FITness frameworks (Fass McEuen, 2000).

C. Information and Communication Technology Literacy

More recently, a group of colleges and universities has partnered with the Educational Testing Service (ETS) to develop ICT Literacy, a model that draws on both fluency with information technology and information literacy. In 2001, ETS convened an international panel to study the relationship of information and communication technologies to literacy, gather information about ICT literacy, and develop an ICT Literacy framework as the foundation for large-scale assessments and diagnostic tools to measure skills and abilities associated with ICT literacy in individuals and groups. The panel defined ICT literacy proficiency as:

> the ability to use digital technology, communication tools, and/or networks appropriately to solve information problems in order to function in an information society. This includes the ability to use technology as a tool to research, organize, evaluate, and communicate information, and the possession of a fundamental understanding of the ethical/legal issues surrounding the access and use of information. (International ICT Literacy Panel, 2002: 11)

Where information literacy focuses on the effective use of information, emphasizing the availability of information in many formats, ICT literacy narrows the focus to effective use of digital information in ICT environments. It also incorporates the use of technology as a tool for information use and communication.

In 2003, seven institutions, including both individual schools and university systems, joined forces with ETS to form the National Higher Education Information and Communication Technology Initiative, with the primary goal of developing a "simulation-based assessment" to measure ICT Literacy in College Students (International ICT Literacy Panel, 2002: 3). The assessment measures seven integrated ICT proficiencies: the ability to identify and appropriately represent an information need (define); the ability to collect and/or retrieve information in digital environments (access); the ability to apply an existing organizational scheme for digital information (manage); the ability to interpret and represent digital information (integrate); the ability to determine the degree to which digital information satisfies the needs of a task (evaluate); the ability to generate information by adapting/applying information (create); and the ability to communicate information properly in its context for use in the ICT environment and for a particular audience and venue (communicate). In 2006, the assessment was a "performance-based, problem-based, Web-based, interactive tool" that consists of tasks at varying levels of complexity, as well as a warm-up and background questionnaire (Brasley, 2006: 44–45).

Librarians and other academic personnel from charter institutions worked closely with ETS through a rigorous design process to create an assessment instrument that can be used for purposes such as tracking students' development throughout their academic careers, comparing students across campuses and disciplines, improving the quality of instruction and educational interventions, and meeting accreditation requirements (Brasley, 2006: 47–48). In addition to significant investments of time and funds to set up and proctor the test, secure a representative sample of students to take the test, and analyze data, institutions must pay ETS for each administration of the proprietary test. As with any assessment, the value of the data and the purposes for which the data will be used should be weighed carefully against the direct and indirect costs.

MEDIA LITERACY AND VISUAL LITERACY

Concurrently with the development of information literacy, educators in fields such as mass communication and fine art have been discussing the knowledge, skills, and abilities required to engage critically with and communicate information in media and visual formats. Conceptions of media literacy and visual literacy intersect in many ways with notions of information literacy, but these conversations are conducted largely in isolation from one another.

The case for media literacy is similar to that made for information literacy: the increasing prevalence of media and technology, sociopolitical and economic systems behind the creation and distribution of information, and the need for individuals to engage critically with media creates a need for a media literate citizenry. A media literate person can "decode, evaluate, analyze, and produce both print and electronic media" (Aufderheide, 1992). Both learning to decode media and learning to produce media are subsets of media literacy (Dorr, 2004). Because educators approach media literacy from a variety of disciplinary orientations, there is no single conceptualization of media literacy. Most definitions "center on the *mass media*, and on *how* and for *what purpose* messages are constructed and consumed by the masses" (Chauvin, 2003: 122). While media literacy focuses on mass media in all formats, visual literacy focuses solely on visual images and includes the fine arts. Chauvin (2003: 125) defines visual literacy as "the ability to access, analyze, evaluate, and communicate information in any variety of form that engages the cognitive processing of a visual image."

As increasing amounts of information are generated in non-text formats, it is likely that conceptions of media and visual literacy will inform the information literacy movement in general, and to those working in visually-driven disciplines in particular.

WHAT TERMINOLOGY SHOULD YOU USE?

Once you have a clear understanding of the scope of the term information literacy, how it aligns with other terminology in use in the higher education community, and the types of pedagogies and initiatives that promote it, you will be better prepared to make decisions about what terminology should be used to discuss and promote information literacy in your own institutional setting.

In making decisions about how to use this terminology in your work with librarians, faculty, and other groups, consider the following questions:

- What initiatives related to information literacy are underway in my own campus environment, and what terminology do they use?
- How are "information literacy" and related phrases currently used at my institution? In the library? By faculty? By other campus units?
- Would it be useful to initiate conversations about the way the phrase is used or the way research and information-seeking behavior are discussed? With whom?
- Are "information literacy" or related terms used in campus documentation such as mission statements, program goals, accreditation documents, program review documents, or other materials?
- What other campus units have a stake in issues around information literacy, and what terminology do they use to discuss these issues?
- What is the accrediting body for my institution, and what terminology do they use?
- To which consortia or educational systems does my institution belong, and what terminology do they use?
- Are related learning skills such as critical thinking, media and visual literacy, and computer literacy discussed on my campus?
- How are issues such as developing learning skills over the course of a program of study addressed?
- Who needs to be involved in decisions about terminology and how it is used in conversations with faculty, in describing the library's instructional role?

CONCLUSIONS:

Information literacy is an important framework for understanding librarians' contributions in the context of broader educational initiatives and trends. As such, it is important that librarians have a clear understanding of the concept of information literacy and how it relates to education as a whole, library instruction, and information technology. These fundamental understandings are critical to effective participation in conversations about program and curriculum development and assessment at the library and campus levels.

What pedagogies and initiatives that promote information literacy look like will depend on many variables including campus history and mission, and curriculum structure and initiatives. With these factors in mind, it may be wise to explore alternative terminologies and conceptualizations of information literacy. Whatever terminology or formulation is selected to frame information literacy initiatives on your own campus, a focus on intentionally developing foundational and transferable learning skills over the course of a student's education, as well as measuring those skills, is an area where librarians should continue to develop and promote their own expertise.

Aligning information literacy with information technology provides some opportunities to advance information literacy programs and make them more visible. "The Standards" specifically address the use of information technologies to locate and manage information, as well as to create products or performances. In exploring the intersection between information literacy and fluency with information technology, care should be taken to retain a focus on values central to information literacy that do not relate to technology, such as effective use of print collections and the role of librarians in the educational process.

In many cases, the phrase "information literacy" and its variants may rarely be used in discussions with faculty and students. Instead, information literacy provides a conceptual framework for understanding and working more effectively with a variety of programs and initiatives to promote student learning on college campuses.

REFERENCES

American Library Association. "Presidential Committee on Information Literacy: Final report." (Last updated 1989). Available: www.ala.org/ala/acrl/acrlpubs/whitepapers/presidential.htm (accessed May 6, 2006).

American Library Association. "A Progress Report on Information Literacy: An Update on the American Library Association Presidential Committee on Information Literacy: Final Report." (Last updated 1998). Available: www.ala.org/ala/acrl/acrlpubs/whitepapers/presidential.htm (accessed May 6, 2006).

Arp, L. 1990. "Information literacy or bibliographic instruction: Semantics or philosophy?" *RQ*, Vol. 30: 46–49.

Arp, L., and B. S. Woodard. 2002. "Recent trends in information literacy and instruction." *Reference and User Services Quarterly*, Vol. 42: 124–132.

Association of College and Research Libraries. "Information literacy competency standards for higher education." (Last updated 2000). Available: www.ala.org/ala/acrl/acrlstandards/informationliteracycompetency.htm (accessed May 6, 2006).

Association of College and Research Libraries, Institute for Information Literacy, Best Practices Initiative. "Characteristics of programs of information literacy that illustrate best practices: A guideline." (Last updated 2006). Available: www.ala.org/ala/acrl/acrlstandards/characteristics.htm (accessed May 6, 2006).

Association of College and Research Libraries, Instruction Section, Teaching Methods Committee. "Information literacy in the disciplines." (Last updated 2006). Available: www.ala.org/ala/acrlbucket/is/projectsacrl/infolitdisciplines/index.htm (accessed May 6, 2006).

Aufderheide, Patricia Rapporteur. 1992. "Aspen Media Literacy Conference—Part II. Proceedings and next steps." Available: www.medialit.org/reading_room/article356.html (accessed May 6, 2006).

Battersby, M., and the Learning Outcomes Network. 1999. *So, what's a learning outcome anyway?* Vancouver, BC: Centre for Curriculum, Transfer, and Technology.

Boyer Commission on Educating Undergraduates in the Research University. "Reinventing undergraduate education: A blueprint for America's research universities. (Last updated 1998). Available: http://naples.cc.sunysb.edu/Pres/ boyer.nsf (accessed September 21, 2006).

Brasley, S. S. 2006. "Building and using a tool to assess info and tech literacy." *Computers in Libraries*, Vol. 26, no. 6-7: 44–48.

Bruce, C. 1997. *Seven faces of information literacy*. Adelaide: AusLib Press.

Bruce, C. 2000. "Information literacy research: dimensions of the emerging collective consciousness." *Australian Academic and Research Libraries*, Vol. 31, no. 2: 93–109.

Chauvin, B. A. 2003. "Visual or media literacy?" *Journal of Visual Literacy*, Vol. 23, no. 2: 119–128.

Committee on Information Technology Literacy. 1999. *Being fluent with information technology*. Washington, DC: National Academy Press. Available: http://newton.nap.edu/html/beingfluent/es.html (accessed May 6, 2006).

Dorr, A. 2004. "Media literacy." In *International encyclopedia of the social and behavioral sciences*, 9494–9497.

Eisenberg, M. B., C. Lowe, and K. L. Spitzer. 2002. *Information literacy: essential skills for the information age*. 2nd ed. Westport, CT: Libraries Unlimited.

Fass McEuen, S. 2001. "How Fluent with Technology Are Our Students?" *Educause Quarterly*, Vol. 24: 8–17.

Grassian, E., and J. Kaplowitz. 2001. *Information literacy instruction: theory and practice*. New York: Neal-Schuman Publishers.

Gratch-Lindauer, B. 2002. "Comparing regional accreditation standards: outcomes assessment and other trends." *Journal of Academic Librarianship*, Vol. 28, no. 1: 14–25.

International ICT Literacy Panel. 2002. "Digital transformation: A framework for ICT literacy: A report of the international ICT literacy panel." Princeton, NJ: Educational Testing Service. Available: www.ets.org/Media/Research/pdf/ICTREPORT.pdf (accessed May 6, 2006).

Jones, E., R. Voorhees, and K. Paulson. 2002. *Defining and assessing learning: exploring competency-based initiatives*. Washington, DC: National Center for Education Statistics. Available: http://nces.ed.gov/pubs2002/2002159.pdf (accessed August 1, 2006).

Moore, Amanda. 2002. "Information fluency in liberal arts colleges." *Arkansas Libraries*, Vol. 59: 4–8.

Rader, H. 2002. "Information literacy 1973-2002: A selected literature review." *Library Trends*, Vol. 51, no. 2: 242–259.

Rockman, I. F. 2002. "Strengthening connections between information literacy, general education, and assessment efforts." *Library Trends*, Vol. 51, no. 2: 185–198.

Rockman, I. F. 2004. *Integrating information literacy into the higher education curriculum: practical models for transformation*. San Francisco: Jossey-Bass.

Snavely, L., and N. Cooper. 1997. The information literacy debate. *Journal of Academic Librarianship*, Vol. 23, no. 1: 9–14.

Webber, S., and B. Johnston. 2000. "Conceptions of information literacy: New perspectives and implications." *Journal of Information Science*, Vol. 26, no. 6: 381–397.

Weimer, M. E. 2002. *Learner-centered teaching: Five key changes to practice*. San Francisco: Jossey-Bass.

Woodard, B., and L. Janicke-Hinchliffe. 2001. "Instruction." In R. Bopp and L. C. Smith (eds.), *Reference and Information Services: An Introduction* (pp. 177–209). Englewood, CO: Libraries Unlimited.

Work Group on Information Competence, S. C. Curzon, Chair. "Information Competence in the CSU: A Report Submitted to the Commission on Learning Resources and Instructional Technology." (Last updated December 1995). Available: http://library.csun.edu/susan.curzon/infocmp.html (accessed August 3, 2006).

Zurkowski, P.G. 1974. The information service environment: Relationships and priorities. Related paper No. 5. Washington, DC: National Program for Library and Information Services.

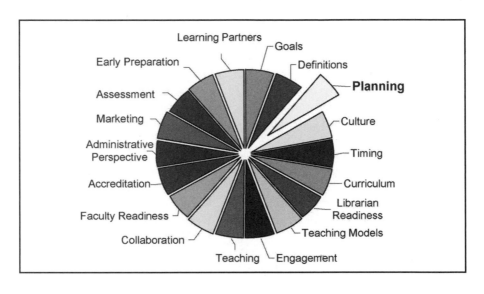

PLANNING

A Word from the Editors

*O*ne of the greatest challenges of an information literacy program is to sustain the program over many years. A common dilemma for librarians is to launch a successful and well-regarded program of information literacy only to find it floundering within just a few short years. So common is this occurrence that we thought it mandatory to address this issue by inviting Judith Peacock, who is widely published in the field of information literacy, to bring her considerable experience to bear on this vital topic. Drawing upon the significant experience of the Queensland University of Technology, Judy, who is the Information Literacy Coordinator for their library, proposes a way to make an information literacy education sustainable. Arguing that it is imperative to think beyond an information literacy "program" to the concept of information literacy education in which we provide learning opportunities, Judy encourages us to develop a composite of strategies across the university that are owned and driven by many. It is a rigorous approach but, if we follow Judy's direction, we will find our efforts flourishing. Writing to the editors, Judy says that "the challenge can be answered through long-term commitment to information literacy education bound to organization-wide, renewable strategic planning and driven through systemic reform." As readers, we are the beneficiaries not only of her life as a practitioner promulgating a holistic, sustainable approach to information literacy education, but also of her many years of consulting, teaching, and participating on the national and international level in the field of information literacy. Judy has a Graduate Diploma of Library Science from the Queensland University of Technology and a Diploma of Teaching from the Townsville College of Advanced Education, now known as James Cook University.

Chapter 3

Beyond the Fashionable:
Strategic Planning for Critical Information Literacy Education

by Judith Peacock

INTRODUCTION

The philosopher, poet, and novelist, George Santayana, warns that "fashion is something barbarous, for it produces innovation without reason and imitation without benefit"—an ominous state since the idea must afterwards be always old-fashioned. Often, significant educational reforms are viewed by stakeholders as "fashionable trends" which answer an immediate imperative but with which one should not trifle too long for fear of wasting effort for no reasonable gain.

Until recently, information literacy has been addressed in higher education as a fashionable learning accessory—a desirable, but non-essential, component of an academic qualification, the next quintessential educational fad. However, information literacy is not (and never has been) a "barbarous" educational fashion. Rather, it is a state of knowing and doing which is fundamental to living in the new knowledge era. The challenge for all educators is to fuse the learning of information literacy to an academic education in such a way that the reasons and benefits are clearly apparent to all concerned.

This challenge can be answered through long-term commitment to information literacy education bound to organization-wide, renewable strategic planning and driven through systemic reform. The key is to deliver systematic and sustainable learning of information literacy for students. It is an approach which demands a macro view of a process generally approached at a micro, or programmatic, level.

This chapter argues that it is only by instigating macro processes for information literacy development that an organization can instigate and sustain true and effective educational reform (Bowman, 1999: 296). By directing the goals and objectives of information literacy education through strategic initiative pathways, individuals can more fully be supported in their efforts to instigate broad implementation at a practical level.

Two fundamental concepts lay at the heart of the discussion in this chapter—strategic planning and systemic reform. Strategic initiatives are defined by Roberto and Levesque (2005: 54) as those which entail the broad implementation of new processes and systems to create new processes, or transform existing ones, to accomplish major goals. These new processes allow organizations to engage in what Tompkins (Bowman, 1999) describes as "continuous paradigm shifting"—a necessary condition for allowing change and growth to occur within the context of an ongoing, continuous process of discovery, learning, growing, evolving, improving, and performing" (Bowman, 1999: 295). This process then has greater potential to cultivate systemic reform, a process which, according to Conley (1994: 12), "involves comprehensive, coherent, and coordinated change." He maintains that a systemic approach challenges fundamental assumptions, practices, and relationships in ways that lead to improved and varied student learning outcomes for essentially all students. In his view, all educators—faculty and librarians alike—"need to commit themselves to the big-picture mentality of systemic reform" (Conley, 1994: 12).

Santayana observes that the process of reform requires the shattering of one form to create another—the two sides of which are not always equally intended nor equally successful. This chapter explores the reconstructive reform of information literacy education in an academic environment by examining how one Australian university—Queensland University of Technology (QUT)—has undertaken a rigorous strategic, systemic approach to information literacy learning and teaching. This analysis explores the characteristics of a strategic approach, and the advantages (or disadvantages), the issues which may arise, and the impact/effect in terms of outcomes.

This chapter will be framed within three fields of discussion. Firstly, it will highlight the broader strategic philosophies and principles that QUT Library uses to align and guide its initiatives within the university context. In keeping with the view of McClamroch, Byrd and Sowell (2001: 372) that "strategic planning takes the long view, the overarching view of what particular activities an organization should undertake to align its mission, vision, and values with its environment," this section will investigate the important role such planning has played in shaping the broader information literacy context, goals, and initiatives of QUT Library.

Secondly, it will look at how these strategic processes articulate into practice by looking at a range of strategies that have been implemented by QUT Library with, and on behalf of, the broader university. It will illustrate how this particular academic library has confronted the realities of a new time, refocused its energies, and allocated its limited resources strategically (McClamroch et al., 2001).

Lastly, the chapter will reflect upon strategic processes in terms of the success and/or failure of those strategies applied at QUT.

STRATEGIC PLANNING FOR SUSTAINABLE CHANGE—THEORETICAL PERSPECTIVES

Drew and Bensley (2001: 62) maintain that, in today's academic institution, rhetoric will be an unacceptable substitute for substance as now, as never before, "the successful management of the functional imperatives . . . necessitates [an] approach that is palpably capable of evolving, adapting, and aligning itself to national and global influences." For Roberto and Levesque (2005), four critical strategic processes assist this approach—chartering, learning, mobilizing, and realigning. These "teleological" processes enable organizations to lay the foundation for the successful institutionalization of strategic change initiatives.

Teleological models are described by Kezar and Eckel (2002) as those which encompass strategic planning, bureaucratic and scientific management, and organizational development. In their study on institutional transformation, they determined that meaningful, systemic change was more prevalent in institutions using robust teleological models as the guiding framework for change. It was these institutions which proved to be more purposeful and adaptive, and more able to move beyond the notion of change as a linear series of sequenced, planned events to one that was interconnected and occurring simultaneously rather than in stages or sequences (Kezar and Eckel, 2002, 318). Their study suggests that balance in the strategies, in the interrelationships between the strategies, and applied to the change process itself, are all critical factors in the capacity for institutions to adopt sweeping changes to established norms of process and behavior.

According to Kaplan and Norton (Harvard Business School, 2005), culture is the foremost factor influencing an organization's ability to change; therefore, for positive change to occur, organizational culture must be tailored to support the strategy. If this is so, then logic dictates that managing strategy and managing change are synonymous and reciprocal states (Harvard Business School, 2005: 73)—one cannot occur in isolation of the other. They also argue that, to successfully execute strategy, an organization must be clear about the new or differing values and expectations they are proposing to ensure strategies are adopted.

For Bowman (1999: 295), educators as leaders must commit themselves to the "big-picture mentality of systemic reform" in order to function as change agents in educational environments. Systemic reform is described by Conley (1994: 12) as that which "involves comprehensive, coherent, and coordinated change" and which has the capacity to "change fundamental assumptions, practices, and relationships in ways that lead to improved and varied student learning outcomes for essentially all students." This is particularly important when one takes the view that "curricula, pedagogy and assessment can no longer be the sole province of individual academic teachers, and that university teaching must become a disaggregated team effort" (Bundy, 2004a: 2).

In this new educational climate, academic institutions must create a new model for information literacy education in which development is not extraneous to the curriculum, but rather is woven into its content, structure, and sequence so that it creates "opportunities for self directed and independent learning where students become engaged in using a wide variety of information sources to expand their knowledge, construct knowledge, ask informed questions, and sharpen their critical thinking" (Bundy, 2004b: 6). Bundy maintains that the progressive universities of the future will be those in which the development and implicit and explicit course integration of graduate attributes, such as information literacy, assures that learning outcomes become liberating (Bundy, 2004b: 11). It is in these universities that content focuses on answers which continually change, rather than on questions which rarely vary (Bundy, 2004a: 8).

In order for information literacy to become an educational construct, owned by all educators within an organization (Bundy, 2004a), it is critical that libraries and their parent institutions adopt a process of systemic—rather than programmatic—reform. To do so requires the support, active participation, and leadership of everyone in the academic institution, with multiple groups taking a lead role in driving, enabling, and/or facilitating the process (Peacock, 2002). It demands a process that McLagan (2003: 52) describes as "distributed intelligence," which occurs when "everyone in an organization, regardless of role or level, proactively solves problems, makes decisions, and takes creative action as the need arises—without waiting to be told what to do."

This collaborative process of sense-making, interpretive strategy, and coalition-building aligns with higher education's tradition of shared governance (ASHE, 2001), creates a sense of shared understanding and interdependency among staff, results in more effective and creative solutions, and engages diverse perspectives and talents (Olson and Singer, 2004). In this model, it is important to appeal to the interests of the stakeholders by making differential appeals, appreciating differences in motivation, and by leveraging modest resources into a broader commitment (Kolb, Williams, and Frohlinger, 2004). As Kolb et al. (2004) also note, it is equally as important to enlist partners with a stake in the decision and with specific expertise to support the case. McClamroch et al. (2001) argue that this approach ensures innumerable opportunities for buy-in and ownership by internal stakeholders, assuring that the long-term benefits outweigh any short-term costs.

However, it is important to understand that not everyone will engage with the process, nor is it necessary that they do—that to move the organization where it needs to go requires only a critical mass, or "tipping point" (Quinn, 2004; McLagan, 2003), at which stage the change becomes mainstream. The challenge is then to sustain the change as the critical mass develops so that the organization can "become a productive community continuously striving to adapt to emerging reality" (Quinn, 2004: 203).

While ambiguity and a non-linear process is important for institutional leaders and change agents (ASHE, 2001), it does create an unsettling situation for those involved in adjusting to a significant cultural change in thought and practice. Quinn (2004: 295) describes this process as "building the bridge as we walk on it," or learning in real time with no definite outcome yet apparent. It is in this process that resistance to the change can force people to revert to old ways of knowing and doing. Covington (2002) warns that it is a virtual certainty that any significant change in the organization is going to shift the balance of power, bring varied rewards, appear threatening to some, and ensure some degree of resistance. It is in the strength of the leadership, combined with clarity of vision, that resistance can be managed and change can occur.

Information literacy is experiencing an "adolescent rebirth" in terms of learning and teaching. As this process develops, it is important that organizations can and do accommodate ambiguity, multiple processes, and adaptive partnerships to ensure that any change in information literacy education is systematically and systemically implemented and tested. At QUT, this process is underway.

QUT OVERVIEW

The Institution

QUT is one of the largest of Australia's 38 universities with an enrollment averaging approximately 40,000 students in undergraduate and postgraduate courses distributed across four campuses. Demographically, the largest proportion of students are drawn from the southeast Queensland regional and Brisbane metropolitan areas, with international students comprising 12 percent of total enrollments. In terms of specific demographics, QUT closely echoes statistical profiles for other Australian higher education institutions—approximately 60 percent are full-time enrollments with the remaining 40 percent consisting of part-time and external students; on average, 37.5 percent are commencing (1st year) students and 55 percent of the student cohort is female (QUT, 2005a). The university offers a broader range of undergraduate degrees than most other Australian universities, and provides flexible options for students to choose a combination of study areas and participation in overseas exchange programs. QUT is the largest provider of bachelor degree graduates into full-time employment in Australia each year, and its graduate employment rate is well above the national average for Australian universities (QUT, 2005b).

Teaching and Learning

The *QUT* "Blueprint" refers to the university's ambition to provide "outstanding learning environments and programs that lead to excellent outcomes for graduates, enabling them to work in, and guide a world characterized by increasing change." It also notes that it has a role to develop the capacity to "generate new knowledge, to foster critical thinking and inquiry," and to provide education that is relevant and demonstrably more than training (QUT, 2004b).

QUT has a well-founded international reputation for quality teaching and learning and excellent graduate outcomes. This reputation is founded in a pedagogy which focuses on student-centeredness, and which reflects in responsive curriculum design, learning environments, and teaching. It states, as its teaching goal, to ensure "that QUT graduates possess knowledge, professional competence, a sense of community responsibility, and a capacity to continue their professional and personal development throughout their lives." Goals are measured through the Key Performance Indicators (KPIs) *positive graduate outcomes* and *graduates* (QUT, 2004b).

In 1998, the West Review produced a useful framework of Australian graduate outcomes which included "research, discovery, and information retrieval skills and a general capacity to use information" (West, 1998: 1). Since that time, all Australian universities have been required to specify their generic graduate attributes in quality assurance and improvement plans submitted annually to the Department of Education, Science and Training (DEST). DEST (2002) reports that, although no university has yet adopted a university-wide strategy for curriculum integration and assessment focused on specific generic abilities, most are now working towards embedding their lists of graduate attributes into curricula, and developing strategies for assessing and recording outcomes.

In support of this ambition, QUT frames the learning of each discipline within the broader development of graduate capabilities, a set of important values, attitudes, knowledge, and skills which QUT expects that graduates should develop as part of their learning. It is expected that these skills will equip them as independent, lifelong learners and assist them to contribute effectively as citizens, leaders in the wider community, and competent professionals within their chosen discipline. QUT recognizes information literacy as a key graduate capability.

QUT LIBRARY: THE ORGANIZATION

QUT Library provides dynamic and innovative access to information resources and services, and extensive educational services supported by the broad knowledge and skills of its staff teams. The senior executive team of the director, library services and two associate directors (Information Resources and Development) oversee a complement of approximately 180 (ongoing and fixed-term) staff in lending, reference, and technical services areas. The library is one of five departments which form the Division of Technology Information and Learning Support (TILS).

Physical resources and services are branch-based and distributed across the four campuses of QUT. The libraries, therefore, are not faculty-specific; rather, they service the needs of multiple disciplines based on each campus (with the exception of the Law Library, which has a single discipline focus and shares the city campus with the Gardens Point Library). QUT Library also provides extensive electronic resources and Web-based services to clients. Services are enhanced through partnerships with clients, university colleagues, and external organizations, and provided by library staff who are committed to providing high-quality service, and whose knowledge and expertise is continually enhanced through an extensive staff development program (QUT Library, 2006).

The accomplishment of the library's vision is addressed through development in four critical areas which mirror the university's strategic focus: teaching and learning, research, community engagement, and resources. The library uses the Balanced Scorecard (BSC) as its quality management framework. This framework integrates performance measurement and quality initiatives as a comprehensive planning tool for the development and implementation of annual initiatives and KPIs.

QUT LIBRARY: INFORMATION LITERACY VISION, GOALS AND OBJECTIVES

The Library's "Information Literacy Statement of Purpose" states that "QUT Library provides leadership in developing and fostering the essential information literacy knowledge, skills, and understanding of the QUT community. The university-wide information literacy strategies promulgated by the library promotes critical thinking and equips individuals for lifelong learning. In partnership with academic colleagues, QUT Library enhances curricula and creates learning environments which support QUT's teaching and learning goals" (QUT Library, 2000).

In support of this vision, QUT Library leads the university towards developing and implementing a strategic, systematic, and sustainable model of information literacy teaching and learning focused on:

- raising the awareness of students and staff to the notion of information literacy as a lifelong learning attribute
- developing a mutual understanding of the inherent principles and practices of information literacy
- effecting attitudinal and cultural change pertaining to the learning and teaching of information literacy

- leading change in learning and teaching practice to ensure that information literacy is a pervasive and enduring part of the learning environment (Carpenter, 1996)
- improving student competence with respect to information knowledge, concepts, and skills

QUT Library emphasizes that information literacy knowledge and skills are most effectively learned when developed recursively within the context of a discipline-related need—i.e., when embedded within the learning experiences (curriculum content and assessment) for each student. To this end, the library undertakes a proactive role in developing, promoting, and implementing a variety of strategies and initiatives which target curricular reform. Through collaborative planning, development, and delivery of concepts and skills, the library contributes to the design of discipline-based curricula which incorporates information literacy as an enabling generic capability. Included in these curricula are advice and assistance on the formulation of authentic assessment tasks which address information literacy learning outcomes.

As information literacy is an ongoing strategic focus for QUT Library, the department undertakes strategic leadership in the development and implementation of initiatives which:

- promote information literacy as a key competency for lifelong learning, fundamental to the teaching, learning, and research focus of the QUT community
- enable and empower students as critical and independent users of information by embedding information literacy skills, as an "emerging skill" and key generic capability, into the whole learning experience
- achieve and promulgate models of effective practice for the implementation and evaluation of information literacy in terms of students' learning outcomes, curriculum structure, and assessment

Internal to the library, information literacy education is a primary responsibility of 21 full-time Liaison Librarians, two dedicated learning and teaching positions, and the shared responsibility of a further 20 full and part-time staff positions (including managers). The library itself provides information literacy educational programs, services, and resources which acknowledge and cater for level, timeliness and mode of study, specific discipline requirements, different learning styles, and the diverse needs and backgrounds of students and staff.

STRATEGIC APPLICATION OF INFORMATION LITERACY AT QUT

Institutional Buy-In

The significant emphasis on lifelong learning and graduate capabilities (including information literacy and technological literacy), coupled with the focus on outcomes-based education and "process-based" rather than "knowledge-based" learning environments, places information literacy learning and teaching as an educational imperative to be addressed by academics, librarians, and administrators alike (Peacock, 2001: 136). QUT educators, recognizing the critical relationship between appropriate curriculum design, effective teaching and learning strategies, and the development of such skills, "strive to provide high quality educational experiences for students that develop the multiplicity of generic capabilities within a discipline context" (Peacock and Bradbury, 2003: 1).

In recent years, information literacy has gained prominence in QUT as a key competency for lifelong learning, fundamental to the university's teaching and learning goal of developing graduates who can "recognize when information is needed, [and] have the ability to locate, evaluate, and use effectively the information needed" (American Library Association, 1989). QUT supports the view that, by knowing "how information is organized, how to find information, and how to use information effectively," (American Library Association, 1989) QUT's graduates will have learned how to learn, for life. In response, the university supports the systematic and systemic development of information literacy as a capability which contributes significantly to positive graduate outcomes and student satisfaction, facilitates secondary-tertiary transition, and minimizes first year attrition. As a result, a number of strategic policies and/or initiatives reflect the university's commitment to the learning and teaching of information literacy.

In 2001, the QUT Teaching and Learning Committee endorsed "Learning for Life: The Information Literacy Framework" (ILF) (QUT Library, 2001) as guiding policy for the development of information literacy. The document was developed by QUT Library to provide a theoretical base and practical direction for implementation of information literacy education. The ILF serves as a guide for QUT administrators, teaching faculty, library teaching staff,[1] and general QUT support staff by promulgating models and strategies for developing and evaluating information literacy in terms of student learning outcomes, curriculum structure, and assessment. The ILF was produced in consultation with relevant library stakeholders, such as faculty liaison librarians, senior library management, and various library committees. Counsel of the broader QUT community was solicited through a formal reference group consisting of nominated university staff with teaching and learning expertise and responsibilities in the area of generic skills development. QUT Library continues to receive widespread recognition of its strategic value to institutional educational outcomes.

With the library's leadership, QUT's information literacy initiatives and activities are closely aligned with the 1st edition "Australian/New Zealand Information Literacy Standards" (ANZ IL Standards), as endorsed by the Council of Australian University Librarians (CAUL) in 2001. The "ANZ IL Standards" provide a framework for embedding information literacy into the design and teaching of educational courses and programs. These standards extend and support the information literacy developmental strategies and initiatives of educators, teacher librarians, and academic librarians in the school, tertiary and TAFE sectors. Due to the close correlation to the "ANZ IL Standards," QUT's information literacy policy and practice stand strongly aligned with global information literacy initiatives and perspectives (Carpenter, 1996).

Inclusion as one of QUT's critical graduate capabilities signals the university's clear recognition of the intrinsic link between lifelong learning and information literacy, as well as QUT's responsibility in developing such a capacity in students and staff. QUT's policy on graduate capabilities states that every QUT course aims to develop graduates who are able to demonstrate "the capacity for life-long learning including: searching and critically evaluating information from a variety of sources using effective strategies and appropriate technologies" (QUT, 2005c).

In parallel with the increasing emphasis on generic capabilities, information literacy has been a focus for comprehensive curriculum reform within the university, and the application of innovative approaches to learning and assessment. With its inherent links to the development of critical thinking and problem resolution, administrators and teaching staff alike recognize the degree to which information literacy contributes to the empowerment of QUT students as lifelong learners and productive, informed employees.

A number of other QUT strategic documents, policies, and initiatives have connections to the effective learning and teaching of information literacy, including the QUT "Learning and Teaching Plan 2005–2010," QUT's "Mission, Goals and Key Performance Indicators," the QUT "Blueprint," the QUT "Online Student Portfolio," and QUT's "Priority Areas" and "Teaching Capabilities Framework."

Organizational Strategic and Quality Processes: Shared Goals

In these times of rapid change, it has become more important than ever for academic libraries to engage in long-term strategic planning (McClamroch et al., 2001). Well articulated strategic plans, according to Wickenden and Huang (2004), must be a realistic response to a situation, set new and clear directions, and for Feinman (1999), must "allow for the strengths and weaknesses within the competitive environment, devote resources to projects that utilize the set of core competencies and primary skills within the organization, identify areas within the social and political environment that require careful monitoring, and recognize the competitive areas that need careful attention" (Feinman, 1999: 1). As academic libraries begin to lead major reform in information literacy education in terms of stronger pedagogical associations and more deliberate moves away from instructional models, a comprehensive teleological framework becomes critical to the success of large and small scale initiatives.

QUT Library not only supports, but actively leads, key university strategies in relation to teaching and learning, and the library continues to strengthen its commitment to client-focused service and continuous improvement in this regard. It is within the critical library and divisional planning and quality assurance infrastructure that information literacy goals, initiatives, and services are referenced and directed. These outcomes are directed and monitored via a number of key policy documents, including:

- Client Charter—The charter describes the standards of service that the library aims to provide for its clients and for which performance is measured against achievement of the targets as specified in the charter, including information literacy.
- Vision and Strategic Plan—The library informs and positions its direction and growth using the Balanced Scorecard (BSC) quality framework in accordance with the four perspectives of client, financials, internal processes, and learning and growth. Information literacy is predominantly represented in the client perspective (for services to, resources for, and partnerships with students and faculty) and learning and growth perspective (in terms of library teaching staff development initiatives). Planning is linked vertically and horizontally to divisional and university planning cycles, and monitored by the Library Planning Forum, assigned to guiding future directions for the library's services and developing the library's renewable three-year objectives.
- Sectional/Functional Plans—Top level planning is supported and extended through planning undertaken at a committee, sectional, and/or functional level. The client services committee and reference services teams incorporate information literacy objectives at a distributed and/or local level. At a specific whole-of-library information literacy planning and review is conducted via information literacy planning retreats, held every two to three years. The retreats provide an opportunity for QUT Library's learning and teaching team to review and reflect on progress and plan future initiatives and strategies. Information literacy initiatives thus remain closely aligned with library, divisional and university strategic planning cycles.
- Key Performance Indicators (KPIs)—KPIs form the critical measures against which the library reviews its performance in key areas. Results are reported regularly and indicators are reviewed and adjusted as necessary. Information literacy is represented by measurements against:
  - client satisfaction—percentage of students who indicate a high/very high degree of satisfaction with the library's generic courses
  - curriculum embedding—percentage of compulsory faculty units within undergraduate courses which show evidence of information literacy implementation and/or curriculum planning and development

- Operational Performance Targets (OPTs)—Faculty/divisional performance each year is marked against the OPTs which are determined within the annual university planning cycle in accordance with guidelines established by the vice chancellor. The targets are determined at a divisional level and achieved at a departmental level, and successful completion of the targets attracts a financial reimbursement to the division. Information literacy has been successfully addressed as an OPT for the division for successive years, thereby further establishing it as an area of significant focus within the university.

Information Literacy Learning and Teaching: A New Model

Through strategic and systemic integration into processes of the broader organization, and by collaborating closely with administrators and faculty, QUT Library has led the development and implementation of information literacy learning and teaching with three broad strategies.

STRATEGY 1: EXTRA CURRICULA (SUPPLEMENTAL)

Extra curricula information literacy learning activities develop *generic* enabling skills and are *supplemental* to the core curriculum of students. Typically, these activities take the form of lectures, workshops, and short courses on basic information skills, which are designed and delivered by library teaching staff and attended at the discretion of each individual student. Information literacy content is generic (i.e., discipline-neutral) and non-targeted (i.e., not aligned with any unit and/or course). If applicable, assessment is formative only and designed to provide immediate feedback to students for their own learning. The outcome is short-term functional application of basic information skills.

STRATEGY 2: INTER CURRICULA (INTEGRATED)

Inter curricula information literacy learning activities develop *specific* enabling skills *linked to* the core curriculum of students. As with Strategy 1, these activities generally take the form of lectures, workshops, and/or short courses on basic information skills which are designed and delivered by library teaching staff but in consultation with, or at the request of, the individual teaching academic. Teaching events are typically attended by groups of students as a study requirement and may be scheduled into unit/course timetables. Information literacy content is generally contextualized within a unit curriculum or discipline and timetable (i.e., discipline-related), and targeted to the broad but immediate needs of students in a single study area. Where required, assessment is generally summative in nature, supplemental to primary assessable requirements and may be assigned a nominal to moderate weighting. The outcome is a task-specific application of basic information skills.

Strategy 3: Intra Curricula (Embedded)

Intra curricula information literacy learning opportunities develop transferable skills embedded within the core curriculum of students. The learning and application of information skills and practice may still occur via varied standard formats. However, these learning opportunities and experiences are designed, delivered, assessed, and evaluated via collaborative partnerships between academic and library teaching staff.

In this strategy, students are engaged in embedded learning of information literacy. Therefore, the approaches to learning and teaching are often invisible to students. Conceptual knowledge and skills development is addressed within the full curricula of a course, in each associated unit of study within that course, and across all year levels. Information literacy content is always contextualized within the content and assessment of a single unit as connected to multiple units within a course (i.e., discipline-driven), and targeted to the specific and immediate long-term needs of students in each unit/course. Assessment elements of the unit/course are a combination of formative and summative mandatory requirements of the unit/course and are weighted accordingly. Through recursive and iterative learning opportunities, the outcome is deep, durable learning, and transferable understanding and application of complex information literacy concepts and skills.

Governance and Engagement: Shared Responsibility, Common Knowledge

Leadership of all information literacy strategies, initiatives, and services is shared between a wide range of the following positions and/or groups within the library, and guided by additional external influences.

Staff Positions

Associate Director, Library Services (Development)

The associate director, library services (development) is responsible for the overall management of the library's information literacy portfolio, within the context of quality client services.

Information Literacy Coordinator (ILC)

The ILC provides advice and recommendations on policies and procedures for the provision of, and client access to, information literacy programs, products, and services across QUT Library and the university. The ILC works collaboratively with faculty and library teaching staff to assist with, and advise on, effective strategies for the integration, delivery, and evaluation of information literacy competencies within the university's curricula, and to network within the university to ensure that information literacy maintains a high profile on the university's teaching and learning agenda.

The ILC reports directly to the associate director, library services (development), and works in close partnership with the liaison librarians, the Advanced Information Retrieval Skills (AIRS) librarian, reference services managers, and branch library managers. External to the library, the ILC maintains regular contact and collaborates with other strategic areas within the university, such as the Office of Research and Research Training, Teaching and Learning Support Services, Information Technology Services (Learning & Development), the Academic Policy and Programs Unit (graduate capabilities and T&L policy issues), the Human Resources Department (staff development issues and initiatives), International Student Services (orientation and special programs), and Equity Services (orientation and special programs).

To ensure that the teaching and learning of information literacy at QUT evolves in step with global trends and models of good practice, the ILC networks widely with professionals from other institutions as well as contributing to the initiatives of wider information literacy-related associations and governance groups. The ILC also monitors and facilitates the ongoing professional development of library teaching staff with regard to information literacy, and teaching and learning in higher education.

LIAISON LIBRARIANS

Liaison librarians constitute the primary teaching and learning interface for the library (as one part of their multifaceted role) and in this capacity work in partnership with designated faculties and divisions as educational practitioners and advisors in all areas directly relating to the library policies and activities which address the information literacy learning needs of students and staff. Liaison librarians lead and actively engage in a range of collaborative teaching and learning partnerships and curriculum development initiatives. By working in partnership with academics, project teams, and course coordinators, liaison librarians contribute to the creation of innovative and authentic information literacy learning experiences for students. Specifically, the liaison librarians:

- collaborate in curriculum and assessment development and design to embed information literacy into the learning of students
- work with academics, tutors, and research assistants to enhance the information literacy comprehension of the wide range of student cohorts
- teach information literacy skills components within undergraduate units and courses and provide structured courses for postgraduate students
- evaluate information literacy programs and services generally, and within faculty/school contexts
- assess student learning against information literacy outcomes

The liaison librarians work in partnership with the ILC towards achieving the information literacy goals and objectives of the library. They report directly to the reference services managers.

ADVANCED INFORMATION RETRIEVAL SKILLS LIBRARIAN

The AIRS librarian is responsible for the teaching, assessment, evaluation, and administration of IFN001: AIRS, a mandatory course for Higher Degree Research (HDR) students. The AIRS librarian reports directly to the ILC.

INFORMATION LITERACY BRANCH COORDINATORS (ILBCs)

Selected liaison librarians from each branch are nominated as ILBCs on a two year basis. The ILBCs form a critical line of communication between branch-based library teaching staff and the ILC. They guide and support strategic and operational information literacy initiatives and planning for the library. The ILBCs monitor and operationalize the delivery and evaluation of branch-based generic information literacy courses. They also monitor information literacy-related quality assurance processes at a branch level.

REFERENCE SERVICES MANAGERS (RSMs) AND BRANCH LIBRARY MANAGERS (BLMs)

The RSMs and BLMs actively facilitate the achievement of the information literacy goals and objectives of the library. Via the direct line management of the liaison librarians and working in partnership with the ILC, they contribute to strategic planning, operational decision-making and resourcing, and promotional processes governing the library's information literacy activities.

Committees and Working Groups

Library staff advocate and lead the learning and teaching of information literacy via engagement in a variety of internal committees and working parties. These include:

INFORMATION LITERACY ADVISORY TEAM (ILAT)

The ILAT is convened by the information literacy coordinator. As a governance group, ILAT undertakes to:

- foster a cooperative and coordinated approach to the support, development, delivery, and promotion of new initiatives and existing generic and branch-specific programs
- provide guidance and leadership with regards to curriculum design, development, and evaluation
- ensure open and clear channels of communication between the branches and the ILC

- undertake collaborative projects to develop information literacy products and enhance services
- manage and implement necessary statistical reporting mechanisms
- oversee information literacy quality assurance and continuous improvement
- identify and recommend staff development opportunities
- serve as a forum for discussion and information sharing

ENDNOTE ADVISORY GROUP (ENAG)

The ENAG works in conjunction with the ILAT. ENAG undertakes to oversee the distribution of EndNote software at QUT and coordination of end-user support and education.

CLIENT SERVICES GROUP (CSG)

The CSG is convened by the associate director, library services (development). As part of its portfolio of strategic planning for cross campus development and delivery of library client services, the group monitors and advises on IL strategic planning, development, and delivery of IL client services, policies relating to IL-related client services operations, procedures, and promotions initiatives.

External to the Library: Institutional

QUT Library participates in a wide range of faculty, divisional, and university committees and working parties in order to ensure that information literacy is addressed in the broader strategic planning and development activities of the university, and incorporated specifically in the design, planning, delivery, and evaluation of course curricula. This includes participation in cross-institutional events, services coordination (such as orientation and careers days), teaching and learning grants support teams, university and faculty/school teaching and learning committees and academic boards, staff development networks, and divisional information exchange teams.

External Institutional Engagement

The information literacy initiatives at QUT are also referenced within a broader global agenda for the learning and teaching of information literacy, and align with the strategic direction and activities of relevant associations, peak bodies, policies, and/or frameworks. These include the Council of Australian University Librarians (CAUL), Australian Library and Information Association (ALIA), and specifically, the ALIA Information Literacy Forum, the Libraries of the Australian Technological Network (LATN),[2] Queensland University Libraries Office of Cooperation (QULOC),[3] and the Australian and New Zealand Institute for Information Literacy (ANZIIL). For the period

2006–2008, ANZIIL will be co-hosted by the libraries of QUT and South-bank Institute of TAFE.

Internal Processes: Administration, Review and Reporting

Within the library's overall administrative processes are embedded a range of systems which support and weave information literacy into the university, divisional, and faculty planning and review processes.

Statistics

QUT Library uses a dedicated database for the collection, collation, and reporting of statistics relating to direct information literacy teaching contact provided by library teaching staff. Statistics are collected to inform the KPIs, rationalize development, govern future planning, and advocate for ongoing support.

Knowledge Management

The activities of the library, while centrally governed, are locally implemented. To support work at a branch and individual level, the library has instigated a range of central systems, such as:

- an intranet portal to resources, information, and programs which assist library teaching staff to plan, design, deliver, assess, evaluate, and report the learning and teaching of information literacy
- coursepacks for the library's generic information literacy courses and classes, prepared by ILAT and made available via the intranet information literacy portal, ensuring consistency across branches in this central service to clients
- an information literacy project management system including project synopses, stages, timelines, staff involved, and links to supporting documentation or related Web sites

Evaluation and Assessment

The library develops, monitors, and implements a range of quality assurance and evaluation processes regarding information literacy products and services. These processes include evaluation and continuous improvement of information skills development activities which reference best practices across the national and international higher education sector to ensure quality learning and to inform future planning and decision-making processes. Regular evaluations of generic undergraduate and postgraduate information literacy classes and courses focus on content and outcomes alignment, relevance, and teacher performance. These methods include student peer and self-assessment and formative and summative assessment methods, such as surveys and focus groups, traditional tests and quizzes, and standardized and/or informal university procedures.

While a rigorous process of evaluation informs the continuous improvement of the library's own courses, successful embedding into the curriculum ensures that student learning, while perhaps less discernible, is prevalent in whole-of-course processes.

Planning, Reporting and Review

The ILC has lead responsibility for collating, coordinating, and/or delivering reports on information literacy activities and initiatives. Reporting and review is via standard library reporting mechanisms, such as quarterly reports, annual action initiatives, divisional annual reports, KPI reports, performance contracts, and performance planning and review processes. To inform information literacy planning, the library also uses data drawn from focus groups and surveys to gain specific insight into information seeking behavior, satisfaction with the library's learning and teaching services and resources, and potentially unmet needs for information literacy education.

Marketing/Promotion

QUT Library implements a range of targeted promotional and marketing campaigns and strategies to ensure that QUT clients are aware of information literacy learning opportunities, and significant attention is given to raising academic awareness of information literacy as a critical generic capability. In this regard, the library Web site plays an important role as a portal to learning services and resources for students and staff. In addition, the library's communications and external relations manager coordinates marketing campaigns which target particular client groups in the university, such as course coordinators or senior administrators. Liaison librarians, the Information Literacy Coordinator, and the AIRS librarian assume a pivotal role in connecting students and staff to appropriate information literacy services and resources. A number of key library and QUT print publications and external QUT reports are also used to disseminate information regarding the library's information literacy services, strategies, initiatives, and achievements.

LEARNING AND GROWTH: TEAM BUILDING AND PROFESSIONAL DEVELOPMENT

QUT Library facilitates and enables ongoing formal and informal professional development of library teaching staff in regard to the acquisition and implementation of teaching and learning theory and practice in higher education. Strategies include completion of formal qualifications in higher and/or adult education, attendance at informal in-house information literacy forums, and maintenance of teaching portfolios. The library's learning and teaching staff also undertake alternative forms of professional development which contribute to facilitating broader reform within the organization, such as provision of information literacy consultancies and facilitation of developmental workshops for other universities and organizations, action research projects within disciplines and/or student cohorts, contribution to the discourse of information literacy via publication in professional journals, and presentations at conferences and symposia.

IN REFLECTION

Admiral Rickover (1900–1986) was quoted as observing that good ideas were not adapted automatically but rather have to be driven into practice by courageous patience. This chapter has explored a large-scale initiative to drive information literacy into the strategic framework of QUT; the question remains—was it a success, how can this be known, and was there value for effort?

From their study, Kezar and Eckel (2002) determined that those organizations that had visible success balanced rational structural strategies with strategies that shaped beliefs and institutional culture, and balanced long- and short-term goals and tasks coupled with long- and short-term plans, created a balance between ongoing efforts and new initiatives, and senior administrative leadership with a collaborative process. To follow a process such as this demands a long-term commitment and a patient, measured approach to change.

For QUT Library, taking a patient approach to changing the way the university relates information literacy to learning has been a complex and rewarding approach in terms of outcomes. By signaling a long-term commitment through strategic initiatives, and sustaining action and development via appropriate internal resourcing and development, information literacy has become well positioned in the educational discourse and practice of QUT. At the same time, it has also proven to be a frustrating process as, while change *has* occurred, it has taken a slower, more divergent route than is necessarily desirable. The library's teaching staff would readily admit that they have accomplished much by building bridges underfoot, and that this has, at times, been a challenging process for highly professional individuals. Needless to say, taking a strategic approach to preparing the ground for change has begun to bear substantial fruit for all concerned, and these achievements will continue to fuel successes in the future.

If institutional legitimacy is a critical force within value-driven organizations in higher education (ASHE, 2001), then aligning with QUT's institutional image and vision has indeed been a lever for positive change. Strategic alignment has resulted in essential advocacy across the university which has, in turn, produced opportunities for engagement in critical learning and teaching initiatives. The QUT "Information Literacy Framework" is an excellent example of the strength of a strategic approach. Its endorsement by the QUT Teaching and

Learning Committee, combined with a targeted marketing campaign, prompted invitations to participate in faculty executive meetings and raised the attention of course planners in the university. In turn, it raised the profile and importance of information literacy, promoted a more common understanding of the concepts and approaches required for learning, affected terminology in key university and faculty policy and planning documents, and thereby effected changes at course level. Ultimately, it attracted an internal teaching and learning grant of AUD$150,000 to reform the undergraduate science curriculum to embed information literacy in the learning and assessment of all major streams in the course.

Incorporating information literacy into the specific strategic planning and quality processes at a divisional and departmental level has, likewise, had a positive impact on the success of broader efforts to introduce and promulgate new models of information literacy education. By tapping into the planning and measurement strategies of the library and the division, and connecting the change process to individual and institutional identity (ASHE, 2001; Feinman, 1999), the library has ensured a common understanding and legitimacy of information literacy which has better assimilated into the goals and objectives of QUT. Adherence and response to such requirements as KPIs and OPTs has elevated information literacy as a critical focus and area of responsibility for others beyond the library.

Actively extending jurisdiction of information literacy within the library and soliciting wider university engagement in developmental processes has prompted a greater common knowledge and understanding of the issues and strategies required, as well as promoted shared responsibility in achieving the strategic goals and objectives of the whole organization. In addition to the obvious strengths of devoting significant individual staff resources to information literacy, involving group governance in the form of committee planning, implementation, and reporting processes has established information literacy as a core functional responsibility of, and within, the library. Strength and capacity has also been increased by linking to the strategic imperatives of groups and agencies external to the library but within the institution, such as the Office of Research, faculty and school Teaching and Learning Committees, university staff development groups, and student agencies such as International Student Services. Linkages to the planning goals of external groups such as the ATN, QULOC, ANZIIL, and CAUL also add veracity to internal decision-making processes.

Attention to internal administrative, review, and quality processes, such as statistical collection and reporting, knowledge management, evaluation and assessment, reporting and review, and marketing and promotion, has provided an infrastructure for, and systems which, support sustainable information literacy development. Finally, a focus on the learning and growth of the human capacity of the library's teaching staff, through team building and professional development activities such as formal and informal workshops and courses, has ensured that the library leads and shares common practices, language, and objectives. It has also built a confidence in the teaching team that ensures excellence in practice and a willingness to demonstrate excellence in the form of action research and scholarly publication.

CONCLUSION

Covington (2002) argues that, while the reasons for undertaking a sweeping change are usually compelling, often any change that occurs is fleeting and—when too challenging—tenuous and likely to force people to revert to the old, familiar ways of tackling issues. He warns that this failure for change to "stick" is often due to a broader failure to prepare the ground adequately—to create a state whereby thinking and actions can be adopted in a meaningful and purposeful way. Leaders, he believes, can and must create this environment for change by following a few simple steps—creating a sense of urgency, building a strong guiding coalition, developing a clear and compelling vision, asking different questions, working the action plan, designing early wins, and embedding the change in the culture. Such a long-term strategic view, by definition, does not bring immediate results, but rather promises long-term gain by invoking organizational ownership and buy-in.

At QUT, endemic change in information literacy education has required just such an approach. For QUT Library, as the lead agency for this process, it has involved developing a strategic vision of how the library can contribute to the learning and teaching goals of the parent institution. It is achieving this objective by supporting this vision through long-term commitment and planning at all levels of the organization, providing resources and support for initiatives, building capacity within the team in terms of knowledge, skills, creative thought, and professionalism, and by rewarding and recognizing all gains as those which contribute to broader, long-term success.

It has been neither a simple nor costless process. Quinn (2004: 9) reminds us that "when we commit to a vision to do something that has never been done before, there is no way to know how to get there . . . we simply have to build the bridge as we walk on it." For QUT Library, it has been a challenging process—one which has demanded a preparedness to function with a degree of ambiguous walking and building in order to shift deeply entrenched corporately cultural expectations of the role of the library as an active participant in the educational business of the university. It has demanded significant visible and invisible expenditure in terms of staff, time, and resources, and challenged deeply held professional beliefs for the faculty and library staff involved.

However, the strategic approach has ensured that information literacy growth and development within the university is sustainable. Closer alignment with the goals, directions, and imperatives of the university, government, and higher education has encouraged and fostered more extensive buy-in. In doing so, it promises long-term commitment and rising value for efforts past and future, and assists in establishing a stronger, more credible learning and teaching role for the library. Ultimately, it will ensure better learning and thus, more capable graduates in the future.

By taking a strategic approach, the library has ensured that a robust process of information literacy development has commenced at QUT which aligns with the vision and goals of the university which, in turn, has the potential to impact positively on student learning outcomes. By thinking and acting strategically, QUT Library has ensured that information literacy—rather than becoming a fashionable accessory—will continue to be woven as a critical thread within the fabric of a QUT education.

NOTES

[1] Also referred to as "Faculty Teaching Librarians" or "Faculty Liaison Librarians." Where teaching is not the primary focus, the latter term will be applied.

[2] The ATN is a consortia of five universities: Curtin University (WA), University of South Australia (SA), RMIT University (VIC), University of Technology, Sydney (NSW), and Queensland University of Technology (QLD).

[3] QULOC is a collaborative organization which provides a framework for information exchange, best practice development, cooperative activities, and the promotion of common interests which support the teaching, learning, and research needs of member institutions. Membership comprises 12 university libraries from Queensland, New South Wales, and the Northern Territory, plus the State Library of Queensland.

REFERENCES

American Library Association. 1989. *Presidential Committee on Information Literacy: Final Report*. Chicago: American Library Association.

Australian and New Zealand Institute for Information Literacy [ANZIIL]. 2002. *Professional Development Group Statement*. Available: www.anziil.org/groups/pd/statement.htm (accessed November 6, 2003).

Association for the Study of Higher Education [ASHE]. 2001. "Research-based principles of change." *ASHE-ERIC Higher Education Report*, Vol. 28, no. 4: 113–124.

Bowman, Richard F. 1999. "Change in education: Connecting the dots." *Clearing House*, Vol. 72, no. 5: 295–297.

Bundy, A. 2004a. "Beyond information: The academic library as educational change agent." Paper presented at the International Bielefeld Conference, Germany, February 3–5, 2004. Available: www.library.unisa.edu.au/about/papers/beyond-information.pdf

Bundy, A., ed. 2004b. *Australian and New Zealand information literacy framework: principles, standards and practice.* 2nd ed. Adelaide: Australian and New Zealand Institute for Information Literacy. Available: www.anziil.org/resources/Info%20lit%202nd%20edition.pdf

Carpenter, K. 1996. "A library historian looks at librarianship." *Daedalus*, Vol. 125, no. 4: 77.

Conley, D. 1994. "Roadmap to restructuring." *ERIC Review*, Vol. 3, no. 2: 12–13.

Covington, J. 2002. "Eight steps to sustainable change." *Industrial Management*, Vol. 44, no. 6: 8–12.

Department of Education, Science & Training. 2002. *Striving for quality: learning, teaching and scholarship.* Higher Education Review Process Issues Paper, released 21 June 2002. Canberra, DEST Commonwealth of Australia 2002. Available: www.backingaustraliasfuture.gov.au/publications/striving_for_quality/pdf/quality.pdf

Drew, G., and L. Bensley. 2001. "Managerial effectiveness for a new millennium in the global higher education sector." *Higher Education in Europe*, Vol. 26, no. 1: 61–68.

Feinman, V. 1999. "Five steps toward planning today for tomorrow's needs." *Computers in Libraries*, Vol. 19, no. 1: 1–5.

Harvard Business School. 2005. *Managing change to reduce resistance.* Boston, MA: Harvard Business School Press.

Kezar, A., and P. Eckel. 2002. "Examining the institutional transformation process: the importance of sensemaking, interrelated strategies, and balance." *Research in Higher Education*, Vol. 43, no. 3: 295–328.

Kolb, D., J. Williams, and C. Frohlinger. 2004. *Her place at the table: A woman's guide to negotiating the five challenges to leadership success.* San Francisco: Jossey-Bass.

McClamroch, J., J. J. Byrd, and S. Sowell. 2001. "Strategic planning: Politics, leadership, and learning." *The Journal of Academic Librarianship*, Vol. 27, no. 5: 372–378.

McLagan, P. 2003. "Distributed intelligence: Change is everybody's business. *TD* (February): 52-56.

Olson, C., and P. Singer. 2004. *Winning with library leadership: Enhancing services through connection, contribution and collaboration.* Chicago: American Library Association.

Peacock, J. 2001. "Drive, revive, survive . . . and thrive: Going the distance for information literacy." In ALIA/RAISS *Revelling in Reference 2001. Proceedings of the Reference & Information Services Section Symposium*, Melbourne, October 12–14 2001, pp. 133–148. Canberra: Australian Library & Information Association.

Peacock, J. 2002. "Reinventing the reference librarian: Information literacy as a change agent." In unpublished proceedings of the *ACURIL XXXII Conference—The New Librarian.com*, Ochos Rios, Jamaica, May 27–31, 2002.

Peacock, J., and S. Bradbury. 2003. *Queensland University of Technology & QUT Library's Information Literacy Framework. Submission for the Australian Award for University Teaching 2003: Institutional Award—Category 1: Innovative and practical approach to the provision of support services (on, and/or off campus) that assist the learning of students)* [unpublished].

Quinn, Robert. 2004. *Building the bridge as you walk on it*. San Francisco: Jossey-Bass.

QUT. 2005a. "Data & information—student summary statistics: 2004." Available: www.frp.qut.edu.au/strat/datainfo/summary/student_enrol.jsp (accessed March 2006).

QUT. 2005b. "University overview." Available: www.qut.edu.au/about/university/ (accessed March 2006).

QUT. 2005c. "MOPP: Manual of policies and procedures: Policy C/1.3 Graduate capabilities." (Last updated January 7, 2005). Available: www.mopp.qut.edu.au/C/C_01_04.html (accessed March 2006).

QUT Library. 2000. "QUT library information literacy statement of purpose." Available: www.library.qut.edu.au/infoliteracy/ (accessed March 2006).

QUT Library. 2001. "Learning for life: The information literacy framework." Available: www.library.qut.edu.au/ilfs/ (accessed April 2006).

QUT Library. 2006. "Client Charter." Available: www.library.qut.edu.au/pubspolicies/client_charter.pdf (accessed March 2006).

Roberto, M., and L. Levesque. 2005. "The art of making change initiatives stick." *MIT Sloan Management Review*, Vol. 46, no. 4: 54-60.

West, R. 1998. *Learning for life: Review committee on higher education financing and policy final report* (The West review). Canberra: Department of Education, Science & Training.

Wickenden, B., and A. Huang. 2004. "Roadmap or roadblock: Strategic information planning." In *Breaking Boundaries: Integration and Interoperability: Proceedings of the 12th Biennial VALA Conference and Exhibition*, 3–5 February 2004, Melbourne Convention Centre. Melbourne: Victorian Association for Library Automation.

KEEP IN MIND

"The most important aspect of a teaching model for an effective information literacy program is the librarians themselves."

— Gabriela Sonntag

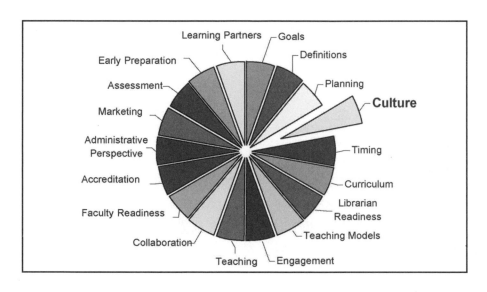

CULTURE

A Word from the Editors

*W*hen most of us want to launch or sustain a program of information literacy, we usually are preoccupied with tangible issues such as staffing, funding, or space. Equally important in the success of a program though are the intangible factors. One of the most powerful of these intangible factors is the culture of the organization. When we see certain behaviors or attitudes, when we face resistance to change, when we see some supporting a program and others not, more often than not we are dealing with the culture of the place. Culture is a powerful influential factor that often guides individual behavior in organizations. But who can understand this sometimes elusive factor? How do we know when we are tapping into a culture that will support our efforts or know when we are about to fly in the face of a prevailing culture? Tackling the challenge of understanding how culture can impact information literacy is Scott Walter, the Associate University Librarian for Services at the University of Illinois at Urbana–Champaign. Through this chapter, Scott takes us through what culture is and what it does and how we can perceive and influence the myriad cultures that can occur particularly in an educational environment. To help us, he also provides us with a framework for asking questions about culture so that we can have a better understanding of our environments. Scott concludes his chapter with an example from Washington State University (WSU), where Scott also took his Ph.D. in Higher Education Administration. Scott's work on information literacy has been presented at national conferences and he is widely published in the field. He is the co-editor with Dawn Shinew of "Information Literacy Instruction for Educators: Professional Knowledge for an Information Age" and co-author with Lisa Janicke Hinchliffe of "Instructional Improvement Programs." Prior to going to Illinois, Scott served as Assistant Dean of Libraries for Information and Instructional Services at the University of Kansas. Scott's M.L.S. is from Indiana University where he also took his M.S. in History and Philosophy of Education.

Chapter 4

Using Cultural Perspectives to Foster Information Literacy Across the Curriculum

by Scott Walter

INTRODUCTION

Why do some libraries seem to have such success in developing powerful partnerships with classroom faculty in support of information literacy instruction, while others struggle so mightily to little effect? There are many factors that influence success in fostering the instructional mission of the academic library, of course, including the skill and commitment of individual instruction librarians, the place that the professionals responsible for instruction hold in the library organization, and the presence (or lack) of instructional leadership at senior levels of the library administration. Another factor that can have a great influence on one's success in promoting information literacy instruction across the curriculum is the degree to which instruction of this sort is supported by campus culture. An understanding and appreciation of the many cultures found on the college campus can provide support for information literacy initiatives sponsored by the academic library, and lack of attention to those cultural perspectives can scuttle the most well-intentioned instructional efforts.

Kuh and Whitt (1988: iii) noted that "[almost] as many definitions of culture exist as scholars studying the phenomenon," but ultimately defined the culture of an institution of higher education as "the collective, mutually shaping patterns of norms, values, practices, beliefs, and assumptions that guide the behavior of individuals and groups... [on campus] and provide a frame of reference within which to interpret the meaning of events and actions on and off campus" (Kuh and Whitt, 1988: 12–13). Patterns of campus culture, they continue, shape decisions about governance, curriculum design, faculty recruitment and retention, and relationships with members of the local community. Efforts to establish a Center for Teaching, for example, may succeed or fail based on whether or not there is strong support for a "developmental culture" (Bergquist, 1992) on campus, just as the opportunity to establish an Office of Civic Engagement may rest on whether or not the campus culture includes a commitment to the land-grant mission (or to a religious tradition emphasizing service to others). Likewise, the success or failure of an effort to create an information literacy component for a general education program may be shaped as much by underlying patterns of support for interdisciplinary instructional initiatives within the campus culture as by the political acumen of a library director or instruction coordinator.

Attempts to apply a cultural perspective to an analysis of the opportunities that exist on campus to promote an information literacy agenda are complicated by the overlap and intersection of the multiple cultural demands made on any given individual, i.e., demands rooted in the culture of the institution, the culture of the discipline, and/or the culture of the professional community. A *campus*, for example, may espouse the value of undergraduate education as part of its institutional culture, but the culture of an academic *department* may place greater value on research than on teaching. As a result of these overlapping (and competing) cultural demands on its faculty members, that department may not present the most fertile ground for a discussion of what information literacy instruction can contribute to undergraduate education. Likewise, while research has shown that the faculty community is often unaware of the scope of the instructional role played by academic librarians (Divay, Ducas, and Michaud-Oystryk, 1987; Oberg, Schleiter, and Van Houten, 1989; Ivey, 1994), it is worth noting that even the professional community of academic librarians does not speak with one voice on the role of the librarian as teacher. This ongoing debate within our own professional culture can have an impact on the instructional services provided by the library to a department, college, or campus. For example, even if the institutional culture of a campus emphasizes collaboration across the curriculum in support of student learning, it is unlikely that information literacy will arise as a successful initiative if the culture of the academic library reflects a commitment to the librarian as collection builder rather than as teacher. These issues rarely present themselves in black and white, but the lesson to be learned in applying cultural perspectives to an analysis of our libraries and our campuses is that, when discussing the "organizational culture" of any institution of higher education, we are actually considering the interplay of multiple campus cultures. Each of these cultural perspectives must be taken into account when planning instructional initiatives in the academic library and promoting information literacy instruction across the curriculum.

This essay will identify issues relevant to academic librarians wishing to take a "cultural perspective" on their work with faculty and other campus communities in order to promote an information literacy initiative across the curriculum. An overview of the application of the idea of "organizational culture" to institutions of higher education will be provided, as will a discussion of faculty culture and its implications for instructional collaboration between teaching faculty and academic librarians. Finally, an example will demonstrate how an appreciation of campus culture can lead to success in promoting an information literacy initiative.

LITERATURE REVIEW

"Organizational culture" may be defined in many different ways (Martin, 1995). At their core, however, most discussions of organizational culture focus on the values, norms, and underlying beliefs that define the appropriate way of conducting business in an organization. Within the context of higher education, one might ask the following questions with an eye for what the answers reveal about campus culture:

- How is excellent teaching rewarded in the promotion and tenure process, as compared with success in the collection of external grants to further one's program of research?
- How are decisions about the curriculum made and disseminated to members of the academic community?
- In what ways (if at all) are new members of the community socialized into the norms and traditions of the campus?

While answers to these questions may seem discrete, they are often bound together by the underlying web of traditions, values, and beliefs that make up the organizational culture of an institution of higher education. Organizational culture may influence the espoused goals of an institution, as well as its strategic priorities, but it may also influence the way in which individuals communicate with one another, the successes that are touted in annual reports, and the rituals through which commitment to the institution is renewed and community is celebrated (Kuh and Whitt, 1988).

Cultural approaches to the study of a variety of organizations (especially corporations) have been popular over the past 25 years (Deal and Kennedy, 1982; Schein, 1985; Trice and Beyer, 1993), but inquiry into the organizational culture (and myriad sub-cultures) of institutions of higher education has been a subject of study for even longer (Kuh and Whitt, 1988). While libraries have rarely entered directly into studies of organizational culture in higher education, Kaarst-Brown et al. (2004) and Budd (2005) have described the importance of organizational culture for understanding the place of the academic library on campus and for making decisions about the allocation of library resources, and the design and delivery of library services. While these studies provide a foundation for inquiry, there are still many unanswered questions regarding the way that campus culture(s) can support (or undermine) efforts to implement a successful information literacy instruction program. By placing information literacy initiatives into their proper cultural perspective, we may achieve a more accurate view of "what works" (or, "what might work") on any given campus.

Cultural Perspectives and the Study of Higher Education

Studies of campus culture(s) have appeared in the literature of higher education for almost 50 years (e.g., Sanford, 1962), but attention to organizational (or institutional) culture, faculty culture, and student culture became more consistent starting in the 1970s, as scholars attempted to confront the sea changes in campus life stemming from the upheavals of the previous decade. Works by Clark (1970), Grant and Riesman (1978), and Thelin (1976), for example, explored how the study of organizational culture could help to identify the unique strengths of "distinctive" academic institutions (Clark, 1970), as well as to explain why curricular reforms or new approaches to campus governance might work on one campus, but not on another. By the 1980s, works by Horowitz (1984) and Thelin and Yankovich (1986) provided examples of how the study of cultural artifacts could add new dimensions to the study of higher education. Thelin (1986), like Clark (1972), also argued persuasively that the research traditions represented in cultural studies (e.g., sociology, anthropology, history) could bring an added dimension to higher education research that would otherwise be defined primarily by empirical studies, and could contribute to effective decision-making by campus leaders. Works by Clark (1987), Horowitz (1987), Bergquist (1992), and Becher and Trowler (2001) have gone beyond the study of broadly-defined campus culture to explore the ways in which multiple student sub-cultures may exist on a single campus, and the ways in which both disciplinary background and institutional type may define a variety of faculty sub-cultures. Given the wealth of research on this topic over the past 35 years, this review of the literature will be highly selective. Interested readers may consult Kuh and Whitt (1988) for a (somewhat dated, but still excellent) introduction to this line of inquiry in the field of higher education.

Cultural Perspectives on Higher Education Administration

The cultural perspective has been applied to a number of questions related to student life and the academic profession, but one of the major concerns for scholars of higher education has been to explore how an appreciation of campus culture can influence (and enhance) educational leadership. A detailed discussion of how the lessons learned in the literature of higher education might apply to the study of library leadership is beyond the scope of this essay, but even a brief review of seminal works may suggest the broader possibilities of applying cultural perspectives to the study of academic libraries.

Some of the most significant early work applying the cultural perspective to higher education administration came from sociologist Burton R. Clark, who argued that organizational culture can have a powerful influence on campus governance structures (1971) and that organizational theory could benefit from the adoption of a cultural perspective (1972). Clark (1971) argued, for example, that most studies of academic governance focus primarily on structural factors such as the formal powers of the president's office and have neglected "ideological" factors such as loyalty and trust. Factors such as these are key to an individual's "normative bonding" with the organization, and the degree to which such bonding occurs can have a significant impact on issues of governance. Clark (1970: 500) argued that normative bonding (adoption of the organizational culture by an individual) is facilitated by the existence within the organization of a powerful "organizational saga," i.e., a "collective understanding of [the] unique accomplishments" of the organization and its members. Clark (1970) also used the idea of the organizational saga as the framework for examining the evolution of three "distinctive" liberal arts colleges, and articulated the role that campus leaders played in fostering the embrace of the organizational saga by members of the faculty, student body, alumni, and general public. Focusing on the management of meaning in order to bring broad support from across an array of constituent groups to an organization in transition, Clark's work has obvious relevance to academic library leaders in the twenty-first century as they struggle to build a campus consensus around the role of the academic library in the Information Age.

Dill (1982) built on Clark's work by identifying the organizational characteristics of institutions of higher education that make the cultural perspective so important for their management. Colleges and universities, he argued, are "value-rational organizations," i.e., organizations in which "members are committed to, and find meaning in, specific ideologies" (Dill, 1982: 310). Because they work in value-rational organizations, educational leaders must be adept at often-neglected skills such as "managing meaning and social integration" (Dill, 1982: 304); in other words, they must be attuned to campus cultures. Libraries, too, are value-rational organizations, with common commitments to intellectual freedom and other ideals espoused in the "Library Bill of Rights" (American Library Association, 2006). Hernon, Powell, and Young (2003) have demonstrated how the management of meaning and other dimensions of symbolic leadership are of ongoing significance to library leaders, and this aspect of library leadership has also appeared in the literature as part of the broader discussion of organizational development in libraries (Holloway, 2004; Sullivan, 2004).

Masland (1985) also built on Clark's work by identifying four "windows" through which the organizational culture of an institution of higher education might be explored: saga, heroes, symbols, and rituals. Masland (1985: 166) concluded that cultural perspectives are critical to effective educational leadership because of the insight they may yield into "conflicting cultural elements" that can lead to negative behavior. Because cultural elements such as shared values are often implicit, Masland provides the reader with valuable tools for bringing these issues to the surface where they can become an explicit part of the planning process and of educational decision-making. Like Clark (1972) and Dill (1982), Masland provides support for the basic notion that an effective leader in any institution of higher education must take cultural perspectives into account as part of what Bolman and Deal (2003) identified as the "symbolic frame" of organizational leadership.

A final foundational entry into this literature can be found in the work of Tierney (1988), who synthesized the early work on organizational culture in order to identify those elements most relevant to management and leadership in the higher education environment. Tierney noted that educational administrators are frequently taken by surprise by the power of local campus cultures, often recognizing significant cultural boundaries only after they have been transgressed. In order to provide both researchers and practitioners with tools for identifying key elements of campus culture prior to such transgression, Tierney (1988: 8) identifies a series of questions that might be asked by anyone seeking to identify the basic framework of organizational culture on campus:

- Environment: How does the organization define its environment?
                  What is the attitude toward the environment?
- Mission: How is it defined?
                  How is it articulated?
                  Is it used as a basis for decisions?
                  How much agreement is there?
- Socialization: How do new members become socialized?
                  How is it articulated?
                  What do we need to know to survive/excel in this
                      organization?
- Information: What constitutes information?
                  Who has it?
                  How is it disseminated?
- Strategy: How are decisions arrived at?
                  Which strategy is used?
                  Who makes decisions?
                  What is the penalty for bad decisions?
- Leadership: What does the organization expect from its leaders?
                  Who are the leaders?
                  Are there formal and informal leaders?

Like the "culture audit" approach advocated by Kuh and Whitt (1988: 103–104), Tierney's framework provides concrete structure for educational researchers and leaders wishing to apply a cultural perspective to their work. As higher education administrators responsible for a core campus resource, approaches such as these are as valuable to academic library leaders as they might be to a department chair, dean, or provost.

Perspectives on Difference: Institutional, Disciplinary, and Professional Cultures on Campus

While much of the work on organizational culture in higher education has focused on broad views of the norms and values that help to bring a campus together, there have also been studies identifying the many student, faculty, and professional cultures that co-exist (sometimes with difficulty) on campus. Works such as Horowitz (1987) have provided excellent studies of distinct student cultures on campus, but studies of the cultures of the academic profession, including Clark (1987) and Bergquist (1992), provide the greatest insight into the cultural differences that can influence the success of an information literacy initiative.

Clark (1987), for example, identified how differences in institutional and disciplinary cultures define the lives of individual faculty members. Beginning in graduate school, he argued, future faculty members are socialized into cultural patterns of behavior defined by their disciplines. Disciplinary cultures define the ways in which knowledge is defined, research is conducted, and professional rewards are distributed. At the same time, differences in institutional cultures— e.g., the difference between being employed in an institution focused on undergraduate teaching as opposed to one focused on research—influence the ways in which individual faculty members approach their day-to-day work. To speak of a unified "faculty culture," Clark concludes, is to gloss over significant and substantive differences in the way the academic profession is approached by those who entered that profession by way of very different paths. The study of disciplinary differences among current and future members of the faculty has been continued by Becher and Trowler (2001), and as part of the "Carnegie Initiative on the Doctorate" (Golde and Walker, 2006).

Where Clark's focus was on the impact of institutional and disciplinary differences in the life of individual faculty members, Bergquist (1992) discussed how competing cultural orientations may co-exist on a single campus. He identified four cultural orientations that may be found to a greater or lesser degree on any campus: 1. collegial; 2. managerial; 3. developmental; and 4. negotiating. For the purposes of this essay, the most important distinctions are between the collegial culture (which Bergquist identifies as the dominant culture on most campuses) and the developmental culture. The collegial culture is one in which individuals find meaning primarily through their disciplines and through the original research that helps to further knowledge in that discipline. The developmental culture, by contrast, is one in which individuals find meaning primarily through their participation in teaching, learning, and professional development activities. More amenable to interdisciplinary approaches to both teaching and research, the developmental culture supports faculty development initiatives aimed at the improvement of instruction (Lewis, 1996; Tiberius, 2002), as well as curricular initiatives such as General Education and Writing Across the Curriculum (WAC).

The differences in institutional and disciplinary culture within the broader rubric of "faculty culture" have obvious relevance for any academic librarian seeking to promote information literacy across the curriculum. Does your campus support a vibrant developmental culture into which you might weave your efforts to help classroom faculty identify student learning objectives focused on information literacy? Do the disciplines (as represented by academic departments) with which you hope to work include approaches to teaching and research amenable to collaboration with librarians as aspects of their cultural matrices? Answering these and other questions rooted in a cultural perspective may help you to identify likely campus partners, as well as to identify potential obstacles to the promotion of your instruction program.

A final consideration for the success of an information literacy initiative is the way in which individual professional cultures interact on campus. Engstrom and Tinto (2000), for example, have identified the distinctive "cultural characteristics" of classroom faculty members and student affairs professionals, as well as how these cultural differences can present barriers to collaboration. Likewise, Divay, Ducas, and Michaud-Oystryk (1987); Oberg, Schleiter, and Van Houten (1989); and Ivey (1994) have explored perceptions of the academic librarians' role on campus among members of the classroom faculty and have found that the librarians' role as teacher is often misunderstood. When applying a cultural perspective to planning for an information literacy initiative, the cultural differences between institutions, disciplines, and professional communities must all be taken into account.

Cultural Perspectives on Information Literacy Instruction

Finally, while there has been no full-scale application of the cultural perspectives found in the literature of higher education to the study of efforts to promote information literacy across the curriculum, there have been studies that explore critical elements of the cultural perspective for what they can tell us about the potential for success of such an initiative.

Hardesty (1991), for example, identified the influence that campus cultures can have on the willingness of members of the classroom faculty to collaborate with academic librarians in support of information literacy instruction. Through his exploration of the "library educational attitudes" of members of the classroom faculty, Hardesty uncovered important differences rooted in both institutional cultures and disciplinary cultures. Likewise, his description of Earlham

College provides a powerful example of how the study of campus culture can identify the "distinctive" elements that can lead to an academic library cementing a place in the instructional landscape of its campus. While Hardesty does not cite Clark (1970) in his exploration of Earlham's unique place in the history of information literacy instruction, his identification of the influence of the Quaker tradition on faculty life and his discussion of the role played by a campus leader (Evan Farber) in the institutionalization of information literacy across the curriculum are consistent with the cultural perspective on curricular reform and campus leadership taken in earlier studies of organizational culture in higher education.

Grafstein (2002) and Simmons (2005) explored the importance of understanding disciplinary cultures (especially as represented in distinct research traditions) in developing and promoting information literacy instruction across the curriculum. Both authors describe the complementary roles to be played by members of the classroom faculty and academic librarians in the design, delivery, and assessment of information literacy instruction. Grafstein (2002) identifies discrete areas of information literacy instruction to be addressed by members of each professional community, while Simmons (2005) describes the role to be played by academic librarians as "mediators" between the individual disciplinary traditions represented among the classroom faculty. Building on earlier studies of faculty culture and on the sub-cultures into which faculty members are socialized as part of their graduate training in discrete disciplines, both authors provide an intellectual framework for defining the place of information literacy in the curriculum, as well as practical advice for teaching librarians hoping to build a bridge between the generic information literacy skills typically taught as part of lower-division undergraduate instruction programs and the specialized research tools and "discourse communities" relevant to the work of upper-division undergraduate and graduate students in the disciplines.

Elmborg (2003) also addressed the notion of discipline-based communities of intellectual discourse in his comparison of the Writing Across the Curriculum movement and the instruction movement in libraries. Looking at how both curricular reforms may be nurtured on a campus with a strong developmental culture, Elmborg provides a framework for understanding the limitations of current theory and practice in information literacy instruction, as well as for thinking about the steps that instructional leaders in libraries might take to help advance the cause in ways similar to those taken over the past two decades by leaders in the WAC movement.

In sum, the cultural perspective allows the academic librarian to ask new questions about "what works" in promoting information literacy instruction across the curricula and allows the librarian to identify both the departments and programs most likely to present opportunities for instructional collaboration, as well as the obstacles that might need to be overcome in planning for the success of the instruction program.

INFORMATION LITERACY INSTRUCTION IN TEACHER EDUCATION

In 2002–03, the author collaborated with faculty members in the Department of Teaching and Learning in the College of Education at Washington State University to integrate information literacy instruction and assessment across the teacher education curriculum. Some aspects of this project were unique, but it was only one in a series of successful instructional collaborations between the Washington State University libraries and various academic departments, interdisciplinary programs, student services, and extra-curricular activities over the past 20 years (Elliot and Spitzer, 1999; Johnson, McCord, and Walter, 2003; O'English and McCord, 2006; Walter, 2005b). Likewise, teacher education, as a discipline, has long provided opportunities for substantive collaboration between librarians and classroom faculty members in support of information literacy instruction (O'Hanlon, 1988; Shinew and Walter, 2003). Why teacher education? Why Washington State University? By applying a cultural perspective to a report of this project, we may find not only answers to the familiar question of "what worked," but also to the equally important question of "why it worked."

The Institutional Setting

Washington State University (WSU) is one of two comprehensive research universities in the State of Washington ("Doctorate-Granting University–Very High Research Activity") and was established in 1890 as the state's land-grant institution. The university maintains its flagship campus in Pullman, a city in the rural, southeastern corner of the state, as well as branch campuses in Spokane, Richland ("Tri-Cities"), and Vancouver. The university also supports ten learning centers located around the state, and cooperative extension offices in each of Washington's 39 counties. In 2002–2003, the Pullman campus enrolled approximately 18,000 FTE students (WSU Institutional Research Data, 2006), while thousands more participated in undergraduate, graduate, and continuing education programs in other locations, or delivered through Web-based instruction.

The College of Education (COE) offers undergraduate and graduate degree programs at each of the WSU campuses, as well as teacher certification through its Center for Collaboration with Schools and Communities (formerly known as the Center for Educational Partnerships) (Education at WSU, accessed: 2006). In 2002–03, the College of Education was comprised of the Department of Teaching and Learning (T&L) and the Department of Educational Leadership and Counseling Psychology (ELCP), and employed approximately 75 FTE faculty members in fields such as teacher education, educational leadership, higher education administration, counseling psychology, school psychology, and athletic training (Accreditation Report: Standard 6, 2002).

The WSU libraries provide a range of collections, information, and instructional services through a network of six libraries on the Pullman campus (Agricultural Sciences, Architecture, Education, Health Sciences, Humanities/Social Sciences, Science and Engineering). In 2002–2003, each Pullman campus library was supported by at least one subject specialist responsible for reference, instruction, and collection management in the relevant disciplines. During this project, the George B. Brain Education Library was staffed by 1.25 FTE librarians and provided an array of instructional services to the faculty, staff, and students of the College of Education, including workshop programs, course-integrated instruction, and a for-credit information literacy course (Gen Ed 300) designed for undergraduate majors in the College of Education. Regular contact points for course-integrated instruction between the WSU libraries and the teacher education program included sessions on how to locate curriculum materials in the library catalog and through other electronic resources (T&L 305), and how to locate biographical information on authors and illustrators of children's literature, and reviews of children's literature (T&L 307). During the academic year prior to the start of this project (2001–2002), over 400 faculty, staff, and students in the College of Education received direct information literacy instruction through these programs (Accreditation Report: Standard 6, 2002).

The CO-TEACH Program

In 1999, the College of Education received a Title II Teacher Quality Enhancement grant from the U. S. Department of Education to support its Collaboration for Teacher Education Accountable to Children with High Needs (CO-TEACH) program. Funded for five years for a total of $9,600,000, the primary goals of the CO-TEACH program were to:

- enhance and improve teacher education programs
- foster active and critical engagement between the teacher education community and the K–12 teachers and administrators in partner schools across the State of Washington
- support the recruitment, induction, and continuing professional development of K–12 teachers and administrators serving in high-needs districts
- integrate technology into classroom teaching
- increase the number of Native Americans pursuing teaching credentials, and enhance the ability of non-Native teachers to meet the needs of Native students (CO-TEACH, 2002)

Focused on developing new approaches to teacher education, fostering collaboration among the many academic departments and programs that contribute to pre-service teacher education, integrating critical thinking instruction across the teacher education curriculum, and promoting pre-service and continuing professional development among practicing teachers in the use of technology in the classroom, CO-TEACH provided numerous opportunities for initiating a discussion of information literacy as an important aspect of teacher education.

One of the major accomplishments of the CO-TEACH program was a thorough revision of the K–8 teacher education curriculum. By the mid-point of the grant cycle, pre-service teachers enrolled in this program followed a cohort model in which they progressed through a series of well-defined instructional "blocks" (see Figure 4-1). Just as many of the overall goals of the CO-TEACH program could be promoted through a discussion of information literacy instruction, the broader environment of curricular reform and pedagogical innovation fostered by grant-related activities provided a unique opportunity for collaboration.

What Worked: Promoting Information Literacy Instruction Through Faculty Development

Because curricular reform and faculty development were two of the primary avenues through which CO-TEACH leaders aimed to meet program goals, our approach to integrating information literacy instruction across the curriculum

---

Block One: Literacy and Language Arts

T&L 305	Fundamentals of Instruction
T&L 306	Survey of Elementary Reading and Language Arts
T&L 307	Children's Literature
T&L 320	Elementary Reading Methods
T&L 402	Instructional Practicum I

Block Two: Content Area Methods

T&L 352	Teaching Elementary Mathematics
T&L 371	Teaching Elementary Science
T&L 385	Teaching Elementary Social Studies
T&L 405	Instructional Practicum II

Block Three: Diverse Learners

ED PSY 401	Classroom Assessment
T&L 310	Classroom Management
T&L 403	Social Foundations of Education
T&L 413	Introduction to English as a Second Language (ESL)
T&L 445	Methods of Educational Technology
T&L 490	Advanced Practicum
SPED 420	Teaching in Inclusive Classrooms

Figure 4-1: K–8 Teacher Education Curriculum, Washington State University, Academic Year 2002–2003

focused on preparing teacher education faculty to integrate information literacy instruction into their own courses.

To facilitate this process, a "Faculty Collaboration Action Plan (ActionPlan)" was submitted for review that identified the following program activities:

- provide a professional development opportunity for WSU faculty and students, as well as teachers from CO-TEACH partner schools, to increase their understanding of information literacy
- develop a strand in the K–8 teacher education program in which preservice and in-service teachers will learn about models of information skills instruction and develop activities or lesson plans that integrate information skills instructional objectives with content area instructional objectives

The "Action Plan" also identified three research questions applicable to CO-TEACH program goals:

1. What are effective strategies for increasing the information literacy skills of pre-service teachers?
2. How do university professors and instructors model information literacy skills in methods courses?
3. How can teacher preparation programs respond to the planned assessment of information literacy competency, as mandated by the State Legislature?

Funded through CO-TEACH based on the "Action Plan," faculty development activities conducted during 2002–2003 included:

- a half-day workshop conducted by WSU librarians on basic concepts related to information literacy instruction and assessment, standards for information literacy instruction at the K–12 and college levels, and current status of information literacy instruction on campus, and specifically, in the College of Education
- a full-day workshop conducted by Mike Eisenberg and Lorraine Bruce from the University of Washington School of Information on the Big6 model of information literacy instruction (www.big6.com) and its applications in the elementary classroom (Eisenberg and Berkowitz, 1999)
- review of revised course syllabi in Block One and Block Two courses to identify existing course assignments that included (implicitly or explicitly) one or more dimensions of the Big6 approach

The goal of these faculty development activities was to develop revised course assignments or syllabi that made one or more dimensions of information literacy into explicit student learning objectives. Moreover, these activities were designed to promote a holistic view of information literacy in teacher education, i.e., a view that addressed the needs of the pre-service teacher as student, as teacher, and as potential instructional collaborator with site-based information professionals (i.e., school librarians) (Walter and Shinew, 2003). While space will not allow a detailed description of each of these components of the faculty development program, it should be noted that each of the participating faculty members from Block One and Block Two courses did submit revised syllabi for review. The process of discussing discrete information literacy components already embedded in existing coursework also provided an opportunity for faculty members to examine a dimension of the teacher education program that had not been explored in previous discussions of the curriculum and of desired student learning outcomes.

Why It Worked: A Culture of Collaboration

A basic requirement for the success of any information literacy initiative is willingness among the classroom faculty to collaborate with librarians on issues related to teaching and learning, and models for effective collaboration have been a prominent feature of the library literature (Dewey, 2001; Haynes, 1996; Raspa and Ward, 2000). A commitment to collaboration is a feature of the institutional culture at Washington State University, and is represented prominently in the current strategic plan, which identifies "Teamwork" as a core institutional value, and which identifies the following among its core institutional goals: "[To create] a university culture that supports efficient and effective collaboration" (Strategic Plan in Detail, accessed: 2006). Likewise, teacher education is an inherently collaborative discipline based not only on collaboration among classroom faculty teaching members of a cohort group in an instructional block of courses, but also on collaboration between faculty in the College of Education and faculty in other colleges providing instruction in content areas such as Mathematics, English, and History (WSU College Partners, accessed: 2006). If collaboration is key to the success of an information literacy initiative, then there is ample evidence that both the campus culture at Washington State University and the disciplinary culture of teacher education support such an effort.

Why It Worked: A Developmental Culture

Bergquist (1992) discussed the impact that a strong "developmental culture" can have on campus, especially in areas related to teaching and learning. There is a strong developmental culture at Washington State University, as evidenced by the existence of programs including General Education and Writing Across the Curriculum, as well as by a number of faculty development initiatives coordinated through the Center for Teaching, Learning, and Technology (Office of Undergraduate Education, accessed: 2006). Likewise, faculty development (especially as related to improvement of instruction) was a focus for the CO-TEACH program. Again, if a developmental culture is one in which interdisciplinary initiatives and initiatives aimed at supporting innovations in teaching and learning should thrive, one would expect both the institutional culture at Washington State University and the culture of the Department of Teaching and Learning to provide support for discussions of integrating information literacy across the curriculum.

Why It Worked: Building Bridges to Disciplinary Culture

Grafstein (2002) and Simmons (2005) have described the importance of disciplinary cultures for the development and promotion of information literacy initiatives, and their work complements the broader discussions of the significance of disciplinary culture in academic life found in works such as Clark (1987) and Bergquist (1992). While the faculty development workshops at the heart of this project focused on many of the "nuts and bolts" of information literacy instruction (e.g., standards, models for instruction, and assessment), the discussion was rooted in the broader concerns inherent to the field of teacher education. Rather than focusing on issues related to the research tradition in the field, the focus was on overarching concerns about the development of competent teachers for the twenty-first century. Among the most important bridges to instructional collaboration between the WSU libraries and the teacher education faculty developed through these workshops were built on discussions of:

- The impact of information literacy instruction on K–12 student learning—participants reviewed the work of the Library Research Service (2006) to introduce the notion that information literacy instruction has an impact on academic achievement among K–12 students.
- The digital divide and the role of information literacy instruction in supporting high-needs students—participants discussed the impact of the digital divide in making the transition to higher education even more difficult for students coming from high-needs schools (the focal point for the CO-TEACH program) to introduce the notion that increasing the number of information literate teachers may provide critical support to students in schools where access to information resources and information technology may be limited.
- Support for teachers in the field—participants discussed the role that school librarians could play in providing instructional support to student teachers and facilitating their success in the classroom and their transition into their first professional positions.
- Assessment and accreditation—participants discussed how a program of information literacy assessment could provide data on student learning outcomes required as part of campus-wide assessment activities, as well as how information literacy instruction could provide evidence of programmatic attention to relevant accreditation standards. Equally important,

content methods faculty members explored included how information literacy standards related to standards for K–12 student learning identified by professional associations such as the National Council of Teachers of English (NCTE).

In short, information literacy was not discussed as an independent learning goal, but rather as a means of achieving recognized goals in the field and in the department. Information literacy, moreover, was discussed not only as a goal for the pre-service teacher, but as an ongoing need for the reflective educational practitioner. Building on the concerns within the disciplinary culture related to the preparation and continuing professional development of K–12 teachers in the 21st century provided a powerful impetus for discussions of instructional collaboration between the WSU Libraries and the College of Education.

Applying the Cultural Perspective

The CO-TEACH information literacy project fostered a year-long discussion of information literacy instruction and assessment among the teaching faculty of the K–8 teacher education program, but it also made information literacy instruction and assessment part of broader discussions across the College of Education about teacher education and the professional development needs both of K–12 teachers and of teacher educators. While it would be easy to suggest that the success of the program was based on the skills and interests of the individuals involved, that would ignore the lessons about promoting information literacy as a departmental or campus initiative that the cultural perspective can provide.

First, *scan your campus for evidence of a developmental culture.* Are interdisciplinary instructional initiatives or programs focused on student learning visible on your campus, e.g., General Education, First-Year Experience, Writing Across the Curriculum? Is there an Honors College on your campus, or a Writing Center? Are faculty development initiatives focused on improvement of instruction supported on your campus, e.g., Center for Teaching Excellence, Center for Teaching with Technology? Each of these programs was available at Washington State University, and the presence of a developmental culture and of faculty members accustomed to participating in professional development programs provided an essential foundation to the success of the CO-TEACH information literacy project (as it has to the success of other information literacy projects at WSU).

Second, *consider the disciplinary culture in which your potential partners have been steeped.* Success in promoting information literacy across the curriculum depends on designing instruction that speaks to the distinct research traditions of a field, but also to broader concerns. The appeal of information literacy to members of the teacher education faculty was rooted not just in the use of discipline-specific research tools, but in making explicit the importance of information literacy for pre-service teachers, in-service teachers, and K–12 students. Student services programs have likewise proven to provide excellent opportunities for information literacy instruction because of the deep commitment within the professional culture of student affairs professionals to supporting student success in the classroom (Walter and Eodice, in press). Even at an institution like Washington State that has made collaboration a key element of its institutional culture, there are certain departments and programs that exhibit disciplinary or professional cultures especially well-suited to the development of an information literacy instruction program. Scan your local environment for evidence of similar cultures and look for your partners there.

Third, *evaluate the culture of your library.* The ability to promote information literacy across the curriculum depends on the degree to which your library peers and your library administration support instruction as a core library service. Walter (2005a) has described the importance of fostering a "culture of teaching" in the academic library as crucial to the continuing professional education of instruction librarians, but also as a critical support for an information literacy program. Whether the measure was allocation of human resources, provision of continuing education opportunities, attention to the evaluation of teaching, or statements by the library administration regarding the importance of the library's role as an instructional center on campus, Washington State University demonstrated a healthy and deep-rooted culture of teaching in its libraries. In what ways—both structural and symbolic—does your library (and your library leadership) demonstrate a commitment to fostering a culture of teaching? Will you have the broad-based support you will need for implementing an information literacy program across the curriculum? If not, how might you build support?

Finally, *identify not only the opportunities made evident to you through the application of a cultural perspective, but also the obstacles.* Engstrom and Tinto's (2000) description of the cultural barriers to collaboration between student affairs professionals and members of the teaching faculty is informative and the further study of the differences between the culture of academic librarians and the culture of classroom faculty may help us to refine our approach to collaboration in support of information literacy instruction across the curriculum.

CONCLUSION

Information literacy instruction programs exist within a complex network of campus cultures. In order to foster the success of an information literacy program, it is important to understand which aspects of the culture of your campus, your partner programs, and your own library support the core values of information literacy instruction. A deep understanding of every campus culture may not be a reasonable expectation to have of the already harried instruction coordinator, but it is important for the instructional leaders of an academic library to be ready to apply a cultural perspective to their work as part of any major information literacy initiative. As the example from Washington State suggests, an appreciation for campus culture, disciplinary culture, and professional culture on campus can help you both to identify your most likely partners, as well as to identify language with which to fruitfully engage some (if not all) of your skeptics.

REFERENCES

"Accreditation Report: Standard 6." (Last updated 2002). Available: www.educ.wsu. edu/ncate/standard6.html (accessed July 19, 2006).

"Accreditation Report: Table of Contents." (Last updated 2002). Available: www.educ. wsu.edu/ncate/toc.html (accessed July 10, 2006).

American Library Association. 2006. "Library Bill of Rights." Available: www.ala.org/ ala/oif/statementspols/statementsif/librarybillrights.htm (accessed July 6, 2006).

Becher, T., and P. R. Trowler. 2001. *Academic tribes and territories: Intellectual enquiry and the culture of disciplines.* 2nd ed. Philadelphia: Open University Press.

Bergquist, W. H. 1992. *The four cultures of the academy: Insights and strategies for improving leadership in collegiate organizations.* San Francisco: Jossey-Bass.

Bolman, L. G., and T. E. Deal. 2003. *Reframing organizations: Artistry, choice, and leadership.* 3rd ed. San Francisco: Jossey-Bass.

Budd, J. M. 2005. *The changing academic library: Operations, culture, environments.* Chicago: Association of College & Research Libraries.

Clark, B. R. 1971. "Belief and loyalty in college organization." *The Journal of Higher Education*, Vol. 42, no. 6: 499–515.

Clark, B. R. 1987. *The academic life: Small worlds, different worlds.* Princeton, NJ: The Carnegie Foundation for the Advancement of Teaching.

Clark, B. R. 1970. *The distinctive college: Antioch, Reed, & Swarthmore.* Chicago: Aldine Publishing Company.

Clark, B. R. 1972. "The organizational saga in higher education." *Administrative Science Quarterly*, Vol. 17, no. 2: 178–184.

"CO-TEACH." (Last updated 2002). Available: www.educ.wsu.edu/coteach/ (accessed July 11, 2006).

Deal, T. E., and A. A. Kennedy. 1982. *Corporate cultures: The rites and rituals of corporate life.* Reading, MA: Addison-Wesley.

Dewey, B. I., ed. 2001. *Library user education: Powerful learning, powerful partnerships.* Lanham, MD: Scarecrow Press.

Dill, D. D. 1982. "The management of academic culture: Notes on the management of meaning and social integration." *Higher Education*, Vol. 11: 303–320.

Divay, G., A. M. Ducas, and N. Michaud-Oystryk. 1987. "Faculty perceptions of librarians at the University of Manitoba." *College & Research Libraries*, Vol. 48, no. 1, 27–35.

"Education at WSU." Available: http://academics.wsu.edu/fields/study.asp?ID=EDUC (accessed July 10, 2006).

Eisenberg, M. B., and R. E. Berkowitz. 1999. *Teaching information and technology literacy skills: The Big 6 in elementary schools.* Worthington, OH: Linworth.

Elliot, P., and A. M. Spitzer. 1999. Lessons of a decade: An instructional experiment matures. *The Reference Librarian*, Vol. 64: 53–66.

Elmborg, J. K. 2003. Information literacy and writing across the curriculum: Sharing the vision. *Reference Services Review*, Vol. 31, no. 1: 68–80.

Engstrom, C. M., and V. Tinto. 2000. Developing partnerships with academic affairs to enhance student learning. In M. J. Barr and M. K. Desler, et al., *The handbook of student affairs administration.* 2nd ed. (pp. 425–452). San Francisco: Jossey-Bass.

Golde, C. M., and G. E. Walker, eds. 2006. *Envisioning the future of doctoral education: Preparing stewards of the discipline.* San Francisco: Jossey-Bass.

Grafstein, A. 2002. A discipline-based approach to information literacy. *Journal of Academic Librarianship*, Vol. 28, no. 4: 197–204.

Grant, G., and D. Riesman. 1978. *The perpetual dream: Reform and experiment in the American college.* Chicago: University of Chicago Press.

Hardesty, L. 1991. *Faculty and the library: The undergraduate experience.* Norwood, NJ: Ablex.

Haynes, E. B. 1996. Library-faculty partnerships in instruction. *Advances in Librarianship*, Vol. 20: 191–222.

Hernon, P., R. R. Powell, and A. P. Young. 2003. *The next library leadership: Attributes of academic and public library directors.* Westport, CT: Libraries Unlimited.

Holloway, K. 2004. The significance of organizational development in academic research libraries. *Library Trends*, Vol. 53, no. 1: 5–16.

Horowitz, H. L. 1984. *Alma mater: Design and experience in ten women's colleges from their nineteenth-century beginnings to the 1930s.* Boston: Beacon Press.

Horowitz, H. L. 1987. *Campus life: Undergraduate cultures from the end of the 18th century to the present.* New York: Alfred A. Knopf.

Ivey, R. T. 1994. "Teaching faculty perceptions of academic librarians at Memphis State University." *College & Research Libraries*, Vol. 55, no. 1: 69–82.

Johnson, C. M., S. K. McCord, and S. Walter. 2003. "Instructional outreach across the curriculum: Enhancing the liaison role at a research university." *The Reference Librarian*, Vol. 82: 19–37.

Kaarst-Brown, M. L., et al. 2004. "Organizational cultures of libraries as a strategic resource." *Library Trends*, Vol. 53, no. 1: 33–53.

Kuh, G. D., and E. J. Whitt. 1988. *The invisible tapestry: Culture in American colleges and universities.* ASHE-ERIC Higher Education Report No. 1. Washington, DC: Association for the Study of Higher Education.

Lewis, K. G. 1996. "Faculty development in the United States: A brief history." *The International Journal of Academic Development*, Vol. 1, no. 2: 26–33.

Library Research Service. "School library impact studies." (Last updated 2006). Available: www.lrs.org/impact.asp (accessed July 19, 2006).

Martin, J. 1995. "Organizational culture." In N. Nicholson, ed., *The Blackwell encyclopedic dictionary of organizational behavior* (pp. 376–382). Cambridge, MA: Blackwell Business.

Masland, A. T. 1985. "Organizational culture in the study of higher education." *Review of Higher Education*, Vol. 8: 157–168.

Oberg, L. R., M. K. Schleiter, and M. Van Houten. 1989. "Faculty perceptions of librarians at Albion College: Status, role, contribution, and contact." *College & Research Libraries*, Vol. 50, no. 2: 215–230.

O'English, L., and S. McCord. 2006. "Getting in on the game: Partnering with a university athletics department." *Portal: Libraries and the Academy*, Vol. 6, no. 2: 143–153.

"Office of Undergraduate Education." Available: https://my.wsu.edu/portal/page?_ pageid=303,159231&_dad=portal&_schema=PORTAL (accessed July 19, 2006).

O'Hanlon, N. 1988. "Up the down staircase: Establishing library instruction programs for teachers." *RQ*, Vol. 27: 528–534.

Raspa, D., and D. Ward, eds. 2000. *The collaborative imperative: Librarians and faculty working together in the information universe.* Chicago: Association of College & Research Libraries.

Sanford, N. 1962. *The American college: A psychological and social interpretation of higher learning.* New York: Wiley.

Schein, E. H. 1985. *Organizational culture and leadership: A dynamic view.* San Francisco: Jossey-Bass.

Shinew, D. M., and S. Walter, eds. 2003. *Information literacy instruction for educators: Professional knowledge for an information age.* Binghamton, NY: Haworth Press.

Simmons, M. H. 2005. "Librarians as disciplinary discourse mediators: Using genre theory to move toward critical information literacy." *Portal: Libraries and the Academy*, Vol. 5, no. 3: 297–311.

"Strategic Plan in Detail." Available: www.wsu.edu/StrategicPlanning/plan-detail.html (accessed July 11, 2006).

Sullivan, M. 2004. "Organizational development in libraries." *Library Administration and Management*, Vol. 18: 179–183.

Thelin, J. R. 1976. *The cultivation of ivy: A saga of the college in America.* Cambridge, MA: Schenkman Publishing Company.

Thelin, J. R. 1986. "The search for good research: Looking for 'science' in all the wrong places." *Review of Higher Education*, Vol. 10: 151–158.

Thelin, J. R., and J. Yankovich. 1986. "Bricks and mortar: Architecture and the study of higher education." In J. C. Smart, ed., *Higher education: Handbook of theory and practice* (pp. 57–83). New York: Agathon Press.

Tiberius, R. G. 2002. "A brief history of educational development: Implications for teachers and developers." *To Improve the Academy: Resources for Faculty, Instructional, and Organizational Development*, Vol. 20: 20–37.

Tierney, W. G. 1988. "Organizational culture in higher education: Defining the essentials." *Journal of Higher Education*, Vol. 59: 2–21.

Trice, H. M., and J. M. Beyer. 1993. *The culture of work organizations.* Englewood Cliffs, NJ: Prentice-Hall.

Walter, S. 2005a. "Improving instruction: What librarians can learn from the study of college teaching." In H. A. Thompson, ed., *Currents and convergence: Navigating the rivers of change: Proceedings of the twelfth national conference of the Association of College and Research Libraries, April 7–10, 2005, Minneapolis, Minnesota* (pp. 363–379). Chicago: Association of College & Research Libraries.

Walter, S. 2005b. "Moving beyond collections: Academic library outreach to multicultural student centers." *Reference Services Review*, Vol. 33, no. 4: 438–458.

Walter, S., and M. Eodice. eds. (in press). "Meeting the student learning imperative: Exploring collaborations between academic libraries and student services programs. [Special issue]." *Research Strategies*, Vol. 20, no. 4.

Walter, S., and D. M. Shinew. 2003. "Information literacy instruction for educators: A global perspective on needs and opportunities." *Behavioral & Social Sciences Librarian*, Vol. 22, no. 1: 1–5.

"WSU College Partners." Available: www.educ.wsu.edu/coteach/wsupartners.html (accessed July 11, 2006).

"WSU Institutional Research Data." (Last updated 2006). Available: www.ir.wsu.edu/db11.asp?tq=b0315&st=Academic_Year&flt=none (accessed July 10, 2006).

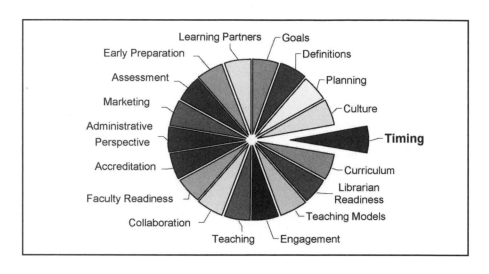

TIMING

A Word from the Editors

*I*n *writing to the editors, Eleanor Mitchell says that "the critical role of timing, while implicit in all planning, has been only rarely and tangentially considered in the now voluminous literature of planning for information literacy." In this chapter, Eleanor, the Director of Library Services for Dickinson College, explores in detail the importance of timing, including when to launch a program, how to build momentum, how to establish timetables, and how to pace the program. This thorough and unique article also explores, as Eleanor goes on to tell us, "the role that pacing and tempo play in the success of a program, and the pace for change and progress that works best." Only slightly with tongue-in-cheek does Eleanor recommend that "somewhere between inertia, momentum and burnout is the right speed." Eleanor has a wide variety of experiences that have formed her approach to and knowledge about the issues of timing. Prior to Dickinson, Eleanor was the Head of the Undergraduate Library at the University of California, Los Angeles, and for three years was the Director of the Information Literacy Initiative including being the founding director. Eleanor, who has written and spoken frequently about information literacy, also worked at Arizona State University, Westchester Community College, and* Newsweek Magazine. *Eleanor's M.L.S. is from the State University of New York at Albany.*

Chapter 5

Readiness and Rhythm:
Timing for Information Literacy

by Eleanor Mitchell

In planning, building, and sustaining a program to support the goal of student information literacy, attention to timing is an essential component for success. The ill-timed effort that fails may derail the incipient program not because it is not needed, but because the timing of launch or the pace of progress was not synchronized with the larger external or local institutional environment. If the timing is off, resources may be wasted, and hopes dashed, setting you back even farther than where you began with the additional burden of a failure to overcome.

The key questions to ask for your institution are "when?" and "at what speed?" What calendars, clocks, rhythms, and pulses drive your institution? They will provide the background for your information literacy plans and efforts. Planning cycles, budget cycles, and hiring cycles: from proposal to completion, from posting to arrival, what is the average timeline for an initiative or project, or the hiring of a much needed librarian or staff member? Determining (or developing) the right time to launch such an effort, sequencing and calendaring activities and projects to build momentum without straining resources, and establishing timetables for assessment, analysis, and retooling are some of the critical timing tasks for the program leader.

Who sets the timeline for information literacy? Is it the campus administration, or the librarians themselves, or the students, or the faculty? What are the imperatives that drive this program? Was it a locally perceived need—first year students with "citation issues," rising juniors unprepared for the demands of their majors? Or is your institution responding to the external climate, reading all about it in "The Chronicle of Higher Education," or listening to the regional accreditation authority, and charging you to make it happen? You may get to choose the moment (based on some calendar, lunar or academic) or it may be chosen for you; the resulting success or disappointment may well reflect your synchronicity with your environment.

The critical role of timing, while implicit in all planning, has been only rarely and tangentially considered in the now voluminous literature of planning for information literacy programs. This chapter will consider how to identify, and/or to create, the most auspicious time to launch an information literacy program, and the function of pace in the successful implementation following the launch. We will consider both external and institutional triggers and signals upon which to build or with which to align your information literacy programs. We will also explore the role that pacing and tempo play in the success of your program, and the pace for change and progress that works best within your library and your institution. Somewhere between inertia, momentum, and burnout is the right speed for you.

EXTERNAL TRIGGERS: KEEPING TRACK, BACKING OFF, BORROWING MOMENTUM

"Librarians need to keep abreast of the professional literature and trends monitored and echoed by campus administrators. Regular review of articles in 'The Chronicle of Higher Education,' 'EDUCAUSE Review' and 'Syllabus,' for example, can give librarians insight into key trends in teaching and learning within institutes of higher education. Recurrent analysis of this literature together with review of key planning documents can help librarians anticipate responses to needs articulated outside of the institution" (Booth and Fabian, 2002: 130). It goes without saying that librarians should keep current with trends within librarianship. Those involved with information literacy planning will find a wealth of invaluable information about successes, challenges, resources, and directions from academic librarians in print, on the Web, on listserves, and at conferences. Academic librarians also need to monitor the events and directions of the higher education community, for both programmatic and pragmatic reasons. Librarians are wise to share faculty and administrative interest in current issues and events that may impact or reflect upon the institution's direction or situation, and to make their awareness of, and engagement with, these issues visible and concrete. This provides evidence that the library staff perceives its own role as institutional rather than departmental, and enforces the idea that librarians are partners in the academic enterprise, rather than independent sub-contractors stepping in, but not staying the course. From federal legislation on student loans, to issues about faculty retention, to funding opportunities and beyond—in realms of governance, curriculum, finance, or personnel—librarians must be seen as not just considering those issues with direct and immediate impact on the library, but as knowledgeable and thoughtful members of the academic community.

In terms of program timing for information literacy, your ongoing scan of the external environment serves at least two purposes, perhaps best expressed as red lights or green, informing you of local, regional, national, and even global issues that may raise concerns about the timing of your program, or that may lend momentum and immediacy to your plans. One example that we all can relate to of a "red light" or at least a cautionary yellow would be chatter in the press (and, ultimately, news releases from your state government) about projected state budget deficits with potential impact on higher education. Unless your information literacy program is already well entrenched, a time when bread and butter activities are under siege is not a propitious moment to introduce something new that will divert funds and focus from other more pressing areas without promise of an immediate payoff.

Once you prove, through measurable outcomes, the value of information literacy to your campus, your program will become a sacred cow that is preserved when budget axes fall. But until that point of validated success, if your information literacy plan calls for reassigning personnel or reallocating resources, particularly if library collections appear to be in any way endangered, news of statewide fiscal uncertainty should prompt you not to necessarily abandon your plan, but at least to think about a more scaled back and incremental approach. Consider instead of a full fledged, campus-wide approach, a pilot program, working with a small team of librarians and a single academic department; think, perhaps, about an evolutionary rather than revolutionary posture, a demonstration project that can test proof of concept and also gather data about the cost of change. Other than budgetary cautionary notes, the announcement of different foci in the state or region might also inform your timing for launching an information literacy program; for example, if there is a big push for economic development, or an announcement about funding for a "year of the arts," you may wisely either alter your timing or, better yet, find a connection, a hook to the new initiative that may allow you to borrow momentum.

External news can also serve as a positive trigger and an impetus for your information literacy planning. In one of the most auspicious coincidences of my own experience, on the very day that I was scheduled to present the foundations for an information literacy initiative plan to the campus faculty committee on the library, the front page article in our city newspaper bemoaned the death of the high school term paper. One of the high school seniors interviewed had never written a research paper, and she exclaimed proudly, was heading for UCLA (my institution!). This provided me with a wonderful introduction for my presentation, and a way to elicit from the faculty their own sense of the preparedness of our incoming freshman for the research related demands of their first year. In this instance, timing was exquisite.

Perhaps the best examples of external events and news that can jump-start your program timing come from research and other organizations whose interests coincide with your information literacy agenda. These reports are less serendipitous than that newspaper article I encountered, often being produced on regular cycles. These may reach a level of campus visibility through general news outlets, or through "The Chronicle of Higher Education"; or you may have to develop your own methods of raising campus consciousness. At one of my former institutions, our information literacy Web site had a section that did just that: called "Nice to know" and "Need to Read," this feature highlighted current news that illuminated or underscored the need for information literacy programming.

One example of an external trigger that may pave the way for your program timing was the publication of the OCLC report, "Perceptions of Libraries and Information Resources" (De Rosa, 2005). For this report, OCLC collected over 20,000 open-ended responses from information consumers, on everything from "content, to community, to coffee and conversation" (De Rosa, 2005: ix). As you look toward building campus consciousness, this kind of data may elicit just the kind of recognition of the common problem that you need. One finding that may resonate with your campus: "Only 10 percent of college students indicated that their library's collection fulfilled their information needs after accessing the library Web site from a search engine" (De Rosa, 2005: 6). While this might seem an indictment of the libraries' collections, it is more likely that this suggests that students are inefficient users of library tools and resources. A report such as this one, widely read and discussed, helps you align your project with national dialogue and reinforces the immediacy of your message.

Another example of a report that will already be familiar to your constituents and which may serve as trigger for your own activities is the "National Survey of Student Engagement," which now surveys over 500 colleges and universities annually to provide "an authoritative source of valid reliable information about the quality of undergraduate education measuring student behaviors and institutional actions that matter to student learning and success in college" (National Survey of Student Engagement, 2005: 6). One statistic culled from this report noted that "seven of ten high school seniors wrote only three or fewer papers five or more pages long; more that one-third (36 percent) of first-year students at four-year colleges wrote at least five papers or reports 5–19 pages in length" (National Survey of Student Engagement, 2005: 30). If your campus administrators read this report with the attention that most do, the importance of this statistic will not be lost on them: your students may be arriving ill-prepared for the research related tasks ahead of them. Your announcement of an information literacy program to address this very gap would be well-timed to build upon such nationally significant statistics; your inclusion of data from this kind of report in your pitch or presentation will underscore the relevance of your response.

Don't overlook controversial or timely articles from the professional and the national presses which demonstrate that the information literacy problems your program is responding to on your campus are broader than your institution; these can be very persuasive to administration, and emphasize that your initiative is in synch with national trends. For example, consider Betsy Barefoot's article, "Bridging the Chasm: First-Year Students and the Library" in *The Chronicle of Higher Education*, which proposes that "the most effective way to ensure that first-year students become information literate is making library instruction an integral part of courses across the curriculum" (Barefoot, 2006: B16). Circulating this article among administrators and faculty, or linking to it from "the Need to Read" column on your information literacy Web pages, serves to put the campus on alert: information literacy is an important issue now, and you (and your library) are all over it. How persuasive, and how positively it reflects on your library, when your campus administrators read this sort of article and recognize that your library already has a plan in place!

There are many other reports and Web sites to watch for the borrowed momentum that may be a springboard for your program; some are national in scope, others regional or local, institutional or discipline based. Begin perhaps by developing your own list of must-read, must-monitor sources; read with an eye for implication and impact, as sometimes it is the story behind the story that provides ammunition for your information literacy cause. While a statistic on Internet usage by students, or a report on the first-year experience may not surface in a key word search for "information literacy," the subtext, the implications, may be very relevant indeed. By building campus awareness of related issues, studies, and programs identified or examined in the literature of the academic and library professional worlds, you will demonstrate the alignment, correspondence, and timing of your information literacy program with broader trends.

RHYTHM AND READINESS: IL TIMING
WITHIN THE INSTITUTIONAL CYCLE

What in your environment is driving the pace and rhythm at this moment? This may be defined fiscally, for example, by your campus' stage in a capital campaign, the multi-year fundraising initiative with its silent and active phases. Is the library included in this campaign? New bricks and mortar may present an opportunity for you to build in a state-of-the-art classroom, or a learning commons to further your goals. Your institutional pace may be perceived via administrative comings and goings, a new chancellor, president, or provost setting a different campus agenda; is there an opportunity for you to make information literacy visible early and often to a new leader on campus? Or, for some institutions, it feels like the predominant athletic season sets the rhythm for the academic year; your information literacy program can even align with this, by targeting freshmen football players for intensive IL intervention, or developing outreach to other athletes who spend a lot of time on the road. Determine what is setting the rhythm, and make sure you are keeping pace.

Most immediately relevant to your timing for information literacy would be the rhythm established by the reaccreditation process, for example, for which many institutions prepare a year or more in advance. The ACRL Web site notes (2003), "Accreditation agencies have lent their support to the information literacy movement by including language in their standards that stress the importance of teaching these abilities in colleges and universities." At one college, information literacy assessment suddenly rose to the top of the provost's agenda as reaccreditation loomed! As your institution is entering this review period, your information literacy expertise may be essential in the process. Booth and Fabian (2002: 134) write, "Campus-wide discussion of national standards, accreditation documents, and academic administrative literature present wonderful opportunities for librarians to suggest ways of achieving campus learning goals while furthering IL agendas. In order to take advantage of these opportunities, however, librarians must join the appropriate conversations through proactive involvement with campus accreditation teams, self-study groups, and sitting on faculty committees with a teaching and learning charge." Timing again is critical here; you cannot wait until the accreditation team is on campus to enter the conversation, but must build these involvements and activities into your strategy early on in order to establish your credibility. Your valued participation may then, in turn, solidify support for a campus-wide information literacy campaign.

Absent a critical driver like an impending accreditation, where do you look for signals and signs, for opportunities? The institutional environmental scan is perhaps your most important tool for identifying the best timing for your program. Grassian and Kaplowitz (2005: 226) note, "It is important to maintain a continuous environmental scan for new trends, new curriculum interests and developments, and new staff at various levels . . . if you sit back and wait, chances are that you and the library will be forgotten and left by the wayside." Listen to your campus: where is the buzz? Read the campus newspaper, check out all bulletin boards. Connect with student organizations, teams, sororities, and fraternities. Talk to people, to departmental secretaries, to facilities personnel, to faculty, and to deans. Read meeting minutes from campus committees and reports to faculty senate. Booth and Fabian (2002: 134–135) describe the variety of administrative and academic documents that should be part of your scan: "Local campus documents are also strategically important for librarians seeking to advance IL initiatives. Documents as varied as institutional mission/vision statements, central campus administration long- and short-term planning documents, reports of local assessment or accreditation teams, general education requirements, state or system-wide standards, and local campus documents on teaching and learning, frequently mirror the trends in higher education . . . librarians need to be proactive in relating IL agendas to these expressed agendas, showing local campus administrators how furthering IL goals will advance their own goals and agendas."

Pick a time when other changes are brewing on campus and you may be able to develop partnerships or collaborations that are mutually supportive of IL goals and partners' goals; being there at the foundational moment of a new program, research center, or initiative may mean the difference between building information literacy in from the start or trying to muscle it in later. Or pick a time when not much else is going on and you may get more attention and visibility for your initiative. "Librarians should also be attentive to the timing of the conversations about information literacy. If there are much higher priorities—for example, budget cuts or a conflict between faculty and administration—this is not the time to launch an information literacy program. First, the discussion will not be heard above the din of the other events, or worse, it might be used as a weapon in the debates on the other issues. When introducing an information literacy program, scan the environment closely and choose the timing wisely" (Curzon, 2004: 37). For example, many librarians staff booths at student orientation and welcome day's events. Our bookmark giveaways don't compete with the water bottles, mugs, trucker hats, and edibles of the athletic departments, the student store, student health, and many other campus entities. Similarly, our message can get lost when broadcast at a time when too much else is going on and attention is elsewhere—the first week of school is probably not the best time for an orientation to the library, nor to try to market information literacy instruction to faculty well enmeshed in the fast pace of the semester.

Readiness—receptivity to the information literacy message and ability, and the opportunity or willingness to respond to it—is another critical factor in timing your program for your institution. Booth and Fabian (2002) write about "institutional readiness" as a pre-requisite for curricular IL integration. "Once collegial partnerships have been established among library peers, faculty, and administrators, the next challenge is to evaluate institutional readiness and to advocate for curricular IL integrations. Fundamental to campus-wide IL implementations are: first, a common understanding of IL standards and their relationship to the curricular goals of the university; and second, an evaluation of readiness in terms of institutional posture and climate for curricular development and redesign" (Booth and Fabian, 2002: 129–130). At one institution, a new interdisciplinary major was being proposed by a faculty member who had previously noted deficits in student research skills. Because the liaison librarian had opened a dialogue with this faculty member on that topic, the groundwork was in place and the timing was right for writing a one-credit information literacy lab into the required courses for this major. In this instance, the information literacy standards dovetailed with the curricular goals of the major; the "readiness" was there in that the preparatory relationship building had taken place; and the timing enabled information literacy to be incorporated at the foundational level rather than added on later.

It is important to be sensitive to the pace of change in your institution. Is yours an early adopter, the campus that distributed iPods years before they became ubiquitous, the place with innovative curricula and buildings that look like they can levitate? Or is your campus more cautious, less likely to get there first, wanting to see proof of concept before committing? Will a revolutionary approach work, or will something more deliberate? "Knowing the type of culture within which you are operating can help give you clues as to the approach you need to take in order to increase the possibility of success. Although each type of culture may view innovation and change differently, all have a way to allow for that change to happen. It may be slower in some than others. Ideas may flourish but implements lag due to the heavy reliance on teamwork and group problem-solving in your culture.... Nothing happens overnight, but developing the right approach for your environment will increase the chance that your idea will succeed" (Grassian and Kaplowitz, 2005: 25).

If you are not at an institution that prides itself on trail blazing, pace yourself and give your program time. Even if resources are not an issue, resistance and reluctance may be. "Make your offerings incremental and modular. This will allow implementation of your plan one piece at a time. While it is wonderful to think about dropping an entire plan into place and making all parts of it run at a selected point in time, it may be necessary and perhaps even desirable to introduce parts of your information literacy plan individually over a period of time. In practical matters such as personnel, funding, and space, this may be the only way in which the entire plan can be completed" (Burkhardt and MacDonald, 2003: 101). Pilot projects are a great incremental way to approach information literacy programming; they may have minimal impact on resources and can be low risk. If you work with one or two individual faculty members or a single department; or focus on one delivery mechanism (an online tutorial or credit course); or isolate a population (freshmen in seminars, transfer students, introductory biology classes), you are limiting damage in a way that a highly-visible and expensive full-scale launch may not. If your pilots succeed wildly, you have excellent examples to use to scale up as you promote the next round of projects. Lessons learned on a smaller scale can inform subsequent stages and projects.

We should not overlook the local practices that may affect the specifics of program timing for your institution. For example, when are new courses or majors proposed and what is the timeline for approval and adoption? If you are proposing a credit information literacy course, or adding an information literacy component to another course proposal, this timing will be critical. How long does it take to get the Institutional Review Board's approval for an assessment? It may take much longer than you thought to obtain the permission to test your students' information competence—so long, in fact, that the juniors you intended to assess may be seniors by the time you actually test them. What is the internal grant timeline? When are new faculty brought on? How are decisions made? Is there a review committee comprised of faculty who disburse to far corners of the world when classes are over (while librarians are hard at work developing proposals and courses that will go nowhere until fall?). Your plans to develop the for-credit information literacy course curriculum over the summer may not mesh with the need for approval before the end of spring. Timing on both the large scale of institutional planning and the detail level of administrative procedures will figure centrally in information literacy programming.

INFORMATION LITERACY WITHIN THE LIBRARY PLANNING PROCESS

What timing issues relate to your library's processes and structure? The strategic planning cycle is key, of course. It is the macro level on which information literacy becomes institutionalized and prioritized within the organization. Having an information literacy strategic initiative means that the concept has been vetted in the administrative hierarchy and has visible top-level support that will lend credibility and viability to your program. It also places it within a timeframe, with "deliverables," elevating information literacy from a value to something tangible and measurable. The importance of this imprimatur goes well beyond resource allocation—it validates the time you and other librarians devote to information literacy activities. In some instances resources are also attached to strategic initiatives; at the UCLA library, three new librarian positions earmarked for information literacy roles came about in support of the strategic plan. Be aware of the planning cycle in your library; if possible, volunteer to participate on a planning task force in order to articulate the importance of information literacy front and center in the final plan. Should this come about, you are then on notice that your process and progress are going to be assessed regularly as part of the cycle. Build into your program or initiative your own benchmarks and checkpoints that will ensure you are on track to accomplish your objectives and prepared to report.

The ACRL document, "Characteristics of Programs of Information Literacy that Illustrate Best Practices," includes the statement that "planning for an information literacy program . . . is tied to library and institutional information technology planning and budgeting cycles" (ACRL, 2003: 1). Beyond additional librarians, your program may have other resource needs that will depend upon aligning with the library's annual budget process. For example, you may need more or different teaching space in your library. Through your instructional improvement efforts, more librarians are using hands-on learning; or perhaps your outreach has been so successful that you cannot meet the demand with current classroom spaces. Both capital improvements and simple renovations are expensive.

Requests with justifications and budgets will have to go through formal channels in just about every library. One staff of librarians realized, after more than one instance of "double booking," that they needed another dedicated space to avoid similar mishaps. The time to make this pitch is not when the classes are coming through the door. Gather data, develop a timely and persuasive proposal, and insert it into the planning process at the right moment.

One information literacy program planned an ambitious online tutorial on plagiarism. Not only was this an enormous commitment of librarians' time, but it called for external programming and design consultation; this support was possible because the request came at the right moment in the budget cycle, before other priorities had consumed the resources. In one program, funds were needed for promotions and publicity, for statistical expertise for an IL assessment, payment for students participating in that assessment, and the printing of pamphlets and other outreach materials. Some of these ideas were planned in advance; others arose from team activities. It would have been too late to request funds at the point when the budget was already set; planning ahead and timing the request appropriately, and building in funds for contingencies and opportunities, ensured at least consideration even if the full amount was not forthcoming.

There are also "drivers" for your program's momentum within the library environment. Is there a new administrator or dean coming on board? This is a key moment for your program. When a new university librarian arrived on campus, as Information Literacy Initiative Director, I was among the first to get on his calendar and make my pitch for his attention to this program; I continued my assault with regular updates to keep this program front and center in his thoughts. Not only was his own support essential to the program, but as a new dean, during the first year he spent a lot of time carrying the library's word throughout and beyond the campus. What priceless visibility for information literacy!

If your library is planning a renovation or a new building, of course there are practical advantages to being in at the ground level, in terms of proposing teaching or consultation spaces, an information commons, or collaborative learning spaces. The construction also gives you a timeline for your publicity campaign for information literacy. You will know that in a year, or two, or more, a spotlight will shine on your new library space; have your programmatic ducks in a row and be ready to showcase IL at the same time.

A moment of significant new or changing technology in the library is an advantageous time for information literacy advances. When our library building reopened in 1996 after several years' renovation, the terminals were replaced with personal computers. The arrival of the Internet gave information literacy a big push; not only did access to resources change in previously unimaginable ways, but suddenly library demos needed to migrate to hands-on sessions! As your library plans a new ILS, course management system, Web site redesign, wiki, blog, RSS feeds, or digital repository, be alert to the impact they will have on information literacy and the ways in which your program needs to have an impact on their selection, design, and implementation. Don't wait until the new technology is rolled out to the campus with big fanfare; be at the table when the issues are being surfaced and the decisions being made. And ensure that the information literacy message will be part of that fanfare.

As on the institutional level, planning for information literacy within the library's cycle also means choosing a time when you are not competing with other mission-critical priorities and programs. If all of the resources and attention are being focused on remodeling special collections, or a scholarly communication initiative, or a structural reorganization, information literacy, for the moment, needs to seek a supporting role within those other endeavors rather than striking out on its own. Not only will you have difficulty recruiting participants and getting resources, but your message will be harder to hear. There are also some very practical issues of timing that can arise when many initiatives are going forward at once. For example, one program was planning to e-mail an information literacy survey to the campus; unfortunately, the Libqual e-mails were scheduled to be sent at the same time, perhaps causing confusion in the part of those surveyed and certainly generating more e-mail "noise" than the library wanted to at one moment. Look ahead for the scheduled completion of long-term projects in your library, and time your program accordingly.

BETWEEN INERTIA AND BURNOUT: THE LIBRARIAN'S LIFE CYCLE

Librarians are both the initiators and the skeptics, even resistors, when it comes to information literacy planning and implementation. In some institutions, previous attempts that have derailed or fizzled have discouraged the librarians involved; in others, programmatic success without additional institutional support has burned them out. Those charged with the mission, perhaps as coordinators for an initiative, lacking direct authority to assign tasks and responsibilities, are often dependent upon their persuasive and coercive skills. Moving librarians beyond reluctance to acceptance (and then to enthusiasm) may be a matter of synchronizing with their professional cycles or their weekly calendars; it can also mean calibrating your programmatic ambitions to their level of comfort with the pace of change. "People deal with change at different speeds and in different ways. Some jump right into it, while others need more reflection time in order to deal with the idea" (Grassian and Kaplowitz, 2005: 25).

When there is any shift or change in staffing, there is an opportunity for information literacy incursions. Being poised to promote your agenda at the right moment will enhance your chance of success. Rewriting or adjusting existing positions is both an administrative and an interpersonal challenge; the process of changing statements of responsibility may be cumbersome, and resistance may be great. However, if a job description is being crafted for a new or changing librarian or technologist position, writing an information literacy responsibility or component may be the beginning of institutionalizing a commitment of human resources to your existing volunteer army. Even altering the wording from "library instruction" to "information literacy instruction" signals movement along the continuum.

Getting librarian participation in your initiative or program depends on their time commitments and also their priorities. Evaluation and review periods are always a time when old commitments are reconsidered and new projects or directions proposed. What is the timeline for the review process for librarians in your institution? When are individual goals set? If you have been able to build support at the top, and see evidence of an information literacy goal in the institutional or library plan, there will be impetus for staff and librarian goals to demonstrate alignment with strategic directions. The library at my former university institutionalized IL by including it in the strategic plan, and then adjusted the individual review process to better support that plan. As director of the Information Literacy Initiative, I received e-mails from several librarians working on their individual goals who sought to commit to participation in the initiative as part of their plans.

Librarians whose goals include improvement of their teaching or outreach performance may be very susceptible to what your initiative can offer them in the way of professional development opportunities. If your initiative includes programs to help them build upon existing strengths and develop new approaches, also build in time for follow-up by giving assignments that will reinforce what was learned and require the application of the workshop content. For example, if you offer a workshop on active learning presented by an outside expert, schedule a debriefing soon after to clarify and reinforce, and a "theory to practice" session weeks later, after participants have had a chance to employ the techniques they learned. If your program can support it, sending librarians to workshops such as the Information Literacy Immersion Institute or an ACRL pre-conference can build the individual's skill base AND create a cohort that can change your local culture. The timing of these programs is predetermined, so your other scheduling (and budgeting) will have to factor that in; plan, too, a time for participants to bring back and share with their colleagues what they have learned. The same iterative process that cements information literacy skills in our students applies also to practitioners: there is no single inoculation but a series of booster shots (and incubation periods!) that take time.

One dean described the rapid process of change in her library as "building the plane while flying it." As an IL program manager, you will need to continue to meet the commitments for your existing instruction programs while in the process of change. Librarians involved in your initiative must often find the time to attend meetings, plan programs, learn new approaches and ramp up outreach, conduct marketing and assessment activities in support of the information literacy program, all while continuing to teach the students before them here and now. Grassian and Kaplowitz (2005: 57) point out that "IL librarians have many demands on their time, and team projects may receive less attention than the many other tasks that fill their days. The IL manager can ensure that team projects do not die of neglect by keeping a friendly eye on the team's progress. If a project seems to be going off course or is not being moved along in a timely manner, it may be time to call the team together to find out if the project is still a viable one... in short, how can the project get moving again, and what, if anything, can the manager do to assist in creating this forward momentum?" This tension between sustaining the existing program and moving forward involves both time as a commodity—Do we actually have enough librarians to teach the classes?—and time as it relates to perceptions—are librarians feeling burned-out, stressed, or overwhelmed by the demands? Managing this tension involves setting a reasonable, but not leisurely pace for your new program; establishing mechanisms for assessing your progress, and correcting or adjusting that pace as needed; providing enough resources so that you can "service what you sell" and meet your commitments; and taking the pulse of your teams and individual librarians to determine the health of the initiative and the participants. Be sure, too, to schedule time to acknowledge progress and celebrate accomplishments on a regular basis.

TWO TO TANGO: THE RHYTHM OF COLLABORATION

Whether you are collaborating with other librarians, administrative or academic units, or specific faculty, you will need an awareness of your partners' priorities and timelines. Are your partners operating on an academic calendar, or a fiscal or annual calendar? This may affect funding cycles, resource use, scheduling of meetings, phasing of projects, and more. You may have very different expectations about the pace of the project, and may have to negotiate when pieces are due or events are scheduled in order to accommodate these differences. If you plan to accomplish most of your work on a tutorial in the slower months of the summer, you may not be able to vet it with faculty or test it on students in time for fall. Even information literacy collaboration between an undergraduate library and the biomedical library, for example, may run into difficulties because the rhythm of the undergraduate library maps to a different research and information seeking process than that of graduate students or medical faculty. Clarifying at the outset the goals, the timeline, the deliverables, and the responsibilities of each party will avoid problems later.

Faculty readiness is also a factor in collaboration for information literacy; laying the groundwork and demonstrating the benefits to the faculty (as well as their students) must precede the specifics of your partnership proposal. Librarians from the Five Colleges of Ohio worked closed with faculty in their three-year, Mellon grant funded program, "Integrating Information Literacy into the Liberal Arts Curriculum," which focuses on increasing student information literacy skills through faculty–librarian collaboration. Grim et al., writing about the collaboration, noted, "although the Mellon grant provided the impetus for the activities . . . in large measure the success of the program has depended upon a general readiness 'on the part of both librarians and faculty' to move the IL agenda forward. . . without the readiness of faculty, the perception that *something* needed to change, *and* the readiness of librarians, the project would have fallen flat" (Grim et al., 2003: 93). When planning your program, don't underestimate the time it takes to demonstrate the importance of information literacy skills to your faculty in order to get their attention and buy-in.

"Creating awareness in the minds of faculty about the need for student mastery of information literacy is not a one-time event. Reports, updates, bulletins, presentations, and many conversations are necessary over an extended period of time to penetrate the collective consciousness of campus faculty and to allow information literacy to rise to the top of the long list of issues confronting campuses today" (Curzon, 2004: 34).

Librarians who are outside of the faculty structure may be unaware of their rhythms or of the calendar that drives their priorities. Whether it is the tenure time clock, or the pace of teaching during the semester—classes, assignments, term papers, finals, etc.,—or committee assignments, or their own research agendas, including sabbatical plans and grant applications—faculty are ruled by different timelines. What presents itself as resistance to your proposed information literacy collaboration may just be the response of a harried professor to yet another demand on his or her time. At one college, librarians looked forward to working with faculty to integrate information literacy into the first year seminar curriculum. Alas, the orientation for this faculty was scheduled for the day before graduation; many would leave campus and not return until the week before the fall semester. Hopes for the kind of close collaboration, reviewing the syllabi and developing information-rich assignments vanished with the awareness that the time that the librarians had to devote to this project—the summer—was not the time that the faculty had planned to spend on those activities. On the other hand, if your program offers something that meets the faculty member's needs at the moment, it may provide just the incentive needed to make that collaboration work. Grim et al. noted, of the Five Colleges' programs, "In some cases, faculty members who are already developing new courses or who are contemplating doing so, hear about the curriculum development grants and are motivated, because the timing is right, to apply for a grant" (Grim et al., 2003: 90).

THE INFORMATION LITERACY INITIATIVE AT UCLA

Why this? Why now? The example of the launching of the Information Literacy Initiative at UCLA in 2001 illustrates the role of timing in planning for information literacy programs. In this example, an alignment of the stars—external triggers and institutional pressures—led to success when previous efforts had foundered.

The UCLA Library had a history of efforts and attempts to address deficiencies in student research skills. Among them were task forces and committees in 1977, 1986, 1994, 1995, and 1996—all charged with essentially the same task, though each reflecting the jargon of the times: to explore the issues surrounding library skills and instruction, and come up with a proposal. These programs correctly identified the problem and the need to involve faculty and the campus in the dialogue. I believe that the reason they did not succeed was more about timing than anything else.

In 2001, the time was ripe and right for information literacy at UCLA. There were both global and local influences that made this the right moment to coalesce disparate efforts and great energy into a single program with multiple facets. There was more information and more access; student needs and deficiencies seemed ever more glaring. There was increasing professional dialogue. Efforts like the ACRL Competencies provided a framework previously not so comprehensively articulated. Other libraries had well developed models to point to and learn from.

Locally, at UCLA, two events drove the launch of the initiative. First, a small team of librarians had completed an information competence assessment that documented the deficits in student comprehension and application of information competencies (Caravello et al., 2001). Among the findings: the average score of the high library-use students (64.2 percent) was higher than the average score of the low library-use students (59.7 percent)). The mean score of undergraduates tested was 61.7 percent, which indicated no clear evidence of mastery of information literacy concepts and skills. Second, the UCLA Library's strategic plan for 2000 identified information literacy as a strategic priority for the library, and put some resources behind it. New public service librarian positions were funded with information literacy written into the statements of responsibility.

With this clear mandate, a director was appointed and a three year timeframe established. A mission was stated: "Our mission is to help members of the UCLA community master conceptual and practical information literacy skills to enrich their educational, professional, and personal lives, and enable them to become independent, lifelong learners." Three goals were developed by participating librarians:

- to increase awareness of information literacy concepts among members of the UCLA community, within the context of changing information needs and environments
- to assess information literacy skills, knowledge, and abilities at UCLA
- to improve information literacy skills, knowledge, and abilities at UCLA (Grassian et al., 2005)

Five interest groups each developed their own goals and timelines; regular meetings of a steering committee comprised of representatives from each group coordinated these activities on the initiative-wide timeline:

- informing, with the objective of increasing campus awareness of information literacy issues
- reaching, which sought new audiences for information literacy and new methods of reaching them
- teaching, which worked to improve the teaching of information literacy concepts and skills
- collaborating, which developed mechanisms to further coordination, communication, and collaboration in support of IL
- measuring, which supported ongoing assessment and evaluation of student information literacy needs and achievement, and of reach and effectiveness of information literacy activities

The approach for the initiative was to seize the momentum. Activities and projects sponsored by the five groups and the steering committee were built aggressively and synergistically; a calendar on the initiative's Web site for participants was essential for tracking all that was going on. While one librarian pled at one point, "I do not see that we need such a 'presto ed agitato' approach. MORE moderato," others shared the sense that a fast advance on many fronts simultaneously was the right pace to, finally, make the information literacy initiative viable, visible, and significant. In 2004, the initiative was formalized as a program, and no longer intended to be just the province of the few, the proud, and the now exhausted participating librarians, but a universally shared responsibility among public service librarians.

CONCLUSION

"Initiation of campus-wide curriculum-based information literacy programs is a multi-layered, incremental, repetitive process whereby librarians undertake to educate not only student populations, but also their administrative and academic colleagues about the goals articulated in the ACRL IL standards" (Booth and Fabian, 2002: 127). The information literacy leader should be aware of the forces at play in the external environment that may further or hinder the initiative, be sensitive to the campus pace and priorities, be politically savvy about the library's strategic direction, budget, human resources, and technology planning cycles, and be able to adjust the tempo as needed in order to work collegially and collaboratively with other librarians, administrators, and faculty. "True change takes time. So the effective leader must temper his or her passion with a healthy dose of patience" (Grassian and Kaplowitz, 2005: 13).

REFERENCES

Association of College and Research Libraries. 2003. "Accreditation: Information literacy and accrediting agencies." Available: www.ala.org/ala/acrl/acrlissues/acrlinfolit/infolitstandards/infolitaccred/accreditation.htm (accessed April 23, 2006).

Association of College and Research Libraries. 2003. "Characteristics of programs of information literacy that illustrate best practices: A guideline." Available: www.ala.org/ala/arcl/acrlstandards/characteristics.htm

Barefoot, B. 2006. "Bridging the chasm: First-year students and the library." *The Chronicle of Higher Education*, Vol. 52, no. 20: B16.

Booth, A., and C. A. Fabian. 2002. "Collaborating to advance curriculum-based information literacy initiatives." In P. Durisin, ed., *Information literacy programs: Successes and challenges* (pp. 123-142). Binghamton, NY: Haworth Information Press.

Burkhardt, J. M., and M. C. MacDonald. 2003. "Inch by inch, row by row...growing an information literacy program." *Integrating Information Literacy into the College Experience: Papers Presented at the Thirtieth National LOEX Library Instruction Conference*, Ypsilanti, MI: 99-102.

Caravello, P. S., E. G. Borah, J. Herschman, and E. Mitchell. 2001. *Information competence at UCLA: Report of a survey project*. Los Angeles, CA: UCLA Library.

"Characteristics of programs of information literacy that illustrate best practice: A draft." (2003) *College & Research Libraries News*, Vol. 64, no. 1: 32–35.

Curzon, S. C. 2004. "Developing faculty-librarian partnerships in information literacy." In Ilene Rockman and Associates, ed., *Integrating information literacy into the higher education curriculum: Practical models for transformation*, 1st ed. (pp. 29–45). San Francisco, CA: Jossey-Bass.

De Rosa, Cathy. 2005. *Perceptions of libraries and information resources: A report to the OCLC membership*. Dublin, OH: OCLC.

Grassian, E., K. Botello, S. Phares, and D. Turnbow. "UCLA information literacy program. Blended instruction course (BICo) task force report." UCLA Library (September 30, 2005). Available: http://repositories.cdlib.org/uclalib/il/04 (accessed August 3, 2006).

Grassian, E. S., and J. R. Kaplowitz. 2005. *Learning to lead and manage information literacy instruction*. New York: Neal-Schuman Publishers.

Grim, J., C. Comer, S. D. Scott, J. C. Gustafson, and J. Vaughan. 2003. "Different models, common goals: Information literacy across the liberal arts curriculum." *Integrating Information Literacy into the College Experience: Papers Presented at the Thirtieth National LOEX Library Instruction Conference*, Ypsilanti, MI: 89–98.

National Survey of Student Engagement. 2005. *Exploring different dimensions of student engagement: 2005 annual survey results*. Bloomington, IN: Indiana University Center for Postsecondary Research.

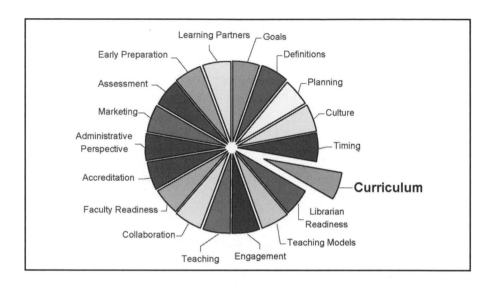

CURRICULUM

A Word from Sue Curzon

*W*hen Lynn and I, as co-editors, were outlining the elements we considered vital for a successful program of information literacy, we wanted especially to look at the role that respect for the curriculum and its processes plays in a successful program. Certainly, one of the best ways for information literacy to be sustained is for it to be embedded into the curriculum. However, the development of or changes to a curriculum are notoriously difficult. So much is at stake with the curriculum including student enrollment, faculty positions, space and equipment resources, accreditation, prestige, and faculty ownership of the content. Librarians do not come into the profession usually with experience in or knowledge of curriculum development. Yet, now with our collective drive for student information literacy skills, we find ourselves in the middle of this process. Sometimes we are successful and sometimes we are left wondering what happened. Lynn Lampert, the Chair of Reference and Instructional Services and the Coordinator of Instruction and Information Literacy at the Oviatt Library at California State University, Northridge, demystifies the curriculum process for librarians. In this chapter, Lynn talks about the importance of librarians knowing and respecting the process, illuminating how the process works, and giving us some best practices in the new trends in curriculum mapping. Lynn is certainly qualified to comment on curricular issues as she serves on the University's Educational Policies Committee and was on the General Education Revision Task Force. Through this process, Lynn was able to achieve a long-time library goal of having core courses certified as courses that are required to contain information literacy skills. Lynn speaks about this experience in this chapter also. Lynn has written and presented widely on the subject of information literacy. Her M.L.I.S. is from the University of California, Los Angeles, where she also took an M.A. in History. She has been very active in ACRL's instruction section.*

Chapter 6

Searching for Respect:
Academic Librarians' Role in Curriculum Development

by Lynn D. Lampert

Whether a librarian is new to the role of information literacy coordination or not, we often hear that attempts at information literacy curriculum integration failed because of discipline faculty's "lack of respect" for librarians, or their reluctance to recognize the benefits of adopting information literacy student learning outcomes. As William Badke quipped, "Academic librarians are the Rodney Dangerfields of the academic world—they can't get no respect," when it comes to trying to persuade faculty about the curricular importance of information literacy (Badke, 2005: 64).

Sadly, Badke's observations sometimes ring true. But the converse and often critically neglected side of the story resides in the fact that many librarians, even those enjoying the faculty status, fail to critically analyze how curricula should be developed within libraries. Librarians and libraries sometimes find themselves scrambling to best illustrate how information literacy instruction meets student learning needs both within and outside their libraries. This problem partially occurs due to librarians' lack of formal training and/or experience in creating curricula. Our lack of preparation tends to lead to short lived and ill-prepared library instructional efforts that fail because they stand alone outside of curricular tie-ins. These efforts often leave students missing the vital information literacy connections that research skills have in associated courses or disparate disciplines. More attention needs to be paid to how curricula is successfully developed outside our domain by faculty, departments, and colleges. Many academic librarians do not make it a practice to examine the concurrent pressures, both external and internal, being placed on curricular reform in order to better gauge their future attempts at garnering curricula integration and/or developing stand-alone courses. Academic librarians and libraries must strategically align themselves with curricular approval entities and assessment processes on their campuses in order to better achieve information literacy integration across the curriculum.

This chapter will provide readers with an overview of the typical ways to implement and incorporate information literacy curriculum into required university course offerings. Attention will be paid to identifying discipline based curricular practices and collaborative opportunities for participation and planning. In addition, both past and present library instructional formats and the concept of curriculum mapping will be discussed to highlight best practices for strengthening information literacy curricular programming. An overview of recent pressures placed upon higher education curricular reform will be discussed in order to provide background on the competing curricular issues that often appear to detract attention away from information literacy. Examples of how curricula are developed with department, college, and university-wide will be explored in order to offer guidance to librarians working to increase the likelihood of success and curricular respect when it comes to integrating information literacy into both the course and programmatic levels of instructional content.

APPROACHES FOR INTEGRATING IL INTO STUDENT LEARNING

For as long as librarians have provided formal instruction on how to utilize library resources, attempts to gain entrance into curricular offerings could adequately be characterized as both hit and miss. Taking stock of academic librarians' development of tours, self-guided workbooks, tutorials, and drop-in sessions and the like, historical sketches of the full arsenal of efforts to educate library users reveal a gradual and often painstaking progress to gain entry into curricular offerings. In programs that have enjoyed the most successes, both historically and presently, academic librarians have spent a great deal of time examining the curricular landscape of their institutions before they attempt to gain a greater share of student instructional hours (Rockman, 2002; Rader, 1995; Kirk, 1974).

While there will always almost certainly be questions about whether or not librarians or discipline faculty should take the lead role in establishing information literacy student learning outcomes and goals, the literature (Jenkins and Boosinger, 2003; Kraat, 2005; Raspa and Ward, 2000) shows that librarian leadership is growing in terms of respect from faculty and success in information literacy programming. However, leadership in the area of curriculum development and information literacy programming must continue to work in collaborative parallels. Patrick Ragains correctly identifies the need for all stakeholders on campus to come to a shared understanding when it comes to curriculum development and information literacy curriculum integration planning and programming. He states that,

> In order for curriculum or campus-wide information literacy initiatives to succeed, faculty and librarians must expand their individual efforts, seek improved understanding of each other's expertise and interactions with students, and support each other's educational efforts. Deans and other administrators must influence programmatic shifts by encouraging the teaching of information literacy beyond isolated courses or pilot projects. (Ragains, 2001: 405–406)

LIBRARY INSTRUCTION CURRICULAR FORMATS PRE AND POST INFORMATION LITERACY

Academic librarians have consistently worked to integrate library instruction and the undergraduate curriculum since the 1950s (Rader, 1995). However, the idea of an academic library offering a curriculum on a college campus is a fairly recent idea in relation to the history of libraries. As Terrence Mech notes,

> Librarians tend to forget that reference services, much less proactive cooperative library instruction efforts, are still relatively recent innovations within American higher education. Until the last half of the nineteenth century academic libraries offered very little to faculty or students . . . reference services did not assume an important role in college libraries until the 1940s and 1950s, and did not become a major activity before the 1960s and 1970s. (Mech, 1990: 82)

What therefore do we mean when we talk about information literacy curriculum? Library instruction within reference and public services units is still a relatively new endeavor that varies in terms of approach from institution to institution. According to *Webster's Dictionary*, curriculum can be defined as the courses offered by an educational institution and/or a set of courses constituting an area of specialization. But if we look past this traditional definition framed around lecture hours and classroom content delivery, curriculum has also recently been defined as the structure of the educational process and the framework for planning educational experiences (Regan, 1980).

The instructional programming of academic libraries certainly falls within the framework of planning educational experiences. However, typically that is where the comparison starts to fade as the majority of academic libraries do not typically offer more than one unit bearing course embedded into the college curriculum. Nor do instructional efforts typically involve strategically balanced offerings of instructional content that aim to avoid repetition and move beyond an orientation to resources both physical and electronic. Without planning and regular assessment, a curriculum cannot likely achieve its targeted educational goals.

John Lubans, Jr. correctly identifies the reasons behind the historical lack of concrete and strategic curriculum development in the area of library and research skills when he writes,

> Most library-use instruction is based on what we as librarians think library users need to know. It is this educated guesswork or perceived need on which many programs (tours, orientation lectures, a multitude of multimedia presentations, and formal courses in bibliography) have been based. . . . Probably the major errors in basing programs only on perceived need is the redundancy inherent in such an approach and that such a shortsighted view does not generally get to the source of many information-use problems: the teacher/librarian relationship. (Lubans, 1974: 232)

Good curriculum development and instructional programming continually evaluates students learning needs in addition to surmising the perceived educational objectives. It should not be solely based on what individual librarians "think" students should know. Assessment and critical inquiry into student information seeking behavior patterns should drive the curricular efforts of reference and instructional services departments.

THE INSTRUCTIONAL MENU OF ACADEMIC LIBRARIANSHIP

With the shift from bibliographic instruction to information literacy, academic librarians are shifting instruction away from resource-based presentations to an instructional focus based on student learning needs in terms of the complete research process. We are also moving away from a purely reactive model of initiating instruction to adopting proactive methods that integrate student information literacy development into course curriculum based on our professional investigations of student learning needs and collaboration with faculty. Grassian and Kaplowitz (2001) identify the initiation of instruction developing in three distinct ways: the reactive mode, the interactive mode, and finally the proactive mode. In the reactive mode, programmatic planning is predominantly motivated by library users' questions. In the interactive mode, a faculty member or an external force typically requests the development of an instructional module. The final model, the proactive model, takes place when librarians plan ahead to develop instructional programming and curriculum that supports their research on existing instructional needs (Grassian and Kaplowitz 2001: 131–132). We can perhaps better visualize what Grassian and Kaplowitz describe is taking place in these three modalities by examining the chart below.

Examples of the Reactive Mode of Instruction Initiation	Examples of the Interactive Mode of Instruction Initiation	Examples of the Proactive Mode of Instruction Initiation
Librarians develop instruction based on repetitive questions posed at reference desk.	A professor requests library instruction and largely controls the instructional design of the session.	Librarians assess and drive what students need to know in terms of the research process and existing curriculum and approach faculty.
Librarians develop instruction based on reception of poorly developed faculty assignments students bring to the reference desk.	An orientation committee assigned with the task of introducing students to campus resources contacts the library for a tour or resources and plans the content of the session.	Through outreach to the disciplines, librarians contact faculty and ask to initiate instruction that correlates to both the course curriculum and identifiable student information literacy needs.

Figure 6-1: Modes of Instruction Initiation

Faculty librarian collaborations and the building of relationships between the library and academic departments help to move the initiation of instruction away from a reactive mode or response to a proactive information literacy instructional mode. Once this change in the engagement of instruction is achieved to ensure the optimal student learning environment, the next step involves addressing how the instructional moment, regardless of its duration, is carried out and connected to long-term student learning opportunities.

THE "ONE-SHOT" VERSUS THE "STANDALONE SEMESTER CREDIT-BEARING COURSE"

When it comes to understanding the array of programmatic offerings that typify an academic library's instructional program, it is important to understand how instruction has progressed within the field of academic librarianship. The typical instructional moment in library instructional programming, the classic "one-shot," usually comes into the foreground. The literature of library and information science is replete with important studies that outline how librarians can better engage students during one-shot formats of instruction through the usage of active learning techniques, attention to diverse learning styles, and critical preparation of lecture content through constructive interactions with faculty (Choinski and Emmanuel, 2006; Sheesley, 2002). However, despite librarians' best attempts to keep the one-shot method engaging and viable as the main format of library instruction delivery,

> It has become clear that the [one-shot] demonstration-style information skills classes delivered out of curriculum context do not necessarily coincide with the students' need for information, are sometimes not valued by students, and do not necessarily prepare them for the challenges of research, problem solving and continuous learning. (Orr et al., 2001: 457)

As Grassian and Kaplowitz (2001) note, the one-shot session has its advantages in terms of often requiring less preparation time than formal stand-alone courses and providing brief and positive interactions with a librarian that may motivate students to return to the library. However, the shortcomings of the format often outweigh the benefits. Within this instructional structure, learners typically only retain some of the covered concepts and attendance is often mandatory, negating the idea of engaging the learner at their best point of instructional need.

Realizing the shortcomings of the one-shot instructional model and working to increase student learning opportunities to improve research and information literacy skills, librarians have worked to increase the success of semester long stand-alone formal courses. While most librarians would rather see these concepts embedded into disciplinary course offerings, great successes at engaging students in courses that solely focus on the area of information literacy instruction have been achieved. Stand-alone formal course offerings that deliver information literacy instructional content can be delivered in many settings. Typically the instruction is synchronous and in-person. However, with the recent adoption of distance learning management systems, such as Blackboard and Web CT, remote instruction often takes place in both synchronous and asynchronous formats.

Semester long and/or formal information literacy credit courses can be related to a designated department curriculum or discipline. At California State University, Northridge, *Chicano/a Studies 230 Introduction to Chicano/a Studies Research Methods* is one example of a stand-alone course that exists in conjunction with a department's targeted information literacy student learning outcomes. Many librarians, who state that they prefer teaching semester long courses, cite the in-depth opportunities they afford for engaging studies in information literacy and research through well designed course assignments. However, many note that the courses are time-consuming in their preparation and that students are often difficult to engage unless the course content directly links to coursework in their major course of study.

Far too often, academic librarians' efforts for information literacy's integration into unit bearing courses have often simply stopped at the creation of stand-alone information literacy courses taught by librarians. These one-unit elective courses typically only attract limited numbers of students. Undoubtedly, one unit library skills courses and one-shot information literacy instructional sessions expose students to critically needed information literacy skills. However, they typically will not garner the same respect given to discipline-based semester long courses that are tied to departmental and programmatic learning outcomes which are assessed and reviewed through consultative processes across departments and sometimes even colleges. For this reason it is important for information librarians to study how successful curriculum is adopted and improved.

HOW IS CURRICULUM DEVELOPED OUTSIDE LIBRARIES?

It is often rare for academic librarians to have a front row seat for viewing how departments, colleges, and the university develop, reform, and improve curricula. In most universities curriculum development begins at the department level with attention being paid to disciplinary demands and standards either accepted regionally or nationally by professional associations, state standards, or often even accrediting bodies. Typically a subcommittee of faculty within a department is charged with overseeing the tasks of new course creation, course and/or program modification, and program review as it pertains to course content. Hopefully these same faculty members are also involved in departmental assessment efforts as they work to ensure that course objectives and student learning outcomes aligned with the curriculum remain relevant and correspond to student learning needs. After a department creates and reviews new curricula or modifications to current course offerings, the body of changes are typically further reviewed by either a college curriculum review board or the campus curriculum approval agency. Peer review is the critical component for success when it comes to the curriculum development process that occurs at the program, department, college, and university levels. Curriculum development also typically involves the participation of school deans, department chairs, and program coordinators, members of educational policy or curriculum review committees, as well as members of the academic affairs side of an institution. It is imperative to the success of information literacy curriculum integration and development for librarians to participate in university governance that works with curricular policies. If this is not possible, librarians should at least try to develop an awareness of the campus curriculum development process and its current pressures.

Hannelore Rader (1995) explained the importance of librarians learning all that they can about curriculum development and reform practices in order to improve the curricular placement of information literacy. She cites the research of Bjorner whom she credits with effectively, "discussing various philosophies of curriculum development discipline-based (found mostly in higher education), student-based (found in elementary schools), social-utilitarian-based (found in vocational training), and social reconstruction (found in religious or other strong ideological focused institutions)" (Rader, 1995: 296).

In my experience as the Information Literacy Coordinator at California State University, Northridge, since 2001, my elected role as a faculty member serving on the campus' Educational Policies Committee has been of paramount importance when it comes to recognizing various and valid opportunities to design curricular integration for information literacy initiatives. The Educational Policies Committee meets twice a month throughout the academic year. Committee members are charged with critically reviewing all of the undergraduate curriculum proposals for new courses, programs, or modifications. From my service on this committee I have developed an awareness of the unique needs that departments are working to meet through their course offerings. My exposure to curricular programming processes across the university continues to help me, in my role as the Coordinator of Information Literacy, identify where needs are for information literacy curricular integration and what model of instructions might best meet a department's needs.

According to the dean of my library, Susan Curzon, "There are nine models for teaching information literacy that can be used on any campus" (Curzon, 2004: 37). These nine models include: the introduction model, the on-demand/one-shot model, the stand-alone information literacy course model, the learning outcomes model, the demonstration of mastery model and/or entrance requirement model, the faculty focus model, the college readiness model, and when possible the General Education model (Curzon, 2004).

For most academic libraries working to integrate information literacy into the curriculum, the *introduction model* requires focusing on freshmen orientations and first year experience learning communities. The *on-demand/one-shot model* typically focuses on covering a targeted lesson plan within a limited time framework, typically 50 to 75 minutes in duration. The one-shot model remains a reactive model that takes place based on instructor requests for instruction. The *learning outcomes model* focuses on developing and then carrying out instruction based on the student learning outcomes that an academic department has adopted into their curriculum and course of study. The *demonstration of mastery model* and the *entrance requirement model* usually utilize a test to certify that a student has attained a pre-determined level of information literacy at a particular point in their undergraduate or graduate course of study or sometimes upon entrance to the university. The *faculty focus model* involves librarians working with faculty to train them on how to individually carry out information literacy instruction on their own through the development of assignments and other instructional methods. The *college readiness model* requires outreach services to work with K–12 teachers in the area to make sure that awareness of information literacy skills needs are clear. Finally the *General Education model* works to embed information literacy student learning outcomes into the required coursework and or section requirements of the courses required in the university's general education program.

In my experience, the one common component faced in bringing any of these models to completion is the difficulty in developing unique information literacy curricula geared to meet the specific information literacy student learning outcomes that have been identified for that learning community or targeted population. This difficulty is a challenge shared by both librarians and faculty members struggling to determine which of the adopted information literacy student learning outcomes will become a focus within the course. Librarians can better prepare for these struggles by internally developing curriculum mapping tools that best illustrate how and when a student should be exposed to an information literacy concept or skills within their course of study.

CURRICULUM MAPPING

Curriculum mapping is a process that allows you to gain control and understanding over educational objectives and the instructional content that your department delivers. Curriculum mapping has been a common practice in K–16 education circles since the 1970s. It has recently gained recognition from library instruction experts as a valuable tool for helping librarians to better plan and implement instructional programming. Bullard and Holden (2006: 1) define curriculum mapping as "a systematic analysis of the content of courses in a curriculum. By using this process librarians can propose the best timing and placement for information literacy concepts across a course of study or the general education curriculum." Additional research also shows that curriculum mapping provides both an internal and external means of communicating with colleagues about long-range and short-term planning, both within and outside one's discipline. The process also helps to clearly identify gaps or repetition in instructional content (Koppang, 2004; Nash, 2004; Hinchliffe, Mark and Merz, 2003; Hayes-Jacobs, 1997).

Examples of libraries that have successfully implemented a curriculum mapping project to better define and reform information literacy curriculum offerings include the libraries of University of Illinois at Urbana–Champaign, the Vogel Library at Wartburg College in Waverly, Iowa, the Leddy Library at the University of Windsor in Ontario, Canada, and the George T. Potter Library of Ramapo College of New Jersey. The libraries at the University of Illinois at Urbana–Champaign state that they view curriculum mapping as a way of "examining a program of study and the courses within that program in order to:

- understand curriculum structures and relationships
- gain insight on how students experience the discipline
- increase awareness of curricular content

- identify common or 'gateway' courses that students are required or choose to take
- reveal opportunities for library integration" (University of Illinois at Urbana–Champaign, 2003)

The drive to improve the instructional efforts and programming of academic librarians has grown over the past decade. Efforts to focus on the pedagogical improvement of instruction librarians and get a better handle on assessment efforts continue to grow and improve. Curriculum development and reform need to be an integral part of this process in academic libraries just as they have been in academic discipline and higher education as a whole. As many university libraries realize, student engagement and learning in information literacy instructional moments depends greatly on the content matching current information needs. In many cases, reform of both library instructional focus and content will be necessary in order to achieve effective delivery across campus curriculum. This is a critical need that must be met to obtain or maintain an information literacy curriculum's integrity and respect with discipline faculty and students. As librarians at the John F. Kennedy Library at California State University, Los Angeles, note,

> While some disciplines and departments have successful instructional liaisons with the library, information literacy skills have not been systematically developed across campus. The case can be made that our students experience unmet needs with regard to information skills instruction. Because information skills are not sequenced, students experience overlap and repetition during library instruction. (California State University, Los Angeles, 2005)

CURRICULUM REFORM PRESSURES WITHIN HIGHER EDUCATION

Over the past two decades, the rapid changes in technology and external calls for accountability have forced the majority of faculty in academe to reexamine the curricular offerings in most academic disciplines in terms of both content and student learning outcomes (Rader, 1998). Calls for integrating life long learning examples into university-wide learning experiences have given rise to community-based service learning programming and calls for innovative collaborative partnerships both within and outside the university nationwide (Riddle, 2003; Lampert, 2003).

The concept and adoption of information literacy as an instructional goal within circles of higher education has propelled countless worldwide movements for curriculum change and educational reform (Bruce, 2002). Calls for information literacy to be embedded into curricular reform models are best achieved when proponents, librarians and/or faculty, have a clear understanding of how they will work across course and modular instructional offerings to give students opportunities for learning and subsequential application and practice of introduced information literacy concepts.

After the fundamental process of mapping course content to information literacy student learning objectives and programmatic goals are underway, librarians and faculty will be much better situated to move onward to the next steps of strengthening the curricular connections between information literacy, general education or required university coursework, and overall campus assessment efforts. Small scale curricular reform must take place both internally within a library instructional program and within department library liaison communication practices. Regardless of whether the approach takes place through course integrated instruction or information literacy course content embedded strategically throughout the disciplines, curricular reform planning is needed in order to infuse information literacy into a broad based curriculum such as a general education program.

GENERAL EDUCATION

When librarians typically think of the ultimate sign of respect for information literacy curricular efforts they usually envision placement and adoption within their campus' general education program. The desire to see information literacy embedded into general education programming stems from many different reasons. Obviously placement within an undergraduate general education program better ensures student exposure to information literacy concepts and practices. In addition, general education programs are also regularly assessed in preparation for institutional benchmarking and accreditation review.

Another important factor that explains the drive to have information literacy student learning outcomes embedded into general education programming stems from the fact that both general education reform and information literacy simultaneously received a great deal of attention in the 1990s alongside the calls for technology's integration into college level coursework steadily entering the literature of higher education.

In the past 15 years many libraries and librarians have worked diligently to have a voice in the direction of their campus general education reform patterns (Jacobson and Mark, 2000). As Ilene Rockman correctly noted, "The reform movement of the 1990s saw some universities develop first-year experiences and seminars for undergraduates with courses focused on communication and composition skills (reading, writing, and critical thinking) as one method to deliver information literacy instruction" (Rockman, 2002: 186–187). For librarians, the challenge in all of these efforts is finding a way to be heard in the cacophony of voices calling for reform in terms of general education and instruction that ensures that students graduate with a mastery of both information literacy and technological competencies.

In my own experience in working to establish my university library's role in our campus's planned general education reform, the important concept to grasp is that regardless of whether or not librarians enjoy faculty status, being an active contributor to the process of curricular reform is never a given. The curricular reform typically involved in overhauling general education programs is a messy business fraught with campus politics and academic departments jockeying for position within the structure of course offerings to guarantee necessary enrollment levels. It is often described in the literature of higher education as a process fraught with compromises and battles that necessitates the skills that a general would need in going to war (Kempcke, 2002).

I worked on California State University, Northridge's General Education (GE) Task Force as an elected member from the library faculty from 2003 until 2005. In comparison to previous campus committee service, my work on the GE Task Force was much more rigorous. All members of the committee were required to learn and study the history of how curricular reform had taken place at the university and within the larger California State University system. Every member of the committee learned to respect and listen to the various positions proposed by different represented disciplines.

My active role in revamping the entire curriculum undoubtedly helped information literacy achieve a stronger status in the newly adopted GE requirements set to take effect in the fall of 2006. Prior to this reform of the General Education Program, information competence was listed as a student learning outcome of the GE curriculum. However, the wording of the policy did not state how students would become progressively more information competent as they moved through general education courses. In short, prior to 2006 there was no way to identify which courses were working to help students improve in the area of information literacy. With the adoption of the newly revised general education plan in the spring of 2005, undergraduates are now required to complete two general education courses that have been designated as Information Competence (IC) bearing by the campus Educational Policies Committee. One IC bearing course must be completed within the Basic Skills section of the GE Program, the other in the Subject Exploration category requirement. Each existing and new course that wishes to be approved and designated as an IC bearing course in the University Catalog must also now undergo a process of certification and assessment on a scheduled basis.

While the strengthening of information competence's role within the general education program at my university is undeniable it is also imperative that librarians do not view a success like this as a *fait accompli*. Just because information competence is now strengthened in its positioning within the campus curriculum, does not mean that the task of curriculum development is complete. Service on bodies like my campus's Educational Policies Committee and the literature of higher education both make it clear that there are currently three types of curriculum in existence on every college and university campus in the nation. These include: designed curriculum (the curriculum proposed for adoption by departments and programs), existing/actual curriculum (what is taught in the classrooms on a daily basis), and achieved curriculum (what students have learned). Continual participation and attention to campus entities responsible for assessment and faculty development in the areas of pedagogical improvement and curricular decision-making will remain a required part of making sure that information competence remains a healthy part of the student learning outcomes within the newly adopted General Education curriculum.

Faculty status certainly helps librarians attain membership on faculty committees, including, among others, curriculum and assessment related committees. But faculty status alone does not mean that this accomplishment will be a given on every campus. Therefore, in their role as department liaisons, librarians must regularly work to achieve successful outreach to faculty involved in ongoing departmental curricular reform in order to integrate information literacy and/or library instruction modules into the curriculum on a small scale. General Education reform is not a consistent part of every university's curricular reform rotation. At some institutions, reform of the General Education program may not take place for several years or perhaps even a decade. Working with faculty serving on department curriculum committees is often another very good way to learn more about the instructional needs that the library can assist in developing.

CONCLUSION

Opinions abound when it comes to theorizing about the "best" ways to develop and deliver information literacy instructional content both inside and outside of library classrooms. Moreover, there will always be competing educational movements and themes that seem to convince academic stakeholders on many campuses that information literacy is not necessarily the top choice for inclusion in current or future planned curricular reform initiatives within departments or across an institution. Convincing the entire campus that information literacy requirements should become a component of a general education program does not take place overnight. It is a long and often arduous process that requires diligence, patience, and attention to instructional programming taking place both within and outside the library.

In their article, "Competing Agendas in Higher Education: Finding a Place for Information Literacy," Loanne Snavely and Natasha Cooper (1997) shrewdly warn librarians of the dangers of ignoring the lessons of past curricular change processes regardless of their successes or failures. Searching for respect for information literacy within existing curricular structures involves understanding the depth of importance that many stakeholders on campus pay to the process. Curriculum is created through the travails of a consultative process that is often laden with historical politics within academe. Citing the words of Snavely and Cooper reminds us of the enormity involved in undertaking curricular change on any college or university campus. "Bok reportedly compared changing a college curriculum to moving a cemetery. Establishing an across-the-curriculum information literacy program is a tall order. Those involved in such an endeavor should take note of the experiences of those who have already been involved in curricular change" (Snavely and Cooper, 1997).

Clearly, participating in curriculum planning, both within and outside of libraries, should provide librarians with clarity about the educational objectives they wish to achieve in the classroom. This clarity is a key component to building a salable argument to include information literacy in curricula both in and outside of library instruction. As the literature on curriculum mapping and curricular decision making shows, it is also imperative for librarians to continually review the curricular requirements and syllabi for the departments they serve and regularly meet with faculty involved in creating new courses and/or revamping existing classes.

These are some of the best ways that librarians can communicate to campus program planners and clearly convey how information literacy instruction can be delivered to their students. Certainly this is no easy task. But it is important to develop a broad and flexible conception of information literacy curriculum that can encapsulate the needs of many departments and programs. Ilene Rockman probably said it best when she wrote,

> So, what does an information literacy curriculum look like? It is campuswide; problem-based, inquiry based, and resource based (that is, it uses a variety of information resources); makes effective use of pedagogies and technologies; is learner centered; and integrated and articulated with a discipline's learning outcomes. It enhances and expands student learning through a coherent, systematic approach that facilitates the transfer or learning across the curriculum. (Rockman, 2002: 16)

It is also important to remember that the key to gaining respect for information literacy curriculum issues lies beyond just agreeing on definitions. The most important thing one can do is learn to listen and responsibly participate in the curriculum development process that is continually taking place on your campus.

REFERENCES

Badke, William. 2005. "Can't get no respect: Helping faculty to understand the educational power of information literacy." In S. Kratt, ed., *Relationships Between Teaching Faculty and Teaching Librarians: Do You Really Get More Flies with Honey?* (pp. 63–80). Binghampton, NY: Haworth Press.

Bruce, Christine. 2002. "Information literacy as a catalyst for educational change: A background paper." In *Proceedings Information Literacy Meeting of Experts*, Prague, Czech Republic.

Bullard, K. A., and D. H. Holden. 2006. "Hitting a moving target: Curriculum mapping, information literacy and academe." Paper presented at the LOEX Conference Meeting, University of Maryland, College Park. Available: www.emich.edu/public/loex/handouts/bullard/BullardHoldenLOEX2006handout.doc (accessed July 18, 2006).

California State University, Los Angeles. 2005. "Toward a working model of information literacy at California State University, Los Angeles: Recommendations for Implementation." Available: www.calstatela.edu/library/infolit/ILplan.pdf

Choinski, E., and M. Emmanuel. 2006. "The one-minute paper and the one-hour class: Outcomes assessment for one-shot library instruction." *Reference Services Review*, Vol. 34, no. 1: 148–155.

Curzon, S. C. 2004. "Developing faculty-librarian partnerships in information literacy." In I. Rockman, ed., *Integrating Information Literacy into the Higher Education Curriculum* (pp. 29–45). San Francisco: Jossey-Bass.

Grassian, E., and J. Kaplowitz. 2001. *Information literacy instruction: Theory and practice*. New York: Neal Schuman Publishers.

Hayes-Jacobs, H. 1997. *Mapping the big picture: Integrating curriculum and assessment K–12*. Alexandria, VA: Association for Supervision and Curriculum Development.

Hinchliffe, L. J., B. L. Mark, and L. H. Merz. 2003. "Bridging the gap between information literacy and campus curricula: Using curriculum mapping to achieve a holistic information literacy program." Available: http://wilu2003.uwindsor.ca/ENGLISH/pres/hinchliffeetal/CM_files/frame.htm (accessed August 18, 2006).

Jacobson, T. E., and B. L. Mark. 2000. "Separating wheat from chaff: Helping first-year students become information savvy: Programs at the University of Albany and Messiah College." *The Journal of General Education*, Vol. 49, no. 4: 256–278.

Jenkins, J., and M. Boosinger. 2003. "Collaborating with campus administrators and faculty to integrate information literacy and assessment into the core curriculum." *Southeastern Librarian*, Vol. 50, no. 4: 26–31.

Kempcke, Ken. 2002. "The art of war for librarians: Academic culture, curriculum reform, and wisdom from Sun Tzu." *Portal: Libraries and the Academy*, Vol. 2, no. 4: 529-551.

Kirk, Tom. 1974. "Problems in library instruction in four-year colleges." In J. Lubans Jr., ed., *Educating the Library User* (pp. 83–104). New York: R. R. Bowker.

Koppang, A. 2004. "Curriculum mapping: Building collaboration and communication." *Intervention in School and Clinic*, Vol. 39, no. 3: 154–161.

Kraat, S., ed. 2005. *Relationships between teaching faculty and teaching librarians*. Binghamton, NY: Haworth Press.

Lampert, L. D. 2003. "Who's afraid of partnerships for information literacy initiatives? Working together to empower learners." *College & Research Libraries News*, Vol. 64, no. 4: 246–248, 253, 255.

Leddy Library, the University of Windsor, Ontario, Canada. 2005. "Curriculum mapping." Available: www.uwindsor.ca/units/leddy/leddy.nsf/CurriculumMapping!OpenForm (accessed July 18, 2006).

Lubans, J., Jr. 1974. "Objectives for library use instruction in educational curricula." In *Educating the Library User* (pp. 211–221). New York: R. R. Bowker.

Mech, T. F. 1990. "Working with faculty in an outcomes-oriented curriculum: Observations from the library." In Hall and Byrd, eds., *The Librarian in the University: Essays on Membership in the Academic Community*. Metuchen, NJ: Scarecrow Press.

Nash, M. 2004. "Information literacy and the learning community." *Nebraska Library Association Quarterly*, Vol. 35, no. 4. Available: www.nebraskalibraries.org/nlaquarterly/2004-4-Nash.htm (accessed August 31, 2006).

Orr, D., M. Appleton, and M. Wallin. 2001. "Information literacy and flexible delivery: Creating a conceptual framework and model." *Journal of Academic Librarianship*, Vol. 27, no. 6: 457–463.

Rader, H. B. 1998. "Faculty-librarian collaboration in building the curriculum for the millennium—the U.S. experience." A paper presented at the 68th Annual International Federation of Library Associations and Institutions (IFLA) Conference in Amsterdam.

Rader, H. B. 1995. "Information literacy and the undergraduate curriculum. (The Library and Undergraduate Education)." *Library Trends*, Vol. 44: 270–278.

Ragains, Patrick. 2001. "Infusing information literacy into the core curriculum." *Portal: Libraries and the Academy*, Vol. 1, no. 4: 391–407.

Raspa, D., and D. Ward, eds. 2000. *The collaborative imperative: Librarians and faculty working together in the information universe*. Chicago: Association of College and Research Libraries.

Regan, R. H. 1980. "Curriculum design: A co-operative venture." *Canadian Vocational Journal*, Vol. 16, no. 1: 37–39, 45.

Riddle, J. S. 2003. "Where's the library in service learning?: Models for engaged library instruction." *The Journal of Academic Librarianship*, Vol. 29, no. 2: 71–81.

Rockman, I. F., ed. 2002. *Integrating information literacy into the higher education curriculum*. New York: Jossey-Bass.

Sheesley, D. F. 2002. "The one-shot multiple section freshman instruction session: Keeping the teaching librarian stress-free and intellectually stimulated." In J. K. Nims, and A. Andrew, eds., *First Impressions, Lasting Impact: Introducing the First-Year Student to the Academic Library, Library Orientation Series: #32*. Ann Arbor, MI: Pierian Press.

Snavely, L., and N. Cooper. 1997. "Competing agendas in higher education: Finding a place for information literacy." *Reference & User Services Quarterly*, Vol. 37, no. 1: 53–62.

University of Illinois at Urbana–Champaign Office of Services University Library. 2003. "Curriculum Mapping, sine nominee, 2." Available: www.library.uiuc.edu/administration/services/news/issue2.htm (accessed July 31, 2006).

Vogel Library, Wartburg College, Waverly, Iowa. "Information literacy across the curriculum." Available: http://wartburg.edu/library/infolit/index.html (accessed July 18, 2006).

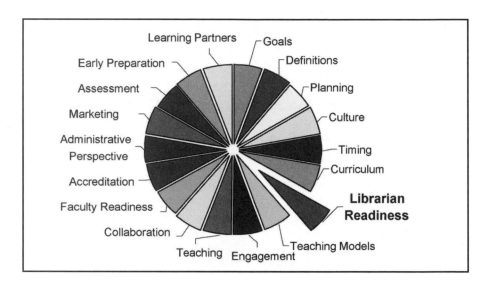

LIBRARIAN READINESS

A Word from the Editors

*T*he emergence of information literacy as a paramount activity particularly of academic and school libraries has created a new dimension for librarians—the librarian as skilled teacher. It is true of course that we have always taught as teaching has always gone hand in hand with our profession. However, teaching on the scale required by an active program of information literacy, and with this urgency, has not occurred until fairly recently in the history of librarianship. Before, we looked to a librarian's skills in information retrieval or information organization as a definition of a professional; now, as often as not, we also include their teaching skills because we know that inculcating information literacy into a student's skill set is dependent upon the teaching abilities of the librarians. The challenge for us is that teaching, while an allied profession, is still a separate profession with its own philosophies, approaches, practices, and methods. In this chapter, Dr. Jeff Liles, Assistant Professor of Education and Chair of the Adolescence Education Department at St. John Fisher College, helps us as librarians to prepare ourselves to be better teachers. Jeff looks at the skills that we ourselves need to engage students and to trigger their motivation towards developing information literacy skills. In this chapter, Jeff provides examples of exercises and pedagogical approaches that librarians can use to engage students in the learning process. Jeff's Ph.D. and M.A. are in Historical, Philosophical, and Sociological Foundations of Education from the University of Oklahoma. He is published widely in such publications as College and Undergraduate Libraries, Educational Studies *and* The History of Education Quarterly. Jeff is much in demand as a speaker and he has conducted presentations and workshops for many libraries and library associations.

Chapter 7

Librarian Readiness and Pedagogy

by Jeff Liles

My current position is that of an Instruction Librarian, so I knew that I would be teaching. I do like to present and train since this is in my background with other positions. However, when I found out there wasn't really much training on teaching techniques to use, ways to present databases to students and how to identify the needs for specific classes, I became less enthusiastic. There also isn't a great deal of information out there on presenting to freshman versus graduate students as far as information literacy goes. I had very little to pull from my graduate school education on teaching library resources. Developing a plan for what to teach and how to teach still proves difficult. Much of the time, I feel it is trial and error or simply falling into patterns in the classroom due to lack of resources. (Dawn Vogler, Personal Communication, March 2006)

This may sound familiar to you. This librarian carries the title of "Instruction Librarian," she has not had much training to be a teacher, and her enthusiasm is challenged by the difficulty of planning and teaching. Teaching is a satisfying but deceptively complex act. Parker J. Palmer (1998: 1) reminds us of this in his book, *The Courage to Teach: Exploring the Inner Landscape of a Teacher's Life:*

I am a teacher at heart, and there are moments in the classroom when I can hardly hold the joy. When my students and I discover uncharted territory to explore, when the pathway out of a thicket opens up before us, when our experience is illumined by the lightning-life of the mind—then teaching is the finest work I know. But at other moments, the classroom is so lifeless or painful or confused—and I am so powerless to do anything about it—that my claim to be a teacher seems a transparent sham. Then the enemy is everywhere: in those students from some alien planet, in that subject I thought I knew, and in the personal pathology that keeps me earning my living this way. What a fool I was to imagine that I had mastered this occult art—harder to divine than tea leaves and impossible for mortals to do even passably well!

Teaching may indeed be too complex to ever truly "master" (this is an important understanding that effective teachers all seem to possess), but there is much that one can do to increase his or her effectiveness in the classroom. There is a lot of information "out there," but as librarians are well aware, finding and organizing the best and most helpful information can be difficult.

Additionally, while librarians are making progress on producing their own knowledge base regarding teaching, there is a dearth of teaching information designed specifically with librarians in mind and directed toward the unique circumstances of information literacy instruction. Librarians are professional people, many of whom have years of successful experience that included little or no teaching. The profession is in transition and there are those who never imagined standing in front of a classroom conducting a lesson. Many librarians never received any instruction about teaching while in library school. Sue Ann Brainard expresses a common refrain among librarians: "I did not take a library course on instruction. They had one, but at the time I was heading toward public library service and I (mistakenly) thought I didn't need it. Imagine my surprise when I became a young adult librarian and I found that I had to speak to classes of teenagers, telling them about library policies, recommending books to read, etc. I was terrified" (Brainard, 2006). Finally, instruction librarians are often expected to deliver a lot of content and teach a lot of skills in abbreviated periods of time. All of these factors should be considered when working with librarians who are learning how to teach. This chapter intends to do just that.

Specifically, this chapter will get you started on the journey of effective teaching. It is for librarians who would like to know what to do next to better prepare themselves, or perhaps others, to be effective teachers. Some of the questions considered are: What does it mean to be ready to teach? What knowledge, skills, and dispositions are required to be an effective teacher? Specifically, you will be introduced to some of the fundamental elements of effective instruction and how to connect them in ways that will facilitate student learning: becoming a student of learning, planning lessons, and creating effective instructional methods.

BECOME A "TEACHER CONSUMER"

Imagine a person who has little knowledge and experience with cooking. She decides she will prepare a special meal for her family, so she gets a recipe from a friend that clearly outlines the ingredients and steps necessary to cook a delicious three-course meal. After collecting her ingredients, she throws it all together, closely following the steps on the recipe. Lacking both knowledge and experience, she is not sure what some of the ingredients are or how to really use them. Consequently, step four reads "chop it and throw it in," so she does. Maybe her creation ends up a disaster, maybe it is a grand success. The important question for our purpose is: Does this experience make our character a chef?

The answer of course is no, she is not a chef. According to an old joke, the difference between a cook and a chef is that the cook has to clean up after himself. Our "cook" probably does have to clean up after herself, but in addition, she is not a chef because she has not had the necessary and required education or experience. A chef has a deep knowledge of ingredients, a broad repertoire of techniques, and an understanding of when and how to use them. A chef also knows the math, chemistry, and physics that are involved in creating the most simple or complex dishes. In short, the chef has a broader and deeper knowledge base from which to work. This breadth and depth allows the chef to work in a more thoughtful, creative way instead of simply being tied to a recipe.

This scenario helps us understand the distinction that educators make between teachers as "consumers" and teachers as "designers" (Sparks-Langer et al., 2004). Teacher-consumers have little or no control over instructional planning or curriculum. They simply follow instructions and curricula created by others. Such a teacher cannot craft the content of a lesson or instructional strategies to suit a variety of contexts or meet the differing needs of students. Also, unable to delineate between important and unimportant content, teacher-consumers are more likely to make mistakes such as trying to teach too much information in superficial ways (Sparks-Langer et al., 2004). A teacher-consumer can only adopt a "one size fits all" approach to planning and instruction, and given the complexity of teaching and learning, a more tailored approach is required.

Teacher-designers, on the other hand, are teachers who have the knowledge, skills, and dispositions necessary to tailor curriculum and instruction to the needs of learners. Teacher-designers are equipped to make a broad range of decisions:

> They make planning decisions by choosing and analyzing content, clarifying outcomes, selecting learning activities and assessing student performance. They make implementation decisions as they design and teach...lessons, assess learning, make adjustments for individual student needs, and enhance their students' thinking skills. Finally, they make decisions about classroom management, applying their beliefs and principles about human beings and communities to create and maintain a positive learning environment. (Sparks-Langer et al., 2004: 2)

The ability to make these decisions is especially important for instruction librarians who not only work with a diverse population of learners, but with a variety of instructors and disciplines as well. Teaching conditions for instruction librarians can vary wildly in a semester, a week, or even a day. Creating an effective "introduction to the library" lesson for a 50-minute one-shot with freshmen, for example, is very different than designing a three-session lesson on conducting research using the deep Web for graduate students. It is clear that a teacher–designer and not a teacher–consumer will be more likely to successfully meet the planning, instruction, and assessment demands of information literacy instruction in today's libraries.

BECOME A STUDENT OF LEARNING

When beginning a study of effective teaching, one might be tempted to start with the methods of teaching and the "bag-of-tricks" approach, i.e., "Just give me a bag of teaching tricks and I will be on my way." This would be a mistake, however, because it is an understanding of how learners learn that should drive our methods of teaching. Because all of the theories in the following discussion are complex and changing, it will help to organize our discussion around three basic, but important questions:

- What is learning?
- How do humans learn?
- How do we know when someone has learned something?

An important principle of teaching and learning to keep in mind is that assumptions about learning give shape to teaching practices. If, for example, one assumes that his dog learns best through a series of questions and answers, then he might reasonably employ the Socratic Method in teaching her how to retrieve the morning paper. If this is not how dogs learn, however, then some may think their friend's Socratic seminar with the dog to be a little crazy, and the dog would be a terrific failure at fetching the paper.

This last example may be "cartoonish," but it highlights a very important point everyone should understand before stepping in front of students in a classroom: understanding how humans learn is at the core of effective teaching. If we want our students to learn, we really need to understand how they learn. Since the early twentieth century, two dominant and competing theoretical frameworks, behaviorism and cognitive theory, have explored human learning and significantly shaped educational practice.

BEHAVIORISM: LEARNING IS OBSERVABLE BEHAVIOR

What comes to mind when you read the names Pavlov, Watson, and Skinner? Drooling dogs? Rats in a maze? Trained pigeons? These were some of the major figures who studied and influenced ideas about learning. These were the behaviorists and their work made it into American classrooms through Edward L.

Thorndike (1874–1949). Thorndike was one of the first to articulate "laws of learning" (Lagemann, 2005). His influence on American education has been profound. Educational historian Ellen Condliff Lagemann asserts that "one cannot understand American education unless one realizes that Edward L. Thorndike won and John Dewey lost" (Lagemann, 2005: 22).

How does behaviorism answer the three questions about learning?

- Learning is observable behavior.
- All behavior is learned through actions of the environment on the learner (stimulus–response), and controlled by the use of reward, punishment, and reinforcement.
- Learning has occurred when behavior has changed.

There are many ways that these assumptions shape educational policies and practices. They are too numerous to list and discuss here. The most prevalent and obvious examples, however, are lecture-driven instruction, teacher-centered classrooms, testing, and grading.

Behaviorism and Information Literacy Instruction

There are many critiques of behavioral teaching practices that should be considered in any discussion of teaching and learning. Alfie Kohn is one of the foremost opponents of behaviorism in the classroom. He contends that behaviorism works if you are primarily interested in short-term results and not meaningful, transferable learning. He also argues that the problem with punishments and rewards is that students learn to behave for punishments and rewards instead of learning truly self-directed appropriate behaviors (Kohn, 1999).

There are some specific reasons that behaviorism is not a good fit for information literacy instruction. Behaviorism relies heavily on external motivation through the use of punishments, rewards, or reinforcers, e.g., grades, tests, quizzes, etc. Instruction librarians are typically not in a situation where they have such "external motivators." Some instruction librarians lament that they cannot "make" students do anything because the students know that their grade will not be affected by performance in an information literacy session. Sadly, because students have learned to reduce learning to the reward, or punishment, of a grade, this holds some truth. Even so, using external motivators is not always possible, and even if it is, it may not be the best route to take.

Another argument against behaviorism in the classroom has to do with relationships. Behaviorism can have a negative impact on the relationship between the teacher and the student. William Glasser (1992) argues that convincing students of the quality of a learning experience brings them closer to us where we can reach them, while rewards, and punishments in particular, push them away. Another angle on this lies in the difference between external and internal motivation in learning. In his study of effective teachers, *What the Best College Teachers Do*

(2004), Ken Bain discusses research which shows that even the motivation of students who have a strong interest and fascination with a subject actually goes down when external motivators are introduced into the learning environment. Bain highlights research showing that "people lose much of their motivation if they think they are being manipulated by the external reward, if they lose what psychologists have called the 'locus of causality' of their behavior (Bain, 2004: 33). Conversely, Bain found that "outstanding teachers generally avoided using grades to persuade students, instead they invoked the subject, the questions it raises, and the promises it makes to any learner" (2004: 36). Librarians enjoy and should strive to maintain supportive, collaborative relationships with students. Librarians want students to come back to the library more often after attending an information literacy class. Instruction librarians, therefore, should avoid behavioral methods in the information literacy classroom, and instead adopt methods that are more likely to develop and maintain positive relationships and encourage student interest and learning. This requires a different way of thinking about learning.

COGNITIVE THEORY: ANOTHER WAY OF "THINKING"

Cognitive theory presents us with a different way of understanding learning and teaching. It is important to note that like behaviorism, cognitive theory is not a complete, monolithic explanation of human learning. The science of learning is diverse and ongoing. As the National Research Council points out: "Today, the world is in the midst of an extraordinary outpouring of scientific work on the mind and the brain, on the processes of thinking and learning, on the neural processes that occur during thought and learning, and on the development of competence" (Bransford et al., 1999: 3). Because, the science continues, it is important that teachers become life-long students of learning. While the search goes on, there are some fundamentally important ideas from cognitive science to consider.

Theorists such as Piaget, Bruner, and Vygotsky answer the questions about learning posed earlier by theorizing and explaining the central importance of the mind. According to them, one cannot understand learning without serious consideration of the mind, a notion, along with the mind itself, which is completely rejected by behaviorists. Cognitive theory focuses on cognitive development and deep understanding rather than observable behaviors and skills. Cognitive theorists offer the following answers to the three questions:

- Learning is the development of new "cognitive structures."
- Learning occurs through the processes of "assimilation" and "accommodation" which resolve disequilibrium.
- Learning has occurred when new, transferable understanding has been developed.

How does this work with an actual learner? A young person is introduced for the first time to a computer. Not knowing what a computer is, the learner slips into a state of "disequilibrium." Learners are naturally in a state of "equilibrium" until they come upon or are presented with new, unfamiliar information. Given the discomfort of this state, the learner seeks to return to equilibrium with two processes: assimilation and accommodation. First, the learner tries to match, or fit the new information into "schemas" that he has already formed. If for example, the learner knows what a typewriter is, but has never seen a computer, then when he sees a computer he will most likely connect the computer, the keyboard in particular, to the "category" of typewriters that he holds in his mind. If the learner has never seen a typewriter and cannot thus assimilate the new information, he will accommodate the new information by creating an entirely new category, or schema. For the cognitive theorist, learning has occurred because of the creation of new schemas, cognitive structures, or understanding (Sternberg and Williams, 2002).

Perhaps the most important contribution of cognitive theory is the idea that learners are developing and active, and not passive recipients in the learning process. Learners, not teachers, are in control of learning. Additionally, one of the important key principles of cognitive theory is that all learners bring prior knowledge, or schema, into the classroom with which they "act." This schema, or prior knowledge, is necessary for new learning to occur and indeed may be the key to unlocking for students the mystery of new knowledge and stimuli. It may also stand in the way of new learning. Should a library instructor ignore the fact that students have only used *Google* to search for information? How might this prior knowledge and experience help or hinder teaching them how to search an academic database? From a cognitive theory perspective, the best thing the instructor can do is "activate" this knowledge with something as simple as a class discussion and use it to facilitate learning. It is evident that cognitive theory moves the instructor out of the center of the learning process and replaces her with the student. This shift is significant because it marks the beginning of student-centered approaches to teaching and learning. Currently, a widely used student-centered theory is constructivism.

CONSTRUCTIVISM: THE CLASSROOM AS A "CONSTRUCTION SITE"

Building on cognitive theory, constructivism explains that the learner is at the center of the learning process. For constructivists, learners are active meaning-makers. This is because the learner's prior knowledge is a fundamental prerequisite to the "construction" of new meanings and understandings. It is important to note that like behaviorism, constructivism is a "theory of knowing" and not a "theory of pedagogy" (Bransford et al., 1999). It offers principles of learning to which educators should pay attention if they are interested in facilitating meaningful student learning. Gagnon and Collay (2001) provide a concise and helpful list of constructivist principles:

- Learners think individually to make personal meaning of learning events.
- Learners think collaboratively to make shared meaning of learning events.
- Learners connect their prior knowledge and previous experiences to learning events.
- Learners pose questions and respond to questions about learning events.
- Learners present their thinking about learning events to others.
- Learners reflect on their collective and individual thinking during learning events.

How does the constructivist theory of knowing translate into practice? To answer this question, we will focus on constructivist conceptions of students, teachers, curriculum, methods, and assessment. First and foremost, teachers should think of students as "active meaning-makers" and search for ways to engage their prior knowledge and direct it toward the construction of new knowledge. Start sessions by finding out what students know, don't know, understand, and misunderstand. An instruction librarian who engages students in a discussion of their previous experiences in libraries and computers will gather a lot of information he can use during instruction. Think again of the example of students who routinely use *Google* to search for information. An instructor will do well to use this as a reference point for teaching how to search library databases. From this discussion of "old" ideas and practices, engaged learners will "construct" new ones. At the very least, starting a class this way as opposed to lecturing to students for half an hour is usually more interesting and engaging for learners of all ages.

For constructivists, the teacher's role is that of a designer, guide, and facilitator. The teacher does not control learning, the learner does. But because the teacher understands the learner and the importance of the knowledge and experiences the learner brings to the table, he can create lessons that will facilitate meaningful learning. This does not, however, mean that a teacher simply provides materials and instructions and then lets the students go. The teacher crafts a learning experience and then guides students through it. Effective teachers interact with students throughout the class, they listen intently to students' discussions while they work, they ask clarifying questions, and provide necessary background information, when needed, in order to stimulate thinking and help students organize their learning.

"Authentic" is the word most often used by constructivists to describe subject matter and curriculum. Generally, this means that the subject of study is connected or otherwise relevant to students' lives. In the context of library instruction this might mean emphasizing for students that beyond learning how to use a specific database to complete an assignment for a passing grade in history class, an immediate level of authenticity, they are developing information literacy skills and understanding that are vital to citizens and professionals in the information age. In this way, the subject matter has an immediate and localized relevance, but also a broader and more universal relevance. Teachers should not expect students to always see relevance. Because students are developing, helping them see and understand the relevance and meaningfulness of subject matter is an important part of what teachers do to motivate students and enhance learning.

Using authentic subject matter also requires using authentic methods of instruction and assessment. Doing so is more a matter of will than difficulty. Assessment does not have to be formal and complex to be useful to both teachers and learners. There is no template for constructivist instructional methods and assessment, but at the very least, for a learning experience to be consistent with constructivist principles, instruction and assessment should be active, social, and begin with learners' prior knowledge. The simplest translation of this into practice might be asking students to work in small groups to complete an exercise that takes them through a database search. While this may seem obvious, there is a lot of instruction not only in library classrooms, but in classrooms across campuses where teachers talk and students just sit and listen (or not).

The following example may help to set one's mind in a constructivist mode of instruction and assessment. Let's say that we want students to learn "A," "B," and "C" in an instruction session. Using a traditional mode of instruction, an instructor will simply plan to "cover" the material through a lecture and perhaps demonstrate it. Many of us have sat through demonstrations where we only watched and listened to the instructor tell us and show us what we are supposed to know and do. Or how about the "follow-the-bouncing-cursor" session where students are expected to follow (and remember?) the instructor's search path as she clicks through dozens of windows. Most, if not all of the instructional time is allocated to this telling and showing. A small amount of time may be set aside at the end for questions. As the research indicates, this is not the best way to facilitate learning.

Compare and contrast this with a constructivist approach. Prior to meeting with the class, the instructor designs an activity in which students "arrive" at "A," "B," and "C" by working together in small groups of three or four. Since students are active meaning-makers and not empty vessels to be filled, the instructor designs activities that will lead students to what she might otherwise tell them. The instructor uses some time at the beginning to explain just enough to get the students started, and perhaps at the end to highlight and review some major points. But the bulk of instructional time is spent with students engaged in learning activities.

What about assessment? For constructivists, assessment is an activity or product that demonstrates student understanding and learning. And unlike traditional assessment which typically occurs after instruction, it can, and should take place throughout instruction (Angelo and Cross, 1993). Discussing students' experiences conducting research in libraries is a simple form of assessment at the beginning of a class. Asking students to complete a written exercise on evaluating Web resources is a form of assessment during class. After the class, the bibliographies students create for their research papers represent a form of assessment. In all of these examples, the students do something or produce something that "shows" what they know and can do. These "products" also provide instructors with data which can be used to inform and improve instruction, another important characteristic of constructivist assessment.

Figure 7-1 provides a convenient overview of how the different theories conceptualize and shape the role of teacher, learner, and teaching methods.

	Behaviorism	**Cognitive Theory**	**Constructivism**
Students	Passive recipients of knowledge; responders	Active, developing minds; prior knowledge; developing; social beings	Active meaning-makers of individual and shared knowledge
Teachers	Primary "knower"; controller of learning	Students of development; facilitators of learning	Designers of learning environments and experiences; facilitators
Relationships	Of little importance; teacher is authority figure and expert	Teacher works with students	Teachers and learners are "co-constructors" of knowledge, equally involved in the learning process
Subject Matter	Standardized; logically ordered; delivered	Complex; developmentally-appropriate	Authentic, "real-world" problems and issues
Methods	Lecture	Interaction with information and environment; social interaction	Present problems; interaction with information and others
Assessment	Teacher-made; objective tests of what students know; summative	Performance-based; ongoing; formative	Authentic; performance-based; use of products i.e., portfolios, exhibits, presentations

Figure 7-1: Theories of Learning

The lesson planning section which follows includes a lesson plan that exemplifies methods of teaching and assessment that reflect some of the fundamental principles of constructivism. As you work through this section, refer back to the table and the previous discussion in order to further develop your understanding of theory and practice.

PLANNING FOR SUCCESS IN THE CLASSROOM

Lesson planning is very important, but there is not one best way to do it. Some teachers plan more than others; most effective teachers have their own idiosyncratic ways of planning, but they do plan. There are very detailed, typed plans and there are plans scribbled on the back of envelopes and napkins. One thing learned from teaching and working with librarians on 50-minute "one-shots" is that the less time one has for instruction, the more important planning becomes. Whether a class is two hours or 50 minutes, doing the right things to facilitate learning is always important. Planning in advance is a great aid and helps make the best possible use of time. The next section of the chapter features explanations and examples of a lesson plan model that works well with information literacy instruction.

The Direct Lesson Plan

The direct lesson plan is widely used in teacher education programs and frequently associated with behaviorism. Since behaviorism, like constructivism, is a theory of knowing and not a theory of pedagogy, it is possible to use a direct lesson plan format along with constructivist ideas and activities. The direct lesson plan model is a good fit with much of information literacy instruction because it is well-suited for "teaching basic skills, concepts, rules, strategies, procedures, and knowledge that lends itself to being presented in steps or sub-skills" (Price and Nelson, 2007: 75). The creation of the direct lesson plan is attributed to Madeline Hunter and is sometimes called the "Hunter Model." There is some debate about how prescriptive Professor Hunter's model was and how many elements it originally included. Some models include five elements, some include seven. What ever the case may be, the following elements can help bring focus and organization to an instructor's planning and help in developing engaging and meaningful learning experiences for students:

- **Anticipatory Set:** Grabs students' attention; sparks their interest; "sets" their focus on the topic of the lesson.
- **Statement of Intended Learning Outcomes:** Articulates what the students will learn; often stated as "know, think, or do."
- **Instructional Input/Modeling:** The instructor provides information and models skills.

- **Check for Understanding:** Strategies used throughout the lesson to monitor students' understanding.
- **Guided Practice:** Activities completed by students with instructor's support and guidance.
- **Independent Practice:** Activities completed independently by individual or groups of students.
- **Closing:** Review outcomes and summarize most important points of lesson.

The direct lesson plan model is also particularly adaptable to lessons that teach skills which fall into Bloom's levels of knowledge, comprehension, and application. It is thus appropriate for many kinds of information literacy instruction. To illustrate, a lesson plan, written and conducted by Instruction Librarian Kim Davies at the State University of New York at Geneseo, for Psychology 251 follows. The plan is for a 50 minute "one-shot" session. The professor of the course has requested the same lesson for several semesters and shared with the librarian that it is very effective. The librarian adds that students bring their handouts from the instruction session to the reference desk while they are conducting their research on their own, and that they already have their search strategies perfectly laid out according to what they learned in the class. There are several other indictors of success here that are worth highlighting. First, in addition to reporting that she is happy with the library session, the professor continues to bring her students to the library for the session. Second, the students are transferring their learning and resources from the instruction session into their independent research for the course. And finally, this effort has recently produced a collaboration with the psychology department where the librarian and professors are developing mini-assignments that will help students practice the skills they are learning in that one-shot session and reinforce the learning. These examples are provided to offer guidance on how to establish and deliver activities in library instruction sessions.

PSYC 251: INTRODUCTION TO BEHAVIORAL RESEARCH METHODS
GOAL
Introduce a few searching techniques that will help students perform effective searches in PsycINFO and Medline, as well as other research databases.

INTENDED LEARNING OUTCOMES
Students will be able to:

- break apart a research topic into major concepts in order to formulate a search strategy (see Figure 7-4)
- brainstorm a number of different synonyms to represent various concepts
- use AND, OR, and NOT effectively in their search strategies

- understand the difference between a subject heading and a keyword search
- use thesauri to determine the correct subject headings for different databases
- apply these searching techniques to effectively perform searches in PsycINFO and Medline, as well as other research databases

ANTICIPATORY SET

Have a picture of a puzzle (or puzzle pieces) displayed on the front screen as students walk into the classroom. Ask students to raise their hand if they have ever worked on putting a puzzle together. Have students volunteer their initial approach to a puzzle after all of the pieces are out of the box and clearly visible on a table. Students will say that they separate the pieces into corner and edge pieces and then they categorize by similar color and/or pattern. Why do they do this? Relate the steps of putting a puzzle together; by first separating out similar pieces and then adding them all back together again, to the steps of a database search. Rather than tackle a complicated research topic head-on, students should first separate out the major concepts of their topic, work with each one individually, and then tie all of the pieces back together again in one sophisticated search strategy.

INFORMATION/MODELING

- While the instructor shows an example topic, in the form of a concept map (see Figure 7-4), on the front screen, students refer to a more generalized concept map (see Figure 7-3) to gain an understanding of how the process works. A blank concept map is provided for the students to work on themselves or in groups. (see Figure 7-2).
- The instructor discusses the components of a complete and solid research statement, whether it be in the form of a question or a hypothesis, and the importance of making a research topic fairly specific.
- The instructor displays the major concepts taken from the original research statement.
- On a white board, the instructor encourages students to brainstorm terms related to the example research concepts (i.e., teenager, alcohol).
- After writing terms suggested by students, the instructor explains how to effectively use AND, OR, and NOT, truncation, and proximity operators to pull concepts together, while also lending flexibility to their search.
- Access to, layout, and special features of PsycINFO are demonstrated.
- Once students have experimented with keyword searching, the instructor explains the difference between keyword and subject searches.
- The instructor further illustrates the difference in subject headings between PsycINFO and Medline, and stresses the importance of knowing the correct terminology.

- After students refine their searches with a focus on subject headings, the instructor discusses the types of articles that have resulted, alternative ways to find other related articles (i.e. by author, through cited references), and how to access articles through the library's holdings or through Interlibrary Loan.

CHECK FOR UNDERSTANDING

- Because this lesson is set up in a step-by-step progression, the instructor takes the students through the process systematically and gauges their understanding with each mini-activity, based on their written and computer work, as well as group discussion.
- The instructor walks around the room as the students work to answer any questions and clarify areas of confusion.
- At certain points in the class, the instructor asks for volunteers to provide suggestions and answers.

GUIDED PRACTICE

- Students work in groups of two on a pre-determined research question (Utilizing Concept Maps A and B in Figures 7-2 and 7-3) to pull out the major concepts and brainstorm related terms.
- After adding Boolean logic, truncation, and proximity operators in the appropriate areas of the search strategy, students enter their search into PsycINFO and evaluate the results as to their relevance to the original research statement.
- Once they have received some instruction on subject headings and online thesauri, students are asked to find the correct subject heading for a pre-determined keyword, either in PsycINFO's or Medline's thesaurus, and write it on a worksheet.
- Students call out certain subject headings based on given keywords to fully illustrate the difference in terminology between PsycINFO and Medline.
- Students are asked to modify their original search strategy to include appropriate subject headings and evaluate the results as to their relevance to the original research statement.
- Students access the holdings of chosen articles and/or determine the need to submit a request through Interlibrary Loan.

ASSESSMENT

- While students conduct keyword searches and then after they modify their searches to include subject headings, the instructor discusses with the entire class any problems that come up in finding a decent set of results.

- Towards the end of class, the instructor asks for volunteers to explain how they modified their search strategy from beginning to end and which search strategy seemed to work best.

CLOSING

- Re-address concepts talked about during the class (show concept maps again).
- Emphasize the fact that the skills learned in this particular class are transferable to other research projects (regardless of subject focus) and other databases, including search engines like Google.
- Remind students to ask for help at the reference desk.

The subject matter of this lesson is fairly typical as are the circumstances in which it is delivered. Here are some elements that contribute to the success of the lesson:

1. Clearly articulated, achievable outcomes.
2. A creative, engaging anticipatory set.
3. Students are engaged early in the lesson.
4. Active, authentic tasks and resources which are well-aligned with the learning outcomes.
5. Opportunities for students to work together.
6. The instructor checks students' understanding throughout the lesson and uses the "data" as a foundation for further instruction.
7. There are various assessments throughout the lesson.
8. The lesson includes a well-organized closing that reviews the important knowledge and skills covered.

Historically, educators have been remarkably consistent at oversimplifying, misconstruing, and just plain missing the mark while attempting to move ideas from theory to practice. This is probably a comment on the complexity of teaching and learning more than it is an indictment of educators. The lesson for us is that no idea or practice can be boxed up and pulled out for use like a set of tools. A project like this one almost inevitably leads us to oversimplify as we attempt to share what we know. It is wise to heed the admonition of philosopher Alfred North Whitehead, who once said, "Seek simplicity, then distrust it." This does not mean, however, that as educators we should fear this complexity and abandon all hope of improving what we do with and for our students. The information in this chapter on becoming a student of learning, planning, and effective methods of instruction and assessment represents only the beginning of a journey to embrace the complexity and continually seek out the information and experiences that will help us do a better job.

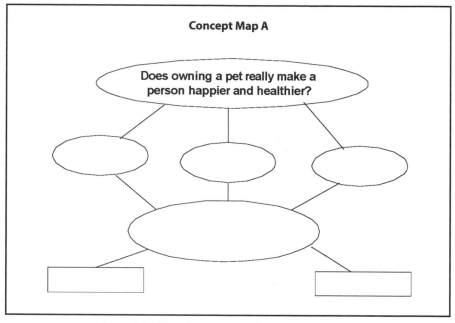

Figure 7-2: Forming a Research Statement: Step 1

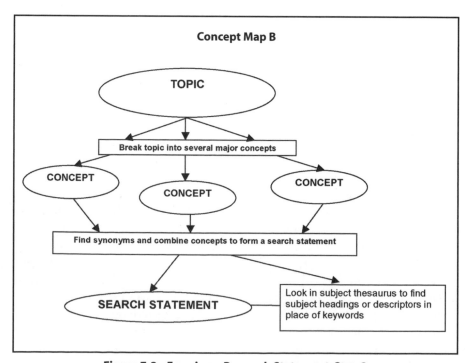

Figure 7-3: Forming a Research Statement: Step 2

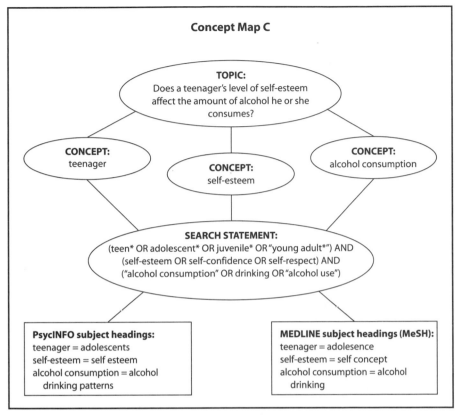

Figure 7-4: Forming a Research Statement: Step 3

PSYC 251: INTRODUCTION TO BEHAVIORAL RESEARCH METHODS
SUBJECT HEADINGS COMPARISON

Keyword	*PsycINFO Descriptor*	*MEDLINE MeSH*
Adultery		
Contraception		
Drunkenness		
Illiteracy		
Marijuana		
Ritalin		
Scholarships		
Sleeplessness		
Talent		
Teenage pregnancy		

REFERENCES

Angelo, T. A., and K. P. Cross. 1993. *Classroom assessment techniques: A handbook for college teachers*, 2nd ed. San Francisco: Jossey-Bass.

Bain, K. 2004. *What the best college teachers do*. Cambridge, MA: Harvard University Press.

Brainard, S. E. 2006. E-mail communication to Jeff Liles, February 17.

Bransford, J. D., A. L. Brown, R. R. Cocking, M. S. Donovan, J. W. Pellegrino, and the National Research Council, eds. 1999. *How people learn: Brain, mind, experience, and school* and *How people learn: Bridging research and practice*. Washington, DC: National Academy Press.

Gagnon, G.W. Jr., and M. Collay. 2001. *Designing for learning: Six elements in constructivist classrooms*. Thousand Oaks, CA: Corwin Press.

Glasser, W. 1992. *The quality school: Managing students without coercion*. 2nd ed. New York: Harper Perennial.

Kohn, A. 1999. *Punished by rewards: The trouble with gold stars, incentive plans, A's, praise, and other bribes*. New York: Mariner Books.

Lagemann, E. C. 2005. "Does history matter in education research? A brief history for the humanities in an age of science." *Harvard Educational Review*, Vol. 75, no. 1: 9–25.

Palmer, P. J. 1998. *The courage to teach: Exploring the inner landscape of a teacher's life*. San Francisco: Jossey-Bass.

Pelligrino, J., N. Chudowsky, and R. Glaser, eds. 2001. *Knowing what students know: The science and design of educational assessment*. Washington, DC: National Academy Press.

Price, K. M., and K. L. Nelson. 2007. *Planning effective instruction*, 3rd ed. Belmont, CA: Thompson Wadsworth.

Scruton, R. 1996. "The eclipse of listening." *The New Criterion*, Vol. 15, no. 30: 5–13.

Sparks-Langer, G. M., A. J. Starko, M. Pasch, W. Burke, C. D. Moody, and T. G. Gardner. 2004. *Teaching as decision making: Successful practices for the secondary teacher*. 2nd ed. Upper Saddle River, NJ: Prentice Hall.

Sternberg, R. J., and W. M. Williams. 2002. *Educational Psychology*. Boston: Allyn and Bacon.

KEEP IN MIND

"Until individual librarians gain a more complete understanding of information literacy in order to become more effective advocates and educators, the full potential of the information literacy movement will remain unrealized."

— Sarah McDaniel

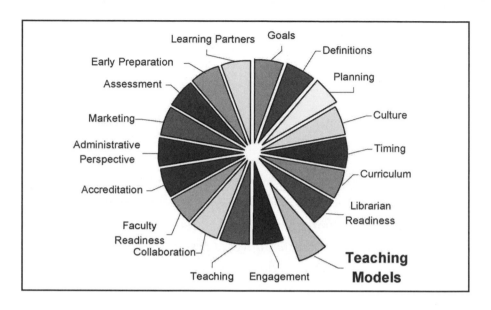

Teaching
Models

TEACHING MODELS

A Word from the Editors

*L*ooking closely at the role that librarians play in the development of student information literacy skills, Gabriela Sonntag proposes the important shifts in awareness, understanding, and behavior that librarians must undergo to move towards being a full partner in the learning enterprise. It is not enough that a library provides services and collections but, in addition, every library must be deeply engaged in helping students learn how to learn. As the Coordinator for the Information Literacy Program and Reference Services for California State University, San Marcos, Gabriela has first hand experience in launching an information literacy program and incorporating information literacy into the general education curriculum. In this chapter, Gabriela speaks with authority about the importance of an academic program for the library that offers standards-based curriculum that parallels the curriculum that students are offered in their majors and about the characteristics of a teaching model for an effective information literacy program. Gabriela brings national experience to her thought–provoking approach through her work as a consultant for information literacy for the Association of College and Research Libraries and also international experience through workshops that she has developed in Mexico, Chile, and Argentina. Gabriela's M.L.S. is from the University of Texas at Austin.

Chapter 8

In Search of Excellence:
Qualities of a Library Teaching Model

by Gabriela Sonntag

INTRODUCTION

The library community defines information literacy as "learning how to learn." Not coincidentally most texts on teaching models place the students' ability to learn and continue to educate themselves as the most important long-term outcome of instruction. The connection between teaching models and information literacy is a strong one. This chapter will outline changes that must occur to develop a teaching model for the library in support of information literacy. It will discuss the academic program of the library, the instruction librarians' role in the learning community, and characteristics of a teaching model necessary for an effective information literacy program.

A LIBRARY TEACHING MODEL

Putting a teaching model in place for an information literacy (IL) program requires some radical changes in the library. Recognizing the academic mission of the university, and the educational role of the library, librarians must begin to see themselves as teachers. This perceptual shift puts instruction as the primary role of the library and the librarians as instruction librarians who also teach at a reference desk or through appointments in their offices. Instruction is no longer an add-on to a long list of duties, but the most important duty, the *raison d'etre*, of the librarian. An argument can be made that the library as an organization splits into two very distinct, yet interconnected sectors. The service sector where such functions as cataloging, acquisitions, systems, or circulation reside; and the teaching sector as described here. Not just organizationally, but philosophically these two sectors are very different. Our teaching model places instruction as the umbrella, the overarching purpose of the academic library. This is not merely a change in language but a fundamental change as the library becomes a teaching/learning center.

This shift is based on the fundamental principle that colleges and universities are learning communities. Faculty, students, and all individuals who form part of this community have certain privileges and responsibilities of membership. Faculty are members that hold certain expertise to share with the community. They are responsible for continuing to learn and to impart this learning to all. Students must accept the responsibility of being active partners in their own learning. The IL program teaching model is in place to help students achieve the full potential of their membership in the community. As members of a learning community, the librarians understand that at the core of the IL program is a strong collaboration between library faculty, disciplinary faculty, and students.

INSTRUCTION LIBRARIANS IN THE LEARNING COMMUNITY

What is the role of the library and more specifically the IL program within the learning community? The library as the heart of the campus may be the model that comes immediately to mind. However a variant model to explore sees the university as a triangle of learning. One angle is the formal learning that occurs in the classroom, the faculty instructor teaching and directly guiding the learning that occurs, mainly focusing on subject content and the related ideas, skills, values, and ways of thinking.

Another learning angle occurs in the library where the students' assignments are vehicles for learning information literacy. Information literacy instruction within the context of the academic program allows the students to develop the skills, attitudes, and abilities that leads them to explore and learn on their own. Campbell and Wesley (2006) look at the very important role that librarians play in developing and strengthening a dialogue among various disciplinary faculty. "Librarians, merely by their roles in an academic community, can foster a broad-based, connected discussion of academic values among diverse faculty" (96). They conclude that "the library plays an integral and *not solely a supporting role* [emphasis added] in the educational priorities of each and every discipline" (96).

A third angle of learning, supported by the other two, is the learning that emerges out of the students' own curiosity piqued by their environment or context and supported by the learning that has occurred both in the classroom and in the library. As active partners in the learning community, students are required not just to interact with the required readings and course material, but also to become engaged in the academic discourse and to become involved in the life of the academic community. Daily experiences and exposure to their surroundings account for an important aspect of students' learning. These experiences give rise to questions and insights, and inspire intellectual curiosity. The students' contribution to the learning community, in fact their responsibility, is to pursue it. Propelled by their formal classroom learning and supported by the information literacy skills learned within the context of the library, students can continue their personal development because they have become independent learners.

The illustration of the learning community in Figure 8-1 visually portrays the role of the library. However the IL program can also be seen as an aspect of all three learning scenarios. Our collaboration with disciplinary faculty provides an opportunity to share the curriculum of a course, to have input into the assignments, to suggest resources that can support the learning in the course, and to acquire materials (books, videos) from which the professor can teach their subject.

The assignments that students receive and the library instruction that, hopefully, accompanies these assignments are the backbone of the libraries' academic program. These are the means by which we are able to deliver our curriculum.

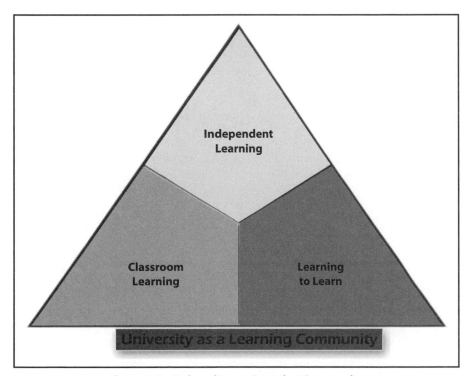

Figure 8-1: University as a Learning Community

The third angle also incorporates elements of the IL program, as more likely than not, students who are pursuing an interest of their own that poses a challenge will contact a librarian for research assistance. This provides us with a teaching opportunity that is invaluable.

The teaching model recognizes the broader role that librarians have in seeing that students become productive members of the academy—of being active participants in the learning community, and of taking responsibility for their learning. We can help teach them many of the important skills needed to understand the intellectual dialogue around any given topic. The librarian is focused on the process of learning whereas the disciplinary faculty tend to focus primarily on the content, the subject matter of the course. Together we can review the product that results from the learning that has taken place. Jointly we can assure that our students are successful. The university community exists because all three angles are strong and mutually supportive, and because the community members have accepted their mutual responsibilities.

FROM REFERENCE LIBRARIAN TO INSTRUCTION LIBRARIAN

Any discussion of teaching models must begin with a look at the historical growth of instruction librarianship as a natural part of the reference function. Librarians took their skills helping people at the desk into the classroom where they oriented students to the library services and resources. This was considered secondary to their job duties and many reference librarians opted to not become involved in instruction. Thus, reference/instruction librarians were asked to do presentations to classes or tours but were not relieved of their reference duties, nor detached from the reference department, nor trained in how to effectively teach. This aspect of a reference librarian's job grew, many times without support either moral or administrative, and without needed resources or training.

In more recent years, instruction has become a larger part of a reference librarian's job and perhaps the most predominant role for all librarians in public service. Recognizing the burden of these responsibilities, some libraries appointed instruction coordinators or hired an information literacy librarian. Their duties were to coordinate the scheduling of instruction or the training of new librarians, while at the same time garnering support on campus for information literacy initiatives. The burden of the program fell on the shoulders of one or two librarians within the organization. The rest of the librarians would take part only on an "as needed basis" or maybe "if I feel like it" basis. Instruction librarians were not recognized or valued because a teaching model did not exist. To this day one can find whole texts discussing instruction, but still referring to the librarians as reference librarians. This reveals that the shift from "librarian as service provider" to "librarian as proactive educator" has not been universal.

Not enough can be said about the need for strong administrative support. A vigorous teaching model must have 100 percent backing from top administrators. An important step is to take the necessary time to discuss issues, trends, and challenges with the administration so that they are more aware of how unique the instruction perspective may be in your institution. The library must become more student-focused, not in the traditional "service" mentality, but in a new model of teaching for lifelong learning. Librarians must demonstrate a commitment to instructional and pedagogical improvement. As Walter (2006: 216) concludes, "Making a commitment to instructional improvement is ultimately the responsibility of every teaching librarian, but helping to foster an environment conducive to making that commitment is one of the responsibilities of an instructional leader" and also of the administration.

Establishing a teaching model is not something that can be done by one administrator or librarian alone. Building consensus among the staff in the library is vital. The entire team is needed when it comes to marketing this model to the rest of the library and to the entire campus. The "teaching library" model must be understood by the whole organization in order to present the vision to the campus with one voice. While it is important to acknowledge individual librarians' teaching styles and guarantee academic freedom, it is crucial that the team carry forward the same message as they promote the instruction program both within the library and elsewhere on campus. It is essential to have all library faculty in agreement about the importance of instruction and the academic program of the library.

THE ACADEMIC PROGRAM OF THE LIBRARY

The information literacy program develops, delivers, and assesses an academic program parallel in many respects to any degree program on campus. Instruction librarians are responsible for managing and monitoring student learning in information literacy. Library faculty have the same role, and similar goals and objectives as disciplinary faculty. As our primary commitment is to students and their learning, we embrace the obligations that the academic learning community requires of us. Most importantly we take every opportunity to improve our teaching and reaffirm our commitment to continuous improvement.

In order for the academic program of the library to succeed, information literacy instruction must be an integral part of the academic curriculum. Having the instruction librarian do tours or general workshops is by and large not as effective and generally must be discontinued as demand for course-integrated instruction increases. Instruction should not be motivated by the need to get people into the library. The educational goal of the instruction program must always be front and foremost in all decision-making. Thus, the first step is for the program to develop a mission statement and goals. Aligning campus documents with the IL program goals and values is a good beginning. The university's mission statement, goals, and planning documents provide a starting place for gathering evidence to support a strong IL program. Information literacy instruction must also figure prominently within the mission, values, and goals of the library organization.

The California State University, San Marcos (CSUSM) IL program mission is to offer instruction integrated throughout the various academic programs and to target the instruction so that classes start in the first year at an introductory level and progress through the core courses for each major at a discipline-specific and advanced level. The teaching program must be course and assignment related and the instruction librarian must be careful to tailor the instruction specifically to what the student needs to know to be successful with that specific assignment, project, or course.

The next step for the IL program is to establish program-level student learning outcomes. Opting to use or modify the *Information Literacy Standards for Higher Education* makes this task a relatively easy one. Ideally, information literacy is also included as a program-level student learning outcome in the various degree programs on campus. If not, this becomes a goal for the IL program.

A curriculum map can be created to show which standards and learning outcomes are taught in specific courses. This curriculum map includes all the various courses where information literacy is included and also where the librarian and the instructor work together to ensure student independent inquiry and the development of IL competency. This curriculum map will also help in ensuring that all the learning outcomes have been adequately covered and that students are information literate at graduation.

Developing this curriculum map requires that the librarians have a strong working knowledge of their liaison departments. This goes beyond the courses to include academic program development and periodic review, the research requirements of students, and the interests of the faculty of their liaison departments. Serving on the campus curriculum committees is one way to develop a strong understanding of the academic programs on campus.

The teaching librarian draws on this knowledge of their liaison departments to identify those courses which will require library research skills, determine the library support needed for student success, and articulate this to the instructor. Librarians have a view of the student to which the faculty are not privy. We see the students as they struggle with assignments or slop together some "research" at the last minute. Sharing this with faculty can help initiate a dialogue so that together changes can be made that really impact student learning. We can engage with faculty in all aspects of instructional design and planning recognizing that they are generally looking to the final product, the students' term paper or project, while we are concerned with improving the process that ultimately impacts the quality of the product.

The final step in developing the academic program in the library is assessment of the student learning outcomes. This is perhaps the most difficult part of the process. Disciplinary faculty also struggle with methods for assessing student learning at the program level. This is especially difficult for librarians who do not always have access to student work. Much of the data gathered by the academic degree programs in their program review process can be helpful to us in evaluating our impact on student learning, especially when information literacy concepts are included in the academic program student learning outcomes.

If information literacy is included as a student learning outcome in the general education program and/or in the various academic programs, then not only can we garner support for the IL program, but we can begin to gather evidence that the IL program is meeting the student learning expectations. An analysis of academic program learning outcomes and corresponding course syllabi may show information literacy instruction and library-use assignments. Statistics can document that librarians provide extensive instruction within these academic programs. Especially important is the instructors' ability to witness, and even measure, the impact of the IL program on their students' work. Close collaboration with our colleagues in the disciplines can open up our options for assessment.

CHARACTERISTICS OF A TEACHING MODEL

The most important aspect of a teaching model for an effective information literacy program is the librarians themselves. Effective teaching models include librarians who have made the transition from the view of librarian as keeper of knowledge to the view of librarian as skilled in locating, evaluating, and using information *and* in teaching others how to do the same. Perhaps equally important is the role of the instruction coordinator as both a leader and a manager (Grassian and Kaplowitz, 2005). The coordinator must be a coach, mentor, teacher, friend, and fan club to the instruction team, creating and nurturing a strong team ethos. The instruction team is comprised of librarians with very important characteristics. These include a commitment to students and their learning, knowledge of our subject and how to teach it, responsibility for managing and monitoring student learning, reflection on teaching practice, a commitment to continuous improvement, and an obligation to the learning community.

Instruction librarians admit that they have learned how to teach on the job. Part of the learning process is thinking systematically about pedagogical practice and learning from experience, including each other's. Here the burden is on the coordinator to serve as a mentor to librarians joining the team. One proven method used at CSUSM is an orientation schedule that includes more than a map and a set of keys, but rather a series of opportunities to discuss and apply best practice in teaching and learning.

The new librarian, whether just out of library school or recently hired from another institution, needs to become acquainted with the teaching model. An orientation schedule begins with a series of meetings and discussions on topics such as the difference between training and teaching, working with adult learners and with the ever-changing first-year student, the attributes of an effective instructor, and assessment of learning.

During their first year, the coordinator and the new librarians work together in meetings and in the classroom to develop in the new librarian a basic understanding of learning theories and effective teaching practice. The instruction librarians learn how to apply the "Standards for Information Literacy Instruction" to actual situations such as using them to initiate a conversation with faculty colleagues, planning a class session, or setting goals for a series of classes. In learning how to plan a lesson, they practice identifying student needs, understanding faculty objectives for the lesson, and how to set appropriate goals and outcomes for the class. The coordinator will team-teach with the new librarian and then coach the librarian in areas that might need improvement. Together assessment/evaluation tools for on-going improvement of instruction are constructed. A continuous examination of practice is crucial, because as our students change, so must our methods and our content.

All the librarians in the instruction team are liaisons to specific academic programs. As their expertise in teaching increases so must their knowledge of their department and of their subject area. Their expertise includes detailed knowledge of any specialized information resources, trends in their discipline as well as impacts these may have on the curriculum and also on instructional practice. This is fundamental for developing the curriculum maps discussed earlier. The librarian must have a fairly comprehensive understanding of the courses offered in their liaison discipline and the learning outcomes of these courses, in order to adequately prepare the required information literacy instruction sessions. They must also know how the courses are sequenced and parallel that sequencing in mapping the information literacy learning outcomes. This is all necessary for the subject liaison librarian to effectively teach the courses in their subject area. It is important not to underestimate the value of this aspect of the teaching model.

Learning does not stop after the first year or happen in isolation. In fact, the entire team is involved as peer teachers and mentors. An open-door policy helps the team understand that the coordinator is there to listen, to assist in planning instruction, to brainstorm ideas, to critique, or support whatever is presented. The coordinator sets the tone for the entire team emphasizing that instruction librarians are colleagues working together to improve professional practice. Facilitating learning and creating a safe environment for sharing practice is an important aspect of the teaching model. We help each other keep abreast of trends in library instruction practices, in the use of technology for instruction, and in educational theory. We share our particular strengths as well as methods found to be successful in reaching and teaching our students.

It is an expectation that all librarians in the team will share their experiences both negative and positive, what worked and what didn't in our classes. At CSUSM, like many other institutions, numerous sections of one course are taught by all the instruction librarians. This provides a common experience, facilitating the open exchange of ideas that foster a culture of teaching. Together we become "teacher-designers" not mere "teacher-consumers" as described by Argentieri et al. (2001: 29). Teacher-consumers can follow a prepared script but designers know pedagogy, teaching and learning styles, and can design a learning experience suited to their students. Designers are able to plan, implement, and assess curricula for their intended audience and can reflect on the impact of their instruction on student learning.

Besides teaching in courses in the various degree programs, the academic program of the library targets special populations providing workshops or clinics to first-year students, athletes, or under-represented students in programs like the Educational Opportunity Program or the program for children of migrant workers. Off-campus groups like AVID (Advancement Via Individual Determination), Upward Bound, or the local high school Advanced Placement classes may be regular visitors to the library instruction labs as the librarian does hour-long activities that teach the steps in doing research.

An especially important aspect of the teaching model is the role of the librarian on campus. It is our obligation to be proactive in looking for opportunities to promote information literacy and to discuss its importance with our faculty colleagues. Additionally, serving on campus committees gives us an important venue for demonstrating that faculty status for librarians is taken seriously. Participation at the campus level provides an opportunity to define mutual interests and to discuss common goals. Being active on campus is a chance to both teach others about the academic program of the library and to learn ways to better collaborate with the campus community.

The instruction librarians must quickly learn to balance a seemingly overwhelming number of professional responsibilities, yet remain motivated, as burnout is a continuous challenge. There are several methods that can be put in place to keep librarians involved and creative. One method is recording daily activities. Team members are asked to keep daily logs using a spreadsheet as shown in Figure 8-2.

The librarian estimates how much time is spent that day in each activity answering the perennial question, "Where did my day go?" This is for personal use, but can be aggregated when the team discusses workload issues. This workday matrix can be especially useful to the librarian when calculating how much of their time is spent on service activities, such as a campus committee on the commencement ceremonies, as opposed to time spent in face-to-face instruction

Date	Library Meetings	Class Prep.	Teaching	Univ. Meetings	Reference	Faculty Meetings	Prof. Develop.	Collection Develop.	Research	Total
3-Feb										0
4-Feb										0
5-Feb										0
6-Feb										0
7-Feb										0
Total	0	0	0	0	0	0	0	0	0	0
%										100%

Figure 8-2: Daily Activities Record

with students. This calculation can help the multitasking librarian decide the best use of time within the framework of the campus promotion and tenure policy. How much weight is given to service activities as opposed to instructional activities? The answer helps us make important decisions about our time and assists in ensuring a balanced workload.

Another method for preventing burnout is to provide opportunities for each team member to renew and regenerate by attending conferences or workshops. Attendance is encouraged and financially supported, as one important duty for the coordinator is securing funding for professional development activities. Often the entire team will attend nearby events taking advantage of the drive time as a chance for team-building or a mini-meeting. Professional development and continuing education are essential for the program to thrive and grow, to stay vibrant and relevant. These opportunities exist on campus through the faculty development centers, the campus information technology departments, and others. Besides the national conferences, local library meetings or workshops, such as those organized by either the Southern California Instruction Librarians or the California Academic and Research Libraries, are excellent opportunities to exchange ideas and meet other librarians who share our interests. The California State University Teacher/Scholar Summer Institutes and the CSU Symposium on University Teaching are also examples of excellent programs. The coordinator must facilitate the teams' participation in these events and look for ways to reward professional growth and continual learning.

Asking instruction librarians to conduct workshops for the team also contributes to learning and prevents burnout. Constantly changing technology can quickly surpass our skill levels if we don't use it on a regular basis. For example, having a librarian explain how upcoming assignments will require the use of certain databases in specific ways allows the team to be better prepared to answer student questions and address their research needs. This type of mini-workshop keeps the team fresh, relieves the stress that comes from not knowing, and more importantly allows us to meet student needs.

Another example of a mini-workshop occurs when a librarian preparing for a conference uses the team meeting to practice their presentation. This not only allows the team to provide comments but keeps all abreast of our colleagues' research, providing support and feedback, while also learning. When the librarian returns from the conference we are interested in hearing how her presentation was received. We also expect to hear about a workshop or a session s/he attended and any other new ideas or methods worth sharing. These presentations are one way to regenerate enthusiasm and stay interesting to our students.

Programs will go through a cycle of enthusiasm, development, decay, and burnout. The teaching model encourages a team where every librarian is both a teacher and a learner. This model is also witnessed in the librarian's research arena. It is not uncommon to see publications that are co-authored. It is also an expectation that the team will support every librarian to find time to complete their research and get published. The coordinator is on alert for both publication opportunities and grants that can support research or other activities that will advance the team members towards promotion and tenure.

It is well understood by the entire instruction team that teaching and doing it well are valued in the library as well as in the university. Librarians develop a teaching philosophy which is prominent in their personnel files. They gather evidence—a teaching portfolio—to show non-instruction librarians and faculty outside the library what their teaching is all about, how it has changed over time, and how they align it with course goals. They demonstrate concern for pedagogy and best practices reflecting on their growth as teaching librarians.

It is important to note that an instruction team can include others who do not teach regularly or who feel uncomfortable in front of a group. These librarians can use their skills in developing online modules, helping create Web guides that complement the in-class instruction, compiling help guides or other instructional materials. They can be part of the team and lend essential support to those that do work directly with the students in a classroom. One method for allowing non-instruction librarians and administrators to better understand the teaching model is to welcome them into the classroom as observers. Being present during an instruction session can help these colleagues better understand the work that we do and perhaps appreciate all that goes into the preparation and delivery of the library's academic program.

There has been much discussion lately about the diminishing number of reference questions asked at the traditional reference desk. The emerging tensions between instruction and reference must be recognized. In a teaching model, these tensions may be alleviated. The focus of the reference interview becomes finding which course has generated the information need, and as much as possible, directing the student to the subject liaison librarian who is best suited to teach the student to find the answer. Many libraries are reviewing a model that sees a combined reference/circulation desk or reference/technology help desk releasing the librarians from this task.

Librarians are the major component of the teaching model. But other pieces must also be in place. Having the appropriate space for teaching is essential. Many libraries were renovated to include a computer area as research began to require them. But these were not necessarily designed with the instruction aspects in mind. Classrooms need to be the right size and shape to allow all students to see the screen and hear the speaker. They also need to have adequate lighting, whiteboards, projection systems, and screens to allow for an optimal teaching environment. Having to share these instructional spaces with other departments such as the computing staff is also a common practice that can cause conflicts. The equipment, technological support, and materials necessary to run the instructional program can be a constant challenge even if the space has been properly planned. Various teaching venues and the accompanying technology challenge us to revisit our teaching and generate new enthusiasm for instructional innovation. Having enough computers to allow all students to do searches allows us to develop hands-on activities that can replace, not supplement, the instruction we provide. Leading the learner to self-discovery has proven to be much more effective than lecturing.

CONCLUSION

A teaching model for information literacy instruction means more than focusing the library on teaching students the skills, abilities, and attitudes for lifelong learning. Developing a strong instruction team and creating a culture of teaching is a key component of this model. A philosophical shift from "library as service" to "library as classroom" is fundamental to support a vibrant information literacy program. This change and all that it implies will allow the library to reclaim its rightful place in the academic learning community.

REFERENCES

Argentieri, L., K. S. Davies, K. Farrell, and J. A. Liles. 2001. "Librarians hitting the books." In J. K. Nims and E. Ownes, eds., *Managing Library Instruction Programs in Academic Libraries*. Ann Arbor, MI: Pierian Press.

Bain, K. 2004. *What the best college teachers do*. Cambridge, MA: Harvard University Press.

Campbell, N. F., and T. L. Wesley. 2006. "Collaborative dialogue: Repositioning the academic library." *Portal: Libraries and the Academy*, Vol. 6, no. 1: 93–98.

Davis, T. M., and P. H. Murrell. 1993. *Turning teaching into learning: The role of student responsibility in the collegiate experience*. Washington, DC: George Washington University School of Education.

Grassian, E. S., and J. R. Kaplowitz. 2005. *Learning to lead and manage information literacy instruction*. New York: Neal-Schuman Publishers.

Walter, S. 2006. "Instructional improvement: Building capacity for the professional development of librarians as teachers." *Reference & User Services Quarterly*, Vol. 45, no. 3: 213–218.

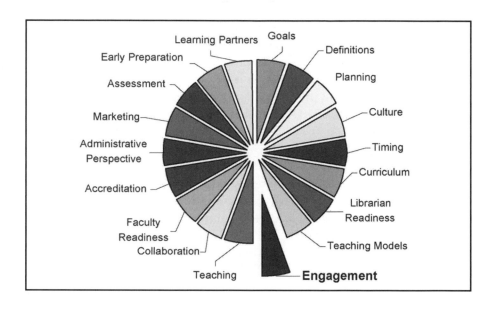

ENGAGEMENT

A Word from the Editors

*I*t is one thing to develop an extraordinary program of information literacy which is widely supported and rich in resources, and quite another to engage students in the study of information literacy. We can put every plan in place, but without students being deeply engaged, our best plans will come to a halt. In this chapter, Margit Misangyi Watts, Director of Manoa Educational Partnerships, reminds us that we have only one purpose in all our efforts—to increase student information literacy skills. In this chapter, Margit looks at the roots of the issue by starting with the purpose of knowledge and then moving us to college readiness and student expectations. Importantly, Margit gives us proven approaches to engaging students in learning with the hope that our collective understanding will reverse the trend of students being disconnected with their learning. Writing to the editors, Margit has said that she is striving to "provide new approaches to teaching and learning in a rapidly changing higher education environment." We all know that is no small challenge, but Margit has brought a rich perspective to this challenge through her work as a member for five years on ACRL's Best Practices Team to her service as a director for first year experience programs at the University of Hawaii. In Margit's current work, she tells us that she strives to "create intellectual and practical synergies between educational constituencies as well as the wider community." Margit is the author of two books* High Tea at Halekulani *and* College: We Make the Road by Walking. *Margit has an elementary teaching certificate from the University of Michigan, and her Master's in Social Work and a Doctorate in American Studies from the University of Hawaii.*

Chapter 9

The Challenge to Engage

By Margit Misangyi Watts

INTRODUCTION

The charge to engage students in higher education has been with us for a long time now. We just aren't listening. Most institutions continue to cling to the traditional notion of a liberal education and turn a blind eye to any suggestion that this might be in direct conflict with what students want. Doling out education as if it were "good for you" like broccoli is good for us isn't working. Faculty who spend years developing "new and improved" general education requirements still have not stepped outside the box and met the challenge of "proving" to students that indeed these requirements are not only new and improved, but relevant to their lives. Until colleges and universities come to terms with the fact that students come to them for a degree and not necessarily an education, then the disconnect will remain.

This chapter addresses the challenges of reversing this disconnect and suggests that one answer might be taking to heart the call by many to develop ways students can be involved in research. Academic librarians together with disciplinary faculty need to offer students opportunities to participate in original research projects. Guidance by both faculty and instructional librarians should foster student engagement in learning. After all, the engine that drives students' ability to do research is information literacy—skills that lead to the "educated" person we all aspire to produce.

OVERVIEW

A human being should be able to change a diaper, plan an invasion, butcher a hog, conn a ship, design a building, write a sonnet, balance accounts,

build a wall, set a bone, comfort the dying, take orders, give orders, cooperate, act alone, solve equations, analyze a new problem, pitch manure,
program a computer, cook a tasty meal, fight efficiently die gallantly. Specialization is for insects. (Heinlein, 1973: 248)

A liberal arts education is about attaining knowledge, wisdom, and understanding, and is meant to promote inquiry, interaction, and collaboration. It is also
intended to be transformative, reflective, and integrative. Above all, it is eventually supposed to give meaning to students' lives. Mark Edmundson, in *Why
Read?*, puts this in perspective well. He states that "... the questions that should
lie at the core of a liberal arts education [are]: Who am I? What might I
become? What is this world in which I find myself? How might it be changed
for the better?" (Edmundson, 2004: 5). But do students want knowledge? Do
they understand what knowledge is for? Do we know what drives them to succeed in their academic endeavors? What inspires and then sustains their motivation? Are they looking to be educated or just wanting a degree that leads to a
high paying job?

The problem colleges and universities are facing nationwide is one of a lack
of engagement by students in their education. This lack of buy-in leads to problems with retention and graduation rates, not to mention the loss of intellectual
curiosity that could lead to a less informed citizenry. In many respects, students
need not be IN an educational system; they should feel that they ARE the educational system. There is also a dichotomy in student thinking. They want it all.
Students want academic challenges but are not prepared for the challenges. They
want the opportunity, in fact demand it, to be independent and then are not pre-
disposed to ask for help when they really need it. Additionally, today's students
process information quickly, have career insecurity, are skeptical but optimistic,
and are technology savvy. They are also visually attuned, activity oriented, affil-
iative, and in their lives no standard rules apply. How do we then, create an academic environment that is both challenging and engaging and one that will meet
the needs of this incredibly diverse, complex, and unique group of students?

Education is a commodity to be traded for a better life and we need to come
to terms with that notion without letting go of our belief in a liberal education
for the "sake" of learning. In his book, *The End of Education*, Neil Postman
(1996) argued that we no longer have a "narrative" to help us answer the question of *why* we should be educated. He suggested that we've lost the "reason" for
going to school and that is why we are not seeing the "engaged" student we'd
like to see. Additionally, the report of the Wingspread Group on Higher Education entitled "An American Imperative: Higher Expectations for Higher Education" (1993) suggested that there are at least three fundamental issues: 1) taking
values seriously; 2) putting student learning first; 3) creating a nation of learners, which should be guiding the direction of our work. Students are asking
"why"; education and universities are slowly trying to answer with innovative

programs, new teaching and learning strategies, and new approaches to the issues of retention and engagement. No matter what discipline, how large the university, or which perspective might drive our palette of educational expectations, we are all challenged to create teaching and learning environments which will not only retain students, but will engage them and open their minds to the intellectual inquiry which is at the core of a higher education.

Some of the response has to be in the form of pedagogical shifts. These can come in the form of: short presentations, reflection as integral to learning, application as a tool for learning, exploration as a key to engagement, and assessment strategies utilized throughout all aspects of an academic experience. In its 1998 report, "Reinventing Undergraduate Education," the Boyer Commission recommended that students be given opportunities to learn through inquiry and that research-based learning should become the standard. The report posits that the engagement of undergraduates in research and creative scholarship and the provision of applied educational experiences, including service learning, are important imperatives for the future of higher education. Most educators would agree that an "educated" person is one who:

- acquires a depth and breadth of knowledge
- develops the ability to communicate in various ways
- learns to think critically
- becomes acquainted with important methods of inquiry
- secures lasting intellectual and cultural interests
- gains self-knowledge
- learns how to make informed judgments
- becomes a competent and involved citizen
- is involved on visual, verbal, and auditory levels
- gains an understanding of history, science, and the arts
- understands that knowledge is essential for a responsible and fulfilling life

What then do we need to do to make certain our graduates become this kind of "educated" citizen?

THE PURPOSE OF KNOWLEDGE

> Isn't it a coincidence of cosmic proportions that it takes exactly the same billable unit of work to learn the plays of Shakespeare and the differential calculus? Or many the guest has been amputated to fit the bed. (O'Banion, 1997: 10)

An institution of higher education is a place where knowledge is kept, created, revised, organized, manipulated, questioned, constructed, deconstructed, and reconstructed. Most students are not invited to participate in any of this, nor do they understand what role they themselves might play, and they regularly miss the relationship between the information seeking process and the actual creation of knowledge. However, it would seem that a university should foster the connection making meaning (creating knowledge out of information) and making a life. Ultimately, the goal of infusing the undergraduate curriculum with research-based learning is to facilitate students' ability to define the meaning of research for themselves. George Kuh, in the most recent National Survey of Student Engagement (NSSE, 2007), reports that what students do during college counts more in terms of desired outcomes than who they are or even where they go to college. His research on college student development illustrates that the time and energy students devote to educationally purposeful activities is the single best predictor of their learning and personal development. The NSSE report endorses the movement toward engaging students more fully in a variety of activities that help students understand scholarship—the creation of knowledge.

Human beings are by nature passionate, curious, intrigued, and will seek to connect, find patterns, and make sense of things. Learning is more effective when new information is made meaningful and linked to personal experience or prior knowledge; when we learn how to evaluate, assess, and connect, information is transformed into knowledge. Unfortunately, most undergraduates experience higher education in the traditional manner, which does not often include direct involvement in original research. In fact, the whole notion of why knowledge is important is probably never dealt with in a clear and concise manner.

> By putting a world of facts at the end of a key-stroke, computers have made facts, their command, their manipulation, their ordering, central to what now can qualify as humanistic education. The result is to suspend reflection about the differences among wisdom, knowledge, and information. (Edmunson, 2004: 10)

Perhaps the first avenue to explore with students is the purpose of knowledge. One way to address this might be to show that the purpose of knowledge encompasses the following:

- survival
- power
- context
- self-realization
- values

Survival is basic. It is about finding food and shelter, keeping warm, and finding water. It is about keeping safe, knowing one's enemy, and having a smattering of common sense. Knowledge is **power** as it gives one a competitive edge, be it regarding corporate secrets, espionage, scientific endeavors, or strategies for a game. Having knowledge means having an edge, knowing more than someone else about any topic. Knowledge helps you develop a **context** for life. Students begin to understand their place in society, where they come from, their heritage, and how family, town, or state fit into the larger scheme of the world. Additionally, the more knowledge one accumulates, the more easily a sense of **self-realization** is attained. Self-realization is deeper and that greater context can be meaningful. This kind of understanding helps get in touch more clearly with why one might be interested in a particular discipline. Finally, knowledge affects personal **values** and the decisions one makes, whether they are moral or ethical decisions. The more one knows about a topic the more "educated" a decision might become. Values and perspectives begin to resonate more clearly when students study about diverse world views.

Preparation for College

> The freshman to be sees photographs of well-appointed dorm rooms; of elaborate phys-ed facilities; of expertly maintained sports fields; of orchestras and the drama troupes; of students working joyously, off by themselves. It's a retirement spread for the young. (Edmundson, 2004: 17)

Jacques Barzun (1991: 154) suggests that the "... name college is magic by itself. Colleges abound and there is no assurance that the graduate from any of them knows anything in particular or knows it well." There is also no assurance that students graduating from high school have a body of knowledge that we can rely on. Faculty is always complaining about the lack of writing, reading, studying, and analytical skills that students have when entering college; students appear to lack the critical intellectual skills necessary to do high level work. In addition, they appear to lack any significant motivation to get them. There is no question that students are coming to college less well prepared than in the past; however, many educators around the country are opposed to offering remedial education at their institutions. From his extensive research, Ernest Boyer discovered that "the separation we found between school and college has led to a mismatch, a disturbing one, between faculty expectations and the academic preparation of entering students" (Boyer, 1987: 3). Pair this with the notion that rather than being excited about just going to college, students now view college as a conduit to the "next thing."

Both students and parents approach college as consumers. News magazines publish lists of colleges that give the most value for the money. In fact, shopping for the best deal is now a standard approach to choosing a college. Students come to the university to "purchase goods that are pre-packaged or made to order" (Douglas, 1992: 163). And how much they need to spend on these "purchased goods" affects students' "take" on academics. How many courses does each institution "require" as part of their general education curriculum? How quickly can a student get "through" these and move on to the important courses (whatever those may be). After all, students are taking longer to graduate and often put the blame on the college or university for requiring so many "unimportant" and "irrelevant" courses in the liberal arts. George Douglas, in his book *Education Without Impact*, addresses this by saying we have to "keep in mind that the prevailing opinion about these lower-level introductory courses is that they are 'service' functions. They are only something to be endured by those who teach them and those who are obliged to take them. There is a shared belief in their unimportance" (Douglas, 1992: 121). Thus, as Mark Edmundson posits, "Universities have become sites not for human transformation, but for training and for entertaining" (Edmundson, 2004: 6).

Getting an Education or Getting a Job?

> Rather, intellect weaves in and out of the main business, which is socialization, entertainment, political activism, and the struggle to get high grades so as to qualify for future employment. (Barzun, 1991: 151)

How well are college students learning what they should be learning? If they come somewhat unprepared yet with high expectations and dreams for a fine future, how will they fare? More importantly, what can we do to help them negotiate this dichotomy? Surely there are competing goals on any campus. Students are looking for that diploma as a ticket to a better job. Faculties see that same diploma leading to an educated person. However, there is a trend toward vocationalism and the value of the traditional liberal education is declining. In 1987, Ernest Boyer declared: "Today's students worry about jobs" (Boyer, 1987: 3). Nearly 20 years later we still have done nothing to address this issue. Is there any wonder we have a disconnect? Arthur Levine suggested, "although they do not believe a college education provides a money back guarantee of future success, they feel it is not possible to obtain a good job without one, much less a lucrative or prestigious job" (Levine, 1993: 115). Richard Paul and Linda Elder agree with Levine and feel that student goals are simple, they are to "prepare for a job, survive their classes in the meanwhile, gain approval from their peers, and satisfy their immediate desires" (Paul and Elder, 2001: 8).

So, what is the difference of being in college for an education or for a degree? Employers are looking for people who can think, write, and communicate well. They want people who are dependable, responsible, and respect diversity. They also want employees who can adapt to change and are good problem-solvers. There must be a way to integrate the development of these important skills with the breadth and depth of knowledge we hope students take away from a liberal education.

Engaging Students

> The faculty members who had an especially big impact are those who helped students make connections between a serious curriculum, on the one hand, and the students' personal lives, values, and experiences, on the other. (Light, 2001: 110)

We want students to retain information, to be able to transfer knowledge to new situations, be skilled at problem-solving, and to be motivated in all of this. However, students focus on grades rather than learning. In fact, they often don't see value in what they are learning. They also feel fragmented and disconnected; there is often no coherence in their educational experiences. Most often, a core curriculum is a scattering of courses across the disciplines with no effort being made to forge connections between ideas. George Douglas suggests that students probably enjoy themselves on campus and even do some maturing, but "for the most part they don't truly interact with the academic world" (Douglas, 1992: 196). That is because we don't invite them to do so.

This situation calls for some major changes in the academy. We need to change from providing instruction to students to providing learning opportunities for students. L. Dee Fink finds that the "basic problem is that, although faculty members want their students to achieve higher kinds of learning, they continue to use a form of teaching that is not effective at promoting such learning" (Fink, 2003: 3). The most important way to transform the educational experience of students is to move from a content-centered to a learning-centered approach. The learning-centered approach leads to students making more meaning of their academic experience. Arthur Levine has found that students are "more likely to prefer concrete subjects and active methods of learning" (Levine, 1993: 129). Unfortunately, faculty still teaches to what they consider a passive group of students, never for a moment considering that they might be contributing to the passivity.

A challenge for faculty is how to find a connection between the life of the academy and the wider human culture. In other words, how do you take the content of your discipline and spin it in such a way that students can see the relevance to their lives and that of their community? The following are some examples of ways of teaching that might engage students more readily. Most of these would fall under the category of active learning. Faculty could use case studies to illustrate ideas and content. Problem-based learning is an excellent way to help students become critical thinkers. Using writing as a vehicle for learning as well as offering many opportunities for self-reflection and assessment during the duration of a course are useful to foster an environment to help students make meaning of what they are learning. Work outside the classroom is always energizing to students. Richard Light (2001: 8) discovered that "when we asked students to think of a specific, critical incident or moment that had changed them profoundly, four fifths of them chose a situation or event outside of the classroom." This kind of work can range from service learning, to individual research, internships, apprenticeships, or even the use of technology to connect with others around the world.

It is doubtful that any institution takes the time to inform its student body of the goals, mission, or strategic plan which guides the decisions made on their behalf. Bringing students in on this information would be a great way to orient them to more than where the cafeteria, pool tables, and sports fields are situated on campus. If students participated in discussions about the mission of their college or university and had opportunities to see the big picture regarding their requirements, perhaps they could see beyond the little boxes they keep checking off—"let's see, one social science, two humanities, only four to go."

Finally, to draw from the author's own experiences of working with an instructional librarian, it is important to note that the need for this kind of collaboration can be a catalyst for developing the kind of academic environment that would engage students, prepare students, and challenge them to take part in the scholarship of higher education. As stated in this author's chapter "The Library as Place Versus the Place of the Library":

> The goal is to give first-year students the tools with which to navigate scholarly narratives, to understand discourse as a conversation over time, and to take part in critically assessing and evaluating information. Students should still be invited to go to the library, ask a librarian, or browse a collection; but, this should now be anchored in an overall collaborative approach to helping students understand both how and why they need to be information literate. (Watts, 2005: 340)

INFORMATION LITERACY AS CONDUIT

"It is possible to store the mind with a million facts and still be entirely uneducated." Alex Bourne

The goal of higher education should be to maintain and strengthen the *context* of learning while enhancing the *content* of a liberal education. The focus needs to be on inquiry, research, and discovery as a frame of mind. One foundation on which this rests is that of creating a series of experiences to build information literacy skills, the hallmarks of being able to do research—the creation of knowledge. It is interesting to note that information literacy skills are completely in line with the kinds of skills students need for their careers. And, by the way, these same skills help create citizens who are able to formulate educated decisions for themselves and their communities.

In the concluding chapter of *Integrating Information Literacy into the Higher Education Curriculum*, Ilene Rockman (2004: 248) states, "information literacy—the ability to recognize when information is needed and efficiently and effectively act on that need—is *the* critical campus–wide issue for the twenty-first century." She brings to life the notion that information literacy needs to be central to the education of students. In other words, the teaching of the skills and abilities inherent to being information literate needs to move out of the traditional library venue and be integrated into courses and programs across the curriculum. Rockman also notes that although information literacy has been embraced by the library association (ACRL) since the late 80s, others are finally beginning to theorize on what is needed in higher education—the language differs, but the end result is the same—how do we help students learn how to learn. In the conclusion Rockman sets forth the imperative that strategies for engaging students in higher education depend on successful integration of information literacy into the foundation of our educational practice. Randy Hensley (2002), in his article, "Learning Communities for First-Year Graduates," comes to the same conclusion. Introducing students to the many facets of information literacy early in their academic experience, especially as part of the greater first year experience at any institution, proves to strengthen their grasp of what it is to be part of the realm of higher education. Mastery of information literacy skills and abilities are essential and we are challenged to transform the curriculum in order to help students to do so.

BUILDING THE SKILLS

> Resource based learning is a common sense approach to learning. If students are to continue learning throughout their lives, they must be able to access, evaluate, organize, and present information from all the real-world sources existing in today's information society. (Breivik, 1998: 25)

So why would the integration of information literacy skills have an impact on student engagement? In part, because there is a solid connection to reality, providing a means for students to finally connect and interact with academic life. Let's review some essential components.

Knowledge Products—Students need to understand that knowledge is most often communicated and/or stored in what can be called "knowledge products." These include books, journals, magazines, and newspapers. Also included are films, videos, television, music, Internet sites, conversations, interviews, government publications and documents, and personal diaries. Most students have had experience with many of these knowledge products, but have never understood the particular kind of information that one can gather from each. For instance, books offer histories, overviews, and pictures; whereas, journals are filled with research studies and analyses, magazines and newspapers have more recent information, and interviews have personal stories and points of view. All of these kinds of "knowledge" are important to understand in context and each type offers unique information and insight.

Keeping the Narratives—These products, or scholarly narratives, are also usually kept in libraries, in various institutions or with individuals, within a variety of disciplines, and out in the community. Access to these narratives (stories) is key to scholarship. It is important to teach students how to find and, more importantly, how to understand them. This includes understanding a variety of database structures that can be accessed by using key words, author names, titles, or subjects. Of course, the way we search in libraries is changing continuously as new computer technologies afford us easier access and multiple databases. Students, therefore, need to be guided to ask: What knowledge resource(s) or product is best for my need? What has been said so far about my topic? How credible and valid is what I find? Finding information resources is about making choices from thousands of possibilities. Students need help with making informed choices.

Engaging Students in Scholarly Narratives—It is imperative that students understand the structure of a scholarly story. Thus, teaching the elements of a scholarly narrative—theory, hypothesis, literature review, methodology, data, interpretation, and significance is the first step toward helping them understand stories within the academic realm. Probably the best approach to this is to connect to the scholarly through personal stories, introduce them to the idea of discourse as a conversation over time, invite them to contribute to discourse, and involve them in original research.

Scholarly and Personal Stories—Students connect with scholarly writing more easily if they are introduced through personal stories. If students are given opportunities to begin researching a topic of personal relevance they can more easily make the leap from a subjective understanding to a scholarly one. For example, a student might be very interested in playing the ukulele. When asked about this, the student reveals that his uncle was a professional ukulele player from Portugal. Carrying this further, the student could begin research on the instrument, move from that to the relevance of the ukulele in Portugal, and finally end up with some excellent research on the significance of ukulele music to a particular culture—moving from the personal to the scholarly.

Discourse: A Conversation Over Time—One method of helping students understand scholarly narratives is to introduce them to the concept of discourse as conversation over time. Having them trace discourse on a particular topic helps them understand that when you insert yourself into a time and place, you are getting a particular perspective on a topic. A first step is telling students that scholarly discourse is a conversation over time about a specific topic by people (often called scholars) who are interested in researching and then adding to a conversation. Students need to understand that scholars have credentials that stem from their education, prior research they might have done, their work history, and validation by others in their field. Giving students examples such as— a scholar begins the conversation on a topic, let's say, *equity in education*, and makes a case one way or the other and publishes it in an academic journal. Someone else comes along and studies the same topic, reads the initial article, then perhaps does a survey or set of interviews of their own, and produces another scholarly product, which adds to the first one. This goes on for years, with the various authors arguing for or against each other, offering new data and new ideas. They therefore create this discourse through connections to others in their field, reviews of the literature, questions they might ask of one another, and contributions they then make to the conversation themselves. By going through this exercise, students can see the bigger picture of how knowledge is created, refined, redesigned, revised, and so forth—it is a moving target.

Contributing to Scholarship—Getting back to the concept of active learning, probably the best way for students to "engage" the world of scholarship is to be asked, or better yet, offered the privilege of contributing to it. Some of the ways students can do this is becoming involved in internships/apprenticeships, service learning, exhibits and presentations, publications, and original research projects.

The term **internship** is commonly used to cover a wide variety of experiential learning opportunities. The primary purpose of an internship is to provide practical perspectives on academic concepts and theories. An internship prepares students for future employment by giving them the opportunity to apply skills learned to a vocational setting. Thus, an internship is a great way to extend education, gain meaningful career contacts, and create significant, differentiating advantages in the job market. Experience in a professional work environment offers increased marketability, a sense of career goals, the creation of a network of contacts and references, and a better understanding of a student's field of interest.

Students make significant contributions to employers' operations, and they gain from the experience and opportunity to discover more about the application of what they have learned in college. Throughout an internship, students actively apply previously acquired knowledge in meeting the expectations of their position. They will demonstrate interpersonal and communication skills, all the while honing oral and written abilities. Students will exercise decision-making and problem-solving skills as they are given self-directed assignments. Finally, internships give them the opportunity to assess career plans and aspirations in relation to their experiences.

Service learning is an educational model that combines experiential learning and community service. Additionally, guided by faculty and community leaders, students participate in planning and executing service projects, which in turn are tied to their academic curricula. The call for service in an educational setting is definitely both a call for practical experience to enhance learning and a reinforcement of moral and civic values inherent in serving others. Additionally, service learning affords students the opportunity to learn how to be creative problem-solvers, members of a team, synthesize information, and make educated and informed decisions.

> Service learning fosters an environment in which students can learn about "others," find out about their lives, thoughts, and struggles, reflect on what their presence in their lives might mean, and, finally, discover who they are. Putting experiences together is what brings insight. Service learning

provides connections to the community to solve real problems; the issues that students address are not the theoretical ones they read about in textbooks, but are those found in real life which need real life answers.

Having students become involved in **exhibits**, **presentations**, and **publications** allow them to do **original research**. The levels of contribution can be just for peers or can be made available to the world. For example, students could create work to exhibit to other students. This could be in the form of sharing papers through peer editing, group discussions, oral presentations, or activities that allow students access to one another's work. Students could also share work with the wider university/college community by participating in forums or debates, organizing a conference, or publishing work in the school newspaper or literary journals. Of course, students could share work with the wider community. They could organize a conference that the community is invited to attend, or work with a local museum and create a museum exhibit. Finally, students could reach the world through telecommunication capabilities by creating Web sites, ezines (online magazines), class related blogs, and so forth.

The possibilities are endless. Academic activities can be transformed into something to share with others. It is a way of allowing students to see that it is the application and dissemination of learning that is most important.

Assess Differently—Of course, if we begin to change the way we teach and help students learn, we must also reevaluate the manner in which we assess. Three ways that are particularly well suited for active learning-based teaching are portfolio assessment, performance-based evaluations, and reflection as connected learning. Most essential to all of this is that assessment strategies need to begin at the beginning and must be revisited throughout the course of a semester. Students and faculty alike have to have clarity on the desirable outcomes for a particular learning endeavor.

Many colleges and universities are beginning to integrate **portfolio assessment** into regular evaluation strategies. The basic concept behind this is that student work is being viewed as a whole. This allows for assessment of growth and change over time. Most often, students are allowed to assemble their portfolio to include revisions and reflections. This offers a faculty member insight into how the student has progressed, has been thinking about their work, and if indeed the student has made the effort to improve.

A **performance-based review** is an excellent benchmark for student learning. Performance-based assessments are a set of strategies for the application of knowledge, skills, and work habits. This type of assessment provides information about how a student understands and applies knowledge. Also, faculty can integrate performance-based assessments into the instructional process to provide additional learning experiences for students. In order to do this kind of assessment, faculty must ask: What concept, skill, or knowledge am I trying to assess? What should my students know? At what level should my students be performing?

What type of knowledge is being assessed? The guidelines for what kinds of evidence will be included in the assessment must be shared with students at the beginning of the course. Rubrics are often excellent ways to outline for the student exactly what kind of work is excellent, average, and not acceptable.

Finally, giving students ample opportunities for **reflection** is an excellent method of assessment and evaluation. Reflection actually should be structured as an official part of course work. It involves taking the time to review, think about, and analyze an experience—be it a reading, a lecture, a discussion, or a field trip—in order to gain deeper understanding. It provides an opportunity to think about the knowledge gained and how attitudes and views might have changed.

The reflective process has three elements. First, it fosters an examination of new knowledge and skills, new information, and alternative ways of knowing or perceiving the world. Secondly, there is the affective component, which examines what students feel in response to new knowledge or experiences (this involves emotions, attitudes, and perspectives). And thirdly, examination of what has been learned in light of the process involved. It allows students the opportunity to think about how the concepts and ideas learned throughout a course or semester might be interconnected.

CONNECTING IT ALL

So yes, something deep inside us made us want to continue to believe that the college or the university was somehow set off from the realm of utility. Even though we no longer know how to build such an institution, we still pine for it. (Douglas, 1992: 12)

The connectedness of knowledge is something that faculty needs to address in all they do. Students will more easily see the relevance of what they are learning if they can connect new knowledge across the curriculum and to their lives. We also need to focus on connecting theory and practice, personal and scholarly, and education and life.

Let's face it—students today are moving faster than ever before. Information (not necessarily knowledge) is being bombarded at them every micro second. They are able to connect with each other and information instantly and thus expect responses (answers) just as quickly. This is in direct contrast to how a college or university curriculum is designed. Most institutions offer at least two years of "grazing" the liberal arts with no explanation beyond "these are good for you" (a little like castor oil was years ago!). And while we continue to offer fields of breadth and depth to our students we are perplexed as to their obvious discontent, disinterest, and inability to connect with what we put on the table.

Everyone who is studying college students today has agreed that our most difficult challenge is engaging them in what we are offering. We've tried learning communities, small seminars, workshops, cohorts, fancier dorm rooms, eclectic course offerings, midnight parties, coffee with the author, access to degree audits, changes in core requirements, jazzy titles to courses, contemporary texts, movies, video, music, and professors dancing on the tops of their desks. Are students engaged? No. Most of them are still here for that ticket to later success—the degree, which they believe will lead to a better (read, high paying) job. And in their way of thinking, the least and most streamlined way they can get there the better.

So what do we do? Most importantly, we have to find a way to combine our institutional mandate to prepare "educated" individuals with the students' goal of "getting a degree." Somehow these two goals need to integrate. This chapter suggests that one clear way to do this is to involve students in original research. What guides this thinking is the theory that an **engaged student** is one who is **involved in the creation of knowledge**, and **information literacy skills** are the engines that drive students' ability to be involved. It's as simple and complex as that. But if we can do more of this in our colleges and universities, we should begin to feel a sea change in student attitudes, their actual work output, motivation, and even the economic issues of retention and graduation rates.

Be assured, students who find themselves intimately involved in the creation of new knowledge will be getting their degrees, but even more importantly, they will magically become educated individuals. And in this way, we all win.

REFERENCES

Ackerman, D. 1999. *Deep play.* New York: Random House.

Barzun, J. 1991. *Begin here: The forgotten conditions of teaching and learning.* Chicago: The University of Chicago Press.

Boyer, E. L. 1987. *College: The undergraduate experience in America.* New York: Harper & Row.

The Boyer Commission on Undergraduate Education. 1998. "Reinventing undergraduate education: A blueprint for America's research universities." Available: http://naples.cc.sunysb.edu/Pres/boyer.nsf/673918d46fbf653e852565ec0056ff3e/d955b61ffddd590a852565ec005717ae/$FILE/boyer.pdf

Breivik, P. S. 1998. *Student learning in the information age.* Phoenix: Oryx Press.

Douglas, G. H. 1992. *Education without impact.* New York: Carol Publishing Group.

Edmundson, M. 2004. *Why read?* New York: Bloomsburg.

Fink, L. D. 2003. *Creating significant learning experiences.* San Francisco: Jossey-Bass.

Heinlein, R. 1973. *Time enough for love: The lives of Lazarus Long; a novel.* New York: Putnam.

Hensley, R. B. 2002. "Learning communities for first-year undergraduates: Connecting the library through credit courses." In J. K. Nims and A. Andrew, eds., *First Impressions, Lasting Impact: Introducing the First Year Student to the Academic Library.* Library Orientation Series No. 32. Ann Arbor, MI: Pierian Press.

Karabell, Z. 1998. *What's college for?* New York: Basic Books.

Levine, A. 1993. *Higher learning in America 1980–2000*. Baltimore, MD: The John Hopkins University Press.

Levine, A., and J. S. Cureton. 1998. *When hope and fear collide: A portrait of today's college student*. San Francisco: Jossey-Bass.

Light, R. J. 2001. *Making the most of college: Students speak their minds*. Cambridge, MA: Harvard University Press.

National Survey of Student Engagement. "2007 Institutional Report." Available: http://nsse.inb.edu/index.cfn

Nozick, R. 1989. *The examined life*. New York: Simon & Schuster.

O'Banion, T. 1997. *A learning college for the 21st century*. Phoenix, AZ: American Association of Community Colleges.

Paul, R., and L. Elder. 2001. *Critical thinking*. Upper Saddle River, NJ: Prentice Hall.

Peters, R. 1994. "Some snarks are boojums: Accountability and the end(s) of higher education." *Change*, Vol. 26, no. 6: 16–23.

Postman, N. 1996. *The end of education: Redefining the value of school*. New York: Knopf.

Rockman, I. F., ed. 2004. *Integrating information literacy into the higher education curriculum*. San Francisco: Jossey-Bass.

Senge, P. 1994. *The fifth discipline fieldbook*. New York: Doubleday.

Simpson, R. D., and S. H. Frost. 1993. *Inside college: Undergraduate education for the future*. New York: Insight Books.

Watts, M. 2005. "The place of the library versus the library as place." In M. L. Upcraft, J. N. Upcraft, J. Gardner, and B. Barefoot, *Challenging and Supporting the First-Year Student: A Handbook for Improving the First Year of College*. San Francisco: Jossey-Bass.

Whitehead, A. N. 1967. *The aims of education and other essays*. New York: Free Press.

Wingspread Group. 1993. "An American imperative: Higher expectations for higher education." Available: www.johnsonfdn.org/AmericanImperative/index.html (accessed September 22, 2006).

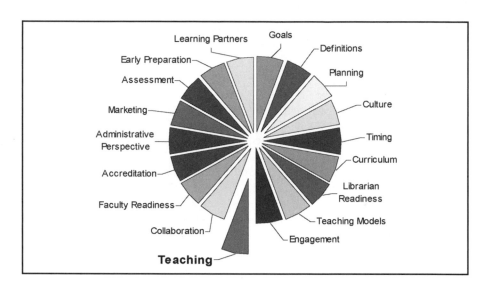

TEACHING

A Word from the Editors

*C*an information literacy be taught in isolation? Can a particular skill within *information literacy, such as the evaluation of sources be taught without any other skills such as the information seeking strategy or the analysis of the information? Can information literacy be taught without students understanding the broad framework of information literacy that takes them from search strategy to evaluation? These are the questions that Dr. Mike Eisenberg, who stepped down as Dean of the Information School at the University of Washington in January 2006 and where he is now Dean Emeritus and Professor, is answering in this chapter. In writing to the editors, Mike has said that his goal is to "offer a complete conceptual and practical approach for successful information literacy instruction." We think you will agree that Mike has succeeded as he explores what he calls "the three essential contexts for successful information literacy teaching and learning: the information process itself, technology in context, real needs—either curricular or personal." Mike has spent his career thinking deeply about curriculum matters, teaching, and learning and we are the latest beneficiaries of his efforts. At the University of Washington, he led the program from a single graduate degree into a broad-based information school. He was a founding director of the Information Institute of Syracuse where he was also a Professor of Information Studies. Along with Bob Berkowitz, Mike created the well-known, widely used, and very successful Big6 approach to information literacy. In this chapter, Mike also reflects on the Big6 in the context of this chapter. Mike's Ph.D. is in Information Transfer from the School of Information Studies at Syracuse University where he also took a Certificate in Advanced Studies. His M.L.S. is from the State University of New York at Albany.*

Chapter 10

Teaching Information Literacy:
Context, Context, Context

By Michael B. Eisenberg

INTRODUCTION: INSTRUCTIONAL STRATEGIES
AS CORE COMPETENCY

Expertise in instruction is now an essential skill for the twenty-first century library and information professional. Every information or library job has some form of presentation, training, or instruction associated with it. Even those in systems or other behind-the-scenes positions are likely to find themselves having to develop a user manual, train a co-worker or new employee, or present to managers or decision-makers. It's even more apparent for jobs in information services with many positions now explicitly listing "instruction" as a desired or required competency.

Instruction and training involves much more than standing up in front of a group of people and lecturing. Instruction and training may take the form of written handouts, Web pages, audio or video recordings, signage, one-on-one discussions, e-mail, or chat. Furthermore, instruction and training takes places in every organization—especially information-focused organizations such as libraries, help centers, and Web-based businesses providing information, answers, or services. Therefore, every information professional must be well-versed in recognizing the need and context for instruction and training, and be able to help meet users' needs through appropriate methods and approaches.

Fundamentally, instruction and training involves skills of communication and collaboration as well as proficiency in instructional design, development, and evaluation. Many accredited library and information science curricula now include a course that focuses on instructional strategies, and at the University of Washington, we have a core, required course entitled, "Instructional and Training Strategies for Information Professionals" (LIS 560). This course provides students the opportunity to learn instructional concepts, strategies and skills, and gain an understanding of how they can be applied in any situation.

The bottom-line is that knowledge and skills associated with instruction and training help information professionals to be more effective in any presentation or working situation. Instructional expertise can be learned—and this paper offers a beginning by providing specific conceptual and practical strategies for effective information literacy skills instruction.

STRATEGY: IT'S ALL ABOUT CONTEXT

In real estate, they talk about the three key elements: location, location, and location. In education, we can say a similar thing about implementing a meaningful information literacy program: context, context, and context.

There are three essential contexts for successful information literacy teaching and learning:

1. the information process itself
2. technology in context
3. real needs—either curricular or personal

Organizationally, for teaching information literacy, these contexts are essential for effective information literacy programs at any level or with any age group. The process provides a structure for applying skills that can seem disconnected; technology within the process gives focus and flexibility; and real needs make information literacy relevant and transferable.

Individually, when students are working on an assignment or solving a problem, it's easy to get lost or confused. They are in a much better position to succeed if, at any point in time, they can identify where they are in terms of the three contexts:

1. Where are they in the information problem-solving process?
2. How does technology boost their capabilities in terms of specific information skills?
3. What is the curricular or personal need being addressed?

The remainder of this chapter will consider information literacy within each of these contexts in more detail.

CONTEXT #1: THE PROCESS

Information is a pervasive and essential part of our society and our lives. Humans are, at their essence, processors and users of information. This is not a recent development. Humans have always been dependent upon information to help them make decisions and guide their actions. Increases in the sheer volume of information and the complexity of information systems, have come about largely because of advances in information technology and the accelerated rate at which we live our lives.

Information literacy is the set of skills and knowledge that not only allows us to find, evaluate, and use the information we need, but perhaps more importantly, allows us to filter out the information we don't need. Information literacy skills are the necessary tools that help us successfully navigate the present and future landscape of information.

There are a number of different information skills standards and models that seek to explain the scope of information literacy including:

- Carol Kuhlthau's information search process
- The Big6 approach of Eisenberg and Berkowitz
- American Association of School Librarians (AASL)/Association for Educational Communications and Techology (AECT) information literacy standards
- ACRL "Information Literacy Competency Standards for Higher Education"

Figure 10-1 is an updated version of various charts authored by Eisenberg and others (Eisenberg and Brown, 1992; Eisenberg, Lowe and Spitzer, 2004) comparing the models of information literacy that were developed through research, practice, and committee, respectively. This side-by-side view of information literacy models shows that there are many similarities among them. In fact, there is more agreement than disagreement among the models, as is true of information literacy research itself. For example, the driving force behind almost all of the models, and many of the findings, is "process"—the understanding that information skills are not isolated incidents, but rather are connected activities that encompass a way of thinking about and using information.

My own approach, the Big6, is the most widely used model in K–12 education, world wide (www.big6.com). With six major stages and two sub-stages under each, the Big6 covers the full range of information problem-solving actions.

The Big6 is an approach that can be used whenever people are faced with an information problem or with making a decision that is based on information. Students—K–12 through higher education—encounter many information problems related to course assignments. However, the Big6 is just as applicable to their personal life.

The Big6 skills comprise a unified set of information and technology skills (see Figure 10-2). Taken together, these skills form a process. The process encompasses six stages from task definition to evaluation. Through the Big6, people learn how to recognize their information needs and how to progress through a series of stages to solve information problems effectively and efficiently.

Kuhlthau Information Seeking	Eisenberg/Berkowitz Information Problem-Solving (The Big6 Skills)	AASL/AECT Information Literacy Standards	ACRL Information Literacy Competency Standards

1. Initiation
2. Selection
 	
4. Formulation (of focus)
	1. Task Definition
	  1.1 Define the problem
	  1.2 Identify info requirements
			1. Determines the nature and extent of the information needed.

3. Explor-ation
(investigate info on the general topic)   5. Collect-ion
(gather info on the focused topic)
	2. Information seeking strategies
	  2.1 Determine range sources
	  2.2 Prioritize sources
	3. Location and access
	  3.1 Locate sources
	  3.2 Find info
	4. Information use
	  4.1 Engage (read, view, etc.)
	  4.2 Extract info
		1. Accesses information efficiently and effectively.	3. Evaluates…sources…critically.
			
			2. Accesses needed information effectively and efficiently.
			5. Accesses and uses information ethically and legally.

6. Presentation	5. Synthesis
	  5.1 Organize
	  5.2 Present
		2. Evaluates information critically and competently.
		3. Uses information accurately and creatively.
			3. Evaluates information… critically.
			5. Understands many of the economic, legal, and social issues surrounding the use of info. and accesses and uses info. ethically and legally.
			3. Incorporates selected info. into his or her knowledge base and value system.
			4. Individually or as a member of a group, uses information effectively to accomplish a specific purpose.

7. Assessment (of outcome/ process)	6. Evaluation
	  6.1 Judge the product
	  6.2 Judge the process		

Figure 10-1: Comparison of Information Skills Process Models

Many problem-solving models provide a set of specific activities, or outline of isolated skills. These models may encourage a lockstep strategy that forces one specific method for problem-solving and decision-making. Like these others, the Big6 approach is systematic, however, it differs in a significant way. Big6 skills provide a broad-based, logical skill set that can be used as the structure for developing a curriculum or the framework for a set of distinct problem-solving skills. These fundamental skills provide students with a comprehensive set of powerful skills to conquer the information age.

But the Big6 is more than a simple set of skills—it is also an approach to helping students learn the information problem-solving process. Learning more about the Big6 as a process and as an approach should make it easier and more useful for instructors and students. For instructors, the Big6 provides a definitive set of skills that students must master in order to be successful in any learning context. Teachers can integrate instructional modules or lessons about the Big6 into subject area content and assignments. For students, the Big6 provides a guide to dealing with assignments and tasks as well as a model to fall back on when they are stuck. The Big6 represents "metacognition"—an awareness by students of their mental states and processes.

From experience and research, we found that successful Big6 information problem-solving does require completing each stage at some point in time: defining the task, selecting, locating, and using appropriate information sources, pulling the information together, and deciding that the task is in fact completed. However, the stages do not need to be completed in any particular order or in any set amount of time. A stage can be repeated or revisited a number of times. Sometimes a stage is completed with little effort, while at other times a stage is difficult and time consuming (see Figure 10-2). However, the Big6 is not linear and prescriptive. It's not necessary to complete the stages in order, however all the stages must be completed for overall success.

Figure 10-3 illustrates that the Big6 is not necessarily a linear, step-by-step process. For example, imagine that after students have defined a task and decided

| 1. Task Definition:
    1.1 Define the problem.
    1.2 Identify the information
        needed.

2. Information Seeking Strategies:
    2.1 Determine all possible sources.
    2.2 Select the best sources.

3. Location and Access:
    3.1 Locate sources.
    3.2 Find information within sources. | 4. Use of Information:
    4.1 Engage (e.g., read, hear, view).
    4.2 Extract relevant information.
5. Synthesis:
    5.1 Organize information from
        multiple sources.
    5.2 Present information.

6. Evaluation:
    6.1 Judge the result (effectiveness).
    6.2 Judge the process (efficiency). |

Figure 10.2: The Big6

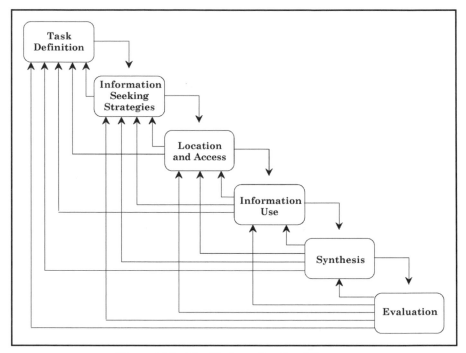

Figure 10-3:   The Big6 as a Feedback Process

on their information seeking strategies in terms of three sources, they find them unavailable. In that case, they would loop back to information seeking strategies to reformulate their plans. Or, suppose when writing a paper (synthesis), students aren't sure if they have done everything the teacher asked. Here, they would jump back to task definition to review the problem and requirements. The point is to be flexible and able to move back and forth in the process, but to be able to do what is essential in each stage.

From a learning perspective, knowing where they are in the process is very helpful for students. It helps them to know what's been completed and what is still to be done. When working on an assignment, project, report, or even an information problem of personal interest, students should be able to identify where they are in the process. For example, are they reading an article related to current events? That's "Use of Information," Big6 #4. Are they searching for sources using a periodical database or search engine? That's Big6 #3, "Location and Access."

From a teaching perspective, it's important to anchor instructional and learning experiences related to information and technology skills instruction within the information process. For example, teaching PowerPoint for organizing and presenting oral presentations—that's "Synthesis," Big6 #5. Working with students to determine the most appropriate and available sources for a project—that's "Information Seeking Strategies," Big6 #2.

Connecting instruction of individual skills or techniques within the overall Big6 process provides students with a familiar reference point. They see the links among seemingly separate skills and are able to reflect on what came before and anticipate what comes after.

Therefore, we recommend continually working with students to help them recognize where they are in the process. Some ways that educators can do this is by:

- identifying for students the various information process stages as they go through them to complete an assignment, project, report, or even to make a personal decision
- using a narrative or self-reflection to point out the Big6 related to the actions of one or more characters
- modeling information process recognition by pointing out when they themselves are engaging in a particular information stage
- asking students, verbally or in writing, to identify which information stage they are working on

Some would call this a meta-cognitive approach. The Big6 (or any other process model) gives students a vocabulary to describe processes and become more self-aware. By continually emphasizing a "process context," students learn to recognize their own styles as well as their strengths and weaknesses. They also have a model to fall back on should they get stuck or have difficulties.

CONTEXT #2: TECHNOLOGY FOR INFORMATION PROBLEM-SOLVING

There seems to be an increased understanding among educators as well as in the general public that technological proficiency is more than simply knowing a particular set of commands or even how to use a particular type of software. We want students to use technology flexibly and creatively. We want them to be able to size up a task, recognize how technology might help them to fulfill the task, and then use the technology to do so. Students need to be able to use computers for a purpose.

Helping students learn to apply technology in these ways requires a change in the way computer skills are traditionally taught. It means moving from teaching isolated "computer skills" to teaching integrated information and technology skills. From an information literacy perspective, that means integrating computer skills within the information problem-solving process. Individual computer skills take on a new meaning when they are integrated within a process, and students develop true "computer literacy" because they have genuinely applied various computer and technology skills as part of learning.

Moving from teaching isolated computer skills to helping students learn integrated information and technology skills is not just a good idea—it's essential if we are to put students in a position to succeed in an increasingly complex and changing world. As early as 1992, Peter Drucker, a well-known management guru, pointed out that many executives today are computer literate but not information literate. That is still true today. Being able to use computers is not enough. Executives must be able to apply computer skills to real situations and needs. Executives must be able to identify information problems and be able to locate, use, synthesize, and evaluate information in relation to those problems. These same needs exist for all people living in an information society.

There are many good reasons for moving from teaching isolated computer skills to teaching integrated information and technology skills. Technology is changing at a breath-taking pace and will continue to do so for the foreseeable future. Bill Gates once said that computing power has increased one million times over the past 20 years and will likely do so again in the next 20 years!

A million times more powerful. Will learning isolated specific skills such as word processing, electronic spreadsheets, and even Web searching suffice? Clearly not. Will learning to use whatever technologies come along to boost our skills within the overall information problem-solving process? Absolutely. That's what it means to look at technology from an information skills perspective.

Consider a common technology—"a pencil and paper." From an information process perspective, how can a pencil and paper help us to be more productive? Clearly, a pencil and paper boosts our ability to present information. In the Big6 process, this is Big6 #5—"Synthesis." What are the electronic equivalents of a pencil and paper—the tools that help us even more to synthesize? Clearly, there's word processing. There's also desktop publishing, PowerPoint, and other presentation software programs. All these are used to organize and present information, Big6 #5.

Reflect on another common technology—"a phone book." The phone book is a tool for accomplishing Big6 #3—"Location and Access." Electronic equivalents to the phone book are online library catalogs, periodical databases, and of course, Web search engines.

Any technology can be analyzed in this way—as part of the information problem-solving process. Web pages, electronic reference resources, Q&A services, are all part of an effective "Information Seeking Strategy" (Big6 #2) and when we engage them and extract relevant information that's Big6 #4—"Use of Information." E-mail, chat, or text messaging is highly useful for linking students with their teachers or with other students for "Task Definition" activities (Big6 #1), and later for "Evaluation" (Big6 #6).

When integrated into the information problem-solving process, these technological capabilities become powerful information tools for students. Figure 10-4 provides a summary of how some of today's technologies fit within the Big6 process and Figure 10-5 flips it around—considering technology within the process. This is the most powerful way to consider technology—as a boost to people's abilities—within the information problem-solving process.

Technology	Big6 Stage	Description
Word processing	5	SYNTHESIS (writing)
	4	USE OF INFORMATION (notetaking)
Spell/grammar checking	6	EVALUATION
Presentation/Multimedia software	5	SYNTHESIS
Electronic spreadsheets	5	SYNTHESIS
Online library catalog	3	LOCATION and ACCESS
Search Engine	3	LOCATION and ACCESS
Full-text electronic resources	2	INFORMATION SEEKING STRATEGIES
	4	USE OF INFORMATION
E-mail	1–6	ALL (particularly TASK DEFINITION, EVALUATION)
Copy-paste (in various programs)	4	USE OF INFORMATION

Figure 10-4: Technological Capabilities and the Big6

CONTEXT #3: REAL NEEDS

As noted earlier, information is a pervasive and essential part of our society and all our lives. Information is pervasive, and so are information skills. Therefore, there are many opportunities for teaching and learning information literacy. From research and experience, we know that the information skills are best learned in the context of real needs—school or personal. Students today, more than ever, want to see connections between what they are learning and their lives. They want to know how something is relevant. We need to take advantage of this and emphasize the applicability of information skills across environments and situations.

In school settings, the context for information literacy instruction is the curriculum. In K–12, this includes the subject area units and lessons of study. In higher education, we focus on courses, class topics, and lectures. Most importantly in both, the emphasis should be on the assignments on which students will be evaluated. Throughout the academic year, teachers and students engage in a rich range of subjects, topics, and assignments. In fact, one of the current problems we face in education is "curriculum information overload"—there's just too much to cover in a limited amount of time.

That's why, in implementing information skills instruction, we do not promote adding new curricular content, units, or topics. There's plenty going on in

Big6 Stage	Description	Technology
1	TASK DEFINITION	e-mail, group discussions (listservs, online forums), brainstorming software, chat, videoconferencing, groupware
2	INFORMATION SEEKING STRATEGIES	online catalogs, info retrieval, networked electronic resources, intranet, Web resources, digital reference services, online discussion groups, blogs, wikis
3	LOCATION and ACCESS	online catalogs, electronic indexes, search engines, browsers
4	USE OF INFORMATION	upload/download, word processing, copy-paste, outliners, spreadsheets, databases (for analysis of data), statistical packages
5	SYNTHESIS	word processing, desktop publishing, graphics, spreadsheets, database management, presentation software, down/up load, e-journals, blogs, wikis, Web-authoring
6	EVALUATION	e-mail, group discussions (listservs, online forums), brainstorming software, chat, videoconferencing, groupware

Figure 10-5: The Big6 and Technology

the curriculum already. The last thing that faculty and students need is more content. Therefore, from an information literacy perspective, the challenge is to determine good opportunities for learning and teaching information skills within the existing curriculum. To do so involves the following actions:

- analyze the curriculum to:
    - select topics and assignments which are well-suited to information skills instruction
    - determine which skills are particularly relevant to the selected curricular topics and assignments
- develop a broad plan that links the information skills program to various curricular topics
- design integrated topic and lesson plans to teach information skills in the context of the subject area curriculum

I strongly advocate a collaborative approach to information instruction. That is, classroom teachers, librarians, technology teachers, and other educators can work together to analyze the curriculum, develop a broad plan, and design specific units and lesson plans that integrate the information skills and class-room content. These educators can also collaborate on teaching and assessment.

Effective information skills instruction starts with selecting existing curriculum units which are best suited to integrated instruction. In the Big6 program, we refer to these units as "big juicies"—those information-rich curriculum units that are filled and dripping with Big6 potential. "Big juicy" units are rich in information needs, resources, and processing. These are the units that offer particularly good opportunities for teaching specific Big6 skills within the overall Big6 process, for example:

- Units or topics that involve a report, project, or product rather than those that rely on a test for assessment.
- Units that require a range of multiple resources rather than only the textbook.
- Units that reach a large number of students and span a reasonable timeframe.

The following is an example of how this might work in practice. It is on the high school level, but the same approach can work in elementary or middle school, higher education, or even in public library, business, or community situations.

High school biology teacher, Ms. Lowe, and library media specialist, Mr. Bennett, meet to discuss how they might collaborate to help students improve their information problem-solving skills while they study biology. They analyze the major units that Ms. Lowe plans to teach during the school year, and agree that there are three key units because they: 1. Result in some form or product of project. 2. Require lots of different types of resources, 3. Involve the whole class, and 4. Span more than just a week or two. In other words, these three units seem to be particularly "information-rich," and are perfect candidates for integrated biology Big6 instruction. These are the "big juicies":

- *The anatomy unit:* Taught early in the school year, takes three weeks, involves significant use of the Web, and results in individual PowerPoint supported oral presentations.
- *The circulatory system unit:* Taught in the second marking period, takes two weeks, involves a series of worksheets that combine to make a study guide, also requires students to identify structures and functions, and to analyze the effect of oxygenation on various other systems (e.g., nervous system, immune system, digestive system).
- *The digestive system unit:* Taught in the third marking period, results in group presentations on the digestive process in different animals, and usually involves extensive information seeking and searching.

What now? Do they select among these units or do they just integrate the Big6 with all three? Do they teach all the Big6 skills with each unit or focus on specific information skills?

These choices depend upon other factors including the time available for Big6 instruction and what else is going on during the school year. We do, however, recommend that while they review and reinforce the overall Big6 process with each unit, Ms. Lowe and Mr. Bennett should provide targeted Big6 skills instruction on one or two of the specific skills. For example:

- The anatomy unit relies on PowerPoint and the Web, so lessons can be taught on both. PowerPoint is a "Synthesis" tool, so that's a Big6 #5 lesson focusing on organizing and presenting principles using PowerPoint. Lessons on the Web might focus on identifying useful types of Web sites ("Information Seeking Strategies," Big6 #2), using keyword search terms ("Location and Access," Big6 #3), and recognizing and extracting relevant information ("Use of Information" Big6 #4).
- The circulatory system unit might be a good unit in which to focus on "Task Definition," Big6 #1, since each worksheet has a different focus. There's also a great deal of targeted analysis, so "Use of Information," Big6 #4, is again important.
- The digestive system unit is a group project and comes later in the school year. This would be a good opportunity to review the entire Big6 process while emphasizing defining tasks and dividing up the work (Big6 #1—"Task Definition") and how to put group presentations together so they make sense and flow easily (Big6 #5, "Synthesis"). "Evaluation" (Big6 #6) can also play a big role in group projects as students may be required to judge themselves and other group members or to assess the final products of other groups.

In actual school settings, selecting topics for integrated instruction and overall information skills planning depends upon the specific needs of the students as well as the setting and situation. The ultimate goal is to provide frequent opportunities for students to learn and practice information problem-solving.

Repetition is crucial. While these skills may seem to be simple or common sense at first, they are actually quite involved and can be difficult to master. This point cannot be overstressed—we learn through repetition. It's not enough to teach a skill or sub-skill once. Students' proficiency with specific skills as well as the overall process will improve over time—if they have regular opportunities to learn and to apply the information problem-solving process.

CONCLUSION

We live in a very complex and often overwhelming information world. As information, library, and education professionals, we have a responsibility to do our best to help people succeed. Our job is to meet people's information needs. The school librarians say it even more boldly and directly: "The mission of the school library media program is to ensure that students...are effective users of ideas and information" (ALA/AECT, 1998). This is an audacious and highly ambitious statement—and it's right on target.

Providing services, resources, and facilities is one way that libraries, schools, and other organizations seek to meet needs. The other way we do so is to teach and to provide opportunities to learn. If we truly believe that information and technology skills are essential for success, then we must make sure that students have frequent opportunities to learn and practice these skills. Systematic planning and delivery of integrated information skills instruction is essential if we are to make a difference.

It's not enough to work with students one-on-one or to offer an isolated lesson in note taking or Web search engines. People need lessons in the full range of skills, delivered in the context of the overall information process, including relevant technologies, and based in real, subject area assignments. Accomplishing comprehensive, integrated information literacy instruction requires library and information professionals in collaboration with others to make a concerted and systematic effort to plan and deliver programs in context.

REFERENCES

American Library Association and Association for Educational Communications and Technology. 1998. *Information power: Building partnerships for learning.* Chicago: American Library Association.

Association of College and Research Libraries. 2000. *Information literacy competency standards for higher education.* Chicago: American Library Association. Available: www.ala.org/acrl/ilcomstan.html

Eisenberg, M., and R. Berkowitz. 2006. "The Big6." Available: www.big6.com

Eisenberg, M., and M. Brown. 1992. "Current themes regarding library and information skills instruction: Research supporting and research lacking." *School Library Media Quarterly*, Vol. 20, no. 2: 103–109.

Eisenberg, M. B., C. A. Lowe, and K. L. Spitzer. 2004. *Information literacy: Essential skills for the information age.* Westport, CT: Libraries Unlimited.

Kuhlthau, C.C. 1993. *Seeking meaning: A process approach to library and information services.* Norwood, NJ: Ablex.

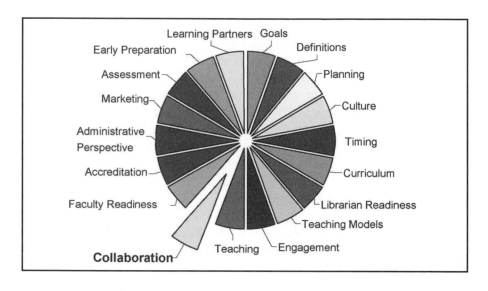

COLLABORATION

A Word from the Editors

*I*n any plan for an information literacy program, there is no room for going it
alone. Collaboration is a keystone for success—a vital element upon which much
else depends. Kendra Van Cleave, the Information/Education Co-Coordinator at the
J. Paul Leonard Library at San Francisco State University, has taken on this important subject to show us how to build a foundation for a successful program. In writing to the editors, Kendra has said that "collaborative partnerships are central to
embedding the vision of information literacy throughout higher education."
Throughout this article, Kendra urges us to "move beyond limited library-centered
efforts." Only in this way can we overcome the territorialism and the lack of broad
support which so often threatens successful information literacy programs. Kendra
gives us many ideas to encourage collaboration. As she has shared with the editors,
"Collaborative partnerships can include working with teaching faculty on designing
curricula, assignments, and assessment methods; integrating information literacy into
electronic course management systems, learning communities, and academic programs; and aligning with, and drawing on support from, campus services such as
writing, tutoring, and information technology." From Kendra's chapter, we see that
our opportunities for collaboration are many and diversified and we also see the
clear rewards for good collaboration. Kendra, whose research includes information
literacy instructional development, was previously the Subject Instruction Coordinator at the University of Southern California. Her M.L.I.S. is from Simmons College
where she also took an M.A. in History.

Chapter 11

Collaboration

by Kendra Van Cleave

S imply defined, collaboration is the act of working together—and yet it has the potential to become a much deeper and richer process. Dick Raspa and Dane Ward (2000: 5), in their aptly named book, *The Collaborative Imperative: Librarians and Faculty Working Together in the Information Universe*, differentiate collaboration from networking or coordination thusly: "... collaboration is a more pervasive, long-term relationship in which participants recognize common goals and objectives, share more tasks, and participate in extensive planning and implementation.... It is a more holistic experience in which we are committed to the enterprise, the relationship, and the process." According to this definition, collaboration contains the key to transformation, which in an information literacy context holds particularly true as collaborative partnerships are central to embedding the vision of information literacy throughout higher education.

WHY COLLABORATE?

Librarians have long been conscious that in order to achieve fully our educational mission, we must broaden our efforts to include campus partners outside of the library. The traditional understanding that information seekers (students) would come to the library for knowledge has been replaced by an urgent mission to bring knowledge to the information seekers. As early as 1974, Evan Farber wrote of the librarian/teaching faculty collaboration at Earlham College, arguing that, "...while the teaching faculty have the central responsibility in the educational enterprise, librarians can help them carry out that responsibility much more effectively and at the same time enhance it" (Farber, 1974:

157). Many early library educational efforts (including library orientations, tours, stand-alone credit courses, and drop-in workshops) were limited in terms of collaboration, relying solely upon librarians for implementation. Change began with the move to course-related and course-integrated instruction, which attempted to improve students' learning by delivering instruction at their point of need and recognized the need to link research skills instruction to the larger context of a course or program. Cooperation and coordination between librarians and teaching faculty became central to supporting what was then termed "library orientation" or "bibliographic instruction;" without the support of teaching faculty, librarians would have difficulty aligning their instruction with course content or assignments, and would not have access to students during class time. Recognizing these connections, Charles Middleton (1976: 40), a history professor at the University of Colorado, wrote, "Alone, faculty members impart knowledge, stimulate the students to want to know more, and provide them with a few of the tools necessary to assist them in the quest for knowledge. In isolation, librarians can teach library skills, but these skills serve no purpose unless they enable students to meet specific goals. It seems self-evident that cooperation strengthens both our endeavors."

The advent of the electronic era has created an ever-growing desire among users, who are no longer constrained by the physical walls of the library, to achieve self-sufficiency in research. At the same time, new pedagogical approaches—particularly constructivist learning theory, which focuses on student-constructed learning based on prior knowledge and authentic tasks, enhanced through social interaction (Cooperstein and Kocevar-Weidinger, 2004: 4)—have transformed the mission of library instruction into one that attempts to proactively develop students' information and research skills, a mission that is encapsulated in the term "information literacy." As librarians continue our efforts to find the most effective methods to facilitate students' information literacy, it has become increasingly apparent that we need to embed these concepts and skills more fully into academic curricula. Not only can integrated programs provide instruction at students' point of need, but they can and do facilitate greater meaning and deeper learning, as students use information literacy skills to solve authentic problems and to enhance their grasp of subject knowledge.

Truly integrated teaching of information literacy and disciplinary knowledge can only take place in a context of collaborative partnerships between librarians and faculty, academic programs, and campus support services. These connections hold the potential to move information literacy efforts beyond simple cooperation or coordination, making it possible for librarians and teaching faculty to blur the boundaries between the teaching and learning of content and process in a way that draws on the expertise of an entire institution. Shared responsibility allows information literacy to move from limited library-centered efforts into full scale campus programs, as librarians and teaching faculty partner to design, deliver, and assess teaching and learning, while administrators and campus services play important roles in supporting these efforts.

GAINING SUPPORT/OVERCOMING TERRITORIALISM

Despite changes in higher education, encouraging collaboration between campus constituencies is not always simple. Often, the biggest stumbling blocks are a lack of an institution-wide focus on information literacy, as well as territorialism over curriculum and classroom control. Although information literacy in its various forms has been one of the most prominent themes in librarianship over the last 20 years, efforts to bring this issue to the attention of teaching faculty, campus administrators, and staff have met with mixed success. The autonomous culture of academia can enable resistance to collaboration from individuals, departments, programs, and services. Scarce resources and a growing number of graduation requirements frequently create a sense of competition for students' classroom time. Teaching faculty, often best trained in and enthusiastic about disciplinary content, are increasingly pressured to incorporate cross-curricular skills and concepts into their courses, such as critical thinking, writing, information literacy, and diversity. Some instructors are loathe to share the role of the expert teacher and class leader, feel that they are already teaching research skills implicitly, assume that students can and should develop information literacy skills on their own (which was often the case in many instructors' own experience), or do not want to give up valuable class time for "extra" information. In addition, regardless of whether librarians hold faculty status at a particular institution, they are often viewed more as a support service for teaching and research than as active educators themselves. At the same time, many librarians want to guard their role as experts in teaching information literacy and designing related curricula.

For true collaboration to take place, territorialism and lack of support must be overcome, often one individual at a time. Unfortunately, there is no magic, one-size-fits-all solution, but there are multiple strategies that have been developed to minimize these issues and to promote a sense of shared responsibility and enthusiasm for information literacy. Cultural change in academic institutions does not happen quickly, and it can feel frustrating to be only one of many interest groups lobbying for campus attention. Patricia Iannuzzi suggests a number of excellent strategies that have proved successful at Florida International University. In particular, she argues that librarians can gain crucial support by changing the focus of their discussions away from how an information literacy agenda can succeed, to instead emphasizing how information literacy can aid other campus initiatives (Iannuzzi, 1998: 99). In other words, aligning information literacy with congruent objectives, such as writing across the curriculum, writing in the disciplines and/or critical thinking, can facilitate the success of all initiatives.

Significantly, Iannuzzi argues that it is precisely through partnerships and collaboration that a campus culture supportive of information literacy will be created.

Many examples exist that illustrate strategies to minimize campus territorialism. Librarians at the University of Lethbridge in Canada, created positive change using strategies that included broadening their awareness of institutional culture and developments in education, fostering their sense of expertise by forming a clear understanding of the educational role of the library, creating peer relationships with teaching faculty, tying information literacy to growing campus concerns about writing and other fundamental skills, and developing personal relationships and a shared vision with teaching faculty (Chiste et al., 2000). Often, some kind of incentive is needed to break through the autonomy of academic life. The California State University system sponsors grants aimed at encouraging the incorporation of information literacy into courses and programs; the 2006 call for proposals requests that grant applications focus on assessment of information literacy as well as development of first-year experience and general education information literacy programs (Reichard, personal communication, April 7, 2006). Similarly, at the University of Cincinnati, teaching faculty members who attended workshops on information literacy were allowed to compete for a grant to create a subject-specific online module for teaching information literacy (Perez, 2005).

Change will not happen overnight. However, by beginning to cooperate and collaborate with willing individuals, and developing our own expertise as instructors, librarians can begin to build a foundation for successful initiatives and programs. As we continue to win converts among teaching faculty, administrators, and campus staff, opportunities for collaborative projects will emerge, programs will grow more comprehensive, and institutional mandates can become possible. Each small step on these paths is, and should be celebrated as, a victory.

OPPORTUNITIES FOR COLLABORATION

Collaborating with Teaching Faculty

A growing number of librarians and other educators argue that students are most successful at learning and retaining information literacy concepts and skills when they are incorporated into students' subject-based curriculum, rather than taught separately. Such integrated programs present an effective model for teaching information literacy, as they facilitate an approach that links the process of exploring, searching, evaluating, and synthesizing information to the learning and production of subject-based knowledge. Ann Grafstein (2002: 200) warns, "The risk [of separating information literacy from disciplinary content] is that of isolating entirely information-seeking skills from knowledge, thereby losing sight of information-seeking skills as a tool whose ultimate goal is the synthesis of information into knowledge." Librarians have long known that students are best able to learn and retain information literacy concepts and skills when they are taught at point of need; integrated subject-based information literacy programs take this idea one important step forward by creating an organic connection between process and content.

Teaching faculty are not only the primary deliverers of instruction, but are also usually in control of decisions about curricula. Because of this central role in shaping and delivering course content and academic programs, they have been and will continue to be among the most essential and effective partners in collaborative information literacy efforts. The "Information Literacy Competency Standards for Higher Education" specifically address this issue of shared responsibility, arguing that librarians, faculty, and administrators all play a role in the teaching and learning of information literacy (Association of College and Research Libraries, 2000). Librarians have reached out to teaching faculty members, and teaching faculty have approached the library, all in an effort to improve students' research skills. The next step is to begin to more fully embed information literacy into students' learning experience via collaborative teaching, curriculum and assignment design, and assessment.

How can librarians gain the attention of busy teaching faculty members, caught in an environment of ever increasing demands on class time? In most instances, librarian-faculty collaborations have been built on personal relationships formed through repeated contact via social and professional interactions (bottom up), rather than administrative mandates (top down). The subject liaison role can create a natural locus for conversations around information literacy, as librarians work with faculty in library instruction sessions, provide one-on-one reference assistance, and discuss collection development processes and needs. Esther Grassian and Joan Kaplowitz (2005: 86) offer a number of excellent strategies to encourage support for information literacy among teaching faculty; in particular, they argue, ". . . we need to remind faculty of the differences between novice and expert researchers and the value of ILI (Information Literacy Instruction) in helping students become more expert researchers. We also need to work toward supporting faculty in integrating IL (Information Literacy) into their own course curricula, rather than teaching all the basics ourselves."

Conversations about students' information literacy skills can prompt collaborative efforts. Many teaching faculty members are concerned about information literacy issues, although they may not use the same terminology that librarians do. At the Institute for Information Literacy's 2004 Immersion program, the professed advice heard again and again from both attendees and instructors was: "Just ask them, 'Are you happy with your students' research skills?' The rest will follow." Plagiarism is an issue of widespread concern across academia, and discussions about solutions can be an excellent way to capture teaching faculty's interest and lead to conversations about information literacy. Collaborative projects often flow naturally from courses and programs that focus on issues and skills related to information literacy, such as those focused on research methods, those with a heavy research or information component, or those that examine issues or ethics related to information and technology.

Many librarians concentrate on developing relationships with key faculty members (for example, department chairs, or those who are in charge of under-graduate and/or graduate programs), and with new faculty members (who may be more amenable to collaboration and/or enthusiastic about information liter-acy issues). Kara Giles (2004) reports that she connected with a teaching faculty member at a dinner for new faculty, resulting in a request to guest lecture for a course and eventually the opportunity to provide research assistance via an online course management system. Librarians who are active in college or uni-versity governance and service, or who participate in campus social activities, obtain many excellent opportunities to meet faculty and administrators and to discuss students' needs. At San Francisco State University, connections made with the associate dean for undergraduate studies via the academic senate led to efforts to embed information literacy tutorials into the online course manage-ment system for first-year experience courses.

The impetus to share responsibility for leading the educational process has supported efforts by teaching faculty and librarians to co-teach courses and ses-sions. Because of frustrations with the limitations of the standard library in-struction session, librarian Linda Stein collaborated with teaching faculty member Jane Lamb (1998) to create a developmental program that included fo-cusing on research skills and topic selection in class lectures, library instruction sessions, assignments, and individual consultations. A number of the teaching methods and objectives that are growing in popularity in academia lend them-selves well to, or even require, collaboration around information literacy. Prob-lem-based learning, whereby learning is centered on solving authentic problems, requires that students be able to search, evaluate, think critically, and solve prob-lems—all skills that are founded on information literacy (Spence, 2004: 491). By designing assignments and leading classes together, teaching faculty member Larry Spence and librarian Debora Cheney were able to move beyond the tradi-tional separation of information literacy instruction from course content, over-come students' resistance to library instruction, and facilitate students' learning of the essential principles related to information searching and evaluation (Cheney, 2004: 501).

In addition to work in the classroom, librarians are collaborating with teach-ing faculty in curriculum and assignment design. At Florida International Uni-versity, librarians worked with their institution's teaching development center to create a series of workshops that covered topics such as "Motivating Students: Using Information Technology and Critical Thinking Strategies to Engage Stu-dents in Course Content," and "Information Literacy and Intellectual Develop-ment" (Iannuzzi, 1998: 102). Librarians at Emporia State University took advantage of their university's professional development program to offer teaching faculty subject-specific workshops in the use of library resources (Akers et al., 2000). The University of California, Berkeley, received a grant to create the Mellon Faculty Institute for Undergraduate Research (2006), an intensive training institute for teaching faculty that focuses on creating effective undergraduate research-based assignments. A master's of library science student, working on a practicum at Los Positas College, created a pilot project to work with teaching faculty on creating assignments that incorporate information literacy concepts; many of these faculty were eager to work with the library because of their own lack of training in instructional design (Inzerilla and Warren, 2006). In addition, colleges and universities are increasingly focused on assessment of student learning, efforts which can present opportunities for collaborative partnerships around information literacy. Librarian participation in designing and implementing assessment measures, at both the class and program level, can provide an opportunity to discuss the inclusion of research skills in assignments, courses, and programs.

More and more instructors are taking advantage of technology to support learning. Electronic learning management systems (also called courseware), such as Blackboard and WebCT, allow teaching and learning to extend beyond the classroom via a collaborative online environment and provide a new venue for information literacy instruction. Library resources and online tutorials can be made available to students in the same way as other course resources. In addition, librarians can work as both instructional designers and teachers, creating assignments that involve information literacy concepts and skills, leading or monitoring class discussion, and providing one-on-one reference assistance to enrolled students. When Dominican University librarian Kara Giles (2004) became attached to a senior-level history course via its Blackboard system, she was able to create relationships with students that allowed her to help them on an individual basis, as well as to be responsive to class learning needs. As distance education grows in popularity at colleges and universities throughout the country, so too does the necessity to support the information literacy requirements of completely online courses. At Austin Peay State University, two librarians collaborated with a teaching faculty member to design and teach a graduate communications course focused on multimedia literacy. Utilizing the online environment to their best advantage, the course included information literacy units that focused on the ethics and effective use of information (Buchanan et al., 2002).

Learning Communities

Learning communities present an exciting opportunity to unite around a truly integrated approach to teaching and student learning. Through such options as linked courses, learning clusters, first-year interest groups, and coordinated studies, learning communities encourage deeper understanding and interdisciplinary learning by connecting previously disparate courses and instructors (Frank et al., 2001: 6–7). Often, learning communities utilize collaborative and cooperative teaching and learning techniques, and combine disciplinary knowledge with an explicit focus on technology-based teaching and learning as well as an emphasis on critical thinking—all of which lead naturally to the inclusion of information literacy. By bringing students together in smaller, more intellectually stimulating communities, and by encouraging team teaching among instructors with diverse expertise, learning communities have the potential to offer students more intense, connected, and nuanced learning.

Librarians often have the opportunity to be involved in learning communities as instructors, and this active educational role holds the potential to transform the teaching and learning of information literacy, disciplinary content, and other concepts and skills. Joan Lippincott (2002) argues that library instruction is highly structured, of limited duration, and focused on the library with a librarian as guest lecturer and expert; in learning communities, information literacy teaching and learning becomes opportunistic, is embedded throughout the course, and focuses on the information environment, while the librarian becomes a faculty partner.

Those institutions that have incorporated information literacy into learning communities have experienced quite encouraging results. An English professor and a librarian at the University of Montevallo were able to integrate information literacy and writing skills throughout a first-year English composition course, using assignments that drew on both writing and research skills (Barone and Weathers, 2004). At the University of California, Los Angeles, liaison activities with general education clusters were meeting with little success at promoting information literacy, so the library instruction coordinator began attending all large lectures in the program. As she began to be called upon as a resource for these courses, the coordinator became positioned to lobby successfully for the addition of a one-unit linked course focused on information literacy (Pedersen, 2003). A similar program exists at California State University, East Bay (formerly Hayward), where a required one-credit library course, taught by a librarian, is linked to theme-based first-year clusters (Pedersen, 2003). At Portland State University, librarians are even more fully embedded into the teaching of course content. The freshman inquiry program consists of theme-based courses taught by faculty from different disciplines and a librarian; librarians teach sessions and create Web resources in support of the course (Pedersen, 2003). A similar program at Indiana University–Purdue University involves librarians who participate in curricular and syllabi planning for freshman seminar learning communities, as well as information literacy instruction in more advanced courses that are linked back to the freshman seminars (Pedersen, 2003). The entire curriculum of Evergreen State College is designed around learning communities; teaching faculty serve as reference librarians (and are involved in information literacy instruction) for one-year stints, while librarians join the pool of instructors who deliver the curriculum (Pedersen, 2003).

Collaborating with Academic Programs

A growing number of librarians and other educators are recognizing the need to establish information literacy in subject-based learning on a programmatic level. A recent open letter from the Association of American Colleges and Universities board of directors (2006) to the chair of the U.S. Secretary of Education's Commission on the Future of Higher Education argued that information literacy was among those key educational aims and outcomes that, "...should be addressed across the curriculum, from the first year experience through the final year of college (and beyond)" (paragraph 21). Meanwhile, Betsy Barefoot (2006) maintains in the *Chronicle of Higher Education*, "The most effective way to ensure that first-year students become information literate is making library instruction an integral part of courses across the curriculum" (paragraph 9). Some institutions are mandating information literacy instruction and encouraging librarians and teaching faculty to collaborate on integrating curricula (see, for example, the California State University system-wide information competence mandate). Not only do subject-based information literacy programs improve students' learning (the most important goal), but they also ensure that instruction is comprehensive and reduce redundancy (for example, by targeting required introductory, methods, and capstone courses).

Collaborating with academic programs can take the form of working with individual faculty; it can also include working with committees, department chairs, deans, and other administrators. While institution-wide requirements are sometimes the goal, individual programs and colleges can prove amenable to creating integrated, articulated information literacy programs on a formal or informal basis. Often, librarians will begin by working to create a program with a department that has a strong history of support for library instruction. Institutional mandates can be necessary for some programs or teaching faculty to be amenable to collaboration, although such directives can be difficult to obtain without the support of key teaching faculty and administrators.

A number of models for discipline integrated information literacy programs exist. At California State University, San Marcos, the College of Business Administration formally incorporated information literacy into their curriculum by identifying key courses for emphasis, as well as by creating an assessment-planning matrix that enables teaching faculty to align their course objectives and methods with information literacy (Fiegen et al., 2002). The California State University system has a history of support for such integrated programs. In 2003, the CSU system offered grants that required that, "...instructional departments integrate information competence into their student learning outcomes, and that this information be visible on their course syllabi. In addition, the grant stipulated that faculty create assignments that would promote the development of student information competence skills and abilities" (Rockman, 2003: 613).

Many campuses are working to embed information literacy in writing programs. Research skills instruction has often been tied to writing, given the concentration on research for writing in course content and the opportunity to reach students via a targeted, developmental program. While stand-alone composition courses have traditionally been a focus for information literacy instruction, the growing emphasis on writing across the curriculum/writing in the discipline (WAC/WID) provides an exciting opportunity. The philosophies of WAC/WID align neatly with information literacy, as both are part of a larger, connected, recursive process, and both focus on critical thinking and process rather than content (Sheridan, 1995; Elmborg, 2003). WAC/WID is differentiated from traditional composition instruction in that it represents an attempt to increase the meaningfulness of writing instruction by embedding it into disciplinary instruction in exactly the same way that information literacy differs from bibliographic instruction. Significantly, WAC/WID is increasingly seen as an imperative at many academic institutions; efforts to pair information literacy with WAC/WID programs can both encourage the learning of subject-based writing concepts and skills and provide the broad-based support necessary to achieving campus-wide buy-in. One example of such a collaborative project is described by librarian Deborah Huerta and teaching faculty member Victoria McMillan (2000), who created a two-course sequence that emphasizes health and natural sciences-specific information literacy and writing.

First-year experience courses are another key academic program that provides a logical focus for librarian-faculty collaboration, given their emphasis on orienting students to higher education, small class size, and interdisciplinary subject content. Librarians at Wayne State University had been involved in teaching information literacy instruction to their campus's freshman seminar program since its inception. To improve the program, librarians and program staff devised a system by which student peer facilitators enrolled in a one-credit information literacy course that prepared them to be more effective mentors (Johnson et al., 2003). In addition, a framework was devised for instructional collaboration between instructors and librarians, which allowed for change in both instructional content and method.

Collaborating with Campus Services

A number of services offered on college and university campuses directly support teaching and learning, and can thus serve as effective partners for collaboration around information literacy. Writing and tutoring centers provide instruction that often touches more or less directly on skills and concepts related to information literacy, and in addition are often organizationally linked to the library, or housed in the library building. Additionally, writing/tutoring center instruction is customized and delivered at the point of need in a one-on-one interaction; as such, the continuum between writing/tutoring center instruction and formal courses is analogous to that between academic library reference and instructional services. Significantly, much of writing/tutoring instruction is performed by student peer tutors. Casey Reid (2005) suggests that libraries should consider training writing center tutors in information literacy, in effect a "teach the teachers" model.

Technology and teaching professionals hold an increasingly important role in most institutions of higher education. Many campuses offer a resource similar to San Francisco State University's Center for Teaching and Faculty Development, which provides (among other offerings) training and support on topics such as electronic learning management systems, assessment, and instructional Web sites, as well as online tutorials on topics like plagiarism. Because of their focus on using technology to support teaching and learning, such teaching centers can serve as an excellent support for information literacy efforts. Joni Warner and Nancy Seamans (2005) describe just some of the potential collaborations between libraries and teaching centers, including training librarians in effective teaching techniques and incorporating information literacy concepts and skills into teaching methods workshops aimed at teaching faculty. Information Technology (IT) professionals can provide crucial support for online teaching. When San Francisco State University implemented an online information literacy tutorial, the courseware selected to support the delivery of quizzes quickly failed; instead, librarians drew upon the campus information technology department to create a customized, in-house system that could support the tutorial (Castro, 2002). In addition, many IT professionals can and do offer technology-specific training that can be drawn upon for information literacy instruction and learning communities. At Northwestern University, librarians partnered with teaching faculty and information technology professionals to create and teach an introduction to electronic resources for incoming graduate students (Lightman and Reingold, 2005).

CONCLUSION

Collaboration is the key to creating truly effective information literacy programs. The opportunities are vast: teaching faculty can serve as partners in designing, delivering, and assessing teaching and learning; administrators can provide the structure to create comprehensive programs; and campus support professionals can extend teaching and learning beyond the classroom. But the opportunities do not stop there: students can assist libraries in designing instructional spaces; advising professionals can join in promoting library resources, instructional offerings, and information literacy requirements; and area high schools and community colleges can join with college and university libraries to create developmental information literacy programs. Whichever directions, strategies, and models are chosen, what is most essential is that librarians continue their efforts to embed information literacy into the vision of higher education through strategic, collaborative partnerships.

REFERENCES

Akers, C., N. Martin, and T. Summey. 2000. "Teaching the teachers: Library instruction through professional development courses." *Research Strategies*, Vol. 17, no. 2–3: 215–221.

Association of American Colleges and Universitities. 2006. "Letter to members of the commission on the future of higher education." Available: www.aacu.org/About/Commission.cfm

Association of College and Research Libraries. 2000. "Information literacy competency standards for higher education." Chicago: American Library Association. Available: www.ala.org/ala/acrl/acrlstandards/informationliteracycompetency.cfm

Barefoot, B. 2006. "Bridging the chasm: First-year students and the library." *The Chronicle of Higher Education*, Vol. 52.

Barone, K., and G. Weathers. 2004. "Launching a learning community in a small liberal arts university." *College and Undergraduate Libraries*, Vol. 11, no. 1: 1–9.

Buchanan, L., D. Luck, and C. Jones. 2002. "Integrating information literacy into the virtual university: A course model." *Library Trends*, Vol. 51, no. 2: 144–166.

Castro, G. M. 2002. "From workbook to Web: Building an information literacy oasis." *Computers in Libraries*, Vol. 22, no. 1: 30–35.

"Center for Teaching and Faculty Development." Center for Teaching and Faculty Development (last updated November 9, 2005). Available: www.cet.sfsu.edu (accessed April 1, 2006).

Cheney, D. 2004. "Problem-based learning: Librarians as collaborators and consultants." *Portal: Libraries and the Academy*, Vol. 4, no. 4: 495–508.

Chiste, K. B., A. Glover, and G. Westwood. 2000. "Perspectives on . . . infiltration and entrenchment: Capturing and securing information literacy territory in academe." *Journal of Academic Librarianship*, Vol. 26, no. 3: 202–208.

Cooperstein, S. E., and E. Kocevar-Weidinger. 2004. "Beyond active learning: A constructivist approach to learning." *Reference Services Review*, Vol. 32, no. 2: 141–148.

Elmborg, James K. 2003. "Information literacy and writing across the curriculum: Sharing the vision." *Reference Services Review*, Vol. 31, no. 1: 68–80.

Farber, E. I. 1974. "Library instruction throughout the curriculum: Earlham College perspective." In J. Lubans, Jr., ed., *Educating the Library User*. New York: R. R. Bowker Co.

Fiegen, A., B. Cherry, and K. Watson. 2002. "Reflections on collaboration: Learning outcomes and information literacy assessment in the business curriculum." *Reference Services Review*, Vol. 30, no. 4: 307–318.

Frank, D. G., S. Beasley, and S. M. Kroll. 2001. "Opportunities for collaborative excellence: What learning communities offer [Electronic version]." *College and Research Libraries News*, Vol. 62, no. 10: 1008–1011.

Giles, K. L. 2004. "Reflections on a privilege: Becoming part of the course through a collaboration on blackboard." *College and Research Libraries News*, Vol. 65, no. 5: 261–263, 268.

Grafstein, A. 2002. "A discipline-based approach to information literacy." *Journal of Academic Librarianship*, Vol. 28, no. 4: 197–204.

Grassian, E., and J. Kaplowitz. 2005. *Learning to lead and manage information literacy instruction*. New York: Neal-Schuman Publishers.

Huerta, D., and V. McMillan. 2000. "Collaborative instruction by writing and library faculty: A two-tiered approach to the teaching of scientific writing." *Issues in Science and Technology Librarianship*, Vol. 28. Available: www.istl.org/00-fall/article1.html (accessed April 15, 2006).

Iannuzzi, P. 1998. "Faculty development and information literacy: Establishing campus partnerships." *Reference Services Review*, Vol. 26, no. 3–4: 97–102, 116.

"Information Competence: A University-Wide Responsibility." (Last updated 1998). Available: www.calstate.edu/AcadSen/Records/Resolutions/1997-1998/2409.shtml (accessed April 25, 2006).

"Information Literacy Competency Standards for Higher Education." (Last updated 2000). Available: www.ala.org/ala/acrl/acrlstandards/informationliteracycompetency.htm (accessed April 15, 2006).

Inzerilla, T., and C. Warren. 2006. "Instructional design: Where does the librarian fit in?" Presentation at the California Academic & Research Libraries Conference.

Johnson, C., S. McCord, and S. Walter. 2003. "Instructional outreach across the curriculum: Enhancing the liaison role at a research university." *The Reference Librarian*, Vol. 82: 19–37.

Lightman, H., and R. Reingold. 2005. "A collaborative model for teaching e-resources: Northwestern University's graduate training day." *Portal: Libraries and the Academy*, Vol. 5, no. 1: 23–32.

Lippincott, J. 2002. "Developing collaborative relationships: Librarians, students and faculty creating learning communities." *College and Research Libraries News*, Vol. 63, no. 3: 190–192.

"Mellon faculty institute for undergraduate research." Mellon Faculty Institute for Undergraduate Research (last updated April 24, 2006). Available: www.lib.berkeley.edu/MellonInstitute (accessed April 25, 2006).

Middleton, C. R. 1976. "Academic libraries and the educational process. In H. B. Rader, ed., *Faculty Involvement in Library Instruction: Their Views on Participation in and Support of Academic Library Use Instruction: Papers and Summaries from the Fifth Annual Conference on Library Orientation for Academic Libraries, Held at Eastern Michigan University, May 15–17, 1975*. Ann Arbor, MI: Pierian Press.

"On Quality and Accountability." (Last updated March 14, 2006). Available: www.aacu.org/About/Commission.cfm (accessed April 25, 2006).

Pedersen, S. 2003. *Learning communities and the academic library*. Olympia, WA: Washington Center for Improving the Quality of Undergraduate Education, National

Learning Communities Project, Evergreen State College; Chicago: Association of College & Research Libraries; Washington, DC: American Association for Higher Education.

Pelikan, M. 2004. "Problem-based learning in the library: Evolving a realistic approach." *Portal: Libraries and the Academy*, Vol. 4, no. 4: 509–520.

Perez, C. C. "Summary: Info. lit. workshop for faculty." Message posted to ili-l@ala.org listserv (April 12, 2005).

Raspa, D., and D. Ward. 2000. "Listening for collaboration: Faculty and librarians working together." In D. Raspa and D. Ward, eds., *The Collaborative Imperative: Librarians and Faculty Working Together in the Information Universe*. Chicago: American Library Association.

Reid, C. 2005. "From cross-referencing to co-construction: Contemplating collaborative potentials for reference and the writing center at Southwest Missouri State University." In J. K. Elmborg and S. Hook, eds., *Centers for Learning: Writing Centers and Libraries in Collaboration*. Chicago: Association of College & Research Libraries.

Rockman, I. F. 2003. "Integrating information literacy into the learning outcomes of academic disciplines: A critical 21st-century issue." *College and Research Libraries News*, Vol. 64, no. 9: 613.

Sheridan, J., ed. 1995. *Writing-across-the-curriculum and the academic library: A guide for librarians, instructors, and writing program directors*. Westport, CT: Greenwood Press.

Spence, L. 2004. "The usual doesn't work: Why we need problem-based learning." *Portal: Libraries and the Academy*, Vol. 4, no. 4: 485–493.

Stein, L., and J. Lamb. 1998. "Not just another BI: Faculty-librarian collaboration to guide students through the research process." *Research Strategies*, Vol. 16, no. 1: 29–39.

Warner, J. E., and N. H. Seamans. 2005. "Teaching centers, libraries, and benefits to both." In W. Miller and R. M. Pellen, eds., *Libraries within their institutions: Creative collaborations*. New York: Haworth Information Press.

KEEP IN MIND

"Collaboration is the key to creating truly effective information literacy programs."

— Kendra Van Cleave

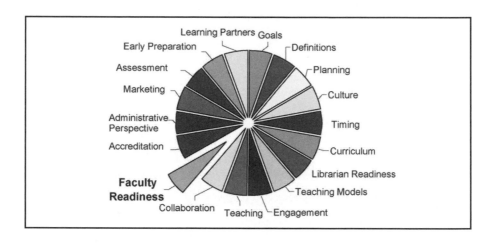

FACULTY READINESS

A Word from the Editors

*T*hree professors have come together to provide us with the story of how one academic department collaborated to integrate information literacy throughout the graduate curriculum, and to incorporate these skills into its learning outcomes. As colleagues in the Department of Educational Psychology and Counseling at California State University, Northridge College of Education, Dr. Rie Rogers Mitchell, Department Chair and Professor, Dr. Merril A. Simon, Associate Professor, and Dr. Gregory C. Jackson, Associate Professor, created a close collaboration to increase student information literacy skills for the nearly 400 students enrolled annually in this graduate program. In writing to the editors, Rie, Merril, and Greg said that "this chapter describes the introductory process with our faculty and students, our work in integrating information literacy skills, and our future plans for further institutionalization into the seven graduate programs in our department." Rie, Merril, and Greg also illustrate how they measured information literacy competencies at the basic, research, and professional levels. The authors go on to say that they have described "the critical contributions of our university librarians" throughout this process. This chapter is particularly important as it gives librarians insight into the perspective of faculty on information literacy and into the inner workings of a department. It also gives us a model if we want to encourage a similar approach throughout other academic departments. Rie is the recipient of The Distinguished Teaching Award from California State University, Northridge, and the Professional Leadership Award from the Association for Counselor Education and Supervision. Rie is widely published internationally in sandplay therapy and related topics. Rie's Ph.D. is from the University of California, Los Angeles, in the field of counselor education. Merril was awarded the California State University, Northridge's Don Dorsey Mentoring Award; her Ph.D. is from the University of Southern California in the field of counseling psychology, specializing in college student personnel services and career development. Merril's academic background includes Master's degrees from California State University, Dominguez Hills, in education with an emphasis on adult education, and in counseling from the University of Southern California. Her research focuses on better understanding psychosocial and career development factors that support success in college, particularly within the first year and with first-generation students. Greg is the former president of the California Career Development Association and received the Judith Grutter Career Development Practitioner of the Year Award. He also received a Certificate of Merit from the National Career Development Association (NCDA). He served a six-year term on the editorial board of Career Development Quarterly, an NCDA's peer-reviewed journal. Greg's Ed.D. is from the University of California, Los Angeles, in the field of higher education, adult development, and work.

Chapter 12

Collaboration to Ensure Mastery of Information Competence Skills

by Rie Rogers Mitchell, Merril A. Simon, and Gregory C. Jackson

To introduce our involvement with information competence, we begin with a vignette that represents the value our graduates now place on becoming an information competent professional.

> Molly checked her departmental brochure against the sign announcing the department's orientation, and walked towards the beckoning door. Just inside she gathered the sheaf of informational papers, moved towards the middle of the room, and took a seat.
>
> Glancing at the papers, she noticed one entitled, "Information Competencies Necessary for Degree Candidates" and another "Information Competency Assessment." Molly thought to herself, "Got that done. I know the Internet and I've got my word processing skills down pat." She then placed her papers aside in order to concentrate on the program information that was being presented.
>
> Later, when potential students were given the opportunity to talk in small groups with current students and graduates of the counseling program, Molly spoke up and shared, "I'm very comfortable with the Internet and word processing, so can I 'test out' of the information competency requirement?"
>
> A current student in the group, Crystal, responded, "I said the same thing when I entered the program. I felt I knew both the Internet and what I thought was necessary about word processing. But in my first class, I found that I had no clear understanding of how to use the Internet to find quality material. Honestly, I didn't know what my instructor was even

talking about when he said he wanted refereed sources, and I certainly didn't know how to find them. I knew nothing about the critical issues involved in identifying and obtaining true professional materials."

Juan, a recent graduate of the program, added, "Second to learning counseling skills, learning information competency skills in the program truly helped me in both my fieldwork and research classes, and certainly in writing my thesis. In fact, I highlighted the certificate I earned in information competence on my résumé. I was often asked about that by prospective employers."

"Oh, really?" queried Molly, with some interest.

"Yes," Juan continued, "during interviews I was asked if I could possibly train and update some of their employees. I felt confident enough to say, 'yes.'"

Molly seemed deep in thought when Juan added, "In my current job, I have to give presentations to groups of administrators, parents, and students. I've found that the quality of information makes a big difference in whether or not the audience takes my opinions, observations, and suggestions more seriously. It's not just having information, and it's not just the breadth and depth of the information that's important; it's also the accuracy and currency of the information that is important!"

Juan saw Molly's reflective look and said finally, "Trust me, it's worth the effort."

In 1995, the California State University system made an explicit commitment to develop a program of information competence (www.calstate.edu/ls/Aboutinfocomp.shtml) to ensure that all students (of the 405,000 in 23 universities) graduate with a mastery of this vital skill. In January 2001, CSU offered grants to departments committed to include information competence in their educational outcomes.

Of those grants awarded, the Department of Educational Psychology and Counseling (EPC) at CSU, Northridge, was the only graduate department to receive this grant. In 2004, our department was awarded a second IC grant to develop instruments to assess IC at various stages. Taken together, these grants provided the opportunity to work with campus and CSU librarians to provide graduate students with skills in information competence within the existing curriculum, as well as develop criteria and assess student learning of IC skills as a prerequisite to receiving a master's degree. This chapter will describe our experience with information literacy at the department level, as well as our collaboration with the university and CSU librarians.

DESCRIPTION OF MILIEU

California State University, Northridge, a learning-centered university and one of the largest of the 23 campuses in the California State University system, is located approximately 25 miles northwest of central Los Angeles in the northern San Fernando Valley, a suburb with a multiethnic population of over 1.8 million people. In fall 2004, the university enrolled over 31,000 students (23,200 FTEs), of which approximately two-thirds are ethnic minorities, immigrants, and/or international students. Over 1,800 faculty members serve in nine colleges that offer baccalaureate degrees in 59 disciplines and master's degrees in 41 fields.

The Department of Educational Psychology and Counseling (EPC), one of six departments in the Michael D. Eisner College of Education, has one of the largest graduate enrollments and is one of the largest academic departments on campus. The nearly 400 graduate students in the department's degree programs (Master of Science in Counseling and Master of Arts in Education) comprise about 9 percent of the total graduate population at CSUN. Within the two master's degrees are seven options: career counseling, college counseling and student services, early childhood education, educational psychology (development, learning, and instruction), marriage and family therapy, school counseling, and school psychology. The department also offers courses towards five post-master's certificates (one of these is online), two state credentials, and two state licenses.

The department is student-centered, and faculty is highly engaged in the development of students as professionals and leaders in the field. Programs and coursework reflect both a developmental life-span approach and an ecological perspective to theory, research, and practice. Our department programs and faculty of 22 full-time and 50 part-time members have achieved national recognition for program design, scholarship, professional leadership, and teaching excellence.

Our graduate programs strive to prepare students for highly effective, ethical, and satisfying professional careers as educators, counselors, psychotherapists, and psychologists, while instilling in our graduates a sense of civic engagement—a commitment to serve all people regardless of economic status or ethnicity and to influence the way in which these services are delivered to ensure access and equity. Therefore, we seek to provide students with a wide range of service-learning opportunities, so they learn to work effectively with diverse individuals, groups, and/or families with a range of issues at varying locations. Our overarching goal is to produce graduates who think critically and engage in reflective, ethical, and legal practice throughout their educational and professional lives.

CSUN's Oviatt Library is a teaching library whose mission includes partnering with faculty in the education of students and in developing the information competence skills of students. To this end, the librarians sustain and develop a very active instructional program to teach students how to use and locate the best resources in their field of study and also to increase their information research skills. Nearly 22,000 students each year go through a library instruction session. The faculty librarians of the library are very student-centered and are very focused on sustaining a positive library experience for students. The librarians maintain close ties with the faculty in the academic departments as well as participating in university-wide academic initiatives. There are 22 full-time and seven part-time faculty in the library.

NEED FOR INFORMATION AND TECHNOLOGY SKILLS

Because of the wide range of students' information and technology skills due to generational and experiential differences, it was seen as necessary and valuable to design an information competence program that could respond to both remediation and professional skill development, while offering an organized, hierarchical program infused throughout the curriculum, supported by collaborative alliances of both discipline and library faculty.

The need to possess IC skills has been recommended by our national accrediting bodies, the Council for the Accreditation of Counseling and Related Education Programs (CACREP), National Council for Accreditation of Teacher Education (NCATE), and National Association of School Psychology (NASP), and professional associations, including the Association for Counselor Educators and Supervisors (ACES) and the National Career Development Association (NCDA). In 1999, ACES developed and endorsed technology competencies (CACREP, 2001) and the NCDA has subsequently developed and adopted the use of career counseling using electronic means of communication.

Accreditation requirements and initiatives by professional groups provided one of the motivators for our department to move toward providing concerted training and education in this area. Also, we believe that, whether students continue their education into doctoral programs or careers in public or private service as educators, counselors, marriage and family therapists, school counselor or school psychologists, information literacy skills are critical in this technological age. On a practical level, we knew that possession of information competency skills would also enable our students to conduct the type of research necessary for the required culminating activity (i.e., thesis, project, or comprehensive exam) for it to be of master's degree quality and be able to use these skills in their future careers, while fostering the lifelong professional skills of reasoning and critical thinking.

DEFINITION OF INFORMATION COMPETENCE

Near the beginning of our journey to infuse information competence throughout our curriculum, the faculty agreed to the following working definition of information competence. An information-competent individual has the ability to locate, evaluate, and use information effectively for a range of purposes (see Figure 12-1). Information competence (or information literacy) is a gestalt, in which becoming competent in the use of each of its parts—tools (e.g., computers), resources, social-structure (e.g., knowledge in differences between refereed journals and Internet information), research, publishing, and professional competencies—results in a whole larger than the sum of its parts. The "whole" in this case represents professional and lifelong learning skills (see Figure 12-2).

IDENTIFYING IC NEEDS OF EPC STUDENTS

In order to prepare EPC students as information competent professionals, it was first necessary to identify the specific needs of this population. Some of the key areas include the need for current and accurate information, ability to use ever-developing technology to access information, skills to conduct research and differentiate between types of information, and the capability to conceptualize and identify important connections among collected information.

Current and Accurate Information

Educational psychology and counseling students have unique needs related to the changing nature of their profession. At one time, the primary focus of counseling

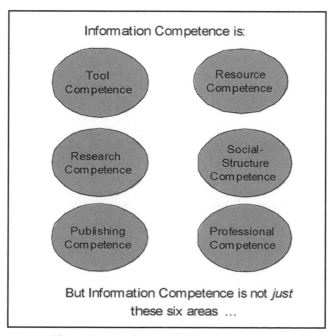

Figure 12-1: Information Competence Is ...

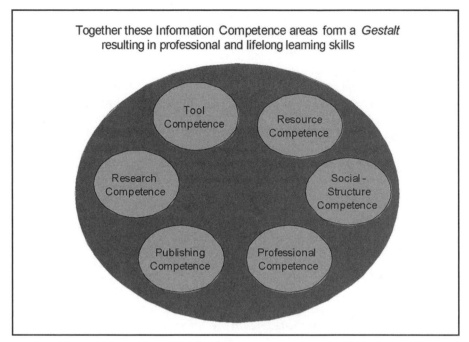

Together these Information Competence areas form a *Gestalt* resulting in professional and lifelong learning skills

Tool Competence

Resource Competence

Research Competence

Social - Structure Competence

Publishing Competence

Professional Competence

Figure 12-2: Information Competence Gestalt

professionals centered on developing listening and facilitation skills, and peripherally, on research and informational literacy. Until the past decade, other professionals' perspectives, commentaries, experiments, and studies were obtained from library books and journal stacks, and most counselors only needed to be consumers of research. Now there is a greater need for assessment and research skills to provide support for the value of counselors and psychologists, particularly in the schools, and to help teachers and clients find resources that are meaningful and accurate.

With the establishment and availability of the Internet and other electronic communication, a new dynamic has appeared. Now, the turn-around time for publication on the Web can be as short as the time it takes for a Web page author to post a page to his or her Web site. The lengthy editorial and peer review is severely shortened, if it occurs at all.

Unfortunately, students are not necessarily careful consumers of information. They have not learned to be discerning between the value of the results of a *Google* search and a peer-reviewed "A-level" journal in the field. To many students, "in print" or "online" means it is acceptable whether or not the source is relevant, appropriate, or accurate.

Knowledge of Technology

In the late 1990s, students in our programs seemed to fall into a bimodal distribution. The younger students were generally proficient in using basic technology, and were unafraid and even welcoming of new technological advances. Nevertheless, they sometimes over-assumed that they knew how to accomplish a technological task and were impatient when it was a struggle. In addition, many of these students lacked ability in typing or word processing, and often did not own or use printers.

Many older students returning for a graduate degree lacked not only technological knowledge, but were also unwilling to learn or use technology. Plus, they had difficulty in finding appropriate technology courses, where the instructor "spoke their language."

However, by 2001, this was beginning to change. Most of our students owned computers, possessed basic keyboarding skills, and used e-mail fairly regularly. Very few, however, had used a statistical package, taken an online course, or used presentation software, such as PowerPoint.

Now, in 2006, it is rare to find a graduate student who is not fairly proficient in keyboarding, surfing the Internet, instant messaging and downloading MP3 music files. In addition, most students register, receive class syllabi and other materials from faculty, and/or take classes via the computer. Faculty no longer even think to ask if special arrangements need to be made for those without access to a computer as most students have easy access to multiple computer laboratories in the college or own computers. In fact, e-mail has been designated by the university as the primary correspondence medium for all university-student communications.

Basic Research and Library Skills

Instructors across campus in various departments report that many students lack research and library skills. Professors in the EPC department have experienced similar voids.

Recently, one of the authors spoke of sharing his love of visiting the library stacks. During an assessment class, he began to talk about the importance of including library texts in their research papers, and shared the feeling he had of perusing the books on the library bookshelves. He spoke of the awe and respect he had for the library and the time he spent there. Pausing a moment, a student called his name and asked, "Professor ____, where is the library?"—followed by a short buzz from a few others in the class, "Yes, where is it? Do you know?" A brief class conversation ensued regarding students' preference for "better utilizing" their time by walking their way through information via their computer. Many students reported that they had relied on Internet searches for articles and sources for papers since middle school without ever entering a library!

Conceptualize and Synthesize

It is no longer sufficient to teach students how to write at a professional level. Our students need to know much more than APA-style formatting, how to conduct literature searches, and how to read and understand peer-reviewed research. Information literacy encompasses those skills and more. As one counselor educator Darcy Haag Granello (2001: 293) said, "What seems to be missing in counselor education literature is a formalized, intentional, and well grounded mechanism designed to teach students how to critically evaluate and synthesize the material they have collected into cognitively advanced reviews of the literature." Our department is addressing those very concerns.

With the department's emphasis on information competence, students see the value of the acquisition of those skills and why they are important for their future as professionals. However, students still struggle to learn conceptualization and critical evaluation and develop synthesis skills. Many are unfamiliar with research methods and basic research tools. When they are asked to survey professional literature and critically evaluate it, they indicate that they feel anxious and lack confidence in their own abilities.

Our goal is not just one-time mastery of IC skills, but to learn transferable skills that can expand with the onset of new technology. To this end, we found the expertise of university librarians critical. Through a collaborative process between department and library faculty, we developed a model that has promoted the integration of information competence, positively impacted student skills, and maximized the potential for lifelong learning.

IMPLEMENTATION OF IC SKILLS

When we received the first IC grant in 2001, we were delighted and almost immediately began to design steps to integrate IC skills into the department's curriculum. At that time, it did not occur to us to collaborate with the library faculty at our university. Now, in hindsight, we know that if we had asked for help, it would have saved us much time and energy. Later, when we began to run into trouble, we did reach out and immediately received the valuable assistance we badly needed.

Planning for the Department Faculty Retreat, August

Our first step was to form a departmental *ad hoc* Information Competence Committee (ICC) of four faculty members. Synchronistically, the committee was comprised of an assistant professor, associate professor, "full" professor, and FERP faculty member (i.e., a tenured professor on an early retirement program). Three of these members demonstrated previous significant commitment to utilizing technology skills and techniques. One member authored the first departmental Web page. The second supervised and coordinated an extensive upgrade of the same Web page, which included the posting of all information and materials for application and program advisement for students.

The third introduced the basic competency of Web page authoring and multimedia skills in his fieldwork classes, and first attended and then later coordinated a national conference on technology skills training for school counselors.

We knew that we also had to gain the support of department faculty in order to accomplish our goal of integrating IC skills in the curriculum. We felt that the most appropriate venue for introducing the subject would be at a two day, off-campus faculty retreat before the academic year began. In preparation for the retreat, the committee members researched and drafted information competence criteria in the areas of technology, research, and professional skills. Our plan was to propose a model to the faculty that infused IC skills into the curriculum paired with three draft lists of competencies: Basic IC Skills, Research Skills, and Professional Skills.

We also identified goals for the retreat, drafted an agenda, carefully scripted our presentations and interactive activities, surveyed the faculty regarding their technological skills, and prepared a packet of materials: agenda, fact sheet on information literacy, departmental IC grant proposal, IC assessment methods by learning domains with examples, faculty technology survey, and draft documents of criteria for basic, research, and professional IC skills.

Although we felt prepared for the retreat, we did not know what to expect. How many faculty members, if any, would be interested in and supportive of this initiative? Would faculty members object? If so, how many and how strongly? We did know that all full-time faculty members (including five FERP faculty) were planning to attend the retreat, except for two faculty members who were out of the country (one was on a Fulbright scholarship in Africa; the other had not as yet returned from a trip abroad). In addition five part-time faculty members were included who were scheduled to teach the research methods course (EPC 602) in the fall 2001. A few faculty members had completed and returned the survey before the retreat (18 out of a potential of about 26), so we also knew that all of the responders regularly used technology; about half of these reportedly had advanced technology skills.

Department Faculty Retreat, August

On the first day of the retreat, we began by asking each faculty member to share a summer experience. We followed this with an ice-breaker about IC that engendered smiles and laughter. Then we launched into the core of the agenda, and talked about goals for the retreat:

1. To feel stimulated and excited about starting the new school year.
2. To come together as colleagues and friends.
3. To identify information competence (IC) skills for master's students.
4. To plan how IC skills can be infused throughout the curriculum.

5. To discuss what types of assignments might be incorporated to increase IC.
6. To discuss how our students' IC skills can be assessed.
7. To examine how we can further develop our own IC skills.

Presentations followed covering topics such as: What is information competence? Why is IC important for our students? Why is it important for the faculty? Why are we discussing IC now? What are its implications for our department? What have various universities and departments done to promote information competence?

We felt relieved when faculty members seemed to be enthusiastic about IC. Lively discussions ensued throughout the day regarding: 1. what skills best fit under the categories of basic, research, or professional competencies; 2. how IC should be infused in the curriculum; 3. what types of assignments would increase IC; 4. how IC could be assessed, and 5. how faculty members could improve their own skills.

At the end of the retreat, we reviewed the goals and were surprised and pleased that all goals had been met:

1. Competency lists of basic, research, and professional IC skills were refined and approved (Goal 3).
2. Faculty members agreed that they would support EPC students in becoming information competent learners before receiving the master's degree (Goal 2).
3. A process model proposed by the Information Competence Committee to infuse IC skills in the curriculum was tentatively adopted with identified modifications to be discussed at the September faculty meeting (Goal 4).

   The model recommended that:

   a. new students be expected to master basic skill competencies before admission
   b. a research skills "strand" be identified for each program option, starting with the statistics course and the introductory class in research methods, followed by courses that require research papers and hands-on research, and culminating with a thesis or project, or comprehensive examination
   c. professional skills be infused throughout the program.
4. Ideas were discussed regarding types of assignments that might be incorporated into the curriculum (Goal 5):

   a. the course mentor for the research methods course volunteered to design a course prototype that included model assignments
   b. further discussion of IC assignments will continue at future faculty meetings.

5. It was also decided to assess basic skills by surveying students registered in a prerequisite class (EPC 451). It was recognized that a sophisticated assessment method would have to be developed in order to assess if, in fact, applicants had mastered basic skills. The faculty agreed that, until this instrument was developed, mastery of basic skills could not be used as a criterion for admission. However, faculty agreed that students admitted next year, fall 2002, would be given a resource list and asked to master basic IC skills before beginning classes (Goal 6).

6. Faculty identified their desired areas of growth, and tentative plans were made for future workshops (Goal 7).

First Faculty Meeting of the Year, September

At the August department retreat, a process model for integrating IC skills in the curriculum had been tentatively approved. This model was again examined and small revisions were made. In addition, faculty voted to include information competence in the department's learning outcomes.

Assessment of Self-Reported Basic Skills, Fall Semester

The directive of the faculty to survey students registered in the prerequisite course, EPC 451 (Fundamentals of Counseling), as to their reported level of competence in basic information skills was carried out during the fall semester. Using a 3-point Likert Scale (1= little or no skill; 2 = some skill; 3= good or strong skills), 56 students registered in two sections of the course were asked to rate their skill level for each of the 61 skills on the department's list of basic IC skills. The skills were distributed into three areas: 1) technology with 32 skills in five categories (i.e., use of: keyboard and mouse, word processing, Windows, e-mail, and Web browser); 2) information resource awareness with ten skills; and 3) accessing research information with 19 skills in six categories (i.e., understanding and using information knowledge, the CSUN Library, online catalog, periodical index, abstract databases, and database searches. Access to technology and use of e-mail were also surveyed.

It was found that:

1. Overall, the mean of the 32 skills in five technology categories was higher (M = 2.6) than the mean of ten skills in awareness of information resource (M = 2.46) and 19 skills in six research information categories (M = 2.13).

2. In the technology category, items receiving the lowest mean scores (suggesting that students on the average knew the least about these skills)

were: 1) subscribing and unsubscribing to list serves; 2) searching archives of listserves; and 3) establishing a group list.

3. Regarding information resource awareness, items receiving the lowest mean scores were: 1) resources not owned by CSUN can usually be obtained through inter-library loan; 2) CSU does not own all the periodicals covered by all the listed databases; 3) when library resources are needed, the library catalog should be used to identify the availability of items within the CSUN Library; and 4) the length of time it takes to receive an item through inter-library loan.

4. With regard to research information, items that received the lowest mean scores were: 1) identifying a specific online database that may include information on a specific research topic; 2) accessing the holdings record to identify specific dates owned, plus various format locations of periodicals within the CSUN Library; 3) recognizing that index/abstract databases may be accessed by an individual through the CSUN Library home page or via a service provider or aggregator; 4) determining availability of resources not owned by CSUN; and 5) locating an inter-library loan form while online or in print form.

5. Regarding access to technology, 52 of the 56 surveyed students (93 percent) stated that they had access to a computer in their home, and 49 (88 percent) also had use of a home printer.

6. Forty-nine of the 56 students (88 percent) used e-mail often or very often; three rarely; and four did not respond.

The results of this survey suggest that the surveyed students viewed themselves as more proficient in using technology than in knowing how to access research using library resources. Also, a large majority of these students have access to a computer and printer and use e-mail on a regular basis.

At the completion of the study, the results of the study were shared with the surveyed students, and appropriate resource referrals were provided for those who wanted to further increase their skills.

Submission of IC Paper to Professional Conference

In October 2001, three members of the departmental ICC submitted a proposal to present a paper on information competence in counselor education at the national conference of the Association of Counselor Educators and Supervisors in Park City, Utah, a year later. Essentially, the paper covered the work we had done in information competence up to this point (e.g., the process we had developed to integrate IC in the curriculum, the basic, research, and professional competencies, survey results, and future plans). In May 2002, the proposal was accepted and was presented on October 17, 2002.

Departmental Web Pages

Information about IC skills and activities was first added to the department's Web site in January, 2002 (www.csun.edu/edpsy/ic/index.html). Among other IC documents, the Web site contains our grant proposals, activities, and deliverables.

Faculty Workshop, February 2002

Based on the results of the faculty needs survey conducted at the fall retreat, a department faculty member delivered a workshop on use of the Statistical Package for the Social Sciences (SPSS) for those who wanted to review the major revisions in this program. Most department faculty attended, as well as faculty from other departments in the college.

Initial Collaboration with Library Faculty, February 2002

Although it seemed that the graduate research methods course (EPC 602) had helped students to improve their research competencies, a formal assessment had not been conducted. Further, the content of the course differed across the six sections offered that semester, even though a prototype syllabus had been developed.

At this point, we felt at a loss and did not know how to proceed. We contacted Susan C. Curzon, Dean of the Oviatt Library, who referred us to a newly hired librarian, Lynn Lampert, who had been recently hired to help develop the university's program in information competence. In a seminal meeting, Lampert suggested that the CSUN librarians develop two to three hour modules for each of the six sections of EPC 602, research methods, offered fall semester, 2002. These modules would: 1) help students acquire both basic and research competencies, and 2) provide a post-test assessment to determine if students had attained the required basic and research skills.

Over the next few months, Lampert, with a team of four instruction librarians, developed outlines and educational materials that were aligned with the learning objectives of the *Library and Information Resource Instruction for Psychology—Guidelines*, the course prototype, the department's research competencies, and assignments developed by the faculty scheduled to teach the research course (Lampert, 2005).

All stakeholders then met to discuss the class, the delivery process, and possible assessment. It was decided to survey the students before the first library session to determine their awareness, comfort, and reported skill level with resources, such as ERIC, PsycInfo, the library catalog, and interlibrary loan. From the results of this survey, content and pace of instruction were determined. By the end of the third library session, most students had developed a literature review that adhered to APA publication guidelines (American Psychological

Association, 2001). When surveyed at the end of the course, students indicated that their comfort level using library resources and knowledge of research skills had increased greatly.

Recent Innovations That Support Information Competence

Seven semesters have now elapsed since the first modules were developed. A number of changes have taken place. Starting in fall of 2003, the department hired a new faculty member coordinator, Reagan Curtis, who fine-tuned the EPC 602 course and developed a common syllabus. Course meetings for the cadre of faculty teaching this course were held on a regular basis, sometimes with library faculty in attendance.

The library also hired an educational psychology and counseling librarian, Stephanie Ballard, to specialize in information competence and resources used by faculty and students in educational psychology/counseling and psychology content areas. Each semester she works closely with library faculty teaching the modules, and also teaches a number of them herself.

The faculty in each of the master's options has identified courses that follow EPC 602. In these courses, students are required to complete research-based assignments in order to practice the research competencies learned in EPC 602. This has further readied students for their culminating experience (i.e., thesis, project, or comprehensive examinations).

Guidelines for the Culminating Experience

One of the challenges we identified through this process was a lack of congruence among the faculty regarding expectations and requirements for students' theses, projects, and comprehensive examinations. Therefore, the department curriculum committee worked for over a year, in consultation with department faculty, to develop a written document for students, "Guidelines for the Culminating Experience" (www.csun.edu/edpsy/resources.html). Faculty members have agreed to adhere to these guidelines.

Writing Assistance

A special course has been developed for students needing to improve their writing skills. Students can either go to the instructor of this special course on an "as needed" basis or enroll in the class to receive on-going help. As we worked with these students to improve their writing, we became increasingly aware that, although all of our students had passed the CSUN writing proficiency examination or the equivalent examination before acceptance to our master's programs, some still needed basic writing support. Therefore, the department curriculum committee has recently designed a plan to identify these students early in the master's program and give them the support they need from the beginning of their program.

Professional Skills

With regard to our third information competence category, professional skills, students complete this category by demonstrating competence in these skills within the context of their regular courses. Faculty has agreed that, when a student demonstrates competency in one of the professional skills, the skill is then "signed off" by the faculty member teaching the class. Some faculty members even require mastery of specific professional skills in order to complete specific classes.

Certificate of Completion

In spring 2003, a Certificate of Mastery in Information Competence Skills was designed for students who evidenced mastery in all three levels of information competence skills (i.e., basic, research, and professional). If desired, the student can cite this accomplishment on his/her professional résumé. Our goal is to help every student qualify for this certificate of completion.

Sharing with Colleagues

A highlight for us occurred when Ilene Rockman, who headed the information competence initiative for the CSU system, asked us to share our IC work with other CSU faculty in our field. Supported by the CSU, a conference was held at Northridge to give faculty members an opportunity to plan their own IC programs and to hear about other programs. In our presentation, we had the opportunity to share our experience of infusing IC into our curriculum. Expansion of knowledge and ability in technology and research skills has been a positive experience, not only by our students, but by our faculty. We also opened ourselves to new ways and systems to conduct research and stay current in our academic fields.

ASSESSMENT OF IC COMPETENCIES

Assessment of Basic Skills

Our original plan called for assessment of basic skills before acceptance to the master's program. However, we were unable to find a suitable instrument for our purposes. We considered creating an online assessment instrument, but this proved costly and would have involved a fee to take the examination.

In 2004, the Basic Information Competence Skills Assessment (BICSA) was developed by an EPC faculty member to assess basic skills of first semester students in use of: keyboard/mouse, word processing software, windows, e-mail, Web browsers, and CSUN library resources. Essentially, students were asked to complete four steps that required technology and library resource knowledge, ending with a short paper in APA format. Using a five-point rubric, the paper was scored based on: 1) how closely the steps were followed; 2) appropriateness of the paper's topic; 3) English usage and clarity of the description of the library sources; and 4) adherence to APA format. However, this proved to be unwieldy for some faculty to administer and did not fit easily into the curriculum of first semester students.

Now, in 2006, we have found that essentially all admitted students have fulfilled our basic technology skill competencies upon arrival. Therefore, we no longer feel the need to assess basic technology skills. However, most new students still do not possess basic research skills. To solve this problem, we have moved the basic research competencies into the research methods course, along with the advanced research skills.

Assessment of Research Skills

With the continuing involvement of library faculty, most of the research skills are acquired in the research class, EPC 602. A rubric has been developed for the assessment of research information competence skills (www.csun.edu/edpsy/ic/). A companion piece, the Research Information Competence Skills Assessment (RICSA), describes the research competencies being assessed by the rubric. This rubric can also be used to evaluate research papers in courses that follow the research course.

Assessment of Professional Skills

The completion of each professional skill is verified by the signature of a faculty member who has observed the student using the skill.

Assessment of IC at the Conclusion of the Culminating Experience

Starting with the Fall 2006 semester, IC skills will be assessed at the completion of the culminating experience, along with the quality of the product (based on the department's guidelines), ethical standards, and department dispositions. Using a common rubric developed by an ad hoc committee of the department curriculum committee, faculty members will complete an online assessment of each thesis, project, or comprehensive examination he or she chairs. This data will then be aggregated for accreditation purposes.

CHALLENGES AHEAD

We are hopeful that our department will become a model for other large and complex departments in how to institutionalize information competence skills throughout a department's programs. Although we have come a long way in our journey, challenges still remain that need to be resolved.

Maintaining Information Competence Standards
Across Courses and Sections

In a large department, some courses have multiple sections taught by both full and part-time instructors with varying degrees of interest and knowledge about information competence.

For EPC 602 (research methods), we have partially solved the reliability problem by requiring a common syllabus (with common goals and assignments), using research modules developed for our students and taught by library faculty, and employing the RICSA description and rubric for assessing research skills. Two other key ingredients that have maximized mastery of information competence skills are: 1) regular course meetings led by a faculty member committed to information competence; and 2) maintaining good communication between department and library faculty.

For courses following the research course, we have encouraged faculty to use the RICSA description and rubric. However, this has been only partially successful. The rubric needs to be expanded to not only evaluate research skills, but also to reflect the goals of each of the follow-up courses. In addition, all sections of a follow-up course need to identify common goals, assignments, assessment methods, and rubrics. In the EPC department, this involves approximately ten courses with multiple sections.

Individualizing Professional Skills

The professional competencies need to be reexamined and modified in light of each program's needs. The faculty in that option should then identify a course(s) in which an identified professional skill or skills would be taught, demonstrated by the student, and then evaluated using agreed upon rubrics across sections.

Agenda for a Future Retreat

It has been almost five years since we first introduced the concept of "information competence" at the faculty retreat. IC has now become a "household word" within the department. Nevertheless, there is still much to develop, maintain, and institutionalize. Perhaps it is time to have another retreat with this same theme. This time we would invite our friends and colleagues from the library faculty as participants and consultants.

Goals for the retreat might be to:

- create a pre-test and post-test that can be used in the research class to determine its effectiveness
- develop common information competence goals, assignments, and assessment methods/rubrics for each section of the follow-up courses (to the research course)

- reexamine the professional competencies list in light of the needs of each option
- identify courses in each option where specific professional skill(s) can be taught and evaluated
- create a rubric to assess professional skills
- develop a plan to institutionalize or further embed IC in the fabric of the department

CONCLUSION

We have made strides in moving toward meeting our long-range goal of every student becoming an information competent scholar. The largest pay-off has been the responses we have already received from supervisors and employers in the field. They greatly value the skills our students have acquired. However, we know that our work is not yet complete. And, the largest challenge is still ahead—how to institutionalize the IC process, so that it is fully embedded in the everyday running of the department.

REFERENCES

American Psychological Association. 2001. *Publication manual of the American Psychological Association.* Washington, DC: American Psychological Association.

Baltimore, M. 2002. "Recent trends in advancing technology use in counselor education." *Journal of Technology in Counseling,* Vol. 2, no. 2. Available: http://jtc.colstate.edu/vol2_2/editor.htm (accessed March 3, 2006).

Council for the Accreditation of Counselor Education and Related Educational Programs (CACREP). *2001 Accreditation Standards.* Washington, DC: CACREP. Available: www.cacrep.org/2001Standards.html (accessed February 24, 2006).

Educational and Behavioral Sciences Section. 1995. "Library and Information Resource Instruction for Psychology"—based on Merriam, La Baugh & Butterfield (1992) "'Library Instruction for Psychology Majors: Minimum Training Guidelines.'" *Teaching of Psychology,* Vol. 19, no. 1: 34–36.

Edwards, Y. V., T. A. A. Portman, and J. Bethea. 2002. "Counseling student computer competencies skills: Effects of technology course in training." *Journal of Technology in Counseling,* Vol. 2, no. 2. Available: http://jtc.colstate.edu/vol2_2/edwards.htm (accessed February 8, 2006).

Farber, E. 1999. "Faculty-librarian cooperation: A personal perspective." *Reference Services Review,* Vol. 27, no. 3: 229–234.

Gore, P. A., W. C. Leuwerke, and J. D. Krumboltz. 2002. "Technologically enriched and boundaryless lives: Time for a paradigm upgrade." *The Counseling Psychologist,* Vol. 30: 847–857.

Granello, D. H. 2001. "Promoting cognitive complexity in graduate written work: Using Bloom's Taxonomy as a pedagogical tool to improve literature reviews." *Counselor Education and Supervision,* Vol. 40, no. 4: 292–307.

Hines, P. L. 2002. "Student technology competencies for school counseling programs." *Journal of Technology in Counseling*, Vol. 2, no. 2. Available: http://jtc.colstate. edu/vol2_2/hines/hines.htm (accessed February 8, 2006).

Lampert, L. 2005. "'Getting psyched' about information literacy: A successful faculty-librarian collaboration for educational psychology and counseling." *The Reference Librarian*, Vol. 43, no. 89/90: 5–23.

Mitchell, R. 2003. "Information competence." Available: www.csun.edu/edpsy/ic/ index.html (accessed February 14, 2006).

Rockman, I., ed. 2004. *Integrating information literacy into the higher education curriculum: Practical models for transformation.* San Francisco: Jossey-Bass.

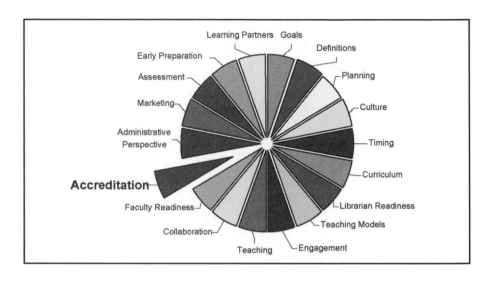

Learning Partners Goals
Early Preparation
Definitions
Assessment
Planning
Marketing
Culture
Administrative
Perspective
Timing
Accreditation
Curriculum
Faculty Readiness
Librarian Readiness
Collaboration
Teaching Models
Teaching
Engagement

ACCREDITATION

A Word from the Editors

*N*o *book on information literacy would be complete without an understanding of the role and impact of accreditation on information literacy and the role and impact of information literacy on educational quality and student achievement. Stephanie Bangert was invited to explore the issues of information literacy and accreditation as a person uniquely poised by background and experience to provide exceptional understanding on the topic. For five years, Stephanie served as Associate Director at the Senior Accrediting Commission of the Western Association of Schools and Colleges (WASC) in Alameda, California. During this time, she provided institutional support and guidance for 40 public and private institutions of higher education in the western region, managed the substantive change process, and developed a number of training programs with colleagues about institutional self-review. In her current position as the Executive Director, Office of the President, Samuel Merritt College in Oakland, California, which is a comprehensive health sciences institution, Stephanie is a key advisor to the president, serving as member of the senior team responsible for policy development, strategic planning, communications and community relations, and support to the governing board. Her introduction to the world of accreditation began while director of the library, and later, dean for academic resources, at Saint Mary's College in Moraga, California. During those 16 years in this comprehensive liberal arts college, she administered the college library, art gallery, and media services. Stephanie earned the M.L.S. from the University of California, Berkeley. Her first professional position was as online librarian at San Jose State University in the early 1980s. In writing to the editors, Stephanie has said that her intent is to "explore fundamental questions about student learning, the relevance of learning outcomes to expectations for a 21st-century educated person, and the role of information literacy in educational effectiveness." In this chapter, Stephanie is looking at the impact of accreditation standards on institutional self-evaluation, with a focus on the relationships among organizational structures and programs, and at the concept of higher literacy. Of particular benefit to us are Stephanie's suggestions about the five strategies for sustaining information literacy programs in today's complex academic environment.*

Chapter 13

Understanding Accreditation:
Student Learning and
Information Literacy

by Stephanie R. Bangert

INTRODUCTION

The quality of student learning is a significant topic in the national conversation about the future of higher education. The Higher Education Act (HEA), the federal legislation that mandates how billions of government dollars are distributed to American colleges and universities, may not pass Congress. Nonetheless, the debate surrounding HEA has sent strident messages to the higher education community. Representative Howard McKeon, Chair of the House Education Committee, was quoted in the *Wall Street Journal* (Hechinger, 2006) stating, "Colleges and universities must remain accountable to consumers of higher education." In another public arena, reported in the *Chronicle of Higher Education* (Bollag and Selingo, 2006), the United States Secretary of Education's Commission on the Future of Higher Education is charged with studying issues considered critical to the quality of higher education. Those issues include accountability, costs associated with attending a college or university, public information about choice and access, and accreditation.

At the heart of the conversation is a key question posed by politicians, educators, and the public at large: What are students learning? Debate generated by the commission has identified a concern that our system of accountability through regional accrediting agencies may not be working. Universal agreement exists, however, that colleges and universities need to provide better evidence

213

about what students are learning. The results of student learning, rather than the mechanism for reporting those results, appear to be the central and common concern across governmental, public, and educational bodies. Critics and supporters recognize that accrediting organizations define the processes used by academic institutions for reporting student learning results. The role accreditation plays in higher education quality, therefore, is significant. The degrees to which information literacy programs are informed by accreditation standards, and more importantly, by analysis of institutional learning results, may determine long-term sustainability of those programs in colleges and universities committed to learning.

Answering the fundamental question (what are students learning?) is complex because it is influenced by the nature and degree of clear and meaningful student learning outcomes as defined by an institution. Institutional capacity for accomplishing student achievement goals, however defined by its learning outcomes, is associated with the way in which a given institution organizes itself around those goals.

The quality of student learning is affected by relationships and interconnections between and among institutional structures and systems. Accreditation standards require institutional accountability for demonstrating alignment and linkage between structures (academic programs, resources and services, and co-curricular offices) and systems (curricular design process, program review, and assessment of learning outcomes). Such alignment is considered by accrediting bodies as partial evidence of educational effectiveness. Information literacy programs, therefore, exist within an academic culture of complex organizational structures and relationships. Connections between and among college or university-wide student learning outcomes, and those articulated for information literacy and other programs, are considered essential to institutional performance and improvement.

STUDENT LEARNING

Colleges and universities create organizational structures to support student learning: academic schools and departments, offices that provide co-curricular activities and support, and an array of academic resources and services such as libraries, teaching and learning institutes, and computer centers. How each school, department, resource, or service center contributes to student achievement determines whether it is perceived as integral to learning, and integral to the fulfillment of the outcomes and competencies associated with earning academic degrees.

Results of student learning appear to be the central theme and focus of our nation's concern about the quality of higher education, and the capacity of colleges and universities to produce graduates able to contribute to an evolving society. Another theme to be explored is the changing nature of what students *ought* to be learning so that they are prepared for the challenges of a global, diverse, and technological world. Accreditation organizations are forces in institutional self assessment; the review processes required by these agencies ask institutions to study what is stated as critical outcomes for student learning and whether those outcomes are achieved.

Research on learning, and perspectives about the multiple ways of knowing, provide for deeper reflection on the core question of what students are learning. Examining these issues suggests the role of information literacy (and other programs) in educating the whole person. This role is as important to institutional performance and student achievement as traditional learning competencies identified with academic disciplines.

Does understanding the context of accreditation and institutional student learning outcomes contribute to the sustainability of information literacy as a core competency in student achievement? Do information literacy outcomes contribute to skills needed by graduates in the twenty-first century? Should student learning goals for information literacy programs integrate into broader institutional learning goals of an institution?

A framework for understanding the role of accreditation in improving quality of higher education, and the parallel role of information literacy in institutional effectiveness and student learning is proposed. This framework should also be considered in the context of what students *ought* to be learning. Because accreditation standards and public expectations call on institutions to keep pace with changing societal needs, student learning outcomes should reflect educational objectives that respond to external forces emerging in the workplace and the environment.

QUALITY OF HIGHER EDUCATION

If two primary roles of accreditation are to ensure and sustain the quality of higher education, understanding what is meant by quality would be useful in seeing the larger context of learning-centered institutions. Knowing how an institution defines its indicators of quality offers developers of student learning programs, i.e., coordinators of information literacy programs, a mechanism by which to link programmatic goals to educational objectives within the entire institution. For the public at large, the institutional level is where accountability for quality of student learning primarily rests. Those at the broadest level of student learning assessment, therefore, need to demonstrate how student learning is enhanced by achievement of learning outcomes at all program levels. Any program not perceived as being aligned with institutional goals may be vulnerable to reduced support, lack of funding or resources, or worst case, closure. Conversely, programs hard-wired to institutional objectives for learning can enable the institution to demonstrate that it functions as an integrated and holistic learning organization focused on successful student attainment.

Regional accrediting bodies encourage, if not require, well-aligned and cohesive systems and structures for institutional effectiveness and student learning. Understanding the role of accreditation and its attendant expectations for institutional performance and effectiveness is critical in developing student learning outcomes, at both institutional and program levels. The influencing power of accreditation, public policy, and commonly-held expectations of student learning has created an agenda for reform in higher education. Reform will have far reaching effects on learning and those programs established to enhance student achievement.

UNDERSTANDING ACCREDITATION

Because of its critical role in American higher education, understanding accreditation is of significant importance. In a quality assurance environment, accreditation is the most visible "report card" regarding the quality of institutional effectiveness and performance. The transformation of accreditation during the last decade has been from a regulatory environment focused primarily on inputs to a collaborative partnership with institutions framing the evaluation process around criteria about educational results (outputs). Coupled with external pressures to demonstrate accountability in achieving stated student learning outcomes, colleges and universities in general use the accreditation process to showcase their effectiveness in teaching and student learning. More commonly, the accreditation review process has become for many institutions the catalyst for faculty and campus leadership to engage cooperatively and comprehensively in studying student learning achievement.

The degree to which libraries are a part of campus engagement before, during, and after accreditation reviews may determine whether the institution understands how information literacy contributes to student achievement. Examining where information literacy fits into the complex picture of institutional learning and student learning is a proposed strategy for sustaining information literacy programs. Figure 13-1 provides a conceptual framework for understanding the relationship of accreditation and information literacy to student learning. The illustration represents interrelationships that exist within an institution where alignment and connections are needed. The diagram also introduces the concept of higher literacy, and information literacy as two of its many components.

WHAT IS ACCREDITATION?

In a useful publication of the American Library Association entitled *Preparing for Accreditation* (Sacks and Whildrin, 1993: 12), the source defines accreditation

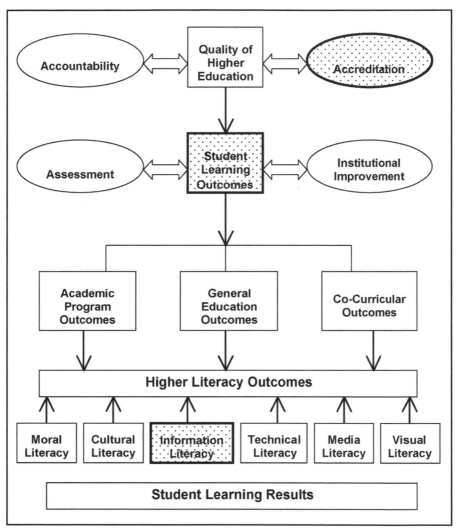

Figure 13-1: Relationship of Accreditation and Information Literacy to Student Learning

as "a voluntary, self-regulatory process for encouraging and assisting institutions of higher education to evaluate and improve their educational endeavors." It further provides a definition of accreditation from the former Council on Postsecondary Accreditation (COPA), stating accreditation as "a process by which an institution or a specialized unit of postsecondary education periodically evaluates its educational activities and seeks an independent judgment by peers that it achieves substantially its own educational objectives and meets the established standards of a body from which it seeks accreditation" (Sacks and Whildrin, 1993: 26).

The Council for Higher Education Accreditation (CHEA) is a voice for accreditation to the public and policy makers, representing over 3,000 colleges and universities and 60 national, regional, and specialized accrediting agencies. It has produced publications to inform the public, legislative groups, and educational institutions about the role of accrediting agencies. CHEA representatives, as well as executive directors of regional accreditation commissions, frequently provide legislative bodies with testimony on the effectiveness of accreditation in assessing higher education quality and student learning.

"The Value of Accreditation: Four Pivotal Roles" (2003) is a published letter from the president of CHEA, Judith Eaton. She defines accreditation as "the primary means by which institutions of higher education in the United States assure and improve quality" (Eaton, 2003). In this work, and restated in remarks to the Commission on the Future of Higher Education in 2006, Ms. Eaton presents the value of accreditation as having four roles: 1) to sustain and enhance the quality of higher education; 2) to maintain the academic values of higher education; 3) to provide a buffer against the politicizing of higher education; and 4) to serve public interest and need.

As the nation's system of quality assurance for higher education, accreditation is described in the CHEA statement as exerting influence on institutions of higher education through "constructive criticism and consultation" (Eaton, 2003: 17). A result of this approach is the strengthening of college and university student learning outcomes and specific program goals, as defined and required by local accreditation standards.

The accreditation review process is on-going and multi-staged. It begins when an institution seeks to be accredited for the first time, and continues periodically in the "renewal" of accreditation, known as reaccreditation. Understanding the accreditation process as multi-dimensional provides an institution and the programs within it various opportunities through which student achievement can be demonstrated. The review process typically requires a college or university to prepare a written self study of its performance with respect to numerous requirements of regional accreditation. While each of the six regional accreditation agencies has issued standards of accreditation unique to its local higher education environment, expectations of quality embedded in all regional standards are remarkably similar.

The accreditation process is also based on peer review. An important element to this review is a site visit conducted by a volunteer evaluation team comprised of faculty, administrators, and other higher education professionals. Teams often include librarians, student affairs staff, academic technology designers, or institutional research officers. Following assessment and evaluation of the institutional self study, an analysis by site visitors of institutional evidence of student work and effective systems is conducted. The result of a comprehensive review is a decision regarding the accreditation status of the institution under review.

The accreditation community also plays a role in putting learning into a broader context. In the "Statement of Mutual Responsibilities for Student Learning Outcomes: Accreditation, Institutions, and Programs" (2003), CHEA states that "learning is more important and more complex than the systems used to account for it." This document maintains that quality of student learning and achievement is a shared responsibility among accrediting agencies, college and university administrators and faculty, and other academic leaders. Accrediting commissions have played a key role in educating "the public, the higher education community, policy makers, and students about the use of student learning outcomes as indicators of quality in institutions of higher education" (CHEA, 2003: 3).

Professional education associations also support the positive force exerted by accreditation organizations on the quality of colleges and universities. The Association of American Colleges and Universities (AACU), in its report from the Greater Expectations Project on Accreditation and Assessment titled "Taking Responsibility for the Quality of the Baccalaureate Degree: A Report from the Greater Expectations Projects on Accreditation and Assessment" (2004: 7), comments,

> But increasingly, the higher education community as a whole is coming to view the achievement by students of desirable learning outcomes as the key indicator of quality. Evidence is also found in accrediting bodies—both regional, which accredit whole institutions, and specialized, which accredit specific programs—that now require collective agreement about the aims of education, the incorporation of demonstrated good practice in curriculum and instruction, and assessment of student learning. Though accreditors have by no means abandoned older measures of fitness, they have steadily increased the pressure on institutions and programs to develop credible strategies for demonstrating the quality of the learning their students master. Their new emphasis requires colleges, universities, and departments to become more focused on effective student learning.

COMMON EXPECTATIONS OF QUALITY IN THREE REGIONAL ACCREDITING COMMISSIONS

American colleges and universities are granted institutional accreditation or reaccreditation from one of six regional accrediting commissions in the United States. For the purposes of this study, the standards (or criteria) of three commissions were examined: The Higher Learning Commission (HLC), a commission of the North Central Association, the Middle States Commission on Higher Education, and the Senior Accrediting Commission of the Western Association of Schools and Colleges.

The Higher Learning Commission summarizes its expectations for quality in five stated criteria: 1. Mission and integrity; 2. Preparing for the future; 3. Student learning and effective teaching; 4. Acquisition, discovery, and application of knowledge; and, 5. Engagement and service. Criterion two (preparing for the future) states that an institution needs to respond to future challenges and opportunities, and that it "realistically prepares for a future shaped by multiple societal and economic trends." Criterion three (student learning and effective teaching) stresses the requirement that an institution's goals for student learning outcomes are clear, supported by effective assessment, and that it "creates effective learning environments." The fourth criterion (acquisition, discovery, and application) states an expectation that an institution "promotes a life of learning," and that the curricula are evaluated by its "usefulness in preparing students to live and work in a global, diverse, and technological society" (Higher Learning Commission, 2003: 7).

The 14 standards defined by the Middle States Commission are organized around two themes: institutional context and educational effectiveness. "Because student learning is a fundamental component of the mission of most institutions, the assessment of student learning is an essential component of the assessment of institutional effectiveness," states the commission in its supplemental publication "Characteristics of Excellence in Higher Education" (Middle States Commission on Higher Education, 2006: 6). This publication focuses attention on assessment as the primary means by which institutions measure, through evidence, that they achieve stated goals for institutional effectiveness (standard seven) and student learning (standard 14). As also common to the other commissions' expectations for quality, the Middle States standards emphasize the responsibility of an institution to define institutional and unit-level (program) learning goals, implement strategies to achieve those goals, and assess the achievement of those goals. A common expectation of the three commissions is the use of the results of the assessments for institutional performance and improvement.

The Middle States Commission on Higher Education has also produced a useful publication for individuals interested in and responsible for the effectiveness of information literacy programs. The booklet is titled "Developing Research and Communication Skills: Guidelines for Information Literacy in the Curriculum," and it provides program planning strategies and assessment techniques (Middle States Commission on Higher Education, 2003). (See Chapter 16 for further reading on assessment and information literacy program development.) A set of information literacy skills is outlined in the publication, informed by the Association of College and Research Libraries publication, *Information Literacy Competency Standards for Higher Education* (2000). In addition to providing a framework for defining learning outcomes for information literacy programs, the discussion provokes thinking about different kinds of integrative and reflective skills complementary, if not parallel, to an equivalent level of cognitive skills normally articulated in institutional learning outcomes for all graduates. Integrative and reflective skills are associated with a suite of desired learning outcomes discussed later regarding an emerging role of *higher literacy* in preparing students for this century.

Over a decade ago, the Western Association of Schools and Colleges began a regional study to explore the core purposes of accreditation that would serve "the region and the public for the year 2000 and beyond." The result of over five years of discussion and research was a new model of accreditation for the western region, captured in the WASC *Handbook of Accreditation* of 2001 (9). Authors of the handbook describe its development as responding to changes in the external environment such as higher expectations for graduate performance, increasing diversity of learners and learning needs, development and impact of online and distributed learning, and concerns that higher education costs are rising while students are self-selecting a variety of educational programs and experiences. The WASC *Handbook* also presents the regional values that underpin the standards organized around the two "core commitments" of institutional capacity and educational effectiveness. Within those commitments, four standards define expectations for institutional performance and improvement. Defining institutional purposes and educational objectives (standard one), achieving educational objectives through core functions (standard two), developing resources and organizational structures to ensure sustainability (standard three), and creating an organization committed to learning and improvement (standard four) define the fundamental expectations of the WASC accreditation process.

Of the four WASC standards, criteria for student learning (standard two) and institutional learning (standard four) frame the self review around educational effectiveness and student learning results. The *Handbook* includes criteria that describe expectations for student achievement in stating, "Regardless of mode of program delivery, the institution regularly identifies the characteristics of its students and assesses their needs, experiences, and levels of satisfaction; this information is used to help shape a learning-centered environment and to actively promote student success" (WASC, 2001: 23). Criteria for creating a learning-centered environment require institutional reflection and planning that is intentionally aligned across the organization. Library resources and information literacy programs, for example, need to be effectively linked to institutional educational priorities for student learning and achievement.

WHAT IS LEARNING?

The focus of national conversation on the quality of higher education is student learning. Since some regional accrediting organizations identify alignment between institutional learning goals and program goals as a key factor in the evaluation of student achievement, better understanding of what students need to learn is useful. Scholars and professional associations have been active in publishing recommendations about student learning outcomes for graduates. Analysis of some of the literature about learning reveals striking similarities among accreditation criteria for student achievement, higher education expectations for the "educated person," and public demand for skilled graduates able to contribute to the workplace.

In *How People Learn: Brain, Mind, Experience, and School* (Bransford et al., 2000), the authors of this important work commissioned by the National Research Council discuss developments in the science of learning that have broad implications for education. The nature of what was considered important to learn in past decades compared to what is expected of students to learn today is dramatically different. Editors John D. Bransford, Ann L. Brown, and Rodney R. Cocking put education and learning in perspective. They write, "In the early part of the twentieth century, education focused on the acquisition of literacy skills: simple reading, writing, and calculating. It was not the general rule for educational systems to train people to think and read critically, to express themselves clearly and persuasively, to solve complex problems in science and mathematics. Now, at the end of the century, these aspects of higher literacy are required of almost everyone in order to successfully negotiate the complexities of contemporary life" (Bransford et al., 2000: 3–4).

HIGHER LITERACY

How People Learn introduces the concept of *higher literacy*. This notion is reinforced in an article appearing in *EDUCAUSE Review* where author, Ron Bleed (2006: 38), suggests an emerging literacy "composed of digital images and of sounds as well as of words and texts." He attributes Daniel H. Pink's 2005 book, titled *A Whole New Mind: Moving from the Information Age to the Conceptual Age*, as important research about changing needs for new skills and competencies. Bleed builds upon the work of Pink and others, arguing that colleges and universities need to revise traditional program outcomes for "the literacy of the twenty-first century" (Bleed, 2006: 38). He suggests programs incorporate course assignments requiring students to use higher order conceptual skills in multi-media environments as one strategy for change.

Perspectives that point to recognizing new knowledge about learning suggest a context for better understanding what students need to learn. How institutional and program learning outcomes are influenced by this new knowledge suggests a strategy is needed to connect programs (information literacy, general education, co-curricular) with disciplines of study. Clear and explicit student learning goals that incorporate intellectual and conceptual skills implied in accreditation standards, and in response to expectations of future employers and the public, appear necessary for educational improvement and reform.

THE EDUCATED PERSON

The notion of the "educated person" is one that has been debated and nuanced since the founding of the first liberal arts college. In recent years, the higher education community has reexamined the nature of undergraduate education and from those studies a number of recommendations have emerged about student learning and preparation for the next century. "Greater Expectations: A New Vision for Learning as a Nation Goes to College" (2002), a report from a national panel organized by the Association of American Colleges and Universities, calls for "meaningful reform in higher education," and outlines "a new vision that will promote the kind of learning students need to meet emerging challenges in the workplace, in a diverse democracy, and in an interconnected world" (para. 2).

The report provides a framework for the kind of reform it believes is needed to answer the question: What should students be learning? Its framework assumes the meta-learning goal that students should be educated to become intentional learners. "In a turbulent and complex world, every college student will need to be purposeful and self-directed in multiple ways. Purpose implies clear goals, an understanding of process, and appropriate action." The recommendation includes a definition of intentional learners: "... integrative thinkers who can see connections in seemingly disparate information and draw on a wide range of knowledge to make decisions" (AACU, 2002: para. 2).

Significant in the study are the recommendations about the intellectual and practical skills needed in student preparation for a world changed substantially by technology. Skills noted in "Greater Expectations" as critical for developing the intentional learner are also recognizable as skills often described in information literacy learning outcomes: "...interpreting, evaluating, and using information; integrating knowledge of various types and understanding complex systems; resolving difficult issues creatively by employing multiple systems and tools; transforming information into knowledge and knowledge into judgment and action" (AACU, 2002: para. 2). The implicit challenge of these recommendations in considering the role of information literacy, however, is the claim that students will need to "think outside the box, and depend on intellectual flexibility, at least as much as on factual information" (AACU, 2002: para. 2).

Information literacy programs may require, therefore, a reform of their own: a reframing of learning outcomes focused on achievement of intellectual skills, not only information skills. John Seely Brown and Paul I. Duguid write about distinctions between knowledge and information in *The Social Life of Information* (2000). Their vision of the future is one shaped by social networks making meaning of information ubiquitously accessible by technology, rather than a future with "tunnel-like focus on information, self-evident and free of context" (Brown and Duguid, 2000: 244). Explicit alignment of information literacy outcomes with broad institutional goals for student learning is a strategy to strengthen perceived value of information literacy programs, especially when those outcomes base their design on integrative and conceptual skills. Information literacy best practices offer a foundation for developing viable and interconnected relationships with institutional structures supporting student learning. Future-oriented examination of current information literacy outcomes, moreover, provides an opportunity for renewing understanding of the role of information literacy.

INFORMATION LITERACY AS HIGHER LITERACY

Understanding accreditation and the issues of quality in higher education have implications for sustaining information literacy programs. Accreditation and national opinion is focused on student learning results. It has been suggested that the quality of student learning is affected by several factors: changing perceptions of what students ought to be learning, the clarity of student learning outcomes and their relevance to external expectations of quality, and the relationships among institutional programs that support learning. A brief study of the literature of learning suggests the concept of higher literacy as a common, integrative element connecting perceptions, expectations, and organizational relationships. Student learning results associated with outcomes attributed to higher literacy may be an overarching strategy for enhancing the quality of student learning. Higher education research is rich with arguments for transforming curricula. Incorporation of higher literacy into the curricula is a critical element of this transformation, and information literacy is intrinsically embedded within it.

The value of information literacy as a higher literacy is a concept consistent with discussions in the professional library literature that proclaim the importance of information literacy to American economic and social well-being. In 1989, the American Library Association (ALA) issued a final report of the "Presidential Committee on Information Literacy." ALA President Margaret Chisholm established the committee with, among several purposes, a central charge of "defining information literacy within the higher literacies and its importance to student performance, lifelong learning, and active citizenship" (ALA, 1989: 1). The report argues that information literacy is a "survival skill in the Information Age," a skill based on a model of learning "active and integrated, not passive and fragmented." Society needs "better thinkers, problem solvers, and inquirers," according to the report, and it (society) "calls for computing literacy, civic literacy, global literacy, and cultural literacy." Information literacy, it concludes, exists to educate students with these critical skills (ALA, 1989: 3).

"Information Literacy Competency Standards for Higher Education" (ACRL, 2000), a seminal publication of ACRL, enumerates professional standards and student learning outcomes for effective information literacy programs. The standards underscore the interrelationship between accreditation and information literacy in its statement that "because information literacy augments students' competency with evaluating, managing, and using information, it is now considered by several regional and discipline-based accreditation associations as a key outcome for college students" (ACRL, 2000). Themes of organizational relationships and linkages within academic institutions are noted: "Incorporating information literacy across curricula, in all programs and services, and throughout the administrative life of the university, requires the collaborative efforts of faculty, librarians, and administrators" (ACRL, 2000). Higher and lower order thinking skills found in the information literacy standards are offered as indicators of student achievement and ultimately, educational effectiveness of the institution. Performance indicators and outcomes defined by the ACRL standards bear further analysis. Within them are concrete expectations for student learning associated with the skills previously described as those needed for the contemporary, intentional learner.

CONCLUSION

Several strategies to strengthen and sustain information literacy programs have been suggested, and a conceptual framework for understanding the relationship of accreditation and the critical issues regarding student learning is offered. Five strategies for reframing development of information literacy programs are to: 1) understand the role of accreditation, and the external issues and forces influencing accreditation and higher education; 2) align information literacy program learning outcomes with broader institutional educational goals; 3) strengthen through organizational relationships and connections how information literacy contributes to student achievement and educational effectiveness; 4) increase knowledge of the science of learning about how students learn, and what they ought to be learning; and 5) explore information literacy as higher literacy, and reframe program goals around new skills called for in educating students for the future.

Information literacy programs, it has been suggested, exist in complex academic environments. Colleges and universities are influenced by public opinion regarding quality of higher education, accountability, and expectations of student learning and learning results. In their regulatory roles, accrediting organizations define how institutions report on educational effectiveness and student achievement. Developers of information literacy programs are encouraged to communicate how outcomes associated with those programs are vital to the quality of the institution through the larger framework of higher education, with its fundamental purpose to educate students for the challenges of this century.

REFERENCES

American Library Association. 1989. *Presidential committee on information literacy: Final report.* Washington, DC: American Library Association.

Association of American Colleges and Universities. 2004. *Taking responsibility for the quality of the baccalaureate degree: A report from the Greater Expectations Project on Accreditation and Assessment.* Washington, DC: Association of American Colleges and Universities.

Association of American Colleges and Universities. 2002. *Greater expectations: A new vision for learning as a nation goes to college.* National Panel Report. Washington, DC: Association of American Colleges and Universities.

Association of College and Research Libraries. 2000. *Information literacy competency standards for higher education.* Chicago: Association of College and Research Libraries.

Bleed, R. 2006. "The IT leader as alchemist: Finding the true gold." *EDUCAUSE*, Vol. 41, no. 1: 33–42.

Bollag, B., and J. Selingo. 2006. "Federal panel floats plan to overhaul accreditation." *Chronicle of Higher Education*, Vol. 52, no. 32: A1–A23.

Bransford, J. D., A. L. Brown, and R. R. Cocking, eds. 2000. *How people learn: Brain, mind, experience, and school.* Washington, DC: National Academy Press.

Brown, J. S., and P. I. Duguid. 2000. *The social life of information.* Boston: Harvard Business School Press.

Council for Higher Education Accreditation. 2003. *Statement of mutual responsibilities for student learning outcomes: Accreditation, institutions, and programs.* Washington, DC: Council for Higher Education Accreditation and Quality Assurance.

Eaton, J. 2003. *The values of accreditation: Four pivotal roles.* CHEA: Letter from the President. Washington, DC: Council for Higher Education Accreditation.

Hechinger, J. 2006. "Higher education bill aims to stir up academia." *Wall Street Journal* (March 30): A8.

Higher Learning Commission. 2003. *Handbook of accreditation.* 3rd ed. Chicago: Higher Learning Commission, a Commission of North Central Association.

Middle States Commission on Higher Education. 2006. *Characteristics of excellence in higher education: Eligibility requirements and standards for accreditation.* Philadelphia, PA: Middle States Commission on Higher Education.

Middle States Commission on Higher Education. 2006. *Characteristics of excellence in higher learning.* Philadelphia, PA: Middle States Commission on Higher Education.

Middle States Commission on Higher Education. 2003. *Developing research and communication skills: Guidelines for information literacy in the curriculum.* Philadelphia, PA: Middle States Commission on Higher Education.

Pink, D. 2005. *A whole new mind: Moving from the information age to the conceptual age.* New York: Riverhead Books.

Sacks, P. A., and S. L. Whildrin. 1993. *Preparing for accreditation: A handbook for academic librarians.* Chicago: American Library Association.

Western Association of Schools and Colleges. 2001. *Handbook of accreditation.* Alameda, CA: Accrediting Commission for Senior Colleges and Universities.

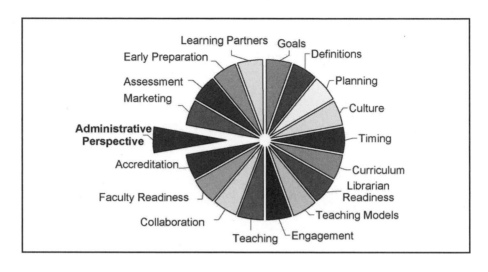

ADMINISTRATIVE PERSPECTIVE

A Word from the Editors

*V*ital to the success of any information literacy program is administrative support. No matter how enthusiastic the librarians are about the program and no matter how receptive the environment might be, support from library administration is critical. From library administration comes resources, time, political support, physical spaces for the program, and guidance navigating through the labyrinths of any organization. Dr. James L. Mullins brings considerable experience as an administrator to bear upon this subject. Currently, he is the Dean of Libraries at Purdue University and his resume also includes experiences at the Massachusetts Institute of Technology, Villanova University, and Indiana University where he also took his Ph.D. Jim has not reflected on his experience alone, however. Instead he has reached out to fellow administrators within research libraries, comprehensive university libraries, and private liberal arts college libraries by conducting a brief survey as to the issues that administrators face when supporting a program of information literacy. This perspective will be especially useful for any librarian who wants to garner the support of library administration. Jim also shares with us the Purdue experience, as well as his personal growth towards understanding information literacy. That journey started with his M.L.S. from the University of Iowa. Jim also has an international perspective from his long participation with the International Federation of Library Associations.

Chapter 14

An Administrative Perspective

by James L. Mullins

INTRODUCTION

If academic library administrators were asked, "Why support a strong, effective information literacy program," the reasons cited would vary considerably from one individual to another. In this chapter, I won't necessarily answer that question, but rather shed some light on the challenges and opportunities that library administrators have in facilitating an information literacy program within their library and campus. To accomplish this, I am going to draw upon my nearly 30 years of experience as an academic library administrator as well as responses to a survey distributed to library administrators within the Association of Research Libraries (ARL), the University Libraries Group (ULG), and the Oberlin Group (OG).

ONE LIBRARY ADMINISTRATOR'S EXPERIENCE

The manner in which I came to value information literacy is likely not unique among those of us who are more senior in the field—those who learned and began our careers long before the advent of the Web forever changed information seeking skills.

More than 30 years ago I was writing an honors thesis at the close of my undergraduate years at the University of Iowa. For my thesis topic I chose the rather esoteric topic of angelology and demonology in the Old Testament and Judaic tradition. Under the guidance of my thesis advisor, I completed the paper and graduated with an honors degree in religious studies.

About a year later, while working on my M.L.S. at the University of Iowa, a requirement for the bibliography in the humanities course was the compilation of an annotated bibliography. I proposed to the professor that I use my honors thesis topic. I will always remember his question, "Do you think you will find additional resources?" With youthful confidence I responded, "Possibly, but not probable since I received an 'A.'"

Well, to my great surprise, and as one of life's lessons to "never say never" new resources began to emerge as I studied one source after another as part of the experience in the humanities bibliography course. I finished my new annotated bibliography with many substantive works that I had not found during my original research process.

Armed with this new richness of information, I visited my honors thesis advisor. When I asked if he knew there were so many additional resources, he responded that he did. I asked him why he hadn't directed me toward them—he commented, "I thought you would find them on your own." But, I hadn't. During my undergraduate education I had not received instruction on how to read catalog entries, how to understand the linking and relationships between citations and notes, and on how to use reference books as a guide for research. Of course, I could have asked a librarian . . .

From that point on, I committed myself to ensuring that students would receive quality instruction and information on best practices in conducting research and in using library and other information resources. Throughout my career—at Indiana University, Villanova University, Massachusetts Institute of Technology, and now Purdue University, I have continued with this commitment, either by instructing one-on-one, or in a classroom environment, or by supporting others in this initiative.

THE EXPERIENCE AND PRACTICE

In the spring of 2006, responses were received to a letter (Mullins, 2006) that I sent to academic library administrators in the Association of Research Libraries, representing research libraries; University Libraries Group, representing comprehensive to research libraries; and the Oberlin Group, who are comprised of liberal arts colleges.

The remainder of this chapter will report on the responses and insights gleaned from the surveys, particularly the administrative experience and practice of the ARL, ULG, and Oberlin Group members. The survey was distributed on February 20, 2006 to the ARL Listserv and to a contact person for ULG and Oberlin who then forwarded it to the respective members. The questions were created to elicit open ended responses. Knowing that information literacy was being interpreted and offered in the various libraries in a myriad of ways, the questions had to allow flexibility for the respondent to answer. The challenges and opportunities between offering information literacy in a research university with an enrollment of 45,000 and a liberal arts college of 1,500 are substantial.

ARL is the largest association of research libraries in the United States and Canada with a current membership of 123 (Association of Research Libraries, 2006).

ULG is comprised of 22 universities in the research and comprehensive categories. Formed in 2000 at Villanova University, the objective of ULG is to "bring together directors of comparable, mid-sized university libraries to share best practices, promote the libraries' interests, develop benchmarks for assessing quality of service, and discuss current trends in the delivery of information to undergraduate and graduate programs in a range of disciplines" (University Libraries Group, 2006).

Oberlin Group is a consortium of 75 selective liberal arts colleges, who through collaboration, determine benchmarks and best practices (Oberlin Group, 2006).

The survey questions, inserted below (and repeated in Figure 14-1), relate to general issues encountered by library administrators when supporting information literacy instruction through the library or through collaboration with academic departments:

1. Commitment of librarians in all disciplines? Preparation of librarians to teach? Reassignment of librarians?
2. Support of university administration: funding?
3. Support and encouragement of disciplinary faculty and department head?
4. Creation of instructional space within the libraries?
5. Balance of classroom instruction with Web-based instruction?
6. Assessment of effectiveness of program?
7. Priority of information literacy when compared to other services: Reference, collections and information resources, other?
8. Other?

While the response was small (10 from ARL, four from Oberlin, and one from ULG), it was sufficient to demonstrate trends regarding common challenges, successes, and opportunities in a variety of academic libraries.

RESPONSE

The first question concerned the commitment of librarians in all disciplines to information literacy and their preparation to teach. The response trended slightly toward the greatest percentage of information literacy instruction being conducted by those who carry the primary responsibility for reference or subject liaison work. Among liberal arts colleges, there was a greater likelihood that all librarians, no matter what position in the library (including the director), participated in the instruction process.

For ten years, the University of Southern California supported an undergraduate-focused, non-discipline-based instruction team. Melanie Remy, Instructional Services Coordinator, reported that this tended to marginalize the information literacy instruction into one unit (Personal Communication, March 17, 2006). Therefore, the instructional team was disbanded in 2005 with team members reassigned to subject-based teams with the expectation that each subject team would then incorporate and "own" instruction equally.

Generally mentioned by survey respondents was the need for pedagogical training for librarians. Consistently mentioned was a lack of preparation, either prior to library school or in the library school experience, for librarians to develop and present an information literacy instruction session. This requires the provision of mentoring and continuing education for librarians in order to help them to become effective and comfortable in the classroom environment. It was mentioned that some librarians were reluctant or wary of working collaboratively with discipline faculty; although it was mentioned less frequently than one might expect.

The second question concerned the level of support the library received from the university administration, either through commitment within the mission of the institution for students to be "information literate," or through the provision of an integrated, comprehensive information literacy curriculum. The question also elicited comments about financial commitment to carry out this goal; the range of responses varied greatly. Some responded that no additional resources were allocated from the college/university administration—although several admitted to not having directly asked for support. Several mentioned that outside support was critical to development of their information literacy programs; this support primarily came from foundations. For example, Carnegie-Mellon University along with several college libraries reported they had realized success with securing foundation support. The most often cited need for support was for preparation of the librarians to teach. This involved funding to send librarians to conferences or workshops, or providing one-on-one training in pedagogical methodologies and effective course content development.

At the University of Illinois at Urbana–Champaign (UIUC), Paula Kaufman, University Librarian, stated, "The campus has recently provided development funds to support course-integrated instruction in a new first-year student program and for the construction of a hands-on classroom. In both cases, the leadership act was to have a proposal ready so that when the opportunity to seek funding presented itself, the Library's response was quick" (Personal Communication, March 1, 2006).

The responses to the third question were also wide ranging, however, a trend did emerge. When asked about the support and encouragement of the disciplinary faculty for the library's efforts in information literacy, the responses ranged from total indifference from some disciplinary faculty to complete understanding and support for information literacy integration. However, nearly all of the respondents stated that the major challenge to integrating information literacy into an existing course is "time." Faculty are very protective of their classroom time, and unless they see a direct connection between their course goals and the information literacy, they are unlikely to commit time for instruction by librarians.

A few respondents offered comments about faculty status for librarians and how it related to acceptance of participation by librarians by the disciplinary faculty. Was it deemed to be beneficial for the librarian to have faculty status? Those who commented stated that it didn't appear to matter, in fact, Mark Emmons, University of New Mexico, stated, "I frequently hear at conferences that not having faculty status can create an unequal power relationship that also causes difficulties—I personally did not find this to be the case when I worked in a college where librarians did not have faculty status" (Personal Communication, March 3, 2006).

One liberal arts college librarian, who wished to remain anonymous, replied that several years ago the information literacy instruction by librarians was combined with information technology training provided by the instructional technologists housed in academic computing. The result has been an effective collaboration of the two professional groups to more effectively support the integration of research methods and technology training into the curriculum.

More than half of the respondents indicated that they had a strong, positive working relationship with the writing center/lab on campus. Through this relationship, collaborative instruction opportunities presented themselves, as well as referrals for students from the writing center/lab to the library for assistance in locating research materials.

Having instructional space within the library was deemed important by all survey respondents, with several stating that they had inadequate or no instructional space within the library facility. Several respondents mentioned having a "wireless" classroom, where notebook computers equipped with wireless connectivity were assigned to students within the reference room with the instruction taking place within the public spaces of the library. One college library stated that the importance of in class instruction is valued throughout the institution. All instruction, whether disciplinary or information literacy, takes place in the classroom, making an instructional space within the library unnecessary.

It was apparent that creating a designated space within a crowded library facility is a challenge for most. Successful incorporation of classroom settings within a library facility was most often the result of a major renovation or addition to the library. Also, some created an information commons from existing computer classroom space. As an example, Indiana University successfully created flexible instruction space within its information commons. Typically, if a separate classroom was provided within the facility, it accommodated 25 to 30 students, and included workstations for all students. The workstation, however, might be a combination of desktop and notebook computers to allow for flexibility of room use.

When asked about the balance between classroom instruction and Web-based instruction, responses were fairly consistent with the majority of the instruction taking place in a classroom setting. Most of the respondents mentioned the need to develop the Web-based component, but that allocating the time needed to create and maintain a Web-based component was a significant obstacle.

Integration into the course content management system was mentioned several times as being one way, or possibly at this point in time, the only way, to reach some students who might not access, or think to access, the library's Web site for assistance. Also mentioned was the need to create subject-based Web-based tutorials that would be generally available and not linked specifically to a particular course.

Assuming that an information literacy program is in place, there is a need to assess the program as to its effectiveness. Only one respondent stated that, although they would welcome a formal information literacy program, their sole collaboration is with the English department teaching first-year students and, as reported by the English faculty, the program does seem to be effective.

Several respondents mentioned that they participated in Standardized Assessment of Information Literacy Skills (SAILS); a few mentioned that it was helpful while others stated they had not studied the data yet, hence it is not possible to assess its usefulness at this point in time. The University of Louisville mentioned being a participant in SAILS and a joint developer of the new Information and Communication Technology test by the Educational Testing Service along with various college and university libraries including Purdue University. The creation and application of the ICT is so recent that its effectiveness in determining initial information literacy skill ability among freshmen and the subsequent impact of an information literacy program cannot be determined at this time. Various universities, including Purdue University, plan to give the test to a cohort of freshmen during the summer of 2006; this will be followed up two years later by retesting to determine the effectiveness of an information literacy instruction program.

The final survey question asked to compare the importance of information literacy instruction to other services provided by the library, such as reference (in-person or online), collections, and information resources, and others. The responses were that it is not possible to separate reference, collections, and information literacy since all are of equal importance; however, several mentioned that if they had to make a choice, information literacy would compete as the number one priority within the library. There was some feeling among the respondents that not all activities within the library can be continued. Several respondents commented upon the need to reassess reference desk time with the reduced demand, allowing reallocation of librarian time to information literacy instruction.

OBSERVATION

Although the sample was small, it still provided an overview of issues that administrators face when supporting and enabling an information literacy program. The primary concern expressed was not whether the faculty or even students perceive the value of information literacy, but rather how does the staff within the library meet the expectations that both the library administration, the faculty, and they themselves place upon instructing students in being able to assess and evaluate information. An undertone did emerge, not overtly, that there was concern that we could be "too" successful and create a demand or awareness of need that the library could not accommodate. One or two respondents acknowledged this openly as a concern, but felt that if the need was there and it was supported outside the library, the college/university administration would provide the additional staff to meet the need. Several of the administrators surveyed indicated their responsibility for conveying this need for support to the college/university administration.

THE PERSPECTIVE FROM ONE UNIVERSITY

Purdue University is a research university that has an international reputation for its research in science, engineering, and agriculture programs, and its professional programs in veterinary medicine and pharmacy. However, Purdue also has a strong liberal arts program, and, in fact, the College of Liberal Arts is second largest at Purdue only after the College of Engineering. Therefore, the breadth of curriculum offered on the undergraduate and graduate levels is comparable to most research universities and is, possibly, broader than many peer institutions in the Association of Research Libraries.

Purdue University and its libraries have had a commitment to information literacy for nearly ten years. In the present strategic plan, created in 2001, one of the core responsibilities of the university is to prepare students to be both information and computer literate. Subsequently, the Purdue University libraries hired a user instruction librarian, whose responsibility is to promote within the libraries and the schools/colleges on campus, a coordinated and collaborative information literacy program. Problem-based learning is an important element in this instruction, enabling students to understand that not only will excellent information seeking skills be important to meet course expectations at Purdue, but that it is an important set of skills for solving problems in their career and their life in general.

About five years ago, a Purdue alumnus provided $100,000 to the libraries to support participation of the Purdue libraries in development of what is now the ETS Information and Communication Technology Test. As mentioned earlier, Purdue will be implementing this test to a statistical sample of incoming freshmen in August of 2006. The reason behind this individual's interest in supporting this initiative was his own work experience as chief financial officer for a major corporation. He was surprised to learn that outstanding, recent hires in the area of engineering and management lacked strong information seeking and evaluative skills. Upon exploring the possibilities for correcting this, he discovered the role that the library could and should play.

The success demonstrated by the Purdue University libraries motivated him in the fall of 2005 to make a planned gift of $2.5 million to fund the first endowed chair in information literacy in the country. This commitment demonstrates to the academic community that industry values information literacy as a skill, and that its importance should not be overlooked.

CONCLUSION

As Dean of the Purdue University libraries, I am continuing the commitment I made over 30 years ago. As an example, the Purdue libraries recently changed the name of the senior administrator for public services to the senior administrator for learning. This was initiated both to bring the libraries in-line with the academic schools/colleges, and to convey to the schools/colleges the important role the libraries play in the learning process with our students.

The response from colleagues throughout the campus has been strongly positive; including an increased understanding of the role and value of the libraries' faculty.

To end with a reflection on the responses from the survey—they provide evidence that the experience at Purdue with information literacy and learning is one shared by nearly all college and university libraries where such programs have been implemented.

From the response to the surveys, it appears that college and university library administrators place great importance on the value of information literacy programs. The ability of each to support, enable, or advance is limited by resources, acceptance by disciplinary faculty, and orientation and commitment of the individual staff librarians. The challenge is obvious, but the need and overall outcome from the effort is acknowledged and appreciated. However, the consistent observation that resonated loud and clear in the results of the survey is that administrators are concerned about resources—financial, facility, and human. The competition that an administrator must always contend with when allocating resources, is balanced by the perceived impact and benefit to students and faculty. Information literacy is obviously at the top of the priority list.

Dear Colleagues:

I have been asked to write a chapter for an upcoming book titled, Proven Strategies for Building a Successful Information Literacy Program, to be published in 2007 by Neal-Schuman, co-edited by Susan C. Curzon and Lynn Lampert. The focus of the chapter is about the issues encountered by academic library administrators in supporting the development and growth of an information literacy program. In order to reflect a cross section of the issues confronting us all, I am asking for your help.

Below are a few questions that I have developed that may engender thoughts on your part about the challenges encountered, either now or in the past, as your information literacy program developed. Also, if your library has decided not to develop an information literacy program, I would like to know about that as well. Any thoughts or comments you would like to share would be greatly appreciated. Please indicate whether you would agree to be quoted or your institution identified, or whether you would rather remain anonymous.

1. Commitment of librarians in all disciplines? Preparing librarians to teach? Re-assignment of librarians?
2. Support of university administration: funding?
3. Support and encouragement of disciplinary faculty and department head?
4. Creation of instructional space within the Libraries?
5. Balance of classroom instruction with web-based instruction?
6. Assessment of effectiveness of program?
7. Priority of information literacy when compared to other services:
   a. Reference—in person or online?
   b. Collections and information resources?
   c. Other?
8. Other?

Figure 14-1: Purdue University Letter and Survey Questions Sent to Directors

REFERENCES

Association of Research Libraries. 2006. "About ARL." Available: www.arl.org/arl/arl-facts.html (accessed May 5, 2006).

Emmons, Mark. Quoted in e-mail from Camila Alire to James L. Mullins. March 3, 2006.

Kaufman, Paula. E-mail to James L. Mullins. March 1, 2006.

Mullins, James L. Letter and survey questions sent to directors of libraries of the ARL, ULG, and Oberlin Group. February 20, 2006.

Oberlin Group. 2006. Available: www.oberlingroup.org (accessed May 6, 2006).

Remy, Melanie. E-mail to James L. Mullins. March 17, 2006.

University Libraries Group. 2006. Available: www.lehigh.edu/~inulg/ (accessed May 6, 2006).

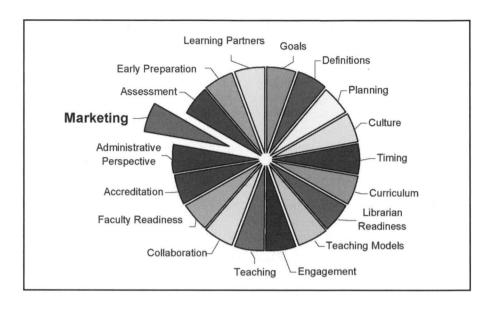

MARKETING

A Word from the Editors

*W*hen we think of marketing, most of us think of developing a brochure about a program or perhaps highlighting a program on our Web pages. Very little in our formal professional development provides us with any depth of understanding of what marketing is and how it can work in libraries. Janeanne Rockwell-Kincanon, Associate Professor and Public Services Librarian at Hamersly Library at Western Oregon University, seeks to correct this issue by providing us with an introduction to social marketing which Janeanne says is the best "construct for advocating information literacy programs." Since most of us do not have a background in marketing, Janeanne also educates us about the different types of marketing, and the different concepts within marketing. Importantly, she focuses on why we should market information literacy programs. Surely their worth should stand by themselves? Not so, says Janeanne, and especially not so when the literature on information literacy is filled with the struggle of getting students and faculty involved in any information literacy program. In writing to the editors, Janeanne says that she wants to "keep the organization of the library prominent in the thoughts of and relevant to our communities." Demonstrating her own beliefs, she was elected as President of the Faculty Senate on her campus. She also served for six years on campus as the Instruction and Outreach Librarian. Janeanne has served as the Communications Coordinator for ACRL, Oregon and was President of this organization for 2006–07. She was in the initial class for ACRL's Institute for Information Literacy. Janeanne's M.S.L.I.S. is from the University of Illinois at Urbana–Champaign, and her M.A. in Education in English is from Wayne State College in Nebraska.

Chapter 15

Using Social Marketing to Promote Information Literacy

by Janeanne Rockwell-Kincanon

In the last few decades, librarians have accepted promotion as a necessary part of developing services that are useful and used by patrons. Promotional activity is now mainstream within the professional consciousness; articles, books, Web sites and conference sessions regularly address the practice, often using the term "marketing" interchangeably with "promotion." Regional and national professional organizations, as well as local library staff promote collections, reference and other information services, facilities and amenities, activities and special events, and even librarians and media specialists themselves. Libraries also advocate certain ideals that are related to their missions: literacy, education and self-help, and freedom to read are perhaps the most prevalent examples of the profession's use of social marketing or concept marketing.

Social marketing is "an organized effort conducted by one group (the change agent), which intends to persuade others (the target adopters), to accept, modify, or abandon certain ideas, attitudes, practices, and behavior" (Kotler and Roberto, 1989: 6). The change in behavior may be in the best interests of the individual adopter or may benefit a community or society. Through ALA Graphics' READ™ posters and bookmarks and its Born to Read™ product line, local libraries promote the ideal of literacy and the behavior of reading. The institution of the library is frequently the subject of social marketing campaigns; it serves as a shortcut referring to the myriad values and services represented by the word "library."

This chapter examines why and how social marketing principles may be applied to information literacy concepts and programs. Those responsible for information literacy can develop marketing plans independently or can incorporate relevant pieces as part of a more general library marketing campaign. Knowledge and practice of these principles can help proponents of information literacy to establish, enhance, and promote their programs.

AN INTRODUCTION TO SOCIAL MARKETING
AND FACETS OF THE MARKETING MIX

Promotional material is the marketing piece that is visible to organizational outsiders. However, marketing is a broader process that is integrated by management into the whole organization and addressed by all levels of a team. Simply defined, marketing entails all processes that speak to meeting audience needs through some sort of exchange. Marketers emphasize audience needs over organizational desires or offerings.

Multiple models of marketing exist, and the models may overlap within a single organization. The most apparent models are commercial product and commercial service marketing, in which the goal is the exchange of money for a tangible item (a car or toothpaste, for example) or for a privilege or benefit (insurance, wireless plans). Organizational or personality marketing seeks to align the public identity of the group or individual with values and interests held by the target audience, in order to gain from that audience trust, loyalty, or support. Organizational marketing is used by businesses as well as by charitable and cultural groups, and by professional, political, and religious associations. The American Library Association employs organizational marketing, as do local libraries. Personality marketing takes the form of a celebrity doing a movie press junket, or, as de Sáez (2002: 9) points out, the bank highlighting its new branch manager in the local paper. Place marketing is yet another model, exchanging the total value of the destination with the audience's time and expense of getting to it. Hotels and tourist areas market with this model, as do local parks and festivals. Libraries, too, frequently engage in place marketing.

The model of social marketing aims to disseminate ideas, to encourage socially-desirable behaviors and practices, and to promote the services of public and non-profit organizations. It is marketing surrounding an issue, cause, or movement. While it is impossible to quantify, social marketing is perhaps more ubiquitous even than commercial product or service marketing; the perception may be the opposite because of heavy concentration of commercial advertisements in mass media channels. However, consider a few of the myriad examples of societal movements that were advanced (or those that are progressing now) because of intentional efforts:

- voting rights, voting encouragement
- energy efficiency
- nature conservation

- fight against breast cancer
- reducing childhood obesity
- seatbelts
- perception of emotional disturbances
- pro-choice, pro-life
- women in war jobs, symbolized by Rosie the Riveter
- shop locally
- support live music
- picking up after dogs
- contemporary church services
- flossing
- sexual harassment
- feminism
- democracy

Social marketers of these campaigns and others may have, in the past, fought multiple fights—that of the cause and that of the propriety of marketing the cause. There remain vestiges of the attitude that "marketing" is a dirty word and that the activity is beneath august institutions such as universities and libraries. However, both types of institutions routinely engage in activities involved in marketing processes, beginning with formulating a mission statement, segmenting and understanding its audience, performing needs analysis, understanding the environment, and developing goals, objectives, and strategic plans. It is quite apparent that while many of the above social campaigns have employed some mass-media advertising, their efforts have included a far broader range of activities. The promotional piece is only one component of the marketing effort, albeit an essential one, to ensure adoption of ideas or behaviors.

Furthermore, social marketing campaigns have an advantage over commercial campaigns that can mitigate opposition to marketing activities. Commercial marketers rely heavily on expensive advertising, which consumers recognize and often discount as a biased source of information. Social marketing campaigns can ethically incorporate many forms of communication besides advertisements, and audiences, while they may disagree with the message, are not likely to disregard it based on the source organization's financial interests. The numerous "Race for the Cure" events every year are promotion for The Susan G. Komen Breast Cancer Foundation. Letters to the editor, editorials, gala events, and parade floats more often than not promote a change in attitude or behavior. Even dentists who hand out a new toothbrush and a container of floss at appointments are engaging in the communicative portion of a social marketing campaign, not promoting their dentistry practice.

Promotion is only one of the standard "four P's" marketing concept, the others being product, place, and price. In theory, a potential customer or client considers the combination of these elements in deciding whether to engage in the exchange. The product—for social marketers, the concept being advocated—is the most important component of the mix. What benefit or need does the product fill, and how completely is the need filled? Place refers to the distance—physical, cognitive, emotional or psychic, or technological—the potential customer would need to cross to partake. Price can of course be monetary, but can also refer to other types of costs incurred by the customer—time, embarrassment or other social forces, inconvenience, etc. Promotion comprises any communication serving to influence the customer.

Fine (1992) considers the four P's insufficient and adds three elements to the marketing mix: producer, purchasers (all audiences to whom the campaign is addressed), and probing (research and feedback). Additionally, while the primary objective for a social campaign is to promote ideas and behavior, there are often tangible elements of the campaign: for example, composting bins as part of a campaign to decrease material going to the landfill. When tangibles are part of the campaign, Kotler and Roberto (1989) add an additional three delivery-related components to the marketing mix: personnel, presentation, and process.

WHY CONSIDER MARKETING IN THE CONTEXT OF INFORMATION LITERACY?

A significant undercurrent running through the information literacy literature recognizes the struggle of getting students, faculty, or other stakeholders to collaborate or participate. In articles and in conference discussions, this frustration boils down to: "We have such great resources and ways of thinking; why don't more people use them?" On the other hand, there are also many accounts of techniques used to successfully convey information literacy concepts and incorporate them into learning. Information literacy is not about students completing a tutorial or even about their using the library. Though variants occur among local definitions, information literacy has as its ultimate goal an improvement in the cognitive behavior, habits, and abilities related to obtaining and processing information. Marketing information literacy is a combination of promoting ideas (that research is a process of exploration and synthesis, for example), practices (to question an author's credentials and biases), and tools (subscription databases, workshops in genealogical search strategies) that aid the adoption of those ideas and practices. The social marketing model is ideal for narrowing the gap between current information ideas, habits, and abilities and an information literate ideal. Adopting such an orientation for an information literacy program promises improvement on several fronts. From a management perspective, it will help organize efforts. It will also increase the likelihood that audiences will have their relevant needs met, and that its values and ideas are more widely adopted.

One interesting characteristic of social marketing campaigns is that those in similar fields tend to overlap and to feed off each other rather than to engage each other competitively. The women's suffrage movement influenced women to fill traditionally male jobs during the Second World War, which encouraged the feminist movement, the sexual revolution, the acceptance of birth control, and the conceptualization of sexual harassment as a social ill. Sargeant, Foreman, and Liao (2002) identify this potential for collaboration with other nonprofits, public sector, and private sector bodies as one of the differences between social marketing and commercial marketing campaigns. This characteristic is significant to those encouraging information literacy because of the potential for influence and integration between it and other educational constructs, such as general literacy, lifelong learning, first-year and capstone seminars, liberal studies, vocational training, and service learning. In addition to promotion of information literacy ideals, marketing a program can also lend strength to related ideas. Librarians should also keep an open mind for engaging with established or emerging initiatives that dovetail with information literacy goals.

THE MARKETING MIX APPLIED TO INFORMATION LITERACY: THE 10 P'S

Librarians and others interested in information literacy have shifted focus from library instruction primarily concerned with information tools, toward a whole information study. However, presentations and use of information tools remain a vital component of information literacy programs, and while many presentations and tools are now electronic, I consider them tangible products. For this reason, I consider Kotler and Roberto's three elements in addition to Fine's seven in an information literacy marketing mix. Of course, I am speaking of information literacy in general terms. Individual programs need a thoughtful analysis of their own marketing mix, dependent upon the established goals, the target audience, and the local environment.

Purchasers (and Market Segments)

Of course, the word "purchaser" is purely theoretical; even in commercial marketing the audience is usually a potential and not an active purchaser. In noncommercial marketing, purchasers simply refers to those whom the producer tries to convince with the campaign. They are the various audiences for the market.

In considering purchasers, commercial marketing is a simple two-point model: the business markets the product or service to the customer, and the customer pays the business (see Figure 15-1).

In a public or non-profit organization (P/NPO), the recipient audience is generally separate from the paying audience. Therefore, marketing for this

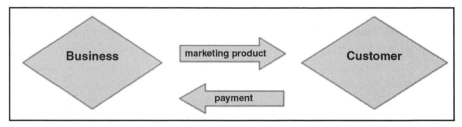

Figure 15-1: Purchasers Model

sector is a three-point model, with the organization marketing in two directions (see Figure 15-2).

Concept marketing also involves multiple audiences in cases where individuals adopt the ideas or actions, but intermediate agencies control policies or access. For example, a campaign that teaches low-income parents about nutrition and encourages healthy meals for their children can only succeed if the local markets carry fresh produce and whole grains and if a local farmers' market accepts food stamp benefits. Information literacy programs also have dual audiences—the individual adopters and any "gatekeepers" for the institution (see Figure 15-3).

So leaders of an information literacy program need to analyze the environment to consider all market audiences, not only the most obvious beneficiaries of the program.

The fact that there are multiple audiences for an information literacy program leads to the need for market segmentation. Marketers look for shared characteristics, needs, ideas, attitudes, and habits among potential adopters in order to formulate more effective marketing plans. Certainly librarians are accustomed to doing market segmentation: for example, we recognize the different

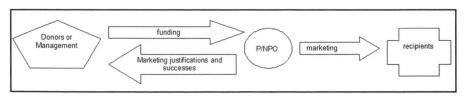

Figure 15-2: Public or NPO Model

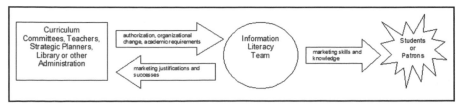

Figure 15.3: Multiple Audiences Model

needs our child and teen patrons have from our adult patrons. Within the context of information literacy, too, the identified segments will have different marketing needs, and they will be attracted to various benefits. Whereas students strive for better grades with less time working, the instructor wishes for her classes as a whole to use more reliable source material. Curriculum review committees and campus administration concern themselves with other outcomes, and the information literacy marketer should address how the program meets those needs. Karp (2006: 117, 120) suggests gathering library use and information literacy data that could speak to typical concerns of an academic institution:

- better semester-to-semester persistence
- better overall retention
- higher graduation rates
- decreased time to degree

Market segments can be defined by other (or additional) factors besides academic role, of course. An information literacy team may choose to identify genealogists and local history buffs as one market segment, and beginning computer users as another. College students are often segmented into first-years who need orientations and basic research skills, those beginning their majors and entering into the disciplinary research, and those who are embarking upon their thesis or dissertation. Market segmentation needs to occur to a point at which the group's similar needs can be met efficiently. Identifying meaningful marketing segments relies on a lowest-common denominator approach and is organization-centric. Good segmentation allows for better communication of purchasers' needs and of the product's relevance to those needs.

Product

What is it we are marketing when we market information literacy? The information literacy team should answer this question as they define the concept for the campus or community. There may be a temptation to define the concept in a straightforward and uniform manner. Instead, to think as a marketer, consider the perspective of each market segment: "What need or problem do I have? How will information literacy make life better or easier? What value does this idea have for me or for the community?" The purchaser should be able to visualize how life could improve if they were to adopt the information literacy ideas and practices. Toothpaste or minivan marketers do not simply define their products in an objective manner; they define them as the solutions to the purchasers' problems (fresh breath and fewer cavities, or room and entertainment for families busy with activities and road travel). Social marketers also define ideas and behaviors as the answers to problems in the social realm: the need to euthanize animals will decrease if pets are spayed or neutered; children who walk or bike to school will likely avoid obesity; brain injuries can be averted by wearing a helmet while biking.

Information literacy is not an end unto itself. Nobody aspires to it. Its habits of mind serve an individual for multiple purposes at varying times, but simply the state of being information literate has no value to anyone. It is also a complex set of concepts and skills, and it is imperative to express what we're doing that is meaningful to the intended audience. Generally in information literacy, the concept being sold is a set of abilities, that of finding relevant information efficiently, of considering the source, bias, format, and limits of the information, and of using the information appropriately in terms of context, standards, legalities, and ethics. From the perspective of a college student, the products of these concepts may lay in more successful assignments or a higher GPA, more time freed from searching, a sense of direction and control, and sanity when dealing with information. For senior citizens, the relevant product could be interesting and cost-effective travel, safety from financial scams, or deeper roots on the family tree.

Producer

In most cases for readers of this text, the primary producer of the information literacy message will be the library. There may be alternate or ancillary designers of the concept, as well, such as instructors of research skills and campus computing units. The marketer should assess the target audience's knowledge and perception of the producer. Does the audience consider the library (or other producer) a "trusted and credible source" (Fine, 1992: 6)? It may be tempting to immediately say, "Yes, of course" to this question. However, it is beneficial to consider the question closely and honestly and in regards to the goals of the marketing campaign. If the audience's knowledge or perception of the message producer is low, the marketer may choose to find a "spokesperson"—it may be an individual or a group—who is more recognizable to the audience or more credible to them.

Place

The marketer considers the various distances (physical, logistical, cognitive, attitudinal, or technological) the customers must traverse to adopt the practice or idea. If the idea is totally new to them, creating the shortest distances possible is important. If it is a familiar idea to the audience, the marketer determines how inclined the audience is to adopt it: the weaker the inclination, the greater the need for short distance. If marketing a subscription database, a consideration of place includes the number of clicks from the patron's opening Web page to the database's search screen, but it also includes the knowledge of and any previous experience using the database. If the information product is a successfully completed assignment, place takes account of the distance between the student and the necessary cognitive skills.

Fine (1992: 8) supplies a related interpretation of "place," which is the position of the producer relative to the target audience, accounting for any intermediaries. In an efficient marketing channel, the intermediaries perform distinct and necessary roles. For a widget, the path from producer to consumer typically includes two institutional intermediaries: wholesalers and retailers. Intermediaries should perform functions that benefit the producer and that help create the shortest distance possible between consumer and product. In considering information literacy concepts as the products, intermediaries could be groups or institutions such as classroom instructors or graduate assistants, campus computing units, database vendors and search sites, or perhaps textbooks. In some instances, the library (as producer of information literacy product) communicates directly with the patron. In many other cases, the library depends upon classroom instructors to communicate the message to the target audience. Some bibliographic database vendors have recently pressed beyond the function of finding information to communicate other aspects of information literacy; providing formatted citations makes it easier for students to use the information ethically, and built-in information management services encourage users to engage in another aspect of information literacy. The library-producer then has, in any intermediary, additional markets to consider.

Price

Price refers to anything of value that the purchaser must give up in exchange for the product. In a social marketing campaign, presuming the purchaser is motivated to change ideas, behavior, habits, and abilities, the cost of such change will often be in terms of time, convenience, comfort, and routine. Furthermore, the level of motivation relates directly to the price the purchaser is willing to incur. If I am mildly interested in changing to a vegetarian diet, I may only accommodate a small disruption in time and convenience in order to shop, cook, and eat according to my new ideal. If I am highly motivated to being vegetarian, however, I may go out of my way for groceries or spend considerable time learning how to cook tasty and enticing tofu.

To improve performance on a primary-source local history assignment, a student might move away from the comfort zone of search engines and databases and delve into the relatively un-indexed world of microfilmed newspapers. If faculty want to see a larger percentage of student bibliographies be to peer-reviewed journals, the price to them may be devoting class time to exposing students to what peer-reviewed journals are and how to find them. The marketer's role here is to know what the price is to the target audience and to make clear to them the value of the product.

Probing

The marketer continually identifies the current and upcoming needs, desires, and values of the target audience. The data mined from careful and current research can provide direction to improve the information literacy products offered, as well as the messages used to promote them. Surveys and focus groups are certainly a few methods of gathering such data, but it is imperative that the data be analyzed and that action result from the findings (Fine, 1992). The librarian involved in marketing information literacy should also pay attention to indicators of information needs—values and trends—such as campus or community news and opinion outlets. Relevant statistics and research can provide clues, as can secondary analysis of other survey data (Kotler and Roberto, 1989).

Personnel

The marketer-librarian has an interest in ensuring that anyone involved in presenting information literacy messages is well trained and uses appropriate interpersonal skills. This applies to student or volunteer employees who work with, in the vicinity of, or for the public as much as it does to the professional librarians. Because information literacy is an intangible product, potential and current audiences do not separate it from those who provide it. Kotler and Roberto (1989) cite five personnel-related expectations identified by Parasuraman, Zeithaml, and Berry in 1985: that personnel be responsive, competent, courteous, credible, and sensitive. These qualities mean that, to promote information literacy, librarians should respect the patron's current information skills and preferences while also trying to strengthen skills such as questioning, searching, evaluating, and using information. They also require that people answering the phone or reshelving materials are approachable, have an appropriate base of knowledge about the concepts and objectives of information literacy, understand the limits of their own knowledge, and know how to effectively refer patrons.

Presentation

Presentation refers to the use of tools, facilities, packaging, and style in the product delivery in order to entice the target audience and to help them adopt the desired idea or behavior. For example, many churches offer contemporary services to attract young worshipers; these services package the church-going experience with presentation software and audiovisual technology, pop music, nursery service, a casual rhetorical style, and alternate worship spaces, times, and materials compared to traditional services. For information literacy, the marketer should consider whether facilities or packaging present any barriers to adoption and should redesign the presentation so that the target audience can identify with and be attracted to the idea or action. Simple technology and friendly service encourages chat reference patrons to continue asking questions. Citation managers support students' need to create well-formatted citations to a complex set of references. And the simplicity of the *Google* search screen had a huge impact on popularizing the search engine, and it is a presentation that some libraries now mimic.

Process

Process comprises the activities and timing involved for someone to take part in the social campaign (Kotler and Roberto, 1989). A process that is well-coordinated by the marketer is more likely to retain those who "trial adopt," than a process that includes perplexing activities and schedules that disrespect the time of the target audience. Particularly for a classroom instructor who has never before scheduled a library session for a specific class, the session's activities need to be relevant to the curriculum, and the time needed to schedule, plan, and evaluate the session needs to be reasonable. To think of an information literacy process with a marketing lens is to consider the target behaviors and skills from the perspective of a student or other intended audience.

Promotion

After considering all other components of the marketing mix, the information literacy marketer may at last delve into promotion, or the actual communication with the target audience. Based on the needs of the market and the objectives of the campaign, promotion entails the type and content of the message as well as the medium through which it is delivered. To develop an appropriate promotion, the marketer considers what reaction the target audience should have. Elliott de Sáez (2002) explains the Attention Interest Desire Action (AIDA) model of desired responses. In a cognitive response, the target audience becomes *aware* of the product and focuses attention on it. The next level of response is the affective and emotional response, in which the audience's *interest* is piqued and they *desire* to know more or to use the service. In a behavioral response, the audience is induced to *act*. This latter type of promotion is generally in the form of a coupon or special deal in commercial contexts; a familiar example of behavioral intent within the social marketing context is the range of premiums offered to public broadcasting donors.

As mentioned earlier in the chapter, social marketers have at their disposal an array of promotional formats. Social marketers can and do run advertisements in media outlets, and flyers and brochures are standard among libraries and other public and non-profit campaigns. But libraries can invest all types of communication with promotion of information literacy. Direct marketing allows for well-timed and personalized messages to individuals identified through good data sources to be likely customers. General e-mail messages are increasingly ignored or blocked as spam, but messages sent through courseware may catch students' attention. Annual reports should address the goals and the current state of the information literacy program, and in addition to administrators, it can be presented (possibly in a modified package) to patrons and potential patrons.

Libraries routinely employ bulletin boards and display cases (within or outside of the library), event booths and parade entries, and take-away communicators such as magnets, pencils, and bookmarks; information literacy marketers can ensure that these tools communicate more than basic literacy and love of the library (however important these ideals are) and that they help keep information literacy messages in front of the target audience.

Regardless of the communication format, storytelling can do much of the promotional work and compel the audience to receive the message. Good promotional materials have characters and action, plot, conflict, and resolution (State Library of Iowa, 2006). The stories can be testimonials from satisfied customers; they can also be fanciful stories that, while untrue in the literal sense, highlight the genuine value of your service or resource. Appropriate visuals enhance storytelling; graphics might be performance charts or candid or posed photos, but they should tell a story unto themselves rather than stand inert. As any children's librarian knows, stories and pictures dramatize the abstract and stimulate emotions; they allow people to understand, believe, and sometimes even act differently.

In the library world, promotions tend to focus primarily on the searching and finding component and ignore other aspects of information literacy such as using and evaluating information. In addition, the vast majority of them use styles and messages that result in audience awareness or interest. Summer reading programs use promotions that reward action; the more the child reads, the better (or more) prizes he or she earns. The challenges for information literacy marketers are to campaign for the higher-order knowledge and competencies and to develop promotions in which the intended responses move beyond knowledge and interest and into behavior.

THE OVERLAP OF MARKETING WITH OTHER ACTIVITIES

This chapter has discussed the several necessary considerations of a complete marketing plan. Rather than conceive information literacy marketing as bookmarks and brochures to announce what we have available, a complete definition of marketing encompasses the activities that we already conduct for information literacy programs and other library services: segmenting our total audience into groups with shared characteristics, setting priorities within the information literacy goals, identification of a target audience, analysis of the audience's knowledge and needs, setting goals for the campaign, planning and implementation, assessment, and monitoring and adapting to product, audience, and environmental changes. In other words, marketing is not an afterthought activity to embark upon when you are ready for your public; the activities of marketing *are* the activities of program development.

As the stakeholders formulate the information literacy mission statement, marketing should be on their minds. What relevance does this have to the audience?

What gaps exist in the audience's knowledge, skills, and motivation related to information literacy? When planners hold the perspective of the audience from the beginning of the process, the work of publicity, when the time comes, is partly done.

The activities involved in general library planning go a long way toward preparing a marketing plan. Planning takes account of the current situation, environment, and activity. The analysis of the present considers strengths and challenges, threats (including current or potential competition), opportunities (including current or potential partners), and trends. A marketing plan should take direction from the mission statement (what the organization strives to do in the short-term) as well as from the vision statement (that which the organization aspires to). Marketing goals and objectives should be integrated with the broader goals and objectives. Doing so will ensure that marketing is not left as an afterthought, and resources such as people, time, partners, equipment and supplies, and budget can be allocated accordingly. Perhaps the whole library plan will take a broad view of marketing, and the information literacy team can use the plan as a springboard into a more focused needs assessment and marketing plan.

EXAMPLES OF MARKETING INFORMATION LITERACY

This section summarizes each of the ten "P" marketing facets in terms of information literacy. It also highlights information literacy marketing campaigns (some general and some named campaigns) that demonstrate how the marketers considered the facet. For simplicity, the word "patrons" is used throughout the definitions, but it always refers to a range of potential target audiences—students, budgeting agencies, or other identified group.

Purchasers: *Patrons (or subgroups of them) whose ideas, beliefs, or actions surrounding information the campaign seeks to change. Also curriculum committees and teachers, planners, managers, and funding sources that impact information policies and access.*

- University of Dayton's Roesch Library flyer for first-year students just moving in doesn't overwhelm them with databases and statistics (Alonzo, n.d.). The flyer meshes promotion of the organization and location of the library and an upcoming event with promotion of information ideas, beliefs, or actions. It is notable for recognizing who the audience is and what information they need immediately and in the near future: recognition of the library building, knowledge of how to pronounce its name, and the fact that jobs are available.
- The Institute for Information Literacy Executive Board (2006) succinctly explains the concepts of information literacy and cites programs and articles of note. The brief guide respects the time of the audience and focuses

on ideas that would be meaningful for a decision-maker new to the idea of an information literacy program.

Product: *The solution to a problem, or the answer to a need, that can be reached if patrons adopt the information idea, belief, or behavior.*

- LibrarySmart's "Rocket" and "Stock Tip" TV ads convey, from the purchaser's point of view, the product of consulting with a librarian or of using library-selected resources—academic or personal successes (Washington State Library, 2001).
- Hocking College Library promotes the availability of feature films, music CDs, and leisure reading at the local Nelsonville Public Library (Ator-James, 2005).

Producer: *The library, information and media center, instructor or other organization or authority figure advocating the information idea, belief, or behavior. A celebrity spokesperson or an average person can substitute as the advocate.*

- Libraries serve as proud producers for many information literacy promotions, including pathfinders, building directional signs, and Web pages.
- The State Library of Iowa (2006) features library patrons' statements of why they value their library; several of them address information literacy concepts. These patrons speak in place of the true producer of the message. (See "John & Shane," "Diane," "Erling," "Kathy," "Deb," "Hannah-Pat-Kayla," "Ray-S," and "Diane M" for information literacy concepts.)

Place: *The reduction of physical, logistical, cognitive, attitudinal, or technological barriers between the patrons and their change in information ideas, beliefs, or behaviors.*

- The placement of links, in as well as outside of the library's Web, to online reference and other electronic resources.
- The KSL Reference Weblog (2006) provides an example of an RSS feed that promotes research techniques and information tools and that has the ability to push information literacy messages to those who have expressed interest.

Price: *The amount of time, convenience, comfort, routine, or money the patron is willing to trade for the product.*

- Ator-James (2005) focuses on the easy directions between the two libraries and the convenience that students only need one library card. The message is that students who use the public library for their leisure materials will not incur a significant price.
- The State Library of Iowa (2006) provides customizable PowerPoint budget presentations which emphasize the informational needs of the

people and of the community, and then examines the personnel and collection funding resources that are required to meet those needs.

Probing: *The identification of needs, desires, and values of patrons in order to develop information literacy products and to improve the promotion of them.*

- As of this writing, over 80 institutions of higher education have administered SAILS, a formal instrument that tests information literacy skills of undergraduate cohorts for benchmarking and for institutional comparison (Project SAILS, 2006).
- Washington State Library (2001) provides the complete and summarized results from its marketing survey on library usage. The questions do not address information literacy directly, but responses to such questions could serve as indicators.

Personnel: *People in a position to optimistically impart or encourage information ideas, beliefs, or behaviors.*

- Lindsay (2003) discusses a program in which select undergraduates study to become peer facilitators for Washington State University's freshman seminar, in which "students learn how to increase their problem-solving skills, develop research strategies, critically evaluate information sources, and use technology to investigate and present information."
- Everyone in the library organization who has direct interaction with either patrons or gatekeepers, should have some ability to kindly encourage, according to their role and responsibility, good information ideas, beliefs, and behaviors. Volunteer shelvers, for example, can guide a patron to a call number if asked, but they should also be trained to personally introduce that patron to a reference librarian when approached with a larger question. The everyday behavior and operations of public service workers impacts the successful promotion of information literacy.

Presentation: *The style, facilities, tools, and packaging used to entice patrons to adopt information ideas, beliefs, or behaviors.*

- Polanka (2003) provides an example of personalized letters that are welcoming and encouraging. She also promotes the chat reference service, which itself is an example of presentation.
- Academic and public libraries create profiles on social networking sites in order to make connections with teenagers and young adults. The sites encourage information literacy by promoting librarian-developed resource pages, inviting reference questions and teaching skills (such as citing sources) through profiles and blogs.

Process: *The activities and timing involved for a patron to adopt information ideas, beliefs, or behaviors.*

- The many online information literacy tutorials involve a process where a patron enters in a series of activities in order to change his or her ideas, beliefs, or behavior regarding information.
- Invitations to ask for research assistance in a variety of ways—in person, by phone, or through e-mail, chat or instant messaging software—allows for a wide range of timing and communication methods that encourage ideas, beliefs, and behaviors surrounding information.

Promotion: *Any communication about the information product directed to the patron by the library or other producer. Promotion includes both the message and its medium, and the intent is that the patron gains awareness, becomes interested, or takes action.*

- All of the communications above are examples of information literacy promotion. In addition, more broadly-defined library campaigns (such as the Campaign for America's Libraries) usually have some promotions that target information literacy concepts specifically.
- Valenza (2004) provides excellent customizable examples of promotional brochures, PowerPoint presentations, letters, instructional worksheets, assessment and other administrative tools whose audiences include students, parents, teachers, teacher-librarians themselves, administrators, and school boards. Information literacy serves as Valenza's common frame for all of the content; as such, she presents a wide variety of promotional communication.

CONCLUSION

Because proponents of information literacy seek improvement in how people understand and interact with the world of information, social marketing is a useful construct for promoting its programs. The model de-emphasizes the commercial connotation of marketing and conforms to the ideals and resources of public and non-profit organizations such as libraries and schools. Social marketing also accommodates the complexity that information literacy encompasses: promoting multiple ideas, practices, and tools; targeting both recipient adopters and sponsoring adopters; and collaborating, not competing, with related movements. Marketing emphasizes the needs and reactions of the audience rather than the offerings and desires of the organization, and as such, it overlaps with the efforts of libraries to become more patron centered. A library or information literacy team that considers the ten facets of the social marketing mix can anticipate that patrons see solutions to their problems and that they adopt these ideas and behaviors.

REFERENCES

Alonzo, A. "Top ten reasons to visit Roesch Library." Unpublished manuscript, University of Dayton, Dayton, OH. Available: www.ohiolink.edu/ostaff/marketing/gallery/UDtoptenflyer.pdf (accessed August 21, 2006).

Ator-James, C. 2005. "One card, two libraries." Unpublished manuscript, Hocking College, Nelsonville, OH. Available: www.ohiolink.edu/ostaff/marketing/gallery/HockingCbrochure05.pdf (accessed August 21, 2006).

de Saez, E. 2002. *Marketing concepts for libraries and information services.* 2nd ed. London: Facet Publishing.

Fine, S. H. 1992. "Introduction to social marketing." In *Marketing the public sector: Promoting the causes of public and nonprofit agencies* (pp. 1–11). New Brunswick, NJ: Transaction.

Institute for Information Literacy Executive Board. "Information literacy for faculty and administrators." In *ACRL information literacy* (last updated February 24, 2006). Available: www.ala.org/ala/acrl/acrlissues/acrlinfolit/infolitoverview/infolitfor-fac/infolitfaculty.htm (accessed August 21, 2006).

Karp, R. 2006. "Seeing the library in the broader context on campus: Marketing our services." In D. R. Dowell, and G. B. McCabe, eds., *It's all about student learning: Managing community and other college libraries in the 21st century* (pp. 101–122). Westport, CT: Libraries Unlimited.

Kotler, P., and E. L. Roberto. 1989. *Social marketing: Strategies for changing public behavior.* New York: Free Press.

"KSL reference weblog." 2006. Available: http://blog.case.edu/orgs/ksl/reference/ (accessed August 21, 2006).

Lindsay, E. B. 2003. "A collaborative approach to information literacy in the freshman seminar." *Academic Exchange Quarterly*, Vol. 7, no. 3: 23–27. Available: www.rapidintellect.com/AEQweb/mo2456may.htm (accessed August 20, 2006).

Polanka, S. 2003. "UDundmusic20.doc." Unpublished manuscript, University of Dayton, Dayton, OH. Available: www.ohiolink.edu/ostaff/marketing/gallery/UDundmusic20.doc (accessed August 21, 2006).

"Project SAILS: Standardized assessment of information literacy skills." (Last updated 2006.) Available: www.projectsails.org (accessed August 21, 2006).

Sargeant, A., S. Foreman, and M-N. Liao. 2002. "Operationalizing the marketing concept in the nonprofit sector." *Journal of Nonprofit & Public Sector Marketing*, Vol. 10, no. 2: 41–65.

State Library of Iowa. 2006. "Telling the library story tool kit." Available: www.statelibraryofiowa.org/ld/tell-library-story (accessed August 21, 2006).

Valenza, J. K. 2004. *Power tools recharged: 125+ essential forms and presentations for your school library information program.* Chicago: American Library Association.

Washington State Library. 2001. "LibrarySmart: When you really need to know." Available: www.librarysmart.com/working/home.asp (accessed August 21, 2006).

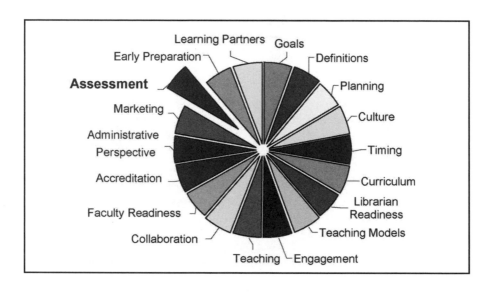

ASSESSMENT

A Word from the Editors

*H*ow do we know that our instructional activities have affected learning? That is the question that Bonnie Gratch-Lindauer answers in this comprehensive and clear look at the role of assessment in the development, revision, and refinement of information literacy programs. Bonnie, currently the Coordinator of Instructional Services at the Rosenberg Library, City College of San Francisco, is a well-known author in the field of information literacy and outcomes assessment. Bonnie's M.L.S. is from Syracuse University and she also has an M.P.A. from the State University of New York, Brockport. Bonnie also has a secondary teaching credential from San Francisco State University. Her article "Defining and Measuring the Library's Impact on Campus-Wide Outcomes" won both the K.G. Saur Award as well as the Association of College and Research Libraries Instruction Section publication award. Drawing from her extensive experience in such activities as the Bay Area information competency assessment project or her service on the executive committee of ACRL's Institute for Information Literacy, Bonnie covers in this chapter the elements of developing an assessment plan, an overview of assessment methods and measures aligned with IL program components, and the importance of communicating assessment results. Bonnie demystifies the features of program assessments, provides a primer for the uninitiated in assessment, and brings forward many thoughtful points for those who already have some background in this area. Writing to the editors, Bonnie cited a quote from Patricia Ianuzzi speaking on "Information Literacy—Laying the Foundations" at the Library Association of the City of New York (LACUNY) Institute in 2000. Bonnie felt this quote summed up the right attitude towards assessment: "Assessment is the means for learning, not just the method of evaluation."

Chapter 16

Information Literacy Program Development:
The Role of Assessment

By Bonnie Gratch-Lindauer

THE ROLES OF ASSESSMENT

In this chapter, the terms evaluation and assessment are used interchangeably, although the author recognizes that for some these terms have different meanings. Assessment with a small "a" and a capital "A" is part of all aspects of a vital information literacy program, from development to revision and refinement. As the chapter quote points out, the primary reason to do assessment is to learn how our instructional activities affect learning. In fact, one of the distinguishing characteristics of an information literacy program plan, as opposed to a bibliographic instruction plan, is the degree to which the statement of student learning outcomes, and learning and assessment opportunities are integrated within the curriculum, demonstrating the shared responsibility required for teaching and assessing information literacy. This chapter covers elements of developing an assessment plan, assessment of specific program components, an overview of assessment methods and measures, and a brief mention about communicating assessment results. Since in-depth coverage of the how-to of assessing student learning outcomes cannot be adequately developed in a chapter, the reader will be referred to several useful books on assessment of learning outcomes that have been published in the past five years.

There are at least three major roles that assessment plays in an information literacy program. Undoubtedly the major purpose is to improve learning—not just student learning, but also faculty and librarians, and others who have a part in designing and revising information literacy learning activities. Moreover, information literacy is integral to learning in any area of study, thus assessment of what learners know and can do related to how they use information is fundamental to their academic achievement, careers, and lifelong learning. Assessing learning and the learning-teaching dynamic is what drives the small "a" in the assessment of IL programs. It is the daily feedback gained from teaching and observing learners engaged in doing information research in the classroom or in the library, as well as the more formal evaluation of instructional program components.

Another role that assessment often plays in information literacy program development and revision relates to building and improving external communication and collaboration, as well as improving internal communication. Information literacy assessment at the course, program, and institutional levels involves outreach and communication, raising awareness, and faculty-librarian collaboration in the design and implementation of assessment activities. This external role has the potential to directly contribute to valued course and program goals and priorities, especially when information literacy abilities/skills are infused in academic programs (e.g., within a major/vocational program); in targeted student programs (e.g., first-year programs, retention programs); and are a part of institutional learning outcomes (e.g., general education/core abilities).

A third role relates to how assessment findings can improve overall services making the library more accessible and responsive. James Madison University's well established program illustrates such service changes. Its online IL tutorial and assessment instrument kept being revised to better reflect IL competencies that faculty came to recognize were important based on assessment findings and curriculum change. The benefits of this several-year process include: "Assessment has influenced decisions from the choice of an online catalog to the design of the library's homepage. It has guided allocation of resources, causing us to bolster important services and keeping us from cutting services that are more useful than we had realized" (Cameron, 2004: 234). To illustrate these roles at one institution, an example is used of how the library staff at Pierce College in Washington used an assessment cycle approach internally and externally to improve communication and collaboration within the library and across campus.

Pierce College Library established a departmental assessment process which "led to identifying public outcomes, assessments, and criteria for all library departments, and setting up a standard assessment process library-wide" (Miller and Pellen, 2004: 192). Starting with rewriting the library mission as outcomes and then specifying indicators of how the outcome would be measured, the staff more clearly recognized their connections and contributions to student success. As one example, the reference librarians identified the following outcome and indicator related to information literacy:

Outcome: Respond appropriately and pedagogically to individuals' reference questions, in order to develop confident, competent and independent information seekers.

Indicator: Model and teach appropriate information-competent behavior and practices. (Miller and Pellen, 2004: 194)

Using periodic student surveys, they found after a year that 90 percent of students, which is 10 percent higher than the assessment criterion they had established, stated that they learned something of value they can apply in the future and that the learning will positively enable their completion of their current project. After a year of various assessment activities, analysis, and discussions about the findings, the library staff found that "once staff members were invested in the assessment cycle, outcomes became a seamless part of how we work instead of the work itself" (Miller and Pellen, 2004: 195).

Pierce College is fortunate to have information competency defined as one of the five core abilities described in the college's strategic plan, and an institutional goal of increasing the number of campus constituents who teach and model the five core abilities. Through a series of workshops, the library faculty worked in collaboration with discipline-based faculty to establish a clearer definition and understanding of information competency within their own disciplines with the goal of increasing the number of courses, assignments, and programs that integrate information competency. After a couple of years of outreach and collaboration, the results have been impressive: in 2002, 42 out of 48 departments (80 percent) participated in integrated library instruction, reaching an increasing number of students and building stronger relationships between librarians and discipline-based faculty (Miller and Pellen, 2004: 202).

The roles and effects of assessing information literacy are many: assessment fuels improvements in learning and teaching; it can help grow and strengthen relationships among all the constituents in the organization; and with time, it offers the potential to change the organizational culture so that it truly becomes the means for learning and change.

PROGRAM ASSESSMENT AND ASSESSING
STUDENT LEARNING: KEY FEATURES

Assessment with a capital "A" encompasses an entire instruction/information literacy program and is most commonly needed for program review, annual reports, and accreditation self-studies. Institutions with information literacy integrated in general education/core competencies and those with IL graduation requirements and/or system-wide or state-wide competency-based requirements, may have an even greater assessment responsibility, and in some cases their institutions' level of funding may even be related to demonstrated IL competencies. Two examples describing this type of state-wide, competency-based situation and the role of assessment include James Madison University Libraries' experience with revising the online tutorial "Go for the Gold" and the development and revision of the information seeking skills test (Cameron, 2004) and the Citadel's Daniel Library, South Carolina, where funding for colleges and universities is determined by how well each meets a set of 37 performance indicators (Carter, 2002).

All program assessments take place in the context of a development-feedback-revision loop process. Nearly all writers on assessment planning describe a cycle of assessment, grounded in the institution's mission and overall educational objectives, which includes the steps of:

Identifying objectives ➜ Gathering evidence ➜ Interpreting evidence ➜

Implementing changes and improvements ➜ Publicizing/reporting findings ➜

Reviewing/revising objectives ➜ and so on, repeating the cycle.

Even when the focus of the assessment is student learning outcomes, it is useful to also look at how other program components may have affected learning. Indeed, the "Principles of Good Practice for Assessing Student Learning" direct attention to not only assessment of student learning outcomes, but also the experiences that lead to learning (Astin, accessed: 2006). Especially at the program level, those experiences that directly contribute to the development of information literate individuals are just as important to measure and assess; such as aspects about the quality of the learning environment, the effectiveness of the instructor and the learning materials, and the quality of the learning opportunities. Assessing the changes and accomplishments of an entire program, or several of the program components at specific points in time, and combining a variety of use data, qualitative data about users' perceptions of specific program components, and findings from different types of evaluations of student learning constitute IL program assessment. In short, the focus is on the whole instead of only one or two of its parts.

Over the past ten years or so outcomes assessment has been emphasized in all segments of education, largely because of accountability concerns and the revised regional and professional association accreditation standards. Outcomes assessment focuses on the achievement of outcomes that have been identified as desirable in the information literacy program's goals and objectives, along with identifying performance measures that indicate how well the program or learner is doing in relation to the stated goals and objectives. Our profession has mirrored the outcomes assessment movement with the publication of several standards and guidelines that include outcomes assessment, such as the "Standards for Libraries in Higher Education," which includes considerable amount of text describing the importance of outcomes and outcomes assessment along with other more traditional measures of program effectiveness (ACRL, 2004); and the "Characteristics of Programs of Information Literacy that Illustrate Best Practices: A Guideline" which distinguishes between assessment of an IL program and student learning outcomes.

For program evaluation:

- establishes the process of ongoing planning/improvement of the program
- measures direct progress toward meeting the goals and objectives of the program
- integrates with course and curriculum assessment, as well as institutional evaluations and regional/professional accreditation initiatives
- assumes multiple methods and purposes for assessment/evaluation
  - formative and summative
  - short-term and longitudinal

For student outcomes:

- acknowledges differences in learning and teaching styles by using a variety of appropriate outcome measures, such as portfolio assessment, oral defense, quizzes, essays, direct observation, anecdotal, peer and self review, and experience
- focuses on student performance, knowledge acquisition, and attitude appraisal
- assesses both process and product
- includes student-, peer-, and self-evaluation (ACRL, 2003a)

Still another is the ACRL document, "Guidelines for Instruction Programs in Academic Libraries," which specifies the need for systematic ongoing assessment and describes five practices essential to good information literacy assessment:

- There should be a program evaluation plan addressing multiple measures or methods of evaluation; such measures may include needs assessment, participant reaction, learning outcomes, teaching effectiveness, and overall effectiveness of instruction.
- The criteria for program evaluation should be articulated in readily available documents pertaining to the program's mission, description, and outcomes.
- Specific learning outcomes should be addressed and specific assessment methods should be identified.
- Coordination of assessment with teaching faculty is important because learning outcomes are a shared responsibility.
- Data for both program evaluation and assessment of specific learning outcomes should be gathered regularly and brought into the program revision process so that the program can be improved continuously, and

specific learning deficits addressed in an ongoing, formative manner (ACRL, 2003b).

The ACRL guidelines/best practices documents referenced above reinforce several key elements that are essential to assessing information literacy programs:

- having an on-going assessment process and/or evaluation plan based on goals and objectives tied to institutional goals and educational priorities and with specified criteria for program evaluation which integrate with course, curriculum/program and institutional assessments
- identifying specific student learning outcomes that focus on student performance, knowledge acquisition, and attitude appraisal and that is addressed by a variety of assessment methods
- using the results of assessment activities for continuous improvement
- coordinating assessment activities with discipline-based faculty and other relevant academic staff because IL and its assessment is a shared responsibility

THE ASSESSMENT PLAN/PLANNING PROCESS

Developing an assessment plan, like all planning, guides the process and helps to ensure improvement of program and student learning goals and objectives. In fact, creating or revising the information literacy plan is the perfect time to incorporate thinking about how the instructional objectives and expected outcomes will be evaluated, thus linking instructional planning and assessment planning. Depending on the size and nature of the institution, libraries might:

1. develop a separate IL assessment plan—e.g., Indiana University—Bloomington Libraries, www.indiana. edu/~libinstr/Information_Literacy/assessment.html *or* Gustavus Adolphus College Library, www.gustavus. edu/oncampus/ academics/library/Pubs/AssessmentPlan.html *or* Suffolk University, Mildred F. Sawyer Library, www.suffolk.edu/ sawlib/plandocs/current_student_assessment_plan.htm
2. integrate assessment plans within a variety of courses and programs—e.g., Weber State University Library, http://faculty.weber.edu/chansen/libinstruct/ILProgram/assessment.htm *or* King's College's Comprehensive Assessment Program, www.kings.edu/ Academics/capprogramcomponents.htm#6 *or* Wartburg College Library, www.wartburg.edu/library/infolit/
3. embed assessment objectives and strategies within an information literacy program plan—e.g., University of Arizona Libraries, http://dizzy.library. arizona.edu/library/teams/InfoLit2000/InfoFluencyProgram%20Plan%20July%202004.pdf

4. integrate information literacy assessment activities in the library's assessment plan or institutional plan—e.g., Paradise Valley Community College Library, www.pvc.maricopa.edu/library/assessment/PVCCLibrary AssessmentPlanSpring2004-Spring2006.pdf *or* University of Northern Colorado Libraries, www.unco.edu/library/assessment/plan.pdf *or* University of Iowa's Strategic Plan 2004–2009, which has a piece relating to information literacy outcomes and assessment, www.lib.uiowa.edu/admin/strategic-plan.html

Peggy L. Maki, higher education consultant on learning assessment, has written extensively about planning for assessment. She refers to an "assessment guide" that can help institutions to conceptualize a plan that integrates assessment into their organizational cultures (Maki, 2002: 12). The elements of this guide are quite comprehensive, containing three major parts with sub-activities that are not necessarily linear or lock-step, but suggest areas about which discussion points need to occur and decisions need to be made:

1. determining the institution's expectations
   - state expected outcomes
   - identify where expected outcomes are addressed in the instructional program
   - determine methods and criteria to assess expected outcomes
   - state institution's or program's level of expected performance (e.g., score on an examination or culminating project)
   - identify and collect baseline data/information
2. determining timing, identifying cohort(s), and assigning responsibility
   - determine who will be assessed
   - establish a schedule for assessment
   - determine who will interpret results
3. interpreting and sharing results to enhance institutional effectiveness
   - interpret how results will inform teaching/learning and decision-making about need for revision (e.g., revise freshman orientation program to include more active learning activities)
   - determine how and with whom you will share findings and interpretations
   - decide how your institution will follow up on implemented changes (Maki, 2002: 9–12)

She provides useful explanations, examples and advice regarding each of these sub-activities. Throughout she stresses the partnerships across the campus that are involved in these sub-activities and the importance of knowing the local organizational culture.

Developing an assessment plan or planning process doesn't have to be overly complicated. An example cited in Hernon and Dugan (2002: 34) captures advice from Suffolk University, which based its plan on ACRL's "Objectives for Information Literacy Instruction: A Model Statement for Academic Libraries":

1. identify goals
2. identify specific objectives for each goal
3. develop performance criteria for each objective
4. determine the practices to be used to achieve goals
5. select assessment methods for each objective
6. conduct assessments
7. determine feedback channels
8. evaluate whether the performance criteria were met and objectives achieved

When a library is getting started with assessment planning, it's useful to explore connecting with other assessment processes and offices/staff at the institution. For example, contact with the staff in the institutional research and testing offices should make it clear what types of assessment plans and activities exist at the institutional and program/department levels. These staff can also advise and share their expertise about survey development and other instruments. Often, they are receptive to librarian review and suggestions of items for institutional, regional, or national student experience questionnaires. Contact with campus curriculum committees is also important for exploring improved linkages of information literacy with the curriculum. For example, the University of Maryland University College is reported to have followed these seven steps in connecting externally with other constituents about its assessment planning process:

1. Establish an information literacy study group. Ensure wide representation from librarians and faculty.
2. Charge the study group to devise a definition of IL, identify standards, and develop a plan for implementation, assessment, and on-going evaluation of IL standards across the curriculum.
3. Present the plan to the curriculum committee for formal acceptance.
4. Implement the recommendations of the study group.
5. Develop an initial course and revise upper-level courses as appropriate.
6. Devise assessment measures and review and evaluate the effectiveness of current offerings.
7. Use assessment results to revise the learning process and improve assessment efforts. (Middle States Commission on Higher Education, 2003: 46)

No matter how comprehensive or basic the assessment plan for an information literacy program is, the following questions should be addressed in the plan or in the choice of assessment approaches:

- Are the assessment goals tied to the institution's mission and goals?
- Will the assessment of information literacy occur at one level or on several levels?
- How will the current bibliographic instruction program be made part of the overall information literacy assessment effort and linked to the course, program, or institutional levels?
- Are there any similarities between the IL assessment efforts and other programs (e.g., writing across the curriculum)? Do these similarities overlap or offer opportunities for coordinated activities?
- Are the goals, benchmarks, and timelines for accomplishing the IL assessment plan reasonable?
- What will be the feedback loop? That is, how will the assessment results be reported and used to improve current practice? (Middle States Commission on Higher Education, 2003: 45)

The structure and content of information literacy assessment plans or assessment sections of the library's information literacy program plan reflect the variety of their host institutions. Most of those examined contain:

- a mission or purpose statement
- overall goals and objectives, typically referring to the "Information Literacy Competency Standards for Higher Education" (ACRL, 2000)
- specific student learning outcomes, sometimes specified by level
- learning opportunities (program components), sometimes linked to specific levels, such as basic skills orientation, first-year program, instruction in the majors, and graduate courses
- specific measures or evaluation methods, sometimes linked to learning outcomes or program component

Assessment plans should also include mention of how the results and findings will be analyzed, used, and disseminated, and who is involved and/or responsible in assessment. An excellent example is Weber State University's Stewart Library's "Information Literacy Program Assessment Plans and Data" that lists and provides links to assessment plans for credit courses, library skills orientation, subject-specific course-integrated instruction, first-year experience, and the entire information literacy program assessment. Each assessment plan has a standard format and includes priority outcomes, how assessed by measures and criteria, and a schedule of data and reports. What is most helpful is the information about how and where the findings will be reported (Weber State University, 2003).

Because collaboration is critical to effective information literacy program development and assessment, it is being singled out here. Evidence of collaboration is found in the increasing number of institutions that are including information literacy among their core abilities in first-year programs, general education courses, and/or identifying information literacy as a graduation requirement. The following statement illustrates this shared role:

> Student learning is a campus-wide responsibility, and assessment is a way of enacting that responsibility. Thus, while assessment efforts may start small, the aim over time is to involve people from across the educational community. Faculty play an especially important role, but assessment questions can't be fully addressed without participation by student-affairs educators, librarians, administrators, and students. Assessment may also involve individuals from beyond the campus (alumni/ae, employers) whose experience can enrich the sense of appropriate aims and standards for learning. Thus understood, assessment is not a task for small groups of experts but a collaborative activity; its aim is wider, better-informed attention to student learning by all parties with a stake in its improvement. (Gardiner et al., 1997: 11–12)

There are many examples of how librarians have collaborated with discipline-based faculty in designing information literacy assessment approaches and instruments. An exemplary program is the King's College comprehensive assessment program, which has an information literacy component. Information literacy, as one of the college's seven core skills and abilities, is integrated throughout the four parts of the assessment program. The first element of the program is the development of educational goals, where faculty and librarians identify and articulate how the transferable core skills and abilities apply to their discipline. The second part of the program is the development of competency growth plans, which are four-year plans that each department develops to "map out how students will transfer skills from the core curriculum into the major and then design pedagogical strategies and assessment criteria to ensure cumulative student growth" (Association of American Colleges and Universities, 2005: 2). The librarians have been involved in designing the assessments in the core curriculum and the faculty have played a key role in the design of assessments in the majors. Brian Pavlac, a history professor who headed King's information literacy project team, notes that "the most significant challenges faced by the program hinge on the involvement of faculty" (AACU, 2005: 2). There are two assessments of information literacy in the major: a sophomore-junior diagnostic project and a capstone seminar project.

Those readers seeking more information about the King's College program and other examples are referred to the AACU news article and the King's College comprehensive assessment program's Web page; the chapter, "Using the Assessment Cycle as a Tool for Collaboration" in the 2004 Miller and Pellen book; the many summary descriptions in the Avery (2003); and the chapter "Assessing Information Literacy" in Rockman (2004).

WHAT CAN BE ASSESSED?

Newly formed, revitalized, and seasoned information literacy programs are comprised of basically the same five components: learners and learning opportunities, learning materials, instructors, and learning environments. Each of these components can be evaluated as part of a library's assessment plan. As explained above, a complete program evaluation would include all of these components for program review, annual reports, and accreditation self-study reports. Similar to other curricula/learning programs, the emphasis should be on measuring the learning outcomes. As pointed out earlier, one of the differences between bibliographic instruction programs and information literacy programs is the adoption and program implementation of student learning outcomes that are broader and connected to institutional goals, which frequently reflect locally defined adaptations of the national "Information Literacy Competency Standards for Higher Education" (ACRL, 2000).

What exactly do these components consist of? The various components are separated below for assessment purposes, but of course they overlap and work together in practice:

Learners—the recipients of instruction programs can be assessed in a variety of ways. Evaluation methods are available to focus on knowledge acquisition/retention; performance as revealed through the process of research and application, whether they are course-embedded assignments, research diaries, papers, multi-media projects, portfolios, etc. One can also measure the effects or impact of these learning experiences on attitudes, behaviors and values, often captured by student self-reports (e.g., journals) and rating scales on surveys. If programs also include faculty and staff/administrator training, they are part of the learners to be assessed.

Learning Opportunities—include separate information literacy courses and those linked to learning communities, group presentations/workshops either linked to the curriculum or as stand-alone offerings, and independent offerings such as reference desk instructional interactions and librarian-developed IL tutorials. Other independent learning opportunities are harder to identify and assess, but they may be even more prevalent, especially with NetGen learners and some adult learners who prefer to figure things out themselves and work in groups to learn from each other. Examples include independent browsing of materials, peer-to-peer learning, help/search tips, information provided by search tools, and other types of Web information that learners find by themselves. Possibly, it might be useful to include a survey item or rating by students about the value and relationship of these types of activities to learning.

There may also be co-curricular formal and informal learning opportunities sponsored by student affairs staff that relate to some aspects of information literacy (e.g., career research skills workshops); by student organizations (e.g., history club session on genealogical research methods); and departmental offerings (e.g., legal studies department about copyright law related to music downloading; or an art department exhibition with handouts on legal use of images for multi-media projects). Being aware of these for potential collaboration and assessment activities is yet another avenue.

Learning Materials—are the various handouts, assignments, online guides/tutorials, course textbook/readings, and so on. Online tutorials and instructional Web pages are included in both the learning opportunities and materials components, since they can be used as a primary component of an instruction program, such as a required multiple-module online tutorial for first-year freshmen or they can be pieces of something larger and used as supplemental learning materials.

Instructors—include both the librarian/library staff presenters and discipline-based instructors who may co-teach the learners as well as observe presentations. In either situation it's important to evaluate the presentational and teaching abilities of whoever is doing the instruction.

Learning Environment—is the physical facilities (e.g., space/room, computers for hands-on practice, projection equipment, types of seating, etc.) and networked facilities (e.g., interactive technologies, wireless network, campus with online courseware such as Blackboard), and the institutional mission/values, organizational culture, and the formal curriculum. It also includes the informal learning environment both in the library and external to the library, such as reference transactions and assistance and handouts provided by other library departments (e.g., archives or government publications); lecture and curriculum-related programs, exhibitions, computer lab training resources, tutorial and writing center lab resources, and so on.

SPECIFIC MEASURES AND METHODS
FOR PROGRAM COMPONENTS

Assessment data and documentation about students' information literacy skills can come from many quantitative and qualitative measures as well as direct and indirect methods of measuring students' skills. Quantitative measures can be represented numerically (e.g., data coming from tests or surveys), while qualitative measures generally relate to quality or kind, such as narrative or text coming from observations, interviews, focus groups, or open-ended items on questionnaires. Direct methods refer to approaches that measure performance and/or knowledge coming directly from what learners know or can do, such as assignments or observation of search behavior. Indirect methods refer to approaches that generate findings related to learning, such as perceptions or self-ratings, but do not measure the learning itself. While nearly all measures will be based on program goals and student learning outcomes, there are other approaches to evaluation, such as goal-free and naturalistic evaluation. Goal-free evaluation refers to the collection and analysis of information related to actual results, rather than pre-established objectives. In fact, a literal understanding of the phrase "learning outcomes" means actual outcomes, not necessarily what was desired or expected. Common usage, however, does not always make this distinction. Naturalistic evaluation usually refers to such qualitative methods as case study, participant observation, and other sociological methods to comprehensively describe program processes and results. Whatever the method used, the measures are designed to yield data and other types of evidence to inform program planning and needed improvements.

Evidence is the data and other findings upon which a judgment or conclusion may be based. The following are characteristics of good evidence:

- It is purposeful and related to specific questions.
- It has been interpreted and reflected upon, not offered in its raw or unanalyzed form.
- It is integrated and presented in the context of other information about the institution that creates a holistic view of the program.
- It is cumulative and is corroborated by multiple sources of data. (WASC, 2004: 10–11)

The data collection methods and types of measures are secondary to the questions that drive the assessment. Spending time clarifying the purpose, the audience and what one wants to learn from the assessment is critical. Figure 16-1: Program Elements with Potential Assessment Methods and Measures illustrates the various program elements with possible methods and measures for collecting data/documentation. The instruments and methods listed include both direct and indirect methods and they yield quantitative and qualitative data and documentation.

There is a great variety of information literacy assessment instruments and measures currently in use. If the 2001 College Library Information Packet Committee (CLIP) "Survey on Assessment in College Library Instruction Programs" were administered today, this author is certain there would be more institutions reporting that they do formal assessments and more would be course-embedded than the 2001 findings, which reported that 59 percent of the 158 responding institutions doing formal assessments cite multiple choice/short answer tests as the most frequently used assessment tool (Merz and Mark, 2002). Activity and lesson-based assessment examples are commonly used in junior/middle and high school settings.

There are several national tests, some standardized, that assess aspects of information literacy. The Information and Communications Technology exam,

Program Elements	Measures/Methods
Learners—What do they know? What can they do? How do they perceive their abilities and what do they value? Do students who participate in IL program opportunities have higher GPAs? —> Start with instructional objectives and desired learning outcomes and match to appropriate assessment measure/method to generate data and/or qualitative information Selection of measure/method also depends on the instructional setting/learning opportunity (e.g., course, workshop, online tutorial, etc.) and overall purpose of assessment **Examples of desired learning outcomes and instructional objective:** • Knows how information is formally and informally produced, organized, and disseminated • Demonstrates an understanding that date, sponsor, or publisher of the information may affect its value in selecting appropriate sources for assignment • Values the variety of information resources and investigative methods, including the librarian and other experts. • After attending two instructional sessions, students will conduct effective searches using two online search tools to find two scholarly sources to compare and contrast in a 500-word essay	Performance (scores, grades, ratings) of: • Standardized or local test/quiz • National licensure examination • Quiz and task items embedded in online tutorial • Course-embedded assignments, papers/projects • Moral/ethical choice exercises • Simulated task performance • Concept mapping • Capstone experience (paper, field project, presentation) • Portfolio analysis of research products using established criteria on checklists or rubrics • National or locally developed freshman survey compared to senior survey • Classroom assessment techniques (CATS) • Online monitoring of searching • Direct observation of research behavior Analysis of: • Self-reflection documented in research log, journals, reflective essays • Items on national or local survey of student engagement/experiences • Items on alumni, employer or graduate surveys • Interviews and focus groups of learners, librarians, course instructors, employers • Correlation studies of GPA of students who do/do not participate in IL workshops, tutorial, courses
Learning Opportunities—What are the learning opportunities, how many, who do they reach and in what programs/curricula? How are they rated by participants?	• Description of variety/number of learning opportunities with usage data and % of curriculum participating in IL instruction • Analysis of assignments based on survey or syllabus/course outline review • Unsolicited feedback from letters, e-mail; anecdotal evidence • Course, workshop, tutorial survey evaluations completed by learners, librarians and/or course instructors

Figure 16-1: Program Elements with Potential Assessment Methods and Measures

Program Elements	Measures/Methods
Learning Materials—What are the learning materials, how are they used and how are they rated?	• Description of types of learning materials and how used to accommodate variety of learning styles and student needs • Student and/or faculty survey of online tutorial and other learning materials • Expert rating of online tutorial/materials
Learning Environment—What is the nature and quality of the learning environment's physical and virtual space? How are instructional technologies used to support teaching and learning? What is the institutional, program and/or course support for information literacy? For example, are there specified learning outcomes related to information literacy in the general education or other academic programs? Is there an IL requirement? What is the extent to which the use of library and information resources is included in course or program descriptions? What is the extent of collaboration between librarians and course instructors and other academic staff? What other campus facilities and services exist that provide assistance related to information literacy?	• Description of aspects of the physical learning environment and how it's used and for which groups of learners; identification of barriers to effective IL instruction and assessment • Description of the institutional and program curriculum linkages to IL • Description of the course linkages to IL and use of library/information sources, possibly based on a syllabus study • Description of the types of collaborations between librarian and faculty/academic staff with a summary of the outcomes of these relationships • Description of other campus facilities and services that provide assistance/training related to IL.
Instructors—How do peers, discipline-based faculty and students rate the teaching and presentational skills of librarians and others doing the IL instruction?	• Peer feedback about teaching and presentation skills, using a checklist of effective behaviors • Student and faculty ratings of presentations • Self-rating of presentation • Self and/or peer analysis of video of presentation • Expert rating of presentation

Note: Many of the methods assessing learners could be administered pre and post to compare performance. The use of a control group and appropriate research design strengthen the findings. A multi-methods approach strengthens evidence.

Examples of CATS are the "one-minute" paper, "the muddiest point," "the one-sentence summary," "what's the principle?," etc. See T. A. Angelo and P. Cross. 1993. *Classroom assessment techniques: A handbook for college teachers*, 2nd. ed. San Francisco: Jossey-Bass.

Figure 16-1: Program Elements with Potential Assessment Methods and Measures *(Cont'd.)*

developed by Educational Testing Service, uses scenario-based tasks to measure both cognitive and applied information literacy skills. The reader is referred to the ETS information literacy Web site for more information about the outcomes this exam is designed to assess (Educational Testing Service, 2006). Another is the "Information Literacy Test," developed at James Madison University as a generic version of their instrument for sale to other institutions through the university's Center for Assessment and Research Studies. It is a 60-item, multiple-choice Web-based test that measures all of the ACRL competencies, with the exception of the standard four, although 68 percent of the test items measure knowledge and 32 percent of the items measure application of IL concepts (James Madison University, 2006). One other is Project SAILS, a test of knowledge of information literacy skills, based on ACRL "Information Literacy Competency Standards for Higher Education." This Web-based tool allows libraries to document information literacy skill levels for groups of students and to pinpoint areas for improvement. Currently, the test is administered from the Project SAILS Web site twice a year at a minimal cost per student, and test administration training workshops are offered at sessions during ALA summer and midwinter (Project SAILS, 2006).

Moreover, national student experience surveys, such as the National Student Survey of Engagement (NSSE), can also yield useful data when addressing assessment questions such as the relationship between certain student behaviors and engagement in learning. The 2006 NSSE contains several experimental items directly related to information literacy and library use. The findings are expected to be analyzed and shared in late 2006. These instruments usually allow institutions to add some of their own items, so that benchmarks can be established and compared over time with local and national norms or institutionally selected peer groups.

Quite a few organizational information literacy Web sites include a section on assessment, some with links to instruments, or a listing of publications including assessment, such as those Web pages created by ACRL sections and the Institute for Information Literacy (e.g., the Institute for Information Literacy's Information Literacy Web site, which has links to "Assessment Bibliography," and "Assessment Issues"); the DORIL Web site ("Directory of Online Resources for Information Literacy"); the National Forum on Information Literacy; the Association for Research Libraries' "ARL New Measures Initiatives"; the Library Instruction Round Table's annual "Top Instruction articles"; and the American Association of School Librarian's "Planning & Assessment," one of the *Resource Guides for School Library Media Program Development.*

The reader is referred to the following publications listed in the "References" section for information about methods and types of instruments, as well as examples of specific instruments and scoring checklists/rubrics: Avery (2003); Grassian and Kaplowitz (2001); Hernon and Dugan (2002); Merz and Mark (2002); Neely (2006); and Shonrock (1996).

In summary, IL program assessment goals, learners, organizational culture, curricular practices, and local expertise are all factors in determining which program components are assessed, how and when. The use of multiple measures, especially when assessing student learning, is essential to generate more robust evidence. Course-embedded assessments, such as research assignments, papers, and other products of student performance are rich sources of student learning at both the course and the program level, and the findings are strengthened when combined with indirect measures of self-ratings or reflections about the information-seeking/research process. When the entire IL program is being evaluated, one should consider having the following combination of measures/methods:

- Descriptive narrative and statistics about progress made in meeting program goals and objectives, as well as use statistics for program components
- Description of the learning environment, especially how changes to it have affected IL offerings and outcomes
- User surveys, and other types of feedback and observational measures about quality of IL instruction, learning materials, and specific learning opportunities
- Learner performance and other Student Learning Outcome (SLO) measures
- Indirect beneficial effects, such as increased awareness and visibility of library/librarians; increase in partnerships between library and its external audiences; inclusion of IL competencies in general education and other program objectives/outcomes

RESEARCH DESIGN AND ANALYSIS

At times, specific components of an IL program may be subjected to a more rigorous assessment study. This type of assessment might occur after earlier, smaller-scale formative assessments have been accomplished and the findings used to improve instructional materials or learning opportunities, laying the groundwork for a research study of the effects of a particular instructional method/mode of delivery, for example, on learning of specific IL competencies. A more formal research study might be undertaken when one hopes to produce evidence that demonstrates the effect between an instructional "treatment" and a resulting outcome by trying to control certain variables so that a causal relationship can be established. Such studies involve more planning, the use of a research design, often a sampling schedule and statistical analysis. A full explanation of this type of assessment is beyond the scope of this chapter, and the reader is referred to the following titles in the "References" which provide chapters about research design, data-gathering instruments, and statistical analysis: *Evaluating Bibliographic Instruction: A Handbook*, authored by Avery, Hernon, Dugan, Schwartz, Powell, and Connaway. One should not be discouraged from undertaking a more formal assessment, even though it will be more time-consuming, as there is always local expertise to help plan the research, design, develop instruments, and conduct the statistical analysis.

COMMUNICATING ASSESSMENT INFORMATION

The assessment cycle discussed above in the section "Program Assessment and Assessing Student Learning: Key Features" makes it clear that assessment findings need to be analyzed, reflected upon and then used to inform program revision and change. As Palomba and Banta (1999: 297) point out, "Assessment information is of little use if it is not shared with appropriate audiences and used in meaningful ways. Much of the value of assessment comes from the systematic way it makes educators question, discuss, share, and observe." Also important to internal and external audiences is to be informed about how the findings have been used to make program improvements. This information not only gives information literacy more visibility in the institution, it also documents how the library is contributing to institutional goals relating to educational excellence, student success, and becoming a learning institution. In fact, one of the most convincing ways to publicize the value of information literacy and assessment is to make others aware of how findings have been used to improve assignments and instruction in particular courses or programs, so that faculty and administrators can better understand the connections between information literacy and the curriculum. Small successes once shared can generate more interest in information literacy and raise the level of faculty commitment. Communication also reinforces the commitment made by faculty who may have been the early innovators, and who may become the models to help prepare other faculty.

Finally, sharing assessment results can lead to recognition at the local, regional, state, and national levels. Communicating with peer or "sister" institutions can help to generate new ideas and approaches, even stimulating collaborative inter-institutional initiatives. Excellent advice about how to communicate assessment findings is found in the Middle States publication "Developing Research & Communication Skills":

> Making the connections between assessment findings, recommendations, or implications and what they may mean for "their students" helps faculty to put a human face on the findings. Disaggregating institutional data and making comparisons by student subgroups or major programs also may assist readers in understanding the information and reflecting on the larger message. (Middle States Commission on Higher Education, 2003: 59)

CONCLUSION

Assessment is as inextricably linked to IL program development and revision, as it is linked to teaching. Assessment findings and results are the raw material for instruction librarians to learn more about students, faculty, and themselves as teachers. What we learn from assessment feeds directly into how we teach, how we design instructional activities and materials, the kind and quality of services we offer, and ultimately it can transform our organizational culture into a culture of outcomes assessment. Outcomes assessment has, in some cases, even redefined how librarians view their role and relate to their institutions. It's a wonderful opportunity for librarians to connect with their colleagues in other programs and departments to help shape the future of teaching and learning. So, there's no question that it's worth the effort and time. Ensuring that assessment is an integral part of an information literacy program can be facilitated by having an assessment plan or regular assessment planning process. The actual development and administration of assessment instruments can be shared with local faculty experts or other appropriate staff. Thanks to the professional development opportunities specifically targeted to information literacy assessment, more librarians are becoming involved with assessment planning and implementation. Some of these professional development opportunities include regional, state and local workshops, and conferences; Association of Research Libraries Institutes; ACRL's immersion program and ACRL's e-learning online seminars, such as "Creating a Comprehensive Plan for Information Literacy," and "Assessing Student Learning Outcomes," and ACRL-TLT Web-seminars and Webcasts, such as "Information Literacy and Assessment."

The roles of assessment in information literacy programs are several and the future looks bright for even more participation in assessment, hopefully with increased sharing of information about findings, both expected and unexpected, so that information literacy programs and learners benefit.

REFERENCES

Association of American Colleges & Universities. 2005. "Feature: AAC&U member innovations: King's College takes a multi-tiered approach to information literacy assessment." *AAC&U News* (January-February). Available: www.aacu.org/aacu_news/AACUNews05/February05/feature.cfm (accessed April 5, 2006).

Association of College & Research Libraries. 2003a. "Characteristics of programs of information literacy that illustrate best practices: A guideline." Available: www.ala.org/ACRLPrinterTemplate.cfm?Section=acrlstandards&Template=/ContentManagement/HTMLDisplay.cfm&ContentID=75392 (accessed April 5, 2006).

Association of College & Research Libraries. 2003b. "Guidelines for instruction programs in academic libraries." Available: www.ala.org/ala/acrl/acrlstandards/guidelinesinstruction.htm (accessed April 5, 2006).

Association of College & Research Libraries. 2000. *Information literacy competency standards for higher education.* Chicago: American Library Association. Available: www.ala.org/ala/acrl/acrlstandards/informationliteracycompetency.htm (accessed April 5, 2006).

Association of College & Research Libraries. 2004. "Standards for libraries in higher education." Available: www.ala.org/ala/acrl/acrlstandards/standardslibraries.htm (accessed April 15, 2006).

Astin, A.W., et al. "Nine principles of good practice for assessing student learning." Available: www.nwhealth.edu/ctl/asmnt/ninepgp.html (accessed April 15, 2006).

Avery, E. F., ed. 2003. *Assessing student learning outcomes for information literacy instruction in academic institutions.* Chicago: Association of College & Research Libraries.

Bibliographic Instruction Section Research Committee, Subcommittee on Evaluation. 1983. *Evaluating bibliographic instruction: A handbook.* Chicago: Association of College and Research Libraries.

Cameron, L. 2004. "Assessing information literacy." In I. F. Rockman & Associates, *Integrating information literacy into the higher education curriculum* (pp. 207–236). San Francisco: Jossey-Bass.

Carter, E.W. 2002. "Doing the best with what you have: Lessons learned from outcomes assessment." *The Journal of Academic Librarianship*, Vol. 28, no. 1–2: 36–41.

Carter, E.W., and R. N. Jefferson. 2006. "Collaborating on information literacy." In P. Hernon, R.E. Dugan, and C. Schwartz, eds., *Revisiting outcomes assessment in higher education* (pp. 303–326). Westport, CT: Libraries Unlimited.

Educational Testing Service. 2006. "Information & communication technology literacy." Available: www.ets.org/portal/site/ets/menuitem.435c0b5cc7bd0ae7015d 9510c3921509/?vgnextoid=b8a246f1674f4010VgnVCM10000022f95190RCR D (accessed September 28, 2006).

Gardiner, L., C. Anderson, and B. Cambridge, eds. 1997. *Learning through assessment: A resource guide for higher education.* Washington, DC: American Association for Higher Education.

Grassian, E., and J. Kaplowitz. 2001. "Assessing, evaluating, and revising ILI programs." In *Information Literacy Instruction: Theory and Practice* (pp. 265–288). New York: Neal-Schuman Publishers.

Hernon, P., and R. E. Dugan. 2002. *An action plan for outcomes assessment in your library.* Chicago: American Library Association.

Hernon, P., R. E. Dugan, and C. Schwartz, eds. 2006. *Revisiting outcomes assessment in higher education.* Westport, CT: Libraries Unlimited.

James Madison University. 2006. "Information literacy test." Available: www.jmu. edu/assessment/wm_library/ILT.pdf#search=%22%22information%20litereacy %20test%22%22 (September 28, 2006).

King's College. "Comprehensive Assessment Program." Available: www.kings.edu/Academics/capprogram.htm (accessed April 5, 2006).

Maki, P. L. 2002. "Developing an assessment plan to learn about student learning." *The Journal of Academic Librarianship*, Vol. 28, no. 1–2: 8–13.

Merz L. H., and B. L. Mark. 2002. *Assessment in college library instruction programs.* CLIP Note #32. Chicago: Association of College and Research Libraries.

Middle States Commission on Higher Education. 2003. *Developing research and communication skills: Guidelines for information literacy in the curriculum.* Philadelphia, PA: Middle States Commission on Higher Education.

Miller, W., and R. M. Pellen, eds. 2004. *Libraries within their institutions: Creative collaborations.* Binghamton, NY: Haworth Press.

Neely, T. Y. 2006. *Information literacy assessment: Standards-based tools and assignments.* Chicago: American Library Association.

Palomba, C. A., and T. W. Banta. 1999. *Assessment essentials: Planning, implementing and improving assessment in higher education.* San Francisco: Jossey-Bass.

Powell, R. R., and L. S. Connaway. 2004. *Basic research methods for librarians.* 4th ed. Westport, CT: Libraries Unlimited.

Project SAILS. 2006. "About the test." Available: www.projectsails.org/abouttest/about Test.php?page=aboutTest (accessed April 5, 2006).

Rockman, I. F. & Associates. 2004. *Integrating information literacy into the higher education curriculum.* San Francisco: Jossey-Bass.

Shonrock, D. D., ed. 1996. *Evaluating library instruction: Sample questions, forms, and strategies for practical use.* Chicago: American Library Association.

WASC–Accrediting Commission for Community and Junior Colleges. 2004. *Guide to evaluating institutions.* Novato, CA: Western Association of Schools and Colleges.

Weber State University. 2003. "Information literacy program assessment plans and data." Available: http://faculty.weber.edu/chansen/libinstruct/ILProgram/assessment.htm (accessed April 5, 2006).

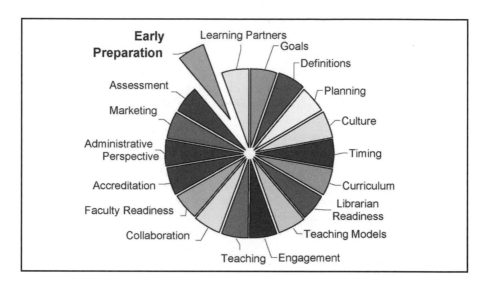

EARLY PREPARATION

A Word from the Editors

*A*s with most skills, students become increasingly skillful in information literacy when they are taught throughout their education the building blocks of information literacy. Dr. Lesley Farmer, Professor at California State University Long Beach, and Coordinator of the Library Media Teacher Program, can speak with authority of the role that school library media teachers play in developing a child's information literacy skills. From the perspective of her Ed.D. in Adult Education from Temple University to her work as a librarian in school, public, special and academic libraries, Lesley is able to provide critical advice in how to develop information literacy skills across the curriculum and how to awaken a child's interest in information research. Importantly, Lesley also places information literacy in the context of two other vital skills—reading and technology literacy—to show how all of these skills overlap and can be utilized to support each other. Lesley also brings an international perspective as a chair of the information literacy special interest group for the International Association of School Librarianship. Lesley has an M.L.S. from the University of North Carolina, Chapel Hill and her most recent books include Librarians, Literacy and the Promotion of Gender Equity *(McFarland, 2005) and* Digital Inclusion, Teens and Your Library *(Libraries Unlimited, 2005). Lesley's M.S.L.S. is from the University of North Carolina, Chapel Hill. Especially librarians in academic settings should read this chapter with an eye to the potential of collaboration with school librarians on information literacy skill-building.*

Chapter 17

The School Library Media Teacher as Information Literacy Partner

By Lesley Farmer

INTRODUCTION

We want our students to be literate. That's a given in today's society, which requires being able to read and write, calculate, and use other appropriate tools to consume and produce ideas. Does a person have to be able to read and write to think critically? No. A person can "read" the clouds, decipher body language, and react to a dangerous sound. But if one cannot understand signs and labels, if one cannot figure out how to use money, if one cannot communicate meaningfully with another person, then that person is not likely to succeed in terms of how today's society measures achievement.

At this point, you may be thinking, "Stop already! It's hard enough to get kids to sit still for story hour!" Fortunately, each seemingly small step can contribute to students' information literacy. You are not starting from scratch; even preschoolers arrive at school with experiences and ways of dealing with their surroundings. By looking at the big picture, you can see how your efforts work in tandem with the rest of the school community.

The library provides access to a wide variety of information with which students can engage. Moreover, you and the rest of the library staff help students access this information intellectually, fostering literacy. The library also has many tools to help students make meaning from their interaction with information: guide sheets, posters, computers, and video cameras. As the School Library Media Teacher (SLMT) your focus is information literacy—the ability to access, evaluate, manage, use, and communicate information purposefully—as your main mission.

The school library program is well grounded in literacies, providing opportunities for students to learn how to comprehend and apply information in a variety of ways for different purposes. School library programs model the conditions for lifelong literate habits of mind: rich and varied resources, individual choice and engagement, thoughtful evaluation of ideas, creative expression, and informed decision-making in a positive social setting. By partnering with the SLMT, classroom teachers can optimize the relevancy and application of their subject matter throughout students' education.

This chapter provides details of the elements of information literacy, and suggests ways for you to provide an effective information literacy program in collaboration with the school community to help students become truly literate, across subject matters and across grade levels.

LITERACIES

Who is the literate person? This is not an easy answer. The term "literate" is derived from the Latin word for letter. As such, it is usually linked with the concepts of reading and writing. Literate first referred to the ability to read a letter or symbol as a way to help remember a story; the letters or signs were memory devices. After a while, as people wrote down their stories, they developed a consistent orthographic system, be it pictographic or alphabetic (as in phoneme-letter association). Thus, a literate person could read an unknown piece of work; literate people could also copy down those stories. Later, the ability to produce *new* text became a benchmark of literacy. The literate person became synonymous with the educated person as text gained status. This kind of definition goes beyond the idea of functional literacy: say, the ability to sign one's name and read a job application.

What about pictures? Doesn't film have its own "language"? Certainly, technological literacy has become a buzzword. At this point, literacy has been linked with several types of skills and knowledge, from emotional literacy to fashion literacy. Still, it is safe to say that literacies deal with information (potentially meaningful data) and a person's engagement with the information. The ability to decipher and comprehend the information, the ability to choose appropriate tools in order to make meaning of that information, and potentially act upon it and produce new information—these are the elements of literacy in general. In the broadest scheme of things, literacy has as its goal the ability of persons to be able to function autonomously within their society.

Information literacy is, paradoxically, a "hot" topic and a misunderstood one. The American Library Association defines information literacy as "the ability to know when there is a need for information, to be able to identify, locate, evaluate, and effectively use that information for the issue or problem at hand" (ACRL, 2000). This definition goes beyond the idea of "library skills" or locational skills to stress the entire process of purposeful interaction with information.

READING LITERACY

Reading literacy may be considered the "default" literacy since it is seen as the cornerstone of enduring ideas and communication. Technically speaking, reading and writing go hand and hand, where reading can be considered the consumer side and writing can be considered the producer side of text. Together, they are necessary elements of information literacy since they constitute the basis for much information input and processing.

Reading fluency has several antecedents: decoding, reading skills, relating reading and language, factors interfering with reading, and the specific acquisition of reading competence (Resnick and Weaver, 1979). The deciphering process is both visual and auditory, which is why students who don't hear well or listen closely have a harder time learning to read. Students have to understand the link between phonemes and text to the point that they can "chunk" letters into words and phrases so they can decode reading easily and progress onto comprehension: understanding the meaning within the text. Predictors of reading success include: vocabulary size, ability to use expressive language, recognizing alphabet and name letters, and knowing the purpose of books. Fluent readers interact with the text purposefully and personally. At that point, reading also depends on students' pre-existing knowledge and societal norms: how the act of reading is valued and applied (Knuth and Jones, 1991; Block, Gambrell, and Pressley, 2002; Pearson and Taylor, 2002).

Reading and writing literacy is considered the job of every classroom teacher, even in the high schools. Elementary teachers are taught reading methodologies; most middle school teachers also get some training, at least in terms of language arts and reading fluency. High school teachers usually get academic preparation in reading and writing domain-specific types of documents, such as technical manuals or critical essays.

While relatively few SLMTs are trained reading diagnosticians, they *are* trained to know children's and young adult literature and other educational sources. They can direct students to just the right book or magazine. Additionally, they know how to find reviews about curriculum-supportive and leveled materials, including reading diagnostic software. Often SLMTs can borrow likely resources from other libraries so they—and other teachers—can examine them before ordering them for the school collection.

Across and beyond the curriculum, SLMTs actively promote the *love* of reading, not just for a grade, but because it is a satisfying way to spend free time. By providing a rich variety of developmentally appropriate and engaging reading material, the SLMT can help each student find the "home run" book that speaks to that child. Noted reading researcher Steven Krashen (2000) and his student Jiyoung Kim found that even one satisfying "home run" book can turn on a child's mental switch to reading enjoyment. Once that switch is turned on, the library can keep that students' reading appetite fed. SLMTs also model the joy of reading, and share their enthusiasm through:

- booktalks and read-alouds
- one-on-one conversations about books
- book clubs, book discussion groups, literacy circles
- reading events such as author visits, read-ins, and poetry slams
- newsletters, flyers, bookmarks, and bibliographies of good reading materials
- displays of books and other reading materials, story characters, and student book reviews
- posters, announcements, and other promotional efforts

Furthermore, they encourage students to share their responses to reading, and promote activities that allow students to express their own ideas. These value-added efforts may be targeted to one child or to the entire school community. As the SLMT, you need to proactively approach classroom teachers to help them foster a lifelong reading habit for their students.

One obvious example of library support of reading is the celebration of reading-related observances, such as National Children's Book Week and Poetry Month. Many elementary libraries plan and implement week-long thematic activities, such as "Get a Clue @ Your Library." Each day students have to guess the title of a book based on clues ("My brother and I solved a mystery about a statue called 'Angel.'" "We ran away, and hid in an art museum."), and they solve word puzzles about books (e.g., word searches of titles). On Friday, a local author speaks to classes about writing mysteries.

To help students improve their reading selection and comprehension skills, Cosburn Middle School in Toronto developed a Passport to Reading program. The SLMT taught students about different literacy genres, and the students created illustrated genre books. The first year, language arts students tended to make alphabet and family histories, which were read to primary classes. By the fourth year, students were producing novels and historical fiction. Reading interest has increased for the students *and* their families, and SLMT collaboration has extended to social studies and science/math teachers (Lawrence, 2005).

INFORMATION LITERACY

Information literacy is the SLMT's stock in trade because it leverages a rich collection of resources and services to meet the academic and personal needs of the school community. It focuses on process: accessing, evaluating, using, and communicating information purposefully. In their information literacy standards (www.ala.org/ala/aasl/aaslproftools/informationpower/InformationLiteracyStandards_final.pdf), the American Association of School Librarians (AASL) also mentions the concepts of independent learning (including appreciation of creative expression) and social responsibility in the overall scheme of information literacy. The underlying idea is to make meaning of the world.

- A student has a question, problem, or task to handle. What does the student need to know to accomplish the purpose?
- What sources of information are appropriate? What strategies should the student use to access those sources?
- Once those resources are located and gathered, how does the student comprehend them and then evaluate them to determine their quality and relevance?
- How does the student extract the useful information, comparing it with other information, including one's own prior knowledge?
- What tools does the student use to organize, analyze, and manipulate the information for the intended purpose? This process may include the production of new information.
- Ultimately, how does the student communicate and act upon the findings?

These queries mark decision points in information literacy, leading the student to the problem solved, the question answered, the task accomplished. It should also be noted that students may focus on just one aspect of information literacy, such as locating magazine articles, rather than trying to tackle everything at once.

A key feature of information literacy is its acknowledgement, indeed appreciation, of the varied formats in which information can be communicated: the printed word, mass media, oral interviews, digital sources, numerical data, images, even meaningful sound (barking dogs, etc.).

- Each of these sources of information involves some sort of strategy to find and understand them: books may be located using library catalogs, magazine articles are found through periodical indices and databases, sources for interviews may be located using directories.
- Each of these media has its communications protocol and "language": film uses lighting and music to evoke a mood, for instance.
- Each format engages learners in different ways: how students interview an octogenarian differs from how they would appreciate film noir.

Why should the beginning teacher care? For several reasons:

- Information literacy provides a systematic way to engage in new ideas.
- Information literacy supports different ways of learning.
- Information literacy is a simple and effective way to link with other curricular areas.

One of the reasons that information literacy has become vital is that students can get overwhelmed by information, much of which is unreliable. Before the Internet, the library collection was carefully selected so that students just had to figure out if the resource at hand was relevant for the immediate task and if they could comprehend it. The SLMT basically controlled the collection, and aimed for a balanced approach to information. With access to the Internet, that kind of control is impossible. SLMTs have to train those same students to evaluate the verity and usefulness of resources for themselves. On a positive note, such training helps students become more self-sufficient and critical learners. By melding such evaluation instruction into the curriculum, you the SLMT, in collaboration with classroom teachers, can develop authentic learning experiences that help students become information literate and savvy decision-makers.

A concrete example demonstrates how the SLMT can collaborate to foster information literacy. Suppose students are studying the U. S. Civil War.

- *The task:* Students can compare Civil War biographical primary and secondary sources in order to understand the concept of point of view and authenticity of documentation. This task reflects the analytical part of information literacy—*and* can be related to diary and autobiographical writing versus biographical novels. The SLMT can work with the social studies teachers in helping students identify the critical features of primary and secondary sources.
- *Access:* The SLMT can show students various forms of primary and secondary sources that can resonate with different learners. The SLMT can also help students use catalogs and indices to locate specific documents.
- *Comprehension and evaluation:* The SLMT and classroom teacher can highlight critical features that show point of view, such as the writer's background and intent.
- *Extraction:* The SLMT may know about similar learning activities in other courses, and can help the classroom teacher tie those intellectual connections to students' prior experiences.
- *Manipulation and organization:* The SLMT can show students how to use graphic organizers to compare and contrast information, and direct students to other sources to verify facts.
- *Communication:* The SLMT can help students produce high-quality documents using technology to present their findings.

As another example, the SLMT at the Hanson/Jewett Elementary Schools (Buxton, Maine) collaborated with upper elementary classroom teachers to have students create their own diary of an animal, inspired by Cronin's *Diary of a Worm*. In order to be successful, students had to learn how to research an animal: finding, comparing, abstracting, and illustrating relevant information. The teachers liked the focus on authentic, first-person writing contextualized in scientific knowledge. On their part, students were enthusiastically engaged throughout the process, and their academic achievement exceeded the work done by prior students (Buzzeo, 2006).

TECHNOLOGY LITERACY

Chances are, your students have grown up in an Internet environment. In a way, they are digital "natives." However, just as a person can be textually illiterate in today's world, so can students be ineffective users of technology. Moreover, students may self-assess their technological skills inaccurately, thinking that "they can find anything on the Net." While they might be able to IM (instant message) easily, they could well be ignorant about using spreadsheet formulas to make predictions about data, for instance. At the least, students need to learn how to use technology to help them think critically and achieve academically.

The International Society for Technology in Education (ISTE) (2000) has set forth six major components indicating technology literacy, each with benchmark indicators for second, fifth, eighth, and twelfth grades: basic computer operations and concepts; social, ethical, and human issues; technology productivity tools; technology tools for communicating; technology tools for research; and technology tools for problem-solving and decision-making (http://cnets.iste.org/students/s_stands.html). Sometimes technology literacy is handled as a separate class (usually taught by a technology or computer specialist), and sometimes it is integrated as part of information literacy, melded across the curriculum. Using the ISTE standards, SLMTs can help students to become technologically literate in several ways:

- Basic computer operations and concepts: SLMTs can demonstrate how to access digital resources, and help them set up relevant fields for each kind of data about plants.
- Social, ethical, and human issues: SLMTs can explain how to credit the authors of the information, thus avoiding plagiarism.
- Technology productivity tools: SLMTs can help students create digital databases using a spreadsheet or database software program.
- Technology tools for communicating: SLMTs can demonstrate how to transform spreadsheet data into a graph format.
- Technology tools for research: SLMTs can help students access information about plants using catalogs, online subscription databases, and search engines.
- Technology tools for problem-solving and decision-making: SLMTs can help students develop a spreadsheet as a database to organize data for analysis.

Clearly, you as the SLMT can serve as a valuable literacy partner by incorporating technology. School libraries often have the most advanced technology on site—with the greatest access for the entire school community. With its rich collection of digital resources and access to online resources such as subscription databases, the library serves as information central. More importantly, though, are the skills you bring.

- SLMTs know both the hardware and software side of technology. They identify relevant criteria to select digital resources that support curriculum, and choose the appropriate hardware to use those resources. They can install and use technology. They can troubleshoot technical problems based on their training and daily involvement.
- SLMTs have been trained in technology-enhanced instruction and resource-based learning. They follow instructional design principles to align concepts, literacies, resources, and delivery. They know that incorporation of technology requires access, engagement, choice, time, flexibility, support, and the human touch. They value student inquiry and manipulation of resources to make meaning.
- SLMTs use technology as a tool for information literacy. They realize that access to resources worldwide is just the beginning; the ability to use technology to help discern the verity of the information—and apply it—is even more important.

As the SLMT, you can show students how to take the best advantage of databases and other technology-based resources, and use them productively. By collaborating with classroom teachers, you can design learning activities that meld technology and concepts for deeper, engaged student learning. For instance, you can locate or help create a WebQuest about ways to combat pollution. Students can create simulation newspapers about ancient times using desktop publishing programs, online images, scanners, and print materials. Students can research social issues using online periodicals and librarian-bookmarked Web sites.

The ISTE standards provide a way to examine a representative instructional design developed by you the SLMT and the classroom teacher. The major topic might be plant life. Besides having each student research a unique plant, the teacher may want them to compare plants along several dimensions in order to identify possible patterns. You might suggest developing a class database, with students researching and inputting data about their plants, and then analyzing the database to uncover trends. The teacher, you, and the students would develop a list of significant factors about each plant (e.g., height, description, growing season, habitat, country of origin, use). Based on the factors, students would then pose hypotheses about plants (e.g., is there a link between height and habitat? Does the use depend on the growing season?). After researching the plants and inputting the data, students would then test their hypotheses, and draw conclusions.

The SLMT at Boston Arts Academy/Fenway High School starts integrating technology into the curriculum with classroom teachers and students at the kindergarten level as students learn how to locate and evaluate Web sites linked with their academic units. For instance, as third-graders studied continents, they consulted atlases and Internet sites. Based on their research, they created informative postcards for families and friends using computers, which strengthened their desktop publishing and Internet skills as well as their scientific background (Gold, 2005).

LIBRARY INSTRUCTION MODES

Library-based instruction can take many forms: signage, reference and guide sheets, research handbooks, Web tutorials, audiocassette tours, videotaped orientations, multimedia presentations, large-group lectures, small group demonstrations, and one-on-one coaching. Instruction can be a formal presentation or a just-in-time intervention. SLMTs take advantage of learning moments, responding to students' immediate intellectual needs. Still, when SLMTs can plan systematically with classroom teachers, they can optimize student transfer of learning across the curriculum through explicit instruction.

Because information literacy crosses all curricular lines, SLMTs can work knowledgeably with all classroom teachers to support their subject matter. Collaboration might be as limited as creating a reserve shelf of relevant books or supplying a bibliographic style sheet—and as deep as developing curriculum together, from content standards to instructional units and assessment of student learning. Even library paraprofessionals can help teachers by identifying student gaps in using the library or doing independent reading, noting what teachers use the library and its resources for student learning, scheduling library time, and finding appropriate resources.

In support of classroom teacher instruction, SLMTs can produce a variety of teaching and learning aids. The most traditional of these is bibliographies of resources on a specific topic; a contemporary version is a Webliography, which typically lists relevant Web sites and can include other digital and print resources as well. When a bibliography provides a research strategy to give students direction, it takes on the form of a "pathfinder." Typically, a pathfinder includes an overview, key words, reference sources, relevant periodicals, books, non-print sources, and Web sites. With an established information literacy curriculum, SLMTs often use and develop learning aids on anticipated topics, such as locating magazine articles, evaluating Web sites, comparing point of views, and so forth. These study guides and worksheets provide a starting point for integrating information literacy into academic domains. SLMTs can also help teachers locate and adopt process and product rubrics that address literacy issues.

On a more substantial level, SLMTs can work with teachers to find and create Web tutorials and WebQuests that meld course content and literacy competencies. WebQuests are particularly interesting because they offer authentic collaborative tasks that incorporate relevant Internet sites in an interactive environment. Librarians also know hosting sites through which students can access these WebQuests at any time.

Sometimes, a separate unit or course focuses on information literacy. This practice resembles teaching multiplication times tables without applying the arithmetic concepts. Occasionally, in primary grades where fixed scheduling occurs and one teacher has the class most of the day, the SLMT may teach specific tool-based prerequisite skills such as physically handling a book or using a dictionary in order to ensure that students can draw upon those skills as appropriate, but it makes more sense to incorporate those skills in light of the curriculum being taught (e.g., learning animal vocabulary, or discovering the ethnic origin of everyday words for a world geography class). While this integrated curricular approach takes more time and effort, the benefits for sustained student learning and application outweigh the challenges of team planning. Certainly in upper elementary grades and up, information literacy needs to be taught as it "naturally" occurs within the instructional program. For instance, middle school teachers often use project-based learning and high schoolers often conduct research. Learning activities fit perfectly with the spirit of information literacy instruction and application as students identify their information task, strategize how to proceed, gather and sift through resources, and create meaningful knowledge.

Michael Hart, principal at Holy Rosary School in Tacoma, Washington, received the 2005 Distinguished Administrator Award from the American Association of School Librarians for his leadership in implementing a school-wide collaborative library program. Every classroom teacher met with the SLMT to discuss curricular areas that might be addressed collaboratively to extend student learning. Instead of teaching isolated computer skills, for instance, students acquired those skills as they worked on a collaborative content project. By the third year, SLMT and teaching staff collaboration was so high that the school adopted a full flexible schedule to facilitate planning and creating meaningful co-teaching. As a result, information literacy skills are taught seamlessly as part of the overall curriculum (Hart, 2006).

INFORMATION LITERACY AS A SCHOOL-WIDE CURRICULUM

By now it should be obvious that these different literacies overlap. For instance, to be a wise "consumer" of mass media messages, students need to be able to decipher visual symbols, understand how technology can modify images, evaluate the authenticity of the source, and read accompanying text. SLMTs can approach information literacy as a whole gestalt or can parse the components of each literacy, focusing student attention on specific concepts and skills. In either case, this process should be done in collaboration with classroom instruction to contextualize the skills and optimize transfer of learning. More importantly, though, information literacy should be considered a school-wide initiative with related student outcomes, not just the library program's shtick; otherwise, it will be difficult for the SLMT to get cooperation and buy-in from the rest of the school community.

In K–12 education, content standards help operationalize literacy. SLMTs see how those content standards are played out in student research projects across the curriculum. Because SLMTs work with all grades and classes, they see in practice how outcomes overlap across the curriculum, and how they articulate across grade levels. The scientific method can be linked to research projects, and analyzing graphical data can apply to social studies. Information literacy standards (to access, evaluate, use, and communicate information purposefully) provides a *lingua franca* across the curriculum. Particularly in high school, the school community tends to think in intellectual silos, so that what is learned in mathematics is not systematically applied in language arts, for instance. As a corollary, then, students tend not to link the two domains, thus reducing the effectiveness of their learning in either subject area. The cross-disciplinary nature of literacies—be it information, technology, visual, or media—often results in no one person taking responsibility for them. Why does this practice persist? Often because classroom teachers have little time to plot out those standards across disciplines. SLMTs, on the other hand, tend to think in terms of *process* and look at literacy issues *across* the curriculum. The more frequently teachers work with the library staff, and have their students use library resources, the more likely that the librarian can relate assignments across courses and grades. For instance, a travel brochure might be a project for a world geography class *and* for a Spanish language class; the beginning teacher is unlikely to know about this duplicative effort. Ideally, the two classroom teachers and the librarian could develop a project that would help students research culture and language seamlessly, taking into account those students having just one of the classes.

Here is a typical scenario. Students may be debating alternative anti-pollution solutions. They have to decide what information they need about the issue: definitions of pollution, factors that lead to pollution, existing alternatives, costs associated with pollution and potential solutions, and so forth. Students need to develop a research strategy for finding the information: what are possible resources, what are associated keywords, how will those resources—and information within them—be found? Journals and scientific studies would probably offer good information, which they can access through periodical indices and online directories using terms such as pollution, smog, ozone, and so forth. Once students locate potential information, they have to evaluate it for accuracy, timeliness, and relevance—once they comprehend what they find. The information that they choose then needs to be analyzed, interpreted, and organized in order to come to a logical conclusion, perhaps using spreadsheets and tables. After synthesizing the findings, students then need to develop a persuasive argument for their debate.

The example above shows how information literacy can be embedded within an academic domain and also cross curricular lines; for instance, developing a hypothesis plays a similar information literacy role to developing a thesis statement. Because SLMTs collaborate with teachers in several subject areas, they can serve as information literacy "translators," facilitating information literacy teaching interdependence and optimizing students' understanding and application of skills.

Addressing information literacy can be done on different scales, ranging from a single pull-out lesson to a K–12 scope-and-sequence curriculum embedded in the school's total curricular program. Likewise, collaborators in designing information literacy learning activities can range from a single classroom teacher to the entire school community. The greater the extent that information literacy is explicitly and systematically addressed throughout the required curricular program, the more students will benefit—and the more that classroom teachers can be interdependent instructors, building on each other's knowledge and practices.

Because collaboration requires trust and risk-taking, beginning SLMTs tend to work with individual teachers to build a positive professional relationship and reputation. By strategically identifying credible key teachers (such as grade level coordinators and department chairs), you the SLMT can leverage these successful collaborations to inculcate connections with the rest of the teaching faculty.

This approach builds a solid foundation for discussing school-wide information literacy initiatives. As schools develop expected student graduation outcomes, incorporating information literacy into that process legitimizes those competencies. Here is a basic outline for the implementation of such a project, with the SLMT taking a leadership role within the school community.

1. The school community identifies the desired information literacy competencies that all students must demonstrate before exiting.
2. The school community determines the indicators and assessments that will operationalize and measure acceptable student performance.
3. The school community maps the curriculum to determine where information literacy is currently being taught and demonstrated.
4. The school community identifies gaps where information literacy is *not* being addressed, and determines at what point in the curriculum the relevant skill is to be taught and practiced.
5. The SLMT collaborates with classroom teachers to make sure that appropriate, targeted instruction and learning activities occur.
6. The school community assesses student learning, and modifies their plan accordingly.

As an entire district initiative in 2004, River East Transcona School Division in Winnepeg developed a scope-and-sequence set of information literacy skills that met curricular content standards. Not only does their document include a framework and checklist, but it also provides rubrics, worksheets, and sample lesson ideas.

ASSESSMENT ISSUES

In order to provide a top-quality information literacy program that supports student learning and school community success, SLMTs assess their efforts— preferably in collaboration with the teachers they serve. Each component of the program is analyzed:

- Resources: Do materials support the curriculum and state content standards in light of information literacy? Are reading and interest levels developmentally appropriate? What curricular gaps exist? Are more materials needed to address curricular units? What formats need to be strengthened: video, audio, digital, etc.?
- Reading promotion: How does the library promote reading? How does the SLMT interact with the school community in promoting reading? What impact do library efforts have on students' reading comprehension and enjoyment of reading?
- Instruction: What other delivery methods should be considered? How effective is SLMT instruction? How can it better support teacher instruction? What effective teaching and learning aids are needed?
- Collaboration: How often do the SLMT and classroom teacher collaborate? What is the extent of their collaboration? What decision-making processes need to be improved? What is the nature of their interpersonal relationship and instructional interdependence? How do SLMTs and teachers negotiate instructional responsibility?
- Impact: How well do students learn and achieve? How do students process their learning and demonstrate their information literacy competence through original products? What helped and hindered student success? How can processes be modified to optimize student learning?

In each case, as the SLMT, you need to know what aspects of the information literacy program influence the school community, and what modifications can be implemented that would improve that influence. Getting input from the school community, especially classroom teachers, and working with them will result in the most beneficial changes for students and the teachers who instruct them. Ways to gather data include informal discussion, observation in the library and throughout the school, analysis of student work, surveys, focus groups, examination of standardized test results, and self-assessments of school community members.

For instance, eighth-graders in Lemmon School District (South Dakota) were surveyed about their research skills. The SLMT found that students liked to use the Internet, but that their skill level was uneven or low. Based on that data, in collaboration with the eighth-grade teachers and former students, the SLMT developed and implemented a unit on evaluating Web sites. As a result of the intervention, students made more informed decisions about the Internet, and appreciated online subscription database sources more. Now the SLMT is expanding that unit to other grades (Heil, 2005).

As this one example shows, while assessment processes occur naturally on an ongoing manner for both librarians and teachers, explicit joint attention to assessment can optimize the library's impact on student information literacy *outside* the library walls—and improve classroom outcomes. When teachers and SLMTs conduct action research projects to improve student achievement, library information literacy programs can support classroom practice, providing mutually supportive learning environments and effective interventions. The results can be significant and lasting with ongoing collaboration—resulting in an effective information literacy program that focuses on student competency.

REFERENCES

American Association of School Librarians (AASL). 1998. "Information literacy standards for student learning: Standards and indicators." Available: www.ala.org/ala/aasl/aaslproftools/informationpower/InformationLiteracyStandards_final.pdf

American Association of School Librarians and Association for Educational Communication and Technology. 1998. *Information power: Building partnerships for learning*. Chicago: American Library Association.

Association of College and Research Libraries. 2000. "Information literacy competency standards for higher education." Available: www.ala.org/ala/acrl/acrlstandards/informationliteracycompetency.htm (accessed May 6, 2006).

Block, C., L. Gambrell, and M. Pressley, eds. 2002. *Improving comprehension instruction: Rethinking research, theory, and classroom practice*. San Francisco: Jossey-Bass.

Buzzeo, T. 2006. "Diary of an animal: Using a children's book as a springboard to collaboration." *Library Media Connection*, Vol. 24, no. 5: 34–37.

Gold, S. 2005. "A tale of two libraries: How two library media centers seamlessly integrate curriculum, information literacy, and technology." *Technology & Learning*, Vol. 26, no. 3: 28–29.

Hart, M. 2006. "Extending the classroom through the school library." *Teacher Librarian*, Vol. 33, no. 4: 70.

Heil, D. 2005. "The Internet and student research: Teaching critical evaluation skills." *Librarian*, Vol. 33, no. 2: 26–29.

International Society for Technology in Education. 2000. *Technology standards for students*. Eugene, OR: International Society for Technology in Education.

Kim, J., and S. Krashen. 2000. "Another home run." *California English*, Vol. 62, no. 2: 25.

Knuth, R., and B. Jones. 1991. *What does research say about reading?* Oak Brook, IL: North Central Regional Educational Laboratory.

Lawrence, G. 2005. "Passport to reading; Passeport a la lecture." *Teacher Librarian*, Vol. 33, no. 2: 33–34.

Pearson, P., and B. Taylor. 2002. *Teaching reading*. Mahwah, NJ: Lawrence Erlbaum.

Resnick, L., and P. Weaver. 1979. *Theory and practice of early reading, volumes I–III*. Hillsdale, NJ: Erlbaum.

River East Transcona School Division. 2004. *Information literacy skills K-S4*. Winnipeg, Manitoba: River East Transcona School Division. Available: www.retsd.mb.ca/site/lrc/resources/literacy_doc.pdf (accessed July 17, 2006).

FURTHER READING

Beck, P. 2002. *Globalinks: Resources for world studies grades K-8*. Worthington, OH: Linworth.

Bishop, K. 2003. *Connecting libraries with classrooms*. Worthington, OH: Linworth

Buzzeo, T. 2002. *Collaborating to meet standards: Teacher/librarian partnerships for 7–12*. Worthington, OH: Linworth.

Buzzeo, T. 2002. *Collaborating to meet standards: Teacher/librarian partnerships for K-6*. Worthington, OH: Linworth.

Callison, D. 2003. *Key words, concepts and methods for information age instruction: A guide to teaching information inquiry*. Westport, CT: Libraries Unlimited.

Carr, J. F., and D. E. Harris. 2001. *Succeeding with standards: Linking curriculum, assessment, and action planning*. Alexandria, VA: Association for Supervision and Curriculum Development.

Church, A. 2003. *Leverage your library program to help raise test scores*. Worthington, OH: Linworth.

Farmer, L. 2003. *How to conduct action research: A guide for school library specialists*. Chicago: American Library Association.

Farmer, L. 1999. *Cooperative learning activities in the library media center*. Westport, CT: Libraries Unlimited.

Farmer, L. 1999. *Go figure! Mathematics through sports*. Westport, CT: Libraries Unlimited.

Farmer, L. 1999. *Partnerships for lifelong learning*. 2nd ed. Worthington, OH: Linworth.

Farmer, L., and W. Fowler. 1999. *More than information: The role of the library media center in the multimedia classroom*. Worthington, OH: Linworth.

Harada, V. 2004. *Inquiry learning through librarian-teacher partnerships*. Worthington, OH: Linworth.

Harada, V., and J. Yoshina. 2005. *Assessing learning: Librarians and teachers as partners*. Westport, CT: Libraries Unlimited.

Henri, J., and M. Asselin, eds. 2005. *The information literate school community 2: Issues of leadership*. Westport, CT: Libraries Unlimited.

Jacobs, H. 1997. *Mapping the big picture: Integrating curriculum and assessment*. Alexandria, VA: Association for Supervision and Curriculum Development.

Keane, N. 2002. *Teaching social studies through literature grades 4–6*. Worthington, OH: Linworth.

Loertscher, D., C. Koechlin, and S. Zwaan. 2004. *Ban those bird units*. San Jose, CA: Hi Willow.

Miller, D. 2005. *The standards-based integrated library: A collaborative approach for aligning the library program with the classroom curriculum*. 2nd ed. Worthington, OH: Linworth.

Miller, P. 2000. *Reading every reader*. Worthington, OH: Linworth.

Northwest Regional Educational Laboratory. 2002. *Learners, language, and technology*. Portland, OR: NWREL.

O'Hara, S., and M. McMahon. 2003. *Multidisciplinary units for grades 6–8*. Eugene, OR: ISTE.

Stripling, B., and S. Hughes-Hassell, eds. 2003. *Curriculum connections through the library*. Westport, CT: Libraries Unlimited.

Thomas, N. 2004. *Information literacy and information skills instruction: Applying research to practice in the school library media center*. 2nd ed. Westport, CT: Libraries Unlimited.

Turner, P., and A. Riedling. 2003. *Helping teachers teach: A school library media specialist's role*. 3rd ed. Westport, CT: Libraries Unlimited.

Weissman, A. 2001. *Transforming storytimes into reading and writing lessons*. Worthington, OH: Linworth.

KEEP IN MIND

"An information literacy program's goals need to be hallmarks for how the program is integrated in an interdependent manner with other aspects of the library organization and with its institutional setting, how the program will change and expand capacity, and how students' needs are incorporated in a continually correcting pattern of measurable outcomes."

— Randall Hensley

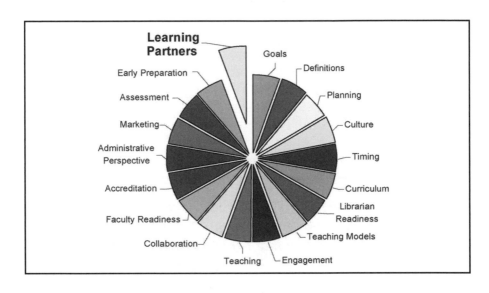

LEARNING PARTNERS

A Word from the Editors

*I*nformation literacy articles and studies are abundant throughout the literature unless we are reading in the literature of public libraries. There the subject is not widely discussed and certainly not with the intensity of the literature for academic libraries. As editors, we asked ourselves why? Public libraries serve vast audiences including, and especially, students of all ages. Their broad access to communities and their high standing with their clientele makes them pivotal in the greater goal of providing information literacy skills for everyone. We turned to the one person who could definitively provide us with an understanding of the role for public libraries in information literacy. Virginia A. Walter, Professor in the Graduate School of Library and Information Studies at the University of California, Los Angeles, served for 25 years as a public librarian including as the Children's Services Coordinator at the Los Angeles Public Library. In this chapter, Ginny looks at the mission of public libraries and how public libraries are interpreting information literacy. Ginny then focuses on one real world example of how the Santa Monica Public Library in California developed a curriculum for information and technology literacy. From this example, Ginny provides us with guidelines for other public libraries interested in providing their clients with twenty-first century skills in information literacy. In writing to the editors, Ginny says that "information and communication technologies have generated many changes in public library information services, including a new imperative to help customers use the new information resources more effectively." Ginny brings a special perspective to her work as she is a past President of the Association of Library Service for Children and was recently a recipient of their Distinguished Service Award. Ginny received her M.L.S. from the University of California, Berkeley, and her Ph.D. in Public Administration from the University of Southern California.

Chapter 18

Information Literacy:
A New Role for Public Libraries?

by Virginia A. Walter

INTRODUCTION

The original mission of the public library was to improve individuals and society as a whole by providing good books for citizens who could not afford to buy their own reading materials. Books and reading remain central to what we do in public libraries. We have even taken on the responsibility of teaching the basics of reading to adults who never acquired those skills as children or who learned how to read in another language as children. We also educate parents and caregivers about how best to nurture the early literacy skills of infants and toddlers.

Of course, books and reading are not the sole mission of any public library. Information services are now well-integrated into basic public library services. Recently the widespread adoption of digital communication and information technology, however, has dramatically changed the ways in which we deliver those services. In the introduction to *21st Century Literacies: Training of Public Library Trainers* (Walter, 2004: 4–5), some of the changes that Internet access has brought to public libraries are spelled out:

- Library users can access information services, including those provided by the public library, from their homes.
- Both library professionals and library users have become increasingly reliant on the Internet as an information source.
- New customers are coming to the public library just to make use of the computers and Internet access. While public libraries appreciate the business, some of these new users pose more of a service challenge than others.

- The uncontrolled content on the Internet has given rise to public (and sometimes staff) outrage about the "inappropriate" materials available to both purposeful and accidental information seekers.
- That outrage has led policy-makers to mandate the use of software filters to reduce the likelihood of access to inappropriate materials.
- Librarians sometimes find their traditional defense of intellectual freedom and first amendment rights at odds with their own values and those of the community.
- Searching for information on the Internet requires new skills for both library professionals and library users, resulting in increased and ongoing needs for staff development and for user education.
- Public service librarians have had to adopt a new educational role as they meet the need to teach library users how to use digital information resources effectively. Using digital information resources effectively requires information literacy skills.

This essay explores this new educational role for public librarians. We have only recently recognized that we share the responsibility for helping people become information literate. Public library information literacy practices are still relatively undeveloped compared with those in school and academic libraries. We have no agreed-upon standards or objectives for information literacy, for example. A search for "information literacy" on the American Library Association Web site produced 19,400 hits (American Library Association, 2000). The first 50 were generated by the Reference and User Services Association (RUSA), the Association of College and Research Libraries, the Government Documents Round Table (GODORT), and the American Association of School Librarians. There were also several hits sponsored by "big" ALA, most of them deriving from the presidency of Nancy Kranich, who made information literacy the theme of her term in office in 2000.

The Public Library Association (PLA) was not responsible for any of the first 50 information literacy hits; and its conference held in Boston in March, 2006, did not offer a single program related to information literacy. Early childhood literacy, yes; information literacy, no. The PLA Web site is filled with useful resources on many topics of interest to its members. There are no resources on information literacy. Interestingly, information literacy is one of 13 service responses that libraries are encouraged to consider adopting in the Public Library Association document "Planning for Results: A Public Library Transformation Process: The Guidebook." A public library that has chosen to focus on this service, based on community needs, "will provide training and instruction in skills related to locating, evaluating, and using information resources of all types. Teaching the public to find and evaluate information will be stressed over simply providing answers to questions" (Himmel and Wilson, 1998: 108).

It is encouraging that information literacy is legitimized in this major public library planning tool as a viable and credible service. It is surprising then that information literacy services do not figure more prominently in the public library discourse. It does not mean, however, that public libraries have opted out of the information literacy business. This author's observations suggest that while public librarians have not yet entered into a public dialogue on the subject of information literacy, they are, in fact, engaging in teaching it. They just don't call it that.

SANTA MONICA PUBLIC LIBRARY

The Santa Monica Public Library (SMPL) is a good example. A new Main Library opened in early 2006. It is a modern building in the heart of the downtown shopping and government district. It is endowed with many of the features we now associate with exemplary twenty-first century public library buildings: "bookstore" displays of new book titles, lots of comfortable seating, a courtyard with a café, quiet rooms and rooms for collaborative group work, a state-of-the-art auditorium, attractive designated spaces for children and teens, a computer classroom, and a computer commons equipped with 50 computers for public Internet usage. There are an additional 37 computers set up especially for database access and one online public access catalog for every six ranges of stacks. The children's area has 20 Internet/database/game computer stations; and the young adults space has ten computers for Internet and database access.

The clientele using the new Main is a good cross-section of the residents of this beach city. There are retired folks with tote bags, well-dressed business people with briefcases, and homeless folks with their shopping bags. Families flock to the children's area, and teens hang out all over the library. It is busy, but the library is so well-designed that the public spaces do not seem overly crowded. People browse in the bookstore-style shelving, search in the stacks, work purposefully in the quiet rooms and the group study rooms, read in the arm chairs, focus intently on the screens in the Computer Commons, and use their laptops everywhere.

Nancy O'Neill is the head of Reference Services for the library. Among other responsibilities, she coordinates the computer classes that are conducted by the reference librarians. Asked why the library has chosen to use precious staff resources to teach these classes, she explained, "People need to know. The information is there; we can give it away if people know how to find it. We have always helped people use our resources. We used to teach people how to use an index in a reference book. Now we teach them how to use the electronic resources as well" (O'Neill, personal communication, 2006). In April, 2006, they offered the following one-hour classes:

- Computer basics—4 sessions
- E-mail—2 sessions

- Internet for beginners—2 sessions
- More Internet searching—1 session
- Microsoft Word—1 session
- Word II—2 sessions
- Internet security—2 sessions
- Reading Group Resources—1 session

A review of the curriculum outline for the basic Internet class reveals content that falls easily under the rubric of information literacy. The instructor explains what the Internet and the World Wide Web are, goes through the common domain names and their significance for evaluating the contents of individual Web sites, and goes into further detail about how to evaluate Web sites. The brief overview of search engines gives some basic limitations and tips for using them effectively.

Most of the people attending the library's computer classes are adults ages 40 and older. Many are significantly older. Senior citizens frequently request assistance in setting up e-mail accounts in order to communicate with grandchildren. Some adults who take these workshops are curious about the Internet, but have had no opportunity to use it at work or at school. There are also library patrons who have been asked to submit job applications or other documents online and need both access and assistance.

O'Neill acknowledged that not all reference librarians feel comfortable teaching the computer classes, and she does not require them to do so if they feel inadequate. This is usually not due to lack of knowledge but rather to a lack of comfort with the teaching role. Some public librarians, particularly those who finished their graduate education many years ago, have no background in teaching or training. Almost all academic librarians who work in public services expect to do some teaching. It is much less common for public librarians to see this as part of their jobs. However, Nancy O'Neill pointed out that at Santa Monica Public Library a lot of informal teaching occurs in the course of routine reference transactions. The computer monitors at the reference stations in the new Main are mounted on posts that swivel, enabling the librarians to show patrons exactly what they are doing as they conduct a search. O'Neill says that she will sometimes make a mistake or embark on a less satisfactory search strategy deliberately, just in order to explain what she is doing and also to make the patron feel comfortable. While many public reference librarians pride themselves on "just giving the answer," others have always shared their search strategies through this kind of "thinking aloud" process. Santa Monica Public Library seems to have institutionalized the ethos of empowering their patrons through both formal and informal educational strategies.

A conversation with Catherine Ronan, the head of the Fairview Branch of the Santa Monica Public Library, confirmed this notion (Ronan, personal communication, 2006). The Fairview Branch, located near a large middle school, serves a mixed population that includes many Spanish speakers. The system's Spanish language outreach librarian is posted here. Of the three branches in the system, this is the only one to have a Youth Technology Center, funded by a grant from a telecommunications firm. The eight laptop computers in the Technology Center are placed around a long table in the children's area of the open floor plan building. After school, homework gets priority here. The Technology Center is staffed by college students from 3:00 p.m. to 8:30 p.m. on school days; they provide homework assistance in addition to technology help. During school holidays and on weekends, the guidelines for using the computers are a little looser; and the teenagers are free to just fool around.

In addition to the one-on-one homework help, the library has at times offered a wide range of workshops, all aimed at exposing middle school students to the basic concepts of information literacy. More than 20 different classes have been offered, ranging from a library treasure hunt that focuses on the library catalog and an orientation to the library's databases, to tutorials on various applications such as Microsoft Word, PowerPoint, and Publisher. One of the projects was to create a PowerPoint presentation about the Technology Center. All of the classes are designed to keep young people interested and on task. One workshop on database searching, for example, was set up as a "CIA Assignment," in which the students pretended they were spies doing research on a country. Another Internet searching workshop focused on colleges.

At the Fairview Branch, staff have also offered classes in Spanish, targeted primarily at adults. The librarians observe that almost all of the children of Spanish-speaking parents are more comfortable in English. Classes aimed at parents help families get on the same page with the new technology.

Catherine Ronan says that most of the staff do not think in terms of information literacy. She feels lucky that she took a course in information literacy instruction when she was in library school at the University of California, Los Angeles. Taught by skilled reference librarians from the UCLA library, it was nevertheless relevant to public librarians. She says it gave her both skills and confidence that may be lacking in some of her colleagues. However, she agreed that all of the public service librarians she works with feel it is their mission to educate patrons about finding good information, often "talking them through the process."

The computer classes at the new Main are aimed at adults while those at the Fairview Branch target middle-school students. The librarians serving children and teens at the new Main do not currently offer any formal instruction for their clientele. Ellen Braby, the Youth Services Coordinator, acknowledges the need, but says that they have chosen to put their energies into storytimes and school visits during these early months in the new building. She recognizes the need for offering workshops for parents and plans to do so in the future. She saw evidence of the need for parent workshops at a recent technology day at the library.

Demonstrations of the kinds of homework resources that were available through subscription databases and online sources were very popular with adults who found that this knowledge enabled them to be better guides to their children. When usage settles down after the initial rush following the opening of the new main library, youth services staff will consider what kinds of information literacy services they might provide (Braby, personal communication, 2006).

LESSONS FROM THE SANTA MONICA PUBLIC LIBRARY

The librarians at the Santa Monica Public Library are good examples of their colleagues around the country, many of whom are improvising ways to teach their patrons more effective twenty-first century information literacy skills. What can we generalize about public libraries and information literacy from the SMPL example?

Lesson One: Public Libraries Have an Important Role to Play as Information Literacy Providers

Most of us would agree that academic settings are an ideal setting in which to learn and hone information literacy knowledge and skills. Working in partnership with faculty, librarians can tailor their instruction to the immediate information needs of students. When examples and skills are grounded in actual curriculum needs, students are much more likely to see their relevance and to remember the principles and concepts being taught. However, many people who are not enrolled in formal educational institutions also need to learn how to access, evaluate, and use information more effectively, particularly in its newer electronic manifestations. Public libraries are the logical agencies to assist these people.

Public libraries serve significant segments of the population who left school long before anybody was thinking about teaching information literacy. As in Santa Monica, people over the age of 40 may never have had any access to formal training in search strategies for the World Wide Web or electronic databases. Even adults who use computer applications such as word processing and spreadsheets on the job may feel at sea when faced with the need to locate information online. *Google* can seem like a wonderful search engine until you need to sort through 15,000 hits to find that restaurant in Santa Fe that had the great sopapaillas when you were there last summer. Even helpful Web sites can seem bewildering when their information architecture is opaque and the link you want is seemingly buried many layers deep.

Senior citizens are an obvious group to target for information literacy instruction. As retired people, they have the time and interest to learn new skills, and they tend to be active users of other library services. Public libraries may find that they can partner with senior citizen centers and tailor workshops to specific needs of this population.

By now we are all familiar with the digital divide. The presence of significant numbers of technological have-nots in our communities is perhaps the single most important reason for public libraries to undertake information literacy initiatives.

The Children's Partnership is a non-profit organization dedicated to extending health and technology opportunities to all children. In a recent study (Lazarus and Wainer, 2005: 20), they document the dimensions of the problem. The percentage of children ages seven to 17 that use a computer to do homework, for example, is significantly different among poor children and wealthy children. For those whose annual income is less than $15,000, only 29 percent use a computer for homework. The percentage for children whose annual household income is $75,000 or more is 77 percent. Race and ethnicity are also factors in digital opportunities. Here are the percentages of young people ages seven to 17 who use word processing or desktop publishing programs on the computer at home:

- Native American: 21 percent
- African American: 22 percent
- Latino: 23 percent
- Asian American: 41 percent
- White: 45 percent

The authors of the Children's Partnership report believe strongly that children and teens need access to Information and Communication Technology at home in order to achieve digital parity. They acknowledge, however, that community programs, including those at libraries, are vitally needed to help bridge the existing divide. They also acknowledge that the new information and communication technologies present serious risks to children, including online pornography, cyberbullying, online predators, overt commercialism, privacy concerns, and the lure of online gambling. The authors provide no solutions or ameliorating situations for these risks. Actually, public libraries could be a big help here. One of the key messages in ALA's "Libraries and the Internet Toolkit" (2000: 1) is that "the best protection for children is to teach them to use technology properly and to make good choices." It is easy to imagine a public library tutorial for young people and their parents that would teach information literacy skills in order to combat the less savory aspects of ICT.

Lesson Two: Public Librarians May Need to Shift Priorities or Redefine Their Missions in Order to Accommodate Formal Information Literacy Instruction into Their Duties

In a public library, reference librarians spend much of their time assisting library patrons. Young adult librarians typically work with teen advisory boards to plan programs and services in addition to providing readers' advisory and reference services. Children's librarians are involved with programming and outreach in addition to their duties at the public service desk. All of these specialists have other "off-desk" responsibilities involving collection development. One never hears any of these librarians complain about not having enough to do. Incorporating formal information literacy instruction for the public into their tight schedules means reordering priorities. At SMPL, we noted that the children's services manager saw the need to offer some kind of instruction in homework resources for parents. At this time, however, she and her staff were focusing on expanding their storytime offerings.

It is certainly good management practice to "stick to the knitting," to focus resources on the core activities of the organization. For public libraries, the core activities have always been reference, collection development, and (especially for children) reading motivation and literacy initiatives such as storytimes. However, good management practice also dictates that we respond to changing environments. Certainly the revolution in digital information and communication technologies is creating changes in the lives of our patrons and in their expectations for service. It would be wrong for us to assume, however, that people's interest in ICT equals their fluency in using it. It might even be irresponsible for us to offer access to the powerful tools of the information age without providing assistance in using them. Perhaps we should think of information literacy instruction as simply an extension of traditional reference services.

We also have seen evidence in any number of surveys that people expect their public libraries to function as educational institutions. The Benton Foundation report, "Buildings, Books, and Bytes: Libraries and Communities in the Digital Age" (1998) was justly criticized for some methodological weaknesses. However, some of its findings had heuristic value, stimulating some useful discussions in the public library community. Of relevance to this discussion was the finding that among five key roles that Americans ranked as very important was "providing a place where librarians help people find information through computers and online services" (Benton Foundation, 1998; 4). This statement is at odds with the report's conclusion that Americans do not see the library as a credible source for the latest technology. The significant fact here is that people evidently see public *librarians* as credible guides to ICT. They are ready for us to teach them what we know.

Lesson Three: Public Librarians Use a Variety of Strategies to Communicate Information Literacy Concepts to Their Patrons

There appear to be three primary forms of information literacy instruction taking place in public libraries currently. One is the computer class, offered as a one-time workshop or less often as a series. Another is the informal one-on-one tutorial given in the context of a reference interview. The third is instruction given as an adjunct to homework assistance, usually informally. We can consider each of these briefly.

The computer class or workshop usually has a subject focus and a specified level of difficulty. It may also have a particular audience, such as senior citizens, reading group participants, or parents. Unlike school and academic librarians, public librarians have not yet formalized any kind of curriculum or expected outcomes for these classes. They may borrow from manuals or guidebooks on information literacy written for school and academic settings, or simply experiment. An informative article in *Public Libraries* (Kelly and Hibner, 2005) tells how two new library school graduates learned by trial and error how to teach basic computer and information literacy skills to older adults. They learned from their early mistakes and eventually developed a winning combination of content and teaching style.

At Santa Monica Public Library, the reference staff have drawn up basic curriculum outlines for each of their workshops, but they expect the librarian who is teaching the class to develop his or her own instructional style. The course outlines for the Youth Technology Center classes are basically just worksheets, handouts that the librarian and students work through together.

Probably most public library patrons are gaining information literacy skills through osmosis while at the reference desk. As noted above, all of the SMPL reference librarians try to "think aloud" while assisting patrons with electronic resources. This is an effective way to demystify the process and to teach skills in context. It is also a different practice from the traditional approach to reference service in which the librarian simply gave the requested information, cited the source, and asked if this completely and fully answered the patron's question.

Interestingly, many public libraries have adopted a new service initiative over the past decade or so. Homework assistance, once thought to be the domain of school libraries, is now provided as a routine after-school service in many public libraries. Cindy Mediavilla (2001: viii–ix) notes that public libraries had actively discouraged student use during the early 1960s in order to control rampant over-crowding during after-school hours. In the late 1980s and early 1990s, however, many public libraries reconsidered their response. Some libraries decided to take a more proactive approach to the problem of unsupervised "latchkey" children and offer constructive programs to meet their needs. They found that unattended children caused fewer behavioral problems when they had a designated place in the library to do their homework. Recently, public library homework centers tend to be anchored by computers equipped with word processing and other applications as well as Internet access. They are often staffed by volunteers or paid employees.

Informal information literacy instruction occurs in the homework centers, much as it does at the reference desk. The author once observed a homework center aide at a Long Beach Public Library branch help a young boy find relevant Web sites for an assignment on national parks. The aide explained to the boy and to his mother why he had selected a particular search engine and why he was using a particular search term. The aide also walked the child through the process of selecting which Web site and which information from the site would be most useful to him. He then helped him download a map and told him how to cite the Web site on his paper. Then he turned the dazzled mother and happy boy over to a librarian to check out some additional print sources. This cross-generational lesson taught all of the essential skills of information literacy seamlessly and painlessly.

It would be an obvious extension of the services of homework centers to offer classes or workshops for both students and parents on topics of perennial interest: resources for Black History Month, country assignments, or Presidents; or college information and term paper strategies. Instructors could lead the students to digital pathfinders and other resources while sneaking in messages about evaluating Web sites, integrating digital information into reports, citing correctly, and the evils of plagiarizing.

While the class, the reference interview, and the homework center are the three primary venues for information literacy at this time, other modes may be emerging. The use of Web sites to provide digital pathfinders is promising. The new *Homework Help* site sponsored by New York, Brooklyn, and Queens Public Library (http://HomeworkNYC.org) is an excellent example of virtual information literacy instruction.

INFORMATION LITERACY: THE NEXT STEPS FOR PUBLIC LIBRARIES

The public library has made tremendous strides in providing public access to computers and information technology of all kinds. In urban areas, at least, public libraries are helping to eliminate some of the disparities created by the digital divide. (Rural areas have other problems to solve, given the geographic isolation of many residents.) Give us an "A" for access; we have done a pretty good job with this. We could still do better, of course. Library hours still restrict people's use of our resources. There are still too few Internet and database-equipped computers in many libraries, resulting in arcane sign-up systems and truncated sessions for many users. Still, public access computing is a public library success story.

The next success story could involve major breakthroughs in patron education. Libraries in my city offer classes in knitting and seminars on living trusts and genealogy. One branch with a well-equipped kitchen has given cooking classes for children. We provide adult literacy instruction and guidance for reading groups. It seems reasonable to assume that we would extend our information services in similar ways. We have taken the first steps in information literacy. The next steps will include the development of best practices, outcomes, and strategies for evaluation.

REFERENCES

American Library Association. 2000. *Libraries and the Internet toolkit*. Chicago: American Library Association (last updated 2003). Available: www.ala.org/ala/oif/iftoolkits/litoolkit/2003internettoolkit.pdf

Benton Foundation. 1998. "Buildings, books and bytes: Libraries and communities in the digital age." Available: www.benton.org/publibrary/kellogg/buildings.html

Himmel, E., and W. J. Wilson. 1998. *Planning for results: A public library transformation process: The guidebook*. Chicago: American Library Association.

Kelly, M., and H. Hibner. 2005. "Teaching computers to seniors: What not to do." *Public Libraries*, Vol. 44, no. 3: 151–155.

Lazarus, W., and A. Wainer. 2005. *Measuring digital opportunity for America's children: Where we stand and where we go from here*. Santa Monica, CA: The Children's Partnership.

Libraries and the Internet Toolkit. 2000. Chicago: American Library Association.

Mediavilla, C. 2001. *Creating the full-service homework center in your library*. Chicago: American Library Association.

Walter, V. A. et al. 2004. *21st century literacies: Training of public library trainers*. Los Angeles: UCLA Graduate School of Education & Information Studies. Available: www.newliteracies.gseis.ucla.edu (accessed May 10, 2006).

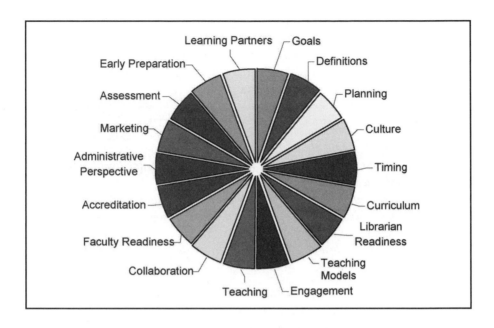

CONCLUDING COMMENTS

From the Editors

*T*he wheel is now complete. In 18 chapters, 20 authors from different backgrounds and different experiences have provided their best advice on how to develop a successful information literacy program. Pulling from case studies, theories and direct experiences, the authors have provided us with proven strategies. From them, we see the real world of information literacy.

However, in the midst of so much valuable information, what special lessons should we carry away with us?

First, we must take a comprehensive approach to developing a new, or to changing an existing, program of information literacy. Addressing one or a handful of components will not make a successful program. Instead, every aspect has to be addressed.

Second, we must really become students of the wide variety of experiences of our colleagues. There is no reason to reinvent the wheel. The field abounds in colleagues sharing their diverse experiences. Anyone looking at their information literacy program should begin with great attention to the experiences of others.

Third, we must recognize the importance of partnering—academic, school and public libraries are a powerful educational force. Additionally, we must partner with faculty who are our key allies in developing information literacy skills.

Fourth, we have to pay attention to the intangible aspects of developing a program. Such issues as timing, culture, respect, readiness, and support are not easy to grasp, but unless we have a grasp on them, the chances of any of these elements working *against our program is likely. Sometimes it is hard to be patient with the intangible, but the intangible will slow us down unless we attend to it.*

Fifth, we have to begin at the beginning. It is very tempting to rush forward with a program, but as the authors have pointed out, setting clear goals and clear definitions, and securing support are vital elements for a program's success.

Sixth, we must remember to look to the wider world and align ourselves with the institution or environment. Information literacy, like libraries themselves, does not exist in a vacuum. It is caught up in educational strategies, technology, accreditation, student preparedness and a host of other issues that dominate the lives (especially) of school and academic librarians.

Seventh, let's remember to tell our story. We can spend a lot of time talking to each other, but not everyone in our environment knows what information literacy is and what it can do to help people in this information rich society. Marketing the program in a way that makes it clear and compelling is essential for success.

Eighth, we must grow and change our programs through the power of assessment. Correctly used and wisely applied, assessment is a formidable tool that keeps us on track and keeps student achievement in focus at all times.

The demands on anyone developing or sustaining a program of information literacy are great. The challenges can be equally formidable from time to time. However, by using proven strategies, we set ourselves on the path towards building a successful program of information literacy.

Recommended Readings

Angelo, T. A., & Cross, P. K. (1993). *Classroom Assessment Techniques: A Handbook for College Teachers. The Jossey-Bass Higher Education and Adult Education Series.* San Francisco: Jossey-Bass Publishers.

American Association of School Librarians (1998). *Information Literacy Standards for Student Learning.* Chicago: American Library Association.

American Library Association. (1989). Presidential Committee on Information Literacy: Final report. Retrieved on May 6 2006 from: www.ala.org/ala/acrl/acrlpubs/whitepapers/presidential.htm

American Library Association. (1998). A Progress Report on Information Literacy: An Update on the American Library Association Presidential Committee on Information Literacy: Final Report. Retrieved 6 May 2006, from: www.ala.org/ala/acrl/acrlpubs/whitepapers/presidential.htm

Argentieri, L., Davies, K. S., Farrell, K., & Liles, J. A. (2001). Librarians Hitting the Books. In J. K. Nims & E. Ownes (Eds.), *Managing Library Instruction Programs in Academic Libraries.* Ann Arbor, MI: Pierian Press.

Association for the Study of Higher Education [ASHE] (2001). Research-Based Principles of Change. *ASHE-ERIC Higher Education Report,* 28(4), 113–124.

Association of College and Research Libraries. (2000). *Information Literacy Competency Standards for Higher Education.* Chicago: American Library Association. Retrieved 6 May 2006, from: www.ala.org/ala/acrl/acrlstandards/informationliteracy competency.htm

Association of College and Research Libraries. Information Literacy Executive Board. (2006). *ACRL Information Literacy Web Site.* Retrieved 15 September 2006 from: www.ala.org/ala/acrl/acrlissues/acrlinfolit/informationliteracy.htm

Bain, K. (2004). *What the Best College Teachers Do.* Cambridge, MA: Harvard University Press.

Bergquist, W. H. (1992). *The Four Cultures of the Academy: Insights and Strategies for Improving Leadership in Collegiate Organizations.* San Francisco: Jossey-Bass

Boyer Commission on Educating Undergraduates in the Research University. (1998). *Reinventing Undergraduate Education: A Blueprint for America's Research Universities.* Stony Brook, NY: State University of New York.

Boyer, E. L. (1987). *College: The Undergraduate Experience in America.* New York: Harper & Row.

Breivik, P. S. (1998). *Student Learning in the Information Age.* Phoenix, AZ: Oryx Press.

Bruce, C. (1997). *Seven Faces of Information Literacy*. Australia: Auslib Press.

Bullard, K.A & Holden, D.H. (2006). "Hitting a Moving Target: Curriculum Mapping, Information Literacy and Academe." A paper delivered at the LOEX Conference 2006: May 4–6, University of Maryland, College Park. Retrieved July 18, 2006 from: www.emich.edu/public/loex/handouts/bullard/BullardHoldenLOEX 2006handout.doc

Bundy, A. (Ed.). (2004). "Beyond Information: The Academic Library as Educational Change Agent." A paper presented at the International Bielefeld Conference Germany 3–5 February 2004. Retrieved from: www.library.unisa.edu.au/about/papers/beyond-information.pdf.

Buzzeo, T. (2002). *Collaborating to Meet Standards: Teacher/Librarian Partnerships for K–6*. Worthington, OH: Linworth.

Buzzeo, T. (2002). *Collaborating to Meet Standards: Teacher/Librarian Partnerships for 7–12*. Worthington, OH: Linworth.

Campbell, N. F., & Wesley, T. L. (2006). Collaborative Dialogue: Repositioning the Academic Library. *Portal: Libraries and the Academy*, 6(1), 93–98.

Davis, T. M. & Murrell, P. H. (1993). *Turning Teaching into Learning: the role of student responsibility in the collegiate experience*. Washington, DC: George Washington University School of Education.

DeSaez, E. E. (2002). *Marketing Concepts for Library and Information Services*. London: Facet.

Edmundson, M. (2004) *Why Read?* New York: Bloomsburg.

Eisenberg, M. (n.d.). *The Big6 Skills Information Problem-Solving Approach*. See www.big6.com

Eisenberg, M. & Berkowitz, R. (1990). *Information Problem Solving: The Big Six Skills Approach to Library and Information Skills Instruction, Information Management, Policy and Services*. Norwood, NJ: Ablex Publishing.

Eisenberg, M. & Brown, M. (1992). Current Themes Regarding Library and Information Skills Instruction: Research Supporting and Research Lacking. *School Library Media Quarterly*, 20(2): 103–109.

Eisenberg, M. (2004). *Information Literacy: Essential Skills for the Information Age*. Westport, CT: Libraries Unlimited.

Farber, E. (1999). "Faculty-Librarian Cooperation: A Personal Perspective." *Reference Services Review*, 27(3), 229–234.

Farmer, L. (2003). *How to Conduct Action Research: A Guide for School Library Specialists*. Chicago: American Library Association.

Fine, S. H. (1992). *Introduction to Social Marketing in Marketing the Public Sector: Promoting the Causes of Public and Nonprofit Agencies*. New Brunswick, NJ: Transaction.

Grafstein, A. (2002). "A Discipline-Based Approach to Information Literacy." *Journal of Academic Librarianship*, 28(4), 197–204.

Grassian, E. & Kaplowitz, J. (2001). *Information Literacy Instruction: Theory & Practice*. New York: Neal Schuman.

Grassian, E. & Kaplowitz, J. (2005). *Learning to Lead and Manage Information Literacy Instruction*. New York: Neal-Schuman.

Harada, V. & Yoshina, J. (2005). *Assessing Learning: Librarians and Teachers as Partners.* Westport, CT: Libraries Unlimited.

Hardesty, L. (1991). *Faculty and the Library: The Undergraduate Experience.* Norwood, NJ: Ablex.

Henri, J., & Asselin, M. (Eds.). (2005). *The Information Literate School Community 2: Issues of Leadership.* Westport, CT: Libraries Unlimited.

Howe, N., & Strauss, W. (2000). *Millennials Rising: The Next Great Generation.* New York: Vintage Books.

Jenkins, J., & Boosinger, M. (2003). "Collaborating with Campus Administrators and Faculty to Integrate Information Literacy and Assessment into the Core Curriculum. *Southeastern Librarian*, 50(4): 26–31.

Karp, R. (2006). "Seeing the Library in the Broader Context on Campus: Marketing our Services." In Dowell, D. R. & McCabe, G. B. (Eds.), *It's All About Student Learning: Managing Community and Other College Libraries in the 21st century.* Westport, CT: Libraries Unlimited.

Koppang, A. (2004). "Curriculum Mapping: Building Collaboration and Communication." *Intervention in School and Clinic*, 39(3): 154–161.

Kraat, S. (Ed.). (2005). *Relationships between Teaching Faculty and Teaching Librarians.* Binghamton, NY: Haworth Information Press.

Kuh, G. D., & Umbach, P. (2004). "College and Character: Insights from the National Survey of Student Engagement." In J. Dalton and T. Russell (Eds.), *Assessing Character Outcomes in College. New Directions in Institutional Research 2004 (122)*, pp. 37–54. San Francisco: Jossey-Bass.

Kuh, G. D., & Whitt, E. J. (1988). *The Invisible Tapestry: Culture in American Colleges and Universities.* San Francisco: Jossey-Bass.

Kuhlthau, C. C. (1993). *Seeking Meaning: A Process Approach to Library and Information Services.* Norwood, NJ: Ablex Publishing

Lampert, L. (2005). "'Getting Psyched' about Information Literacy: A Successful Faculty-Librarian Collaboration for Educational Psychology and Counseling." *The Reference Librarian*, 43(89/90), 5–23.

Maki, P. L. (2002). "Developing an Assessment Plan to Learn about Student Learning." *The Journal of Academic Librarianship*, 28 (1-2), 8–13.

McDonald, R. H. & Thomas, C. (2006). "Disconnects between Library Culture and Millennial Generation Values." *Educause Quarterly*, 29(4), 4–6.

Merz, L. H., & Mark, B. L. (2002). *Assessment in College Library Instruction Programs.* CLIP Note # 32. Chicago: Association of College and Research Libraries.

Miller, D. (2005). *The Standards-Based Integrated Library: A Collaborative Approach for Aligning the Library Program with the Classroom Curriculum.* Worthington, OH: Linworth.

Neely, T. Y. (2002). *Sociological and Psychological Aspects of Information Literacy in Higher Education.* Lanham, MD: Scarecrow Press.

Neely, T.Y. (2006). *Information Literacy Assessment: Standards-Based Tools and Assignments.* Chicago: American Library Association.

Palmer, Parker J. (1998). *The Courage to Teach.* San Francisco: Jossey-Bass.

Palomba, C. A., & Banta, T. W. (1999). *Assessment Essentials: Planning, Implementing and Improving Assessment in Higher Education.* San Francisco: Jossey-Bass.

Pedersen, S. (2003). *Learning Communities and the Academic Library.* National Learning Communities Project Monograph Series. Olympia WA: The Evergreen State College, Washington Center for Improving the Quality of Undergraduate Education, in cooperation with the American Association for Higher Education and the Association of College and Research Libraries.

Rader, H. (1995). "Information Literacy and the Undergraduate Curriculum. (The Library and Undergraduate Education)." *Library Trends,* 44, 270–279.

Rader, H. (2002). "Information Literacy 1973–2002: A Selected Literature." *Library Trends* 51(2), 242–259.

Rockman, I. (Ed.). (2004). *Integrating Information Literacy into the Higher Education Curriculum.* San Francisco: Jossey-Bass Publishers.

Sacks, P. A., & Whildrin, S. L. (1993). *Preparing for Accreditation: A Handbook for Academic Librarians.* Chicago: American Library Association.

Senge, P. (1990). *The Fifth Discipline: The Art and Practice of the Learning Organization.* New York: Doubleday.

Sheridan, J. (Ed.). (1995). *Writing-across-the-Curriculum and the Academic Library: A Guide for Librarians, Instructors, and Writing Program Directors.* Westport, CT: Greenwood Press.

Simmons, M. H. (2005). "Librarians as Disciplinary Discourse Mediators: Using Genre Theory to Move toward Critical Information Literacy." *Portal: Libraries and the Academy,* 5(3), 297–311.

Thompson, G. B. (2002). "Information Literacy Accreditation Mandates: What They Mean for Faculty and Librarians." *Library Trends,* 51(2), 218–41.

Walter, S. (2006). "Instructional Improvement: Building Capacity for the Professional Development of Librarians as Teachers." *Reference & User Services Quarterly,* 45 (3), 213–218.

Watts, M. (2005). "The Place of the Library Versus the Library as Place." In (Eds.), M. Lupcraft & J. N. Gardner & G. O. Barefoot & Associates. *Challenging and Supporting the First-Year Student: A Handbook for Improving the First Year of College.* (pp. 339–355). San Francisco: Jossey-Bass.

Index

About the Editors

Dr. Susan Carol Curzon is Dean of the Oviatt Library at California State University, Northridge, an urban Los Angeles campus of nearly 33,000 students. Previous positions include Director of Libraries for the Glendale Public Library and Regional Administrator for the County of Los Angeles Public Library. She also has experience in a corporate library. For seven years, she was Chair of the California State University's committee on information literacy, which brought a program of information literacy to the 23 campuses of the system. Her doctorate is in Public Administration from the University of Southern California. Her M.L.S. is from the University of Washington. She was *Library Journal*'s Librarian of the Year in 1993. She is the author of two previous books entitled *Managing Change* (Neal-Schuman, 2006) and *Managing the Interview* (Neal-Schuman, 1995). She has also written articles and made many presentations on the subject of information literacy and the management of libraries.

Lynn D. Lampert is Chair of Reference and Instructional Services at the Oviatt Library at California State University, Northridge. Since joining the faculty at CSUN in 2001, she has also served as the Coordinator of Information Literacy and Instruction. In her work with the California State University, Lynn has served on system-wide committees responsible for strategic planning related to information literacy and the development of the ETS-ICT assessment instrument. Before joining the faculty at CSU, Northridge, in 2001, Lynn worked as a librarian at California Lutheran University in Thousand Oaks, California.

Lynn has authored many publications, appearing both within and outside the field of library and information science, focusing on information literacy, the role of the librarian in combating student plagiarism, and other issues within academic librarianship. Lynn frequently presents on critical issues in information literacy practices and library instructional programming at both the national and regional level. She is an active member of ALA, serving on ACRL's Instruction Section and the California chapter of ACRL, CARL (California Association of Research Libraries). Her M.L.I.S. in Library and Information Science and M.A. in History were both awarded by the University of California, Los Angeles, in 1998.